# THE END OF
# LAISSEZ-FAIRE

# THE END OF LAISSEZ-FAIRE

## NATIONAL PURPOSE
## AND THE GLOBAL ECONOMY
## AFTER THE COLD WAR

## ROBERT KUTTNER

UNIVERSITY OF PENNSYLVANIA PRESS
Philadelphia

Originally published 1991 by Alfred A. Knopf, Inc. and Random House of Canada, Ltd.
Paperback edition published 1992 by University of Pennsylvania Press by arrangement with Alfred
A. Knopf, Inc.

10 9 8 7 6 5 4 3 2


Published by
University of Pennsylvania Press
Philadelphia, Pennsylvania 19104-4011


Library of Congress Cataloging-in-Publication Data

Kuttner, Robert.
    The end of laissez-faire: global economy and national purpose after the Cold War/ Robert
Kuttner
    p.    cm.
    Includes index.
    ISBN 8-8122-1401-3 (alk. paper)
    1. United States—Economic policy—1981-   I. Title.
HC106.8.K88                    1991               ·
338.973'009'048—dc20                                              90-5174
                                                                   CIP

FOR ADELE S. KUTTNER,
WORLD CITIZEN

In the science of economics, theory and practice are virtually divorced from one another—to the detriment of both. Economists condemn practical men as mere followers of routine who fail to appreciate either the truth or the grandeur of the doctrines enunciated by economists. Practical men, on the other hand, regard economists as mere doctrinaires who ignore the facts of life and inhabit a dream world of economic theories that exists only in their imagination.

—FRIEDRICH LIST,
*The Natural System of Political Economy,* 1837

It is *not* a correct deduction from the Principles of Economics that enlightened self-interest always operates in the public interest . . . Many of the greatest economic evils of our time are the fruits of risk, uncertainty, and ignorance. It is because peculiar individuals, fortunate in situation or abilities, are able to take advantage of uncertainty or ignorance, and also because for the same reason big business is often a lottery, that great inequalities of wealth come about; and these same factors are also the cause of the unemployment of labour, or the disappointment of reasonable business expectations, and of the impairment of efficiency and production. Yet the cure lies outside the operation of individuals; it may even be to the interest of individuals to aggravate the disease.

—JOHN MAYNARD KEYNES,
"The End of Laissez-Faire" (essay), 1926

The idea of a self-adjusting market implied a stark utopia. Such an institution could not exist for any length of time without annihilating the human and material substance of society. . . . To allow the market mechanism to be the sole director of the fate of human beings and their natural environment, indeed, even of the amount and use of purchasing power, would result in the demolition of society.

—KARL POLANYI,
*The Great Transformation,* 1944

# CONTENTS

# ACKNOWLEDGMENTS

I began work on this book in 1985. I put it aside to write a short book on liberalism and the Democratic Party in 1986–87 *(The Life of the Party),* and again in 1989 to launch a new magazine, *The American Prospect.* As the Cold War ended and a new era of pluralism dawned, the delay proved fortuitous, for my premise is now in better sync with global events. The United States no longer needs to shoulder a disproportionate share of global defense burdens; its diplomacy can address its own national economic interests and a more realistic set of rules for the international trading system. The book represents a continuation of my longtime search for greater understanding and balance in the interplay of politics and economics, this time in the international realm.

Particular thanks are due the John Simon Guggenheim Foundation, which provided a fellowship to begin work on the book, and to my editor, Elisabeth Sifton, for improving the manuscript in countless ways. She continues to be the rare editor who insists on editing every word, with great insight and wit. Her literary ear has perfect pitch. Thanks also to the Economic Policy Institute and its president, Jeff Faux, for underwriting two monographs that served as drafts of portions of chapters 5 and 7, on trade policy and on export controls; to the German Marshall Fund, which underwrote a reporting trip to Europe; and to the Ditchley Foundation.

Among my editorial colleagues and friends, I am grateful to Paul Starr and Robert Reich, co-founders of *The American Prospect* and collaborators in the enterprise of resurrecting the case for a mixed economy; to Hendrik Hertzberg and Martin Peretz of *The New Republic,* to Jack Pluenneke and Steve Shepard of *Business Week,* to Marjorie Pritchard and Marty Nolan of the Boston *Globe,* to Bill Dickinson and Anna Karavangelos of the Washington *Post* Writers Group, to Richard Medley of *The*

*International Economy,* to Alan Webber, Robert Howard, and Bernard Avishai of the *Harvard Business Review,* and to Irving Howe of *Dissent* for continuing to publish and help refine my journalistic output, many of whose themes reappear in this book.

Amy Mace Stackhouse, editorial assistant on *The American Prospect* and occasional research assistant to this book, deserves a special thank-you. Thanks also to Robert Blecker, John Brockman, Wolfgang Hager, Roger Hickey, Ella Krucoff, Rochelle Lefkowitz, Larry Mishel, Lee Price, David Smith, Lee Smith, and Alan W. Wolff, for a variety of kindnesses.

I owe an intellectual debt to several eclectic thinkers whose work has enriched my understanding of international economic relations, several of whom I also count as friends: Fred Block, Barry Bluestone, Frank Bourgin, David Calleo, Rudy Dornbusch, John Eatwell, Michael Emerson, Richard Gardner, Robert Gilpin, Peter Gourevitch, Bennett Harrison, Albert Hirschman, John Ikenberry, Robert Keohane, Charles Kindleberger, Paul Krugman, George Lodge, William Lovett, Walter Russell Mead, Clyde Prestowitz, Richard Rothstein, John Gerard Ruggie, Ajit Singh, Paul Streeten, Laura Tyson, Richard Valelly, Karel van Wolferen, and Chris Wilkinson.

I also appreciate the many courtesies extended by several economists whose views are sometimes foils for my own: Fred Bergsten, Jagdish Bhagwati, Gary Hufbauer, Robert Lawrence, Jeff Sachs, Jeff Schott, Larry Summers, and John Williamson, among many others.

My wife, Sharland Trotter, read every chapter and served as a reality-check whenever the prose became too mired in technical detail or too full of itself. The text was immeasurably improved by her gentle reminders: "What is this supposed to mean?"

R.K.

# THE END OF
# LAISSEZ-FAIRE

# INTRODUCTION

The *end* of laissez-faire? Surely the collapse of communism, the globalization of commerce, and the triumph of capitalist ideas all signal a new golden age of laissez-faire. The remarkable events of 1989–90 have been widely heralded as a victory for the free market—a vindication of laissez-faire in general and American-style capitalism in particular. Indeed, it has become a cliché to declare that the United States is now the only nation that remains both an economic and a military superpower. But that conclusion, I suspect, is far too facile as a guide either to ideology or to policy. In the new era now unfolding, the pursuit of laissez-faire as an optimum goal, for the global system or for the United States, would do grave harm to both.

In this book, I explore the logic of the end of laissez-faire—as theory, as policy, and as the object of U.S. economic diplomacy. I contend that the pursuit of laissez-faire had much to do with American dominance of the noncommunist world in the years since World War II, and that in turn had much to do with the Cold War. Paradoxically, therefore, the collapse of Marxism and the end of the Cold War portend the end of laissez-faire, too. My subject is in a sense the *second* end of laissez-faire, for the ideal of a self-regulating economy seemingly had been dispatched once and for all after the bitter lesson of the global Great Depression, the ensuing World War II, and the explanatory power of Keynesian economics. The reader will note that I have borrowed my title from a short essay by Keynes written in 1926. The intriguing question is why the utopian vision of a pure market economy proved so potent—why it came back to life, after being so thoroughly discredited by events half a century ago and after most advanced nations successfully built their postwar societies very much in the spirit of a mixed economy rather than a laissez-faire one. Most of this book is devoted to exploring that question.

The doctrine of laissez-faire, as explicated in Adam Smith's *Wealth of Nations*, holds that market economies, when left alone, are essentially self-regulating. Sellers, left to their own devices, will produce goods and services in response to the demands of buyers. The interplay of supply and demand will generate the right signals, in the form of prices, of what ought to be produced. Correct prices will "clear the market," as in an auction. The unfettered operation of the price system leads to an optimal allocation of resources and the most efficient possible distribution of production, based on the logic of specialization, in which each producer gets to do what he does best. The resulting distribution of income and wealth is also efficient, and hence implicitly just. Even Smith, however, recognized that government had a function in all this—in caring for the needy, in building public works, in education and public health, and in preventing merchants from conspiring against the public interest.

In the 215 years since the publication of *The Wealth of Nations*, modern economic theory has striven for a world even more utopian than Smith's. Although Keynes's *General Theory* had immense influence on policy, orthodox economists in the end absorbed the Keynesian critique of Smith's classical economic view only to the extent of admitting that entire national economies might find demand out of balance with supply (the realm of "macroeconomics"); they continued to cherish the idea that governments should not interfere with the price system. That meant disdain for regulation, for substantial public investment, for industrial policy, or for measures to allocate investment or redistribute income and wealth. If and when governments did intervene, their actions should be as "marketlike" as possible. Keynes was relegated to a footnote, in effect, and the majestic ideal of a self-regulating economy marched on. The equations grew ever more intricate, but the basic idea persisted. So if laissez-faire was sidelined by the Depression, by wartime planning, and by postwar recovery, it lived on in the hearts of economists.

The case against laissez-faire as a principle for operating a national economy has been made in a voluminous literature and in human experience. In brief, pure free-market economies can be criticized for their instability as well as for their inequity. As theory, the *locus classicus* of the counterargument is John Maynard Keynes. As history, it is Karl Polanyi, who saw the entire collapse of Western civilization after 1914 as resulting from the century-long utopian endeavor of substituting market relations, which are contingent and transitory, for a more reciprocal and sustainable organization of human society. Though laissez-faire capitalism professed to be liberalism itself, market relations carried to an extreme drove out other necessary forms of relation and led to deeply antiliberal spasms of response. Laissez-faire, in short, wrecked the civil society on which capitalism depended. There is also, of course, an extensive Marxian literature that takes issue with classical capitalist economics. My quarrel, however, is not with capitalism itself, only with its utopian variation, and I quarrel in the spirit of Keynes and Polanyi.

If orthodox economists continued to harbor dreams of a self-regulating marketplace, practical statesmen carried the day in the postwar era, building modern welfare states, tempering the instability of a pure market system with both Keynesian management of total purchasing power ("aggregate demand") and a dose of national economic planning. In the United States, much of the planning was done under military auspices and the welfare state was less fully developed, but for the quarter century after World War II, Americans, like Europeans, practiced a mixed rather than a laissez-faire brand of capitalism.

My purpose here is not to reiterate the arguments against laissez-faire as the best principle for managing a domestic economy. There are entire libraries on the subject, and I have added my own observations in an earlier book, *The Economic Illusion* (1984). Rather, I am here concerned with the international economy, a realm in which the forces of private commerce are far more difficult to tame, for the obvious reason that the reach of the nation-state ends at its borders. One must look to the international realm to understand why laissez-faire rose from the dead, and to appreciate why American diplomats led the resurrection.

After all, for most of its history, the United States has pursued policies that went beyond simpleminded laissez-faire. Alexander Hamilton created a major economic function for government in banking and in industrial development. Thomas Jefferson, usually classed as the more classically liberal of the two, was also something of a planner. He made sure that the land-tenure policies of the young Republic favored small freeholders rather than large land speculators. Like Hamilton, he supported government policies to encourage the scientific, agricultural, and mechanical arts—the sum and substance of commerce of the day. Government also invested extensively in canals and railroads and in mapping new territories. And early America necessarily industrialized behind tariff walls; otherwise, it would have continued to be an economic ward of Great Britain.

To be sure, one can point to an opposite tradition: American culture has always been individualistic. Americans as a people are deeply ambivalent about government. Our nation began as a revolt against the British Crown. Our Constitution was a unique act of statecraft whose essence was limitation on state power. Unlike, say, Britain or Sweden or Japan, our nation was not a monarchy with a tradition of strong government that was gradually democratized and converted to public purposes without losing its ability to act in the national interest. Nonetheless, despite all of these unique cultural and historical antipathies, Americans still had a barn-raising tradition that often required surprisingly activist use of government for economic development purposes—even in Jefferson's day, not to mention the era of the New Deal—in programs as diverse as social insurance, homesteading, and public works.

America's intermittent enthusiasm for laissez-faire grew into a diplomatic obsession and a global ideal only after World War II, when the United States was the world's premier military and economic power. There is a logic to this stance: the nation best positioned to exploit its own commercial leadership becomes a crusader for the most open possible global markets in capital, raw materials, and finished goods and services; Britain, the leading nineteenth-century commercial power, had done this earlier. After World War II, the United States' commitment to laissez-faire as the principle for global trade was somewhat offset by the reality that Americans were practicing a mixed economy at home. If a mixed economy was necessary domestically to compensate for the imperfections of Adam Smith's invisible hand, it didn't make sense to strive for perfectly free markets globally. And in the 1940s and 1950s global commerce was still so encumbered by leftover wartime restraints—perfect free trade was such a long way off—that this latent contradiction was not yet a problem.

As the postwar era evolved, the balance of domestic political forces within the United States shifted. The elements of the Roosevelt coalition, which provided the constituency for a mixed economy, gradually weakened. The business community, which had been constrained politically both by the Depression and by government planning during the war, recovered its influence. The Vietnam War undermined the liberal coalition and set in motion an inflationary cycle, which discredited both Keynesian economics and liberal Democrats—the architects of a mixed economy. The OPEC oil price increases and the economic distress of the 1970s administered the coup de grace: a decade of turbulence could be blamed on Keynesian economics. When Ronald Reagan succeeded Jimmy Carter in January 1981, the marriage between political conservatives and laissez-faire economists was waiting to be consummated.

Unfortunately, however, the moment of laissez-faire came round again at just about the time the United States was losing its global commercial leadership. If it made pragmatic sense for America in the 1950s and 1960s to preach the freest possible markets, it made far less sense in the 1980s and 1990s. Yet by 1980, as laissez-faire hardened from self-interest into dogma, the world was turning into one big marketplace, outrunning the macroeconomic policies of individual nations. During the 1950s and 1960s, the potential instabilities of a global market system were tempered by the reality that the economic power of the United States and the American dollar gave ballast to the world economy; a quarter century later, that was no longer true. And the Cold War and U.S. military expenditures serving as instruments of planning and stabilization is a phenomenon that is fast vanishing as well. It has been more than half a century since the world economy tried to operate according to principles of laissez-faire—and the 1920s and 1930s hardly offer models to emulate.

The years ahead should be a post-laissez-faire era for several distinct reasons. First, there is the stability of the system itself. Thirty years of steady postwar economic growth and relative political stability is a record in the history of the world. But it depended to a large extent on the United States' hegemony, and far from being a unique force for global economic stability, the United States today is only one great power among many, a source of instability, and new stabilizing institutions are necessary. Economies are not self-regulating within any one nation-state, and they do not suddenly become so just because commerce and finance are globalized—on the contrary, when commerce and finance are genuinely global and economies more interdependent than ever, a free market is newly vulnerable. We need a new generation of countervailing institutions and processes, for reasons of efficiency and stability as well as equity.

Second, world commerce as practiced is already a far cry from laissez-faire, except in the minds of orthodox American economists and their political allies. It is wishful thinking to celebrate the collapse of communism as a victory for simple nineteenth-century economic liberalism. When the restive citizens of Eastern Europe contemplated the attractions of the West, they had in mind not Dickensian capitalism, but modern social democracies in which the citizen enjoys protections against the ravages of markets as well as the excesses of states. The successful, dynamic economies of the late twentieth century have never subscribed to the Margaret Thatcher or Milton Friedman brand of simple free markets. Japan, Korea, and other economically vigorous Asian nations use an explicitly developmental state; the instruments that safeguard social health are largely cultural, but certainly they do not have free markets in the Western sense. The European Community practices a mix of managed and free markets and is not at all reluctant to support farm prices, subsidize new commercial technologies, and condition free entry to its domestic markets upon reciprocal bargains. Even the most "conservative" nation of the EC, the Federal Republic of Germany, spends nearly half its gross national product in the public sector, and it offers its citizens generous universal welfare-state support. Though commerce and finance in the late twentieth century are substantially globalized, our era is increasingly one of transnational joint ventures and consortia, heavily driven by technological learning and heavily influenced by state involvement. This is not the economy of Adam Smith or David Ricardo.

If the United States could not export its conception of laissez-faire to the world at a time when its economy was supreme, it can hardly do so when its relative economic power is more modest. The end of the Cold War signals an end not only to Soviet dominance in the East but to U.S. dominance in the West. The coming of age of Japan and the European Community increases the influence of forces that neither preach nor practice U.S.-style classical liberalism, and the United States needs to come to terms with this reality.

Third, there is the crucial matter of America's own national interest in an era no longer defined by the East-West geopolitical conflict. It is easy enough to declare that geopolitics must now give way to geo-economics. Defining what that really is, what conception of ideology and national interest applies, and what policies logically follow is rather more complex. That is the subject of much of this book. In a nutshell, my thesis is that America's devotion to laissez-faire as an ideal for either the U.S. economy or world commerce has become a serious hazard. It impedes the tasks of defining our strategic goals in the world, restoring our own economy to health, and organizing a sustainable, plural new economic order. The end of American hegemony does not have to signal the beginning of American decline. On the contrary, it ought to signal an opportunity for American national renewal.

The end of the Cold War invites a strategic shift in the economic as well as the military posture of the United States. The epochal changes in the Soviet Union and Eastern Europe come not a moment too soon, for the global grand strategy of the United States can no longer be sustained by the American economy. It has become conventional to assess the costs of the Cold War mainly as the economic strain of military leadership— Professor Paul Kennedy's "imperial overstretch." But as I shall argue, America's military leadership, its relentless promotion of laissez-faire, and the costs to its own economy are also linked in other, more subtle and complex ways.

Until the revolutionary events of 1989–90, the idea that the United States should revise its conception of national security to emphasize geo-economics rather than geopolitics had a certain logic, but it was a very difficult case to make in domestic politics. For even if the American economy was admittedly deteriorating, the high politics of Cold War remained paramount so long as Soviet policy seemed to threaten Western Europe, or peripheral areas of the world, or the nuclear balance. Moreover, the central role of the United States as propagator of the faith in liberal commerce made it awkward to commend economic nationalism as the policy of choice for the United States itself. As a result, politicians who favored any form of planning, or industrial policy, or "conversion" from military to commercial prowess, or a new emphasis on economic renewal, were dismissed, not as proponents of a dissenting school of political economy but as jingoists, simple protectionists, and geopolitical naïfs. Of course, the apparent "nationalism" of the dissenting view is not jingoist or anti-foreign, but simply a recognition that until world government arrives the nation state is the necessary locus of social contracts between market and society. As long as individual wealth is bound up with the wealth of a particular nation, then it matters immensely who produces what, and whether major nations play by the same rules.

The end of the Cold War and the dawn of many forms of pluralism unlock new possibilities. Pluralism in the former Eastern bloc means that the East-West balance ceases to be the defining strategic reality. And the economic coming of age of Western Europe and Japan signals a new pluralism in the West, which allows responsibility for the norms of the trading system to be shared, rather than being the prime responsibility of the United States. Yet at this writing, these dramatic changes have not yet produced fundamental reappraisal or initiative in U.S. geo-economic policy, other than a willingness to begin gradual arms reduction. The basic American conception of its global interest tenaciously resists revision.

Since the late 1940s, the American stance in the world has been built on two bedrock premises: that communism must be contained and that world commerce and finance must be organized according to principles of laissez-faire. The corollary of resolute anticommunism seemed to be an equally fierce unreconstructed capitalism. This symmetry of anticommunism and pro-laissez-faire may seem so obvious as to be axiomatic, but its dynamics are complex and worth investigating. Western Europe and Japan, after all, are also resolutely anticommunist but have never crusaded for classical economic liberalism, nor have they habitually sacrificed their own economic well-being to promote system-wide goals. However, for the United States, the Cold War and the laissez-faire imperative were mutually reinforcing—in several respects.

Geopolitically, an anti-Soviet grand alliance under American auspices engendered a satisfying deference to the United States among the liberal capitalist nations. On matters of "high politics"—national security—America's allies tended to follow its lead. The United States, in turn, paid for its leadership by bearing a disproportionate share of the costs of the Cold War. On economic matters, the United States took the lead in promoting an ever greater liberalization and integration of the global market system. But as guardian of that system, it was constrained, paradoxically, to tolerate a good deal of covert mercantilism among its trading partners and to subordinate its own national economic interest to free-market goals for the system as a whole, which it viewed almost as an extension of itself. Dollar hegemony, likewise, offered geopolitical benefits but escalating economic costs.

It was not surprising, therefore, that many officials in the Bush administration at first expressed real unease bordering on nostalgia when the Cold War began to end. For, as Deputy Secretary of State Lawrence Eagleburger declared poignantly in a lecture of September 13, 1989, at Georgetown University, these twin goals—containing communism and promoting American-style capitalism—had offered a certain security and predictability, as well as a reliable hierarchy of foreign-policy goals. "For all its risks and uncertainties," said Eagleburger, "the Cold War was characterized by a remarkably stable and predictable set of relations among the great powers."

Geopolitics after World War II was at its core about limiting the reach of the Soviet Union. That goal became so fundamental to American diplomacy that policy operated almost reflexively and provided a dependable calculus of American national interest. Peripheral conflicts were deemed significant mainly on the basis of whether they helped or harmed the Soviet Union. Our ostensible commitment to liberal capitalist democracy could be subordinated to accommodate fairly nasty right-wing regimes (in Chile, El Salvador, South Africa) and even wayward communist ones (Yugoslavia, China, Cambodia) so long as they blocked Soviet expansionism. In the American political mainstream, the only serious policy disputes of the Cold War era all hinged on whether the Soviet connection in a given regional conflict was strong enough to justify U.S. intervention (Vietnam, Cuba, Nicaragua). Seldom did we debate whether these conflicts intrinsically threatened our own national security, and never whether Russia itself should be contained. That bedrock goal was bipartisan and beyond dispute.

The logic of the postwar system also offered a hierarchy of geo-economic goals. These were less explicit, understood more intuitively, and seldom examined or challenged. America's own economic power was assumed as a given. Explicit industrial goals were eschewed as unnecessary, as contrary to our stated ideology, and as a bad example for our trading partners. Hardly anyone acknowledged or addressed the contradiction between practicing a mixed economy at home and promoting a laissez-faire economy globally. American manufacturers and bankers saw advantage for the leading capitalist nation in the freest possible movement of goods and money. And U.S. diplomats were pleased to offer America's Cold War allies the prize of free entry to the world's biggest market. The two goals complemented each other perfectly.

Both ideology and geopolitics reinforced the nearly fanatical loyalty to "free trade" that has characterized the members of America's bipartisan foreign-policy establishment. Yet this logic led the United States into policy dead ends, bad for the U.S. national interest and confusing for the global trading system. The prevailing ideology of economic liberalism has eschewed having industrial goals in the United States: in principle, it is none of the government's business where steel, or automobiles, or semiconductors, or VCRs, or civilian aircraft are produced; if production migrates abroad, this must be the market speaking, and if foreign industrial policies are the guiding, not invisible hand of global markets, this is deemed to make no significant difference. In practice, this makes America's industrial fate partly the captive of other nations' industrial strategies. Yet classical trade theory holds that if other nations are stupid enough to subsidize their export industries, American consumers ought to welcome the gift. The continuing disdain for having national industrial objectives makes it impossible to have any U.S. trade goals either, other than to exhort other nations to practice laissez-faire in the American image.

The United States continues to view itself as the political leader of the Western world, but U.S. administrations are reluctant to force other nations to play fair, lest they alienate key geopolitical allies. When exhortation fails to achieve equitable results, or to open markets, they are reluctant to resort to explicit market-share remedies, because this, of course, would be a version of the managed trade they claim to disdain and would violate the very ideology they promote. Finally, perhaps most seriously, our devotion to the ideal of laissez-faire means that those departures from liberal trade which do intermittently occur are undertaken guiltily and without strategic purpose, and are considered unfortunate concessions to domestic politics rather than economic development initiatives.

If our trading partners at least appreciated us as the only good free trader in the system, that might be a worthwhile outcome, but they don't. To most of the world, the theory seems utopian and the practice hypocritical. America seems to practice a chaotic ad hoc mercantilism—weapons procurement, farm price supports, textile quotas, and various "voluntary" restraints extracted from trading partners—while it stridently preaches free trade.

The United States after World War II enthusiastically embraced the role of, in Professor Charles Kindleberger's term, geo-economic "hegemon," much as Britain did in the middle and late nineteenth century. In Kindleberger's "theory of hegemonic stability," first spelled out in 1973 and since embellished by Stephen Krasner, Robert Keohane, and John Ruggie, among others,[1] the global economy tends to be systemically unstable, for much the same reason that an unregulated domestic economy is unstable. An unstabilized market economy is vulnerable to cycles of overproduction and underconsumption, as well as to panics that originate in the financial sector, which in turn lead to monetary contractions that only reinforce the macroeconomic propensity to boom and bust, as they spread to the "real" economy.

Domestically, this tendency could be leavened by activist macroeconomic policy, as well as interventionist central banking and other regulatory measures intended to contain financial instability. These could be explicitly Keynesian, via appropriate public budget deficits and surpluses; or they could involve an implicit Keynesianism of countercyclical military spending, social insurance, and multiyear union contracts, all of which serve to stabilize purchasing power across the business cycle.

But internationally, there is no Keynesian mechanism because there is neither a central monetary authority, a central currency, nor a central government capable of enforcing a common macroeconomics. There is also a proclivity for individual nations to solve their domestic economic problems by periodically deflating or by resorting to mercantilist devices, both of which restrict the market for other nations' products. The laissez-faire tendency to overproduction, to competition based on cheap wages, and to a resulting shortfall in aggregate demand is only intensified when nations attempt, strategically, to capture advantage in particular products at the expense of other nations. The classical liberal remedy for the multiple dilemmas of global commerce is simply free trade. But free trade by itself does not solve the Keynesian problem and may in fact worsen it.

Kindleberger and others have suggested that in the absence of a world government the global economy can be stabilized when a powerful nation plays the role of flywheel. The hegemon, in this conception, performs several functions: it serves as quasi-central banker, providing the system with financial liquidity in times of stress, as well as credit to temper exchange-rate instability; it serves as market of last resort and encourages other nations to keep their markets relatively open; being a rich and technologically advanced nation, the hegemon is a net source of development capital as well; and it also has a special responsibility for keeping the peace. A hegemon, in Kindleberger's sense, is relatively benign. Affiliation with its system is not coerced, but invited on the basis of benefits that the hegemon offers other member nations. Indeed, what differentiates hegemonic leadership from Caesarism is precisely that the hegemon uses carrots rather than sticks and makes sacrifices to preserve the system. Chief among these is that the hegemon endeavors to be the system's best-behaved free trader.

The nineteenth-century version of this system worked roughly as the theory describes, though it coexisted with such anomalies as empires, as well as German, French, American, and Japanese protectionism. It also had the notable disadvantage of being based on a gold standard, which achieved stability at the price of periodic deflation and left financial liquidity dependent on the vagaries of new discoveries of gold. After World War I, when a weakened Britain ceased to be the world's central banker and a hesitant United States was not yet willing to play the role, dissension and eventual anarchy reigned. The system slid toward depression and autarky, followed by crude nationalism and war, precisely because it lacked a benign hegemon.

The trouble with the hegemonic role is that over time it takes a toll. In the nineteenth century, Britain gradually got into the habit of exporting capital rather than goods, which depleted its own industrial base. In the spirit of Cobden and Peel, it practiced unilateral free trade; even nations with protective tariffs could export freely to England, just as the theory of free trade commended. Gradually, Germany and post–Civil War America, which were protectionist, caught up with and surpassed Britain's industrial productivity. After World War I, Britain briefly endeavored to retain the hegemonic role despite immense debts, and attempted to value the pound at its prewar parities, severely deflating its economy. Its military outlays also exacted both a direct fiscal toll and an indirect one in the militarization of much of its industry.

Of course, the hegemonic role confers benefits as well as burdens, and let us pause for a moment to note them. To begin with, the hegemonic role is immensely satisfying. If your nation is the leading one, it means that your currency is as good as gold, and other nations' currencies tend to be cheap in comparison. The hegemon characteristically permits other nations' currencies to be slightly undervalued, in order to temper its own payment surplus. Its allies, looking to expand exports, appreciate this, which in turn reinforces their deference to the hegemon. In the first three postwar decades, American GIs, tourists, and businessmen were delighted to find Western Europe a place where it took only a few dollars to buy fistfuls of local play money. A presentable meal cost five shillings in London or six francs in Paris, sailors could find sexual entertainment for the cost of a pair of nylon stockings, and the American middle class could actually tour Europe on the incredible pittance of Five Dollars a Day. Americans had the further satisfaction of seeing English become the lingua franca. The American abroad enjoyed a privileged status, and could generally be bailed out of any minor trouble by the local U.S. consulate.

As long as the hegemonic economy has a large capital surplus and the most productive manufacturing base, the world is an oyster for the hegemonic industrialist. After World War II, American entrepreneurs and bankers, armed with dollars and with that self-consciously American resource "know-how," spread out to all corners of the globe in search of markets. Rather than exporting products from high-wage America (which would have been churlish, given America's towering trade surplus), they set up shop locally, bearing financial and physical capital for local development. As late as 1967, the French journalist Jean-Jacques Servan-Schreiber could warn of an insurmountable *défi américain,* made up of U.S. capital and technological and entrepreneurial supremacy. The notable exception to this pattern, interestingly, was Japan, which largely closed its borders to American capital and American industrial investment, much to the consternation of U.S. economists, who offered grim warnings that poor Japan was shooting itself in the foot.

The hegemonic nation also gains a variety of political and economic advantages from being the provider of the system's key currency. That currency, by definition, is typically the system's "hardest" currency, the one treated with the most respect in the world's money markets. The technical literature terms this special advantage "seigniorage," in an updated usage of an archaic term that originally meant the profit that the sovereign makes for his own treasury from minting the coin of the realm. As applied to global political economy, seigniorage refers to the extra benefits of monetary hegemony. The seigniorial nation, for example, is able to borrow from abroad in its own currency, leaving other nations with the exchange-rate risk of possible devaluation. The monetary hegemon, uniquely, can print extra currency to cover payments deficits, leaving trading partners with imported inflation. Its currency is the one used for most commercial transactions, which gives its bankers advantage. Even at moments of extreme payments imbalance, America never had to submit to the indignity of IMF stabilization reviews, as did such once-mighty nations as Great Britain. For the most part, the seigniorage of the dollar was borne stoically by America's allies, as part of the recompense for American responsibility for the collective defense. The notable exception was General de Gaulle, who publicly railed against what he called the "exorbitant privilege" accorded dollar seigniorage, and uniquely among the leaders of allied nations deliberately exchanged dollars for gold in order to undermine the dollar's dominance.

Needless to say, the supremacy of the dollar in such institutions as the

IMF and the World Bank, as well as the dollar's role as principal currency both in commercial transactions and in the official reserves of nations, also gave the United States political benefits. American geopolitics—with the United States considered the bulwark against Bolshevism, the nation that viewed anticommunism in the most sacred terms—gave the United States further reason to value the diplomatic leverage conferred by its economic hegemony. Only in the 1960s, for the first time, did a major European ally (France) cross the United States on a fundamental question of East-West strategy. And General de Gaulle's insistence on developing an independent French nuclear *force de frappe* was notable mainly because it was so exceptional. Britain and West Germany, by contrast, generally did America's strategic bidding where the East-West strategic balance was concerned. Differences openly arose only over policies toward peripheral areas—the Suez invasion (in which Britain and France were humiliatingly made to back down); Vietnam (where the United States got less than the deference it wanted); the Falkland Islands (where the British lion indulged in one last atavistic imperial roar).

Until only a few years ago, the United States essentially ran the IMF, the World Bank, the GATT, the Coordinating Committee on Multilateral Export Controls (CoCom), NATO, and other nominally international agencies of hegemony, usually through foreign national surrogates. This meant that its preferred financial policies, as well as its geopolitical politics, were most likely to carry the day. All of this suggests why hegemony, once experienced, is so very hard to give up—even when its costs are excessive.

In the revisionist memory of orthodox economists, the postwar reconstruction that began at the Bretton Woods conference of 1944 was nothing more than the restoration of classical economic liberalism, based on free movement of capital and goods. But at the time, the goal was seen as something else entirely. The statesmen of the 1940s were activists. They were mindful of the need to invent an alternative to the two extremes that recent history had burned into their consciousness: the escalating instability of laissez-faire capitalism during the 1920s and the destructive retreat into autarky and currency blocs during the 1930s, which in turn led to popular revolt against democratic rule, to extreme nationalism, and to a second world war. The postwar system, in John Gerard Ruggie's nice phrase evoking Karl Polanyi, was not intended to be classical liberalism but rather "embedded liberalism"—a market economy acknowledging social realities and tempered by stabilizing institutions.[2]

As we shall see in Chapter 2, none of the architects of postwar recovery on either side of the Atlantic placed much credence in laissez-faire. The

Great Depression had discredited the idea that markets were self-regulating. The war had demonstrated the power of economic planning and the possibility of full employment. Virtually every Western leader of republican conviction, whether nominally Social Democratic, Christian Democratic, plain Democratic, or even high Tory, believed government had a major function to perform in the economy, as stabilizer, as planner of public investment, as guarantor of high employment, as arena of social bargaining, and as custodian of a benign welfare state. In 1944, the statesmen of Bretton Woods attempted to design a world economic order biased toward full employment and high rates of growth.

The Keynesian remedy was to share a degree of sovereignty with a new global monetary authority. Nations might borrow liberally from that source to cover temporary payments deficits, rather than responding in the traditional way by deflating. The Keynesians hoped that this regime would both permit domestic economic policies of full employment and gear the international system as a whole toward plentiful credit and rapid growth. To the extent that the Keynesians were qualified free traders, they considered the systemic commitment to high growth, planning, and full employment necessary to make porous domestic markets politically endurable. In the absence of such a global regime, nations might have to limit free movement of capital and goods in order to practice Keynesianism-in-one-country.

But to borrow from T. S. Eliot, between the conception and the creation fell the shadow. Once Roosevelt died and the war ended, neither the Truman administration nor the Congress was prepared to cede that degree of sovereignty to international institutions, least of all to institutions likely to be dominated by foreigners of dubious collectivist persuasion. The actual International Monetary Fund turned out to be rather more modest, partly because forces of financial orthodoxy had regained influence in both Britain and America and partly because of the concerns about sovereignty. A parade of bankers, led by the president of the New York Federal Reserve Bank, Benjamin Strong, testified against the already watered-down IMF design for a global regime based on cheap credit, which seemed reminiscent of cranky nineteenth-century populist monetary schemes. In 1946 and 1947, the United States retreated from its bold commitments to a new global financial order, and Europe descended into recession. What rescued global Keynesianism—of a sort—was the Cold War.

American power came to be the stabilizer that was briefly envisioned for the IMF and World Bank. The dollar, not Keynes's imagined reserve currency "Bancor," gave the system liquidity and a bias toward growth. The Marshall Plan and America's Cold War spending, not a large-scale World Bank, balanced America's chronic export surplus and provided capital for postwar reconstruction. On paper, a degree of sovereignty had passed to a new generation of supranational bodies that seemed to be a vast improvement upon the frail institutions of the Versailles regime. But in practice, the U.S. Congress was willing to cede such authority only because the new international institutions were well understood to be proxies for the United States.

There was now a sharp disjuncture between the forms of a moderately Keynesian global regime, the geopolitical realities, and the understanding of what had been ventured. Though the global economic system invented in the mid-1940s was emphatically a mixed regime, with Keynesian and social democratic stabilizers, the regime's guarantor, the United States, paradoxically had the least enthusiasm for either abandoning classical liberalism or ceding sovereignty. Thus, the very departures from laissez-faire that helped to anchor a mixed system were not entirely acknowledged by the system's prime sponsor. Conservative Americans accepted nominally supranational institutions only because they were surrogates for American power. They tolerated restrictions on the free flow of capital and goods only as transitional measures necessary for early postwar reconstruction. They accepted the Keynesian welfare states of Western Europe as necessary anticommunist allies, not as ideological soul mates. And when laissez-faire was fashionable again, and private capital became fully mobile, and planning fell into disfavor, it was in the United States that the resurrection of classical liberalism was greeted with special glee—for this supposedly was the ultimate aim of American doctrine.

Yet as the ethic of laissez-faire gained ground, it did so almost in lockstep with the relative decline of its prime sponsor, the United States of America. America's endeavor to inject its own norms into the policies of other nations and rules of the trading system, while retaining its own status as system leader, came at increasing cost to its own (poorly understood) national interest. As other industrial nations gained strength, the cost to the United States of maintaining American hegemony escalated. However, American leaders were reluctant to alter their fundamental global policy objectives so long as Soviet communism was a perceived and often real security threat. With the ascendance of Ronald Reagan, the twin commitment to laissez-faire economics and anti-Sovietism as the fundamental policy goal intensified, and so did the costs to the U.S. economy.

The history of this deepening crisis is discussed in Chapters 3 and 4. The costs of hegemony have been conventionally understood mainly in military terms, as the unsustainable fiscal expense of maintaining a military protectorate. In official circles, there is long-standing clamor for "burden-sharing" of military costs with U.S. allies. But that analysis overlooks two other kinds of costs that directly flow from America's hegemonic role—the structural costs to domestic industry, which are discussed in chapters 5, 6, and 7, as well as the macroeconomic strains of supplying the world's currency and serving as engine of world demand, which is treated in Chapter 8.

The structural costs include the penalties that America incurs as the necessary exemplar of laissez-faire trade. America permits itself a closet form of strategic industrial planning only as an incidental by-product of military spending. Most government-sponsored R&D outlays are funneled through the defense establishment, compared with less than 10 percent in Germany and Japan. Commercially oriented industrial targeting, of the sort practiced by both Japan's Ministry of International Trade and Industry and the European Community, is ideologically verboten, and can be accomplished only incidentally. American trade negotiators chronically find themselves in the ludicrous position of earnestly denying that U.S. supremacy in aircraft has anything to do with the trillion dollars expended on purchases for the Air Force. The end of the Cold War drags all of these issues out of the closet. The United States now must face head-on the ideological questions of what deliberate technology policy we desire, to what national ends, and subject to what global ground rules.

Oddly enough, for a decade the United States has preached an ever more devout adherence to laissez-faire while practicing a perverse, unacknowledged Keynesianism, at ever-escalating cost to its own well-being. With much of the world suffering from debt, high unemployment, and stagflation, the one source of fiscal stimulus to the global economy was the U.S. budget deficit, which contributed extra purchasing power to the world economy—at long-term cost to America. As Japan and West Germany tended their own gardens and fiercely resisted the pressures of imported inflation, the dollar remained in its anomalous role as global currency. In theory, Reaganism preached an economics of free markets and fiscal restraint. In practice, Reaganism offered a fiscal stimulus to the United States and the world, driven first by increases in military spending and later by a structural deficit borne of tax cuts.

Supposedly, the post-1973 regime of floating exchange rates would force each nation to bring its macroeconomic policies into harmony with those of trading partners or suffer runs on its currencies. But the United States, as monetary hegemon, was the one nation able to borrow in its own currency. It was thus oddly exempt from the discipline, at least in a short run that turned out to be distressingly long. By the early 1980s, foreign capital flooded into U.S. money markets, attracted by Federal Reserve chairman Paul Volcker's monetarist anti-inflation remedy of double-digit interest rates. This, of course, bid up the value of the dollar. A high dollar, in turn, abruptly priced U.S. goods out of world markets—just when the productive strength of rival economies was also making U.S. goods less competitive.

But thanks to this hegemonic exemption, as the U.S. balance of payments deficit widened and the trade accounts worsened, the value of the dollar, instead of going down, kept going up. American products were ever more uncompetitive, while the first Reagan administration kept insisting that the "free market," by definition, had to be getting the value of the dollar right and that there was no problem. A high budget deficit exacerbated the problem by requiring the United States to suck in even more foreign capital. A related ideological stubbornness—a dedication to low taxes and high military spending—precluded a macroeconomic remedy.

When, early in the second Reagan administration, Treasury Secretary James Baker belatedly conceded that markets could indeed be getting the value of the dollar wrong, the strategy changed but the larger ideology did not. The Plaza Accord of September 1985 committed the five leading nations to a rough management of exchange rates and a coordinated effort to drive down the value of the dollar. However, the "Group of Five" (the United States, Japan, West Germany, Great Britain, and France) stopped well short of devising a new Bretton Woods or constructing an expansionary solution to the Third World debt. It was a moment that cried out for bold statecraft, but the leaders of every major capitalist nation save France were conservatives who did not believe that markets required major structural interventions. The traditional policy goals of the United States— ever greater deregulation and liberalization of the global system and disdain for policies of economic stabilization or industrial targeting—were reemphasized.

A cheap dollar coupled with persistent budget deficits failed to solve America's trade imbalance. Contrary to standard theory, the structural damage to U.S. competitiveness caused by the period of dollar overvaluation did not instantly reverse itself when the dollar cheapened. At the end of the 1980s, the U.S. trade deficit was still in excess of $100 billion a year. Nations eager to hold the market shares they had captured proved very adept at "pricing to market" and compensating for the cheaper dollar. When the yen appreciated 50 percent against the dollar, the price of Toyotas did not rise proportionally. Despite a macroeconomic imbalance, the United States was able to import the capital it needed to finance its budgetary and trade deficits, but it did so more and more by selling real assets. With its twin deficits, it therefore continued to be a Keynesian engine sustaining a moderate pace of global growth—but at escalating cost to its own economic health.

. . .

There is an orthodox account of the cause and cure of America's economic slide, and a dissenting account. The orthodox account is the product of an extremely potent alliance—of Cold Warriors, private capitalists, and traditionalist economists. The Cold Warriors like American markets to be as open as possible because this is part of the glue of alliance, in which the low politics of trade takes second place to the high politics of national security. When U.S. priorities place geopolitics ahead of geo-economics, America's trading partners are only too happy to oblige. The private capitalists like global laissez-faire for the obvious reason: they wish to pursue markets, materials, and earnings wherever they choose and to escape the discipline of national regulation. Orthodox economists complete the triad by preaching that the least regulated market is the most efficient one, and they certify the scientific soundness of laissez-faire. Neoclassical economists, industrialists, and investment bankers flow in and out of government jobs, where they share the premises of the Cold Warriors about America's hegemonic responsibilities. American industry, in turn, supports researchers known for respectable, internationalist thinking, which is to say laissez-faire. All these links create a club of like-minded people that marginalizes or excludes heretics.

In the orthodox account, America's industrial decline is mainly the result of macroeconomic factors—a low savings rate, an excessive budget deficit—which in turn require domestic interest rates to be too high and suck in foreign capital. Standard economics insists that structural factors such as industrial organization, technology policy, public investment, and training systems only barely affect the competitiveness of nations and in any case cannot (by definition) improve on the market. The standard account holds that it would be self-defeating for America to respond to its worsening competitive standing by resorting to sectoral policies or strategies of managed trade. Such measures are dismissed as wrongheaded theory, as self-serving pressure from injured interest groups, and as irritating to allies.

The orthodox school also holds that foreign investment in the United States is an unambiguous blessing, and that concern about foreign ownership of factories, farms, real estate, and proprietary technologies is anachronistic in a globalized economy, if not nativist. Finally, it insists that trade policy, again by definition, can make no difference. If the United States turns up the diplomatic heat and coerces Japan to buy more supercomputers, say, American consumers will compensate by purchasing some other import so long as the macroeconomic fundamentals are unchanged; the same trade balance will persist.

The dissenting account of America's economic predicament is less neatly packaged and less ideologically coherent, but it is rapidly gaining credibility. It emphasizes that a variety of structural factors—including the dynamics of American capital markets, the organization of American firms, the short-term perspective of American investors, the quality of American schooling and job training—have combined to hobble the competitiveness of U.S. industry. It doesn't deny that savings rates, budget deficits, and the value of the U.S. dollar matter, but it insists that they don't tell the whole story.

Ideologically, the dissenting camp is diverse. For example, business leaders frustrated by Japanese mercantilism find the macroeconomic account of America's declining competitiveness unconvincing. Trade unionists find that the integrated global economy is relentlessly undercutting good jobs at good wages. Most specialists on Japan find the economists' denial of Japan's intricate mercantilism absurdly deductive; empirical studies of the structure of the Japanese economy have identified a complex web of relationships that effectively resists imports. This emerging view is ideologically inchoate, for some of its most provocative representatives (Clyde Prestowitz, Chalmers Johnson, Kevin Phillips, among others) consider themselves essentially conservative Republicans, while others (Lester Thurow, Robert Reich, Laura Tyson, and James Fallows) are liberal Democrats. They have something basic in common, though they haven't quite acknowledged it: they don't believe in laissez-faire.

Until very recently, the logic of American hegemony, both as protector of military security and as advocate of global free markets, was so potent that the dissenters could not receive a serious hearing. When it comes to trade policy, most Democratic economists as well as Republican ones are resolute defenders of classical liberalism. In the last Democratic incumbency, the most potent opposition to both industrial policy and aggressive trade policy came from within the administration, not from the Republican opposition. Politically, the ascendancy of laissez-faire and the disrepute of Keynesianism have caused candidates with interventionist instincts to couch their views mainly in terms of having to get tough with America's trading partners. In the 1988 election, the press treated Richard Gephardt as a simple Japan-basher, and not as a candidate offering a different theory of political economy, and Gephardt himself was not quite sure just what his dissenting theory might be.

But all of this is at last changing, and rapidly. The old laissez-faire iron triangle of industrialists, diplomats, and economists is wobbling. Industry is no longer unanimously supportive of the laissez-faire agenda, and the skepticism goes far beyond the "loser" industries of the orthodox account. America's most advanced manufacturing industries are now supporters of both a more collaborative relationship between industry and government and a more assertive approach to trade. The Bush administration may not care whether America's last large manufacturer of semiconductor fabricating equipment is sold to the Japanese, but IBM cares, even though IBM is the quintessential "internationalist" American company. The principal lobbyist for disbanding export controls is now the U.S. Chamber of Commerce. And for the diplomats, with the Cold War ebbing, the East-West conflict ceases to be the overriding determinant of policy. Even the economics profession has made room for a dissenting view of trade, as well as giving grudging recognition to the truth that the organization of the firm, and of financial markets, and of educational and training systems, do affect a nation's ability to compete.

If the Cold War ended on November 9, 1989, the day the Berlin Wall came down, the post–Cold War era began on August 2, 1990, the day Iraq invaded Kuwait. The Mideast crisis that ensued signaled the outlines of a new geopolitical order in several ways. It suggested a concert of great powers, essentially status quo nations that believe in liberal capitalist democracy, upholding world order against a small group of nations with radical, system-threatening aims. It suggested that the Soviet Union, eager to ingratiate itself with Western powers and giving priority to its own economic recovery, would behave like a status quo power. It was startling to hear spokesmen for the Soviet Union—which after all had annexed Estonia, Latvia, Lithuania, and portions of Finland, Poland, Germany, Romania, and Czechoslovakia in the 1940s, which had invaded sovereign Eastern European nations as late as the early 1980s—railing against Iraq's aggression and defending the sanctity of national borders. And, remarkably, the United Nations, so recently attacked by U.S. administrations, was used to American advantage as an instrument of collective security.

At the same time, the Kuwait crisis underscored the United States' continuing image of itself as a hegemonic power while its major allies retained the habit of acting as free riders on the system. It was the U.S. that took the diplomatic lead, engineered the Security Council resolution, persuaded the Saudis to let in U.S. troops, urged the Egyptians to form an anti-Iraq bloc within the Arab League, and coordinated the embargo. It was the United States that initially committed ground troops. Japan, long accustomed to viewing its global interests in purely commercial terms and reluctant to alienate any trading power, had to be pressured into honoring the blockade of Iraq. America's NATO allies committed only token naval and air forces and resisted sending ground troops. The U.S. was hesitant to gear up the machinery of the United Nations as the vehicle of military action, and, as hegemon, remained the key source of electronic intelligence on Iraq's battle plans and troop movements.

So, the system still tends to operate, by default, as a Pax Americana, and will continue to do so as long as the U.S. allows it to. Yet, with the Cold War over, for the first time since 1944 there is now an opportunity to build a true multilateral system. We have come full circle back to Roosevelt's vision of a system of collective security using international institutions anchored by great-power cooperation. Geopolitically, there is no need for the world's major nations to spend upward of a trillion dollars a year on an East-West arms race. The new challenge is how to prevent proliferation of chemical and nuclear weapons, and how to contain and mediate regional conflict, in the absence of an alliance system.

Economically, the challenge is also the one identified in 1944 by Keynes: how to gear the world toward high growth and full employment, and how to reconcile national sovereignty with a global marketplace. In the late 1940s, the United States was reluctant to cede sovereignty to international institutions because it was so strong; empowering organizations controlled by foreigners seemed an affront. Today, there is resistance to a new round of institution building because America seems too weak. It is easier to cling to the habits of American economic hegemony, and the false ideal of laissez-faire, even as those illusions corrode America's own well-being.

But to rebuild the world system and to redefine America's national strategy within that system requires the same boldness and imagination as possessed by the statesmen of 1944. First, we need to acknowledge the reality of pluralism. One hopes, contrary to Professor Kindleberger, that the role of hegemon can be played by a concert of great nations, for no single nation currently has the combined political and economic stature to do the job single-handedly. Such a system would require nations to pool sovereignty and financial authority in several functional areas: in an international trade organization with real enforcement powers; in a genuine global public central bank or regional banks with a Keynesian bias toward high growth.

U.S. influence in the Bretton Woods generation of monetary institutions is fading. Instead of clinging to the perquisites of former hegemony, we should welcome that shift. In exchange for letting Europe and Japan have more influence (which is coming anyway), we should insist that they take on more responsibilities. At Bretton Woods, Keynes rightly attempted to structure incentives that would force nations with chronic surpluses to expand, rather than placing the burden on debtor nations to deflate. It is unacceptable that a few nations, such as Germany and Japan, should run immense trade surpluses year in and year out. As chronic surplus nations, they enjoy high-employment economies with tight monetary policies, low real interest rates, and low inflation. That intensifies the competitive advantages enjoyed by their firms, and it exports deflation to other nations. Japan and Germany (and of course Germany is now the leading nation of a larger entity, the European Community) have come of age, and they should shoulder more responsibility.

We need to acknowledge that laissez-faire is a false idol, for both domestic and global political economy. The global intelligentsia may think of itself as stateless, and global capital may see nation-states as anachronistic encumbrances. But the state remains the locus of the polity, notwithstanding the best successes of supranational institution building. And the polity remains the structure best suited for counterbalancing the excesses of the market. Therefore it does matter if American workers have access to high-productivity jobs, and it matters whether enterprises that provide those jobs are located in the United States. The EC, for example, is right to insist that foreign-owned companies that operate within Western Europe as "European" companies meet some threshold tests, such as whether they produce "high end" components in Europe or merely slap together final assembly. This may strike some purists as distastefully mercantilist, but until the millennium of global government comes or until all nations have roughly the same labor and social standards, it is a necessary accommodation to the reality of political economy. The United States would do well to address explicitly which key industries it hopes to retain and what mixture of foreign-owned and domestic companies is appropriate. One pursues such policies not because one dislikes foreigners but because the invisible hand does not produce equitable outcomes and the visible hand remains a national one.

Somewhere, in between the failed utopias of pure socialism and pure laissez-faire, a practical middle ground exists where economies can operate dynamically and civil society can flourish. It was the challenge of the generation of the 1940s to rebuild liberal society and keep totalitarianism at bay. It is our challenge, half a century later, to renew the promise of a mixed economy and a social conception of citizenship. In the coming decades, we will live in a post–Cold War world, which no great power will dominate. It is likely to be a post-laissez-faire world as well.

one

RELUCTANT STATECRAFT:

BRETTON WOODS AND THE

POSTWAR SYSTEM

A remarkable half-decade of statecraft began at Bretton Woods, New Hampshire, where, in the stately Mount Washington Hotel, representatives of forty-four nations spent the first week of July 1944 designing a system to restore the world's flow of money and commerce after the disruptions of World War II. Years later, the system established at Bretton Woods would be depicted as a triumph of liberal internationalism—a resurrection of free-market forces, the economic counterpart to a restored democratic politics. But in 1944, with the economic upheavals of the 1930s fresh in everyone's mind, few participants at Bretton Woods were disposed to go back to simple laissez-faire; that had been tried after World War I and found disastrously wanting. Rather, the planners of Bretton Woods wanted something quite new: to restore the flow of global commerce, but within a framework of economic intervention. The aim was to allow for domestic planning and full employment within each nation and to avoid the instability created by a global system driven purely by market forces.

The mixed economic system ventured at Bretton Woods was created partly by design, partly by force of circumstances. The design was substantially that of the century's most original economist, John Maynard Keynes. The circumstances were historical, ideological, and geopolitical. Everyone remembered the practical disgrace of laissez-faire economics in the 1920s and the contrast with the successful wartime economic planning of the 1940s. And everyone sensed the emerging dominance of the United States of America.

The United States had entered both world wars reluctantly and still behaved more as an upstart than as an imperial power. But Roosevelt's administration was determined not to withdraw from postwar reconstruction as the United States had done in 1919. The nation was still suffused with Wilsonian idealism, now leavened by a more mature sense of *Real-politik.* Americans were in an uncharacteristic mood of interventionism, both economic and political. Yet the new sense of global responsibility was caught between opposite self-images—the United States as a reluctant peacemaker that intervened only long enough to put things right versus the United States as Atlas, a deliberate long-term guarantor of world stability. These contradictory notions seemed briefly to fuse, in a bold moment aimed at building a universal world order with multilateral rules, in which the United States accepted the need for systematic intervention in both the private marketplace and the collective security of nations. The goal was not American dominion, but a stable, prosperous, and well-ordered world in which American soldiers would not have to intervene to settle foreign wars every generation.

Roosevelt relished the prospect of injecting American ideals into world politics, and doing so in a more pragmatic and effective fashion than the hero of his youth, Woodrow Wilson. His country was an improbable hegemon, skeptical of the role of power in world affairs, wary of European intrigue, touchingly constitutionalist. It was also an improbable banker, for the nation had been built on cheap land and cheap money. As Walter Russell Mead has observed, America was suddenly a creditor nation but still had the mentality of a debtor nation.

John Maynard Keynes had been an early critic of the disastrous, bungled effort to restore a global economic order after World War I. In his prescient 1920 book, *The Economic Consequences of the Peace,* he had inveighed against both the attempt to reestablish the prewar gold standard and the draconian reparations extracted from defeated Germany. The worsening instability of the global economy during the 1920s vindicated his criticism, and by the time of the cataclysmic world depression, the mature Keynes was fashioning his insights into his magisterial *General Theory.* Keynes persuasively refuted Say's law, which held that supply had to generate demand. He demonstrated that supply often exceeded demand, leading to mass unemployment, idle resources, social conflict, and a needless waste of human potential. The costs were not merely economic: the ensuing social and political chaos led directly to war.

For Keynes, the international realm of the laissez-faire economy displayed a special version of his general theory, especially vulnerable to instability and depression and resistant to stabilization. An individual nation, with a relatively self-sufficient national economy, enjoyed the perquisites of sovereignty within its borders; its government could manipulate total demand to generate adequate rates of savings, investment, growth, and employment. But an open global economy of cross-national trade in different currencies, mediated only by private merchants and bankers, tended to intensify periodic depressions. If one nation stimulated its economy by itself, some of the extra demand "leaked" into the purchase of imports, leaving that nation with an unsustainable payments deficit. Yet walling off a domestic economy only deprived the global economy of that nation's purchasing power. Nations with payments deficits had usually balanced their accounts by shrinking their domestic output or by closing their borders, and hence exporting deflation and depression to the rest of the world. Depression intensified the temptation to pursue economic recovery at the expense of one's neighbors. The 1930s had shown an extreme example of this dynamic.

It would be hard to exaggerate how central to the planners of 1944 were the lessons of Versailles and the Great Depression. For them, the end of the second great war was a unique moment when, by historical standards, the victorious nations were in a rare mood to be both benign and bold. To the British and the Americans, their war effort was a triumph of democratic planning, as well as proof of Keynes's point that people can be put back to productive work if the level of demand is kept high. In the United States, unemployment had melted from 13.8 percent to less than 2 percent in the first six months of mobilization; by 1945, the *civilian* economy was producing 50 percent more than it had in 1940, even though nearly half of the GNP in 1942–45 had gone for the socially unproductive task of making war.

Keynes began work on his blueprint for a postwar economic system as early as 1941. As senior adviser to the British Treasury—the same post he had held in World War I—he had been intimately involved in negotiations with the Roosevelt administration on Lend-Lease throughout the war and then on plans for postwar economic reconstruction. As leader of the British delegation, Keynes came to Bretton Woods with an ingenious design to replace the deflationary gold standard and laissez-faire internationalism with a global counterpart of his domestic economics—an internationalism that made room for domestic economic planning. His grand goal was to keep the level of worldwide demand high, and to create the space for planners in each nation to run high-demand domestic economies, free from the constraints of imported deflation. A global financial system with plentiful credit would liberate nations from having to solve balance-of-payments problems by practicing deflation or protection and would thus free the system from the cumulative effect of cascading national austerities. It was a wholly new conception of the international economy—a third way.


Before Keynes, there were two opposite conceptions of the role of the state in a capitalist global economy—liberal internationalist versus protectionist. Prior to the era of industrial capitalism, internationalism had been illiberal. It had often taken the form of religious universalism—the Crusades or the Holy Roman Empire. Occasionally internationalism had been merely a grandiose extension of nationalism, as in the imperial pretensions of Charlemagne or Napoleon. However, as capitalists became the new internationalists in the early nineteenth century, internationalist came to be synonymous with liberal. To be a liberal internationalist meant that one supported republican political institutions and laissez-faire economics at home, free flows of capital and goods across national frontiers, and a hopeful, irenic sense of world community.

As the historian Karl Polanyi explained it, laissez-faire, or classical liberalism, required three interrelated tenets: "that labor should find its price on the market; that the creation of money should be subject to an automatic mechanism; that goods should be free to flow from country to country without hindrance or preference; in short, a labor market, the gold standard, and free trade."[1] Domestically, laissez-faire capitalism required that wage workers be available to entrepreneurs; to be available, they had to be economically vulnerable. Liberal internationalism required a gold standard both as a common denominator of monetary value and as a source of financial discipline. In an open trading system anchored by a gold standard, every nation's currency could be freely exchanged for gold at a price determined primarily by markets and kept relatively stable by newly emergent central bankers, close allies of private financial forces. A nation that grew at an "excessive" rate or that tolerated domestic inflation was likely to run a trade deficit as it sucked in more goods than it exported. The resulting deficit in the national balance of payments triggered speculation against the offending nation's currency and compelled it to sell gold reserves. Eventually, this constraint would force the deviant nation to raise its domestic interest rates, which would both depress the domestic appetite for imports and attract foreign capital, restoring external balance. A central bank could help facilitate this discipline. And free trade—the freest possible movement of capital, goods, and services—was the linchpin of the entire theory.

This model more or less operated between the mid-nineteenth century and World War I, at least as an ideal. It comported nicely both with the classical economist's love of self-adjusting systems and with the private merchant's desire for open commerce, labor discipline, and fiscal restraint. A Marxist might underscore the point that it also allowed capitalists with an international perspective to discipline national work forces—by keeping the domestic unemployment rate high enough to promote labor discipline and punishing nations whose economies grew faster than their neighbors'.

Geopolitically, the system was based on the open-door principle of universal access to world markets. Liberal internationalism could coexist with surmountable trade barriers such as tariffs, but these were supposed to be transparent and "nondiscriminatory," which meant that they were supposed to apply equally to all trading partners. If country A imposed a 20 percent tariff on shoes against country B, it was not supposed to cut a separate side deal for a lower tariff with country C. Trade and investment opportunities were supposed to apply equally to all comers, and barriers were likewise supposed to be uniform.

In the century after David Ricardo's famous treatise on the virtues of comparative advantage, published in 1817, this view of open trade and monetary relations gradually became codified and acquired a characteristic baggage of concepts, institutions, and moral claims. Most liberal internationalists added the further contention, after Montesquieu, Sir James Steuart, and Richard Cobden, among others, that where open commerce flowed, war became less likely.[2] World War I, a uniquely savage carnage among close trading partners, did amazingly little to dampen that claim.

But, of course, the classical system was never fully operational. Something approaching classical liberalism operated within Europe for perhaps thirty years, beginning with Britain's repeal of its tariffs on imported grain, the Corn Laws, in the 1830s, which ushered in a period of reciprocal reductions in trade barriers, as well as a formalization of the gold standard. Yet even in its heyday, the system was complicated by bilateral concessions, by empires, and by a variety of mercantilisms. France and Germany were already moving toward economic nationalism by the 1860s; liberal trade remained a *beau idéal*. But to the extent that a gold standard and relatively open movement of goods and capital did operate, they exercised severe constraints on domestic economies.

Among the several disadvantages of the classical system was its unfortunate bias toward economic contraction. In effect, individual nations were penalized if they grew faster than the system as a whole. The system also left nations vulnerable to external shocks, in the form of imported bouts of inflation, financial panic, and depression. In addition, it tended in the short run to favor the industries of the nation that currently enjoyed a technological lead. Some commentators termed this "the imperialism of free trade."[3]

In the usual formulation, the opposite of liberal internationalism is nationalism. Economically, nationalism is usually mercantilist and protectionist. In the nineteenth century, the catch-up nations were mercantilist, viewing the free traders as merely wrapping the self-interest of currently dominant nations in an ideological cloak of high-mindedness. Obviously, if there were no barriers to commerce, the private companies of the leading power (Britain in the nineteenth century, the United States in the mid-twentieth) would dominate world commerce, and their technological lead and market power would only widen. Nations as diverse as Germany, France, Japan, and the United States all practiced varying degrees of protectionism in the late nineteenth century, just as Asia's newly industrial nations were mercantilist in the late twentieth.

The intellectual father of nineteenth-century mercantilism was a Swabian, Friedrich List, whose treatises *The Natural System of Political Economy* (1837) and *The National System of Political Economy* (1841) argued for state-led industrialization to keep the then dominant nation (Britain) from becoming industrially preeminent. List, interestingly, was a liberal in many respects. He favored political democracy. He insisted that before economic development could take place, a country needed to abolish slavery and serfdom, establish the rule of law for both persons and property, provide public education of young people and training of artisans, and establish a professional civil service. However, he argued that wealth depended not on a natural global division of labor but on the "productive powers" of a nation. And these could not be developed if lesser nations passively deferred to the dominance of the leading industrial nation—Great Britain.

> As a nation becomes more industrialized it becomes more necessary to secure the services of suitable trained people in the factories and workshops. Such people are now able to command higher salaries and wages than was formerly possible. It will be easier for them to devote themselves entirely to a particular branch of knowledge. . . .
>
> The greater the advance in scientific knowledge, the more numerous will be the new inventions which save labour and raw materials and lead to the discovery of new products and processes . . .
>
> The cosmopolitan theorists [Adam Smith, David Ricardo, Jean-Baptiste Say, et al.] do not question the importance of industrial expansion. They assume, however, that this can be achieved by adopting the policy of free trade and by leaving individuals to pursue their own private interests. They believe that in such circumstances a country will automatically secure the development of those branches of manufacture which are best suited to its own particular situation. They consider that government action to stimulate the establishment of industries does more harm than good.[4]

List not only made the classic "infant industry" arguments for state assistance, but made a far more subtle case that only when there was a world government would the theoretical preconditions of laissez-faire be fulfilled; that, absent a functioning world government, laissez-faire would engender economic dislocation and social chaos. List's treatise, almost unknown in the Anglo-Saxon world, had immense influence in its day in Germany and, later, in Japan. And it sounds remarkably like the philosophy pursued today by the developing nations of East Asia.

Of course, Americans like Alexander Hamilton or Abraham Lincoln needed no economic text to appreciate that the young industries of a young nation needed subsidies to promote their own "mechanical arts" and high tariffs to keep out cheaper, more technically advanced British goods. Nor did Japan, Korea, and the later mercantilists rely on any body of theory to justify their instinctive sense that domestic industries would be slow to develop if their markets were swamped with American imports.

In a century noted for intense nation-building, mercantilism often came wrapped in the same package with the uglier forms of nationalism. In their desire to chart an economic course independent of the imperialism of free trade, some nations, invoking nationalistic pride, found it convenient to add colonies; an empire was a quite natural concomitant of economic nationalism, for it provided a closed circle of raw materials and markets, a currency bloc, linked militarily, satisfyingly color-coded on maps, and nicely insulated from metropolitan competitors.

In the dichotomy of liberal internationalism versus simple protectionism, the United States began shifting in a more liberal direction in the 1890s. As American industry and agriculture became more productive and competitive, companies seeking export markets began to challenge the prevailing protectionist policies. The United States became a crusader against the covert bilateral concessions wrested by European powers from China and other quasi-colonies, and an advocate of the Open Door. The idea was that access to overseas markets, raw materials, and investment opportunities should not be governed by bilateral deals and spheres of influence, but should be available to all contenders. This doctrine, originally formulated as a China policy, was soon generalized into high principle. By the time of Woodrow Wilson's presidency, the politics of the Open Door was viewed as not simply a natural expression of the self-interest of a newly emergent exporting nation, but as a universal and transcendent virtue. This penchant for idealism and universalism often made it extremely difficult to calculate just what the national interest was as circumstances changed. Though Wilson represented the apotheosis of the American discomfort with *Realpolitik,* the American insistence on finding idealistic reasons for the most calculating and nationalistic policies long outlived him.

In the American experience, the opposite of liberal internationalism was not only protectionism but, often, isolationism. The American self-image envisioned a nation blessed with special virtues in a wicked world; the practical choice was either to export American principles to the world or else to withdraw from it. After Wilson's failure to persuade his countrymen that the United States should share responsibility for the postwar reconstruction of the 1920s, much American opinion reverted to conservative isolationism. Yet it was an isolationism with more than a tinge of imperialism. Henry Cabot Lodge, for example, the scourge of the Versailles Treaty, was no simple isolationist; he was eager for the United States to become a strong naval power, to assert its influence in China, to annex Hawaii, Cuba, and the Philippines.

America's liberal internationalists saw their mission as projecting U.S. power into the world—but in order to teach universal virtues, not to pursue narrow nationalistic goals. Wilsonians thought of their program as the antidote to both isolationism and imperialism, foreign and domestic. This universalist internationalism invariably went hand in hand with laissez-faire economics. In the first half of this century, Cordell Hull, who became Roosevelt's Secretary of State, was the purest and most influential exemplar of a liberal internationalist. Hull not only embraced the traditional nineteenth-century economic arguments for free trade but, like Wilson, believed it was America's duty and destiny to convert cynical European diplomatic conceits—spheres of influence, secret concessions, empires, and currency blocs—into a system of universal open commerce. He also believed, with Montesquieu and Cobden, that openness and free trade promoted political democracy, increased prosperity, and lessened the risk of war. And he added the characteristically American idea that free trade would be a useful form of antitrust, a natural enemy of homegrown monopolies.

Only in the 1930s, in response to the Great Depression, did a new approach to the global political economy emerge—liberal, but not laissez-faire. When FDR took office, the global system of payments and trade was in shambles. In response, the major powers had retreated into protectionism and competitive deflation. The first major international parley facing the new administration was the London World Economic Conference of 1933, which President Hoover and the European forces of financial orthodoxy had conceived as an effort to restore a functioning gold standard. But Roosevelt was a sufficiently intuitive Keynesian to know that the deflationary influence of an international gold standard would undercut his program of domestic economic recovery, and that recovery was the first order of business. To the great embarrassment of Hull (and the applause of Keynes), Roosevelt abruptly took the United States off the gold standard and torpedoed the London Conference.

Roosevelt did not yet have a clear vision of what sort of world system was consistent with his domestic economic program. Like so much of the New Deal, his international economic policy was a pragmatic amalgam of opposites. Only a year after the London Conference came apart, Hull was able to persuade the administration and Congress to enact the Reciprocal Trade Agreements Act, which embodied the sacred free-trade ideal of nondiscrimination and the "most favored nation" principle. Congress, which had hitherto reserved to itself the writing of tariff schedules, gave the President the power to negotiate reciprocal reductions in tariffs and accepted the idea that barriers to trade ought to be reduced. This reflects the two distinct tendencies coexisting uneasily throughout the New Deal. One emphasized domestic reconstruction, embraced economic planning, allocated capital, favored organized labor, redistributed income, and regulated the private economy; it was implicitly mercantilist in its understanding that international laissez-faire would wreck domestic stabilization. The other tendency—Hull's—was classically liberal, favoring free trade globally and free markets at home. At Bretton Woods these two opposite tendencies were briefly reconciled in the Keynesian vision. As John Gerard Ruggie observed in his classic 1982 essay on international regimes: "This was the essence of the [postwar] compromise: unlike the economic nationalism of the 1930s, it would be multilateral in character; unlike the liberalism of the gold standard and free trade, its multilateralism would be predicated upon domestic interventionism."[5]

For less visionary men than Keynes, the immediate goal at Bretton Woods was simply to restart the flow of international payments and commerce in the traditional manner. There was thus a tension between the forces of orthodoxy, who merely hoped to restore business as usual, and the Keynesians, who wanted something radically new. The ideological divisions at Bretton Woods were further complicated by bureaucratic rivalries within each delegation and by divisions of perceived national interest. The British, for example, wanted to preserve their empire and to retain preferential trading and financial relationships within the countries of the "sterling bloc"—those nations that used the British pound to settle their accounts. The U.S. State Department, in contrast, wanted a universal system of open trade. The British wanted a long transitional postwar period with plenty of cheap credit to finance their staggering war debts. The Americans wanted to clear up the war debts and return to a system of freely convertible currencies as quickly as possible. And as late as 1946, many in the Roosevelt-Truman administration clung to the pre–Cold War vision of One World anchored by U.S.-Soviet cooperation.

Some viewed British plans as nothing but a cover for the traditional imperialism of trade and currency blocs. In reality, the British proposals braided together an old strand of imperialism with a new one of Keynesian planning.

The heart of Keynes's design for the Bretton Woods system was an "international clearing union" that stopped just short of being a world central bank.[6] This fund, capitalized at $26–$32 billion, would issue its own reserve currency, which Keynes called Bancor, from the French words for bank and gold. The plan would allow countries having payments deficits to incur loans on the books of the clearing union, euphemistically termed "overdrafts." Rather than having to undergo real contractions of their economies, "have-not" countries could borrow more or less at will, subject to the limits of their credit line. However, the "have" countries—those that ran chronic surpluses in their balance of payments—would have their currencies declared "scarce," which would give other nations the right to discriminate against their exports, thus compelling the surplus countries to expand their economies and absorb more imports. The central, radical innovation was this: where the traditional gold standard placed pressure on deficit nations to contract, Keynes's system put pressure on creditor nations to expand.

The plan also provided for fixed and stable exchange rates supported by interventions of the clearing union and the central banks of member nations. While nations with temporary payments imbalances could freely borrow from the clearing union, a nation with a long-term imbalance would eventually have to devalue its currency, but that process would also be lubricated by advances from the clearing union. Where traditional global finance had been run by private forces serving narrow creditor interests, this new order would be administered by new transnational public institutions committed to high growth and the general good. Keynes thus wrapped the orthodox objective—restoration of free commerce and payments—in his own grand design for a world economy biased toward growth.

In an early published draft of the plan, Keynes wrote in April 1943:

> We need an instrument of international currency having general acceptability between nations, so that blocked balances and bilateral clearings are unnecessary . . .
>
> We need an orderly and agreed method of determining the relative exchange rates of national currency units, so that unilateral action and competitive exchange depreciations are prevented.
>
> We need a quantum of international currency . . . neither determined . . . by the technical progress of the gold industry . . . nor

subject to large variations depending on the gold reserve policies of individual countries; but is governed by the actual current requirements of world commerce . . .

We need an agreed plan for starting off every country after the war with a stock of reserves appropriate to its importance in world commerce . . .

We need a central institution, of a purely technical and non-political character, to aid and support other international institutions concerned with the planning and regulation of the world's economic life.[7]

This was all in marked contrast to the interwar experience, in which no coherent monetary system existed and private bankers with creditor mentalities dominated the management of periodic crises, leaving nations to serve their own welfare with a variety of beggar-my-neighbor moves. These included competitive bouts of devaluation, in which nations hoped to gain temporary advantage by cheapening their currencies, as well as tariff wars and other devices to reduce imports and promote exports. Keynes hoped to prevent a repetition of this disastrous history: a system biased in favor of growth and plentiful credit would enable each nation to practice a Keynesian economics of full employment, high growth, and social security at home, and be relatively open to each other's exports.

The idea that a world central bank, of all things, could be "purely technical and non-political," was splendidly naïve. It expressed the wartime planners' supreme confidence that the power of insight, goodwill, and persuasion could overcome the politics of national and institutional interest. In reality, Keynes's insights about the dynamics of international commerce were astute, but the execution of his design was infinitely complicated by both domestic politics and geopolitics.

Beginning with the Lend-Lease Act of 1940, providing American war loans in exchange for the use of military bases, the British war effort had been heavily dependent on American wealth. By 1944, it was clear that the major architect and financier of postwar reconstruction would be the United States, not Britain. Under Lend-Lease, the United States supplied Britain with some $30 billion of war matériel and received about $6 billion in goods and services in return. During the war, Britain lost about one-fourth of its entire national wealth, liquidated most of its foreign-exchange reserves, and lost many of its foreign investments; it emerged owing nearly £3 billion in external debt and had an internal national debt equal to more than a year's gross national product.

A contemporary bit of doggerel insisted that British shrewdness would best American money:

> In Washington Lord Halifax*
> Once whispered to Lord Keynes
> "It's true *they* have the money bags
> But *we* have all the brains."[8]

But the Americans were not without brains. Keynes's American counterpart at Bretton Woods was Harry Dexter White, a left-wing New Dealer and protégé of Treasury Secretary Henry Morgenthau. Ordinarily, Treasury people represent economic orthodoxy, but in the Roosevelt administration the usual roles were reversed. Treasury was increasingly a sanctuary for radical ideas—Morgenthau once proposed "to drive . . . the usurious money-lenders from the temple of international finance'"[9]—while the State Department and Secretary of State Cordell Hull continued to champion the orthodoxy of laissez-faire internationalism. Much has been made of the differences between White's blueprint at Bretton Woods and Keynes's. However, White was an American Keynesian: like Keynes, he wanted an international central banking institution biased toward high growth, which would leave running room for domestic programs of high demand, full employment, social welfare, trade unionism, and economic planning. In essence Keynes and White were on the same side of the fundamental debate. The opponents of the Keynes-White view were the financial traditionalists, both English and American, who wanted neither the loss of sovereignty that a global central bank entailed, nor the abandonment of the conservative discipline of the gold standard, nor the brand of domestic planning cum full employment that Keynes favored.


As Keynes and White conceived the Bretton Woods arrangements, the central objective was to uncouple domestic economic policy from the deflationary influence of a simple global gold standard, yet still maintain some discipline and encourage the restoration and expansion of world commerce. Keynes and White both imagined that nations would cede a significant degree of sovereignty to the two planned institutions. At the time, this did not seem wildly visionary, because in 1944 the air was thick with talk of a United Nations Organization, an Anglo-American union, and other radical departures from ordinary national sovereignty. The proposed departures from the traditional world monetary system were radical both in their expansionary (Keynesian) bias and in their public character, since the power of private banks and national treasuries was to be substantially ceded to new supranational and public institutions. Not surprisingly, the eventual Bretton Woods system fell somewhat short of the ideal.

*Halifax was British Foreign Secretary.

It was perhaps inevitable that the American working paper, rather than the British, became the draft blueprint at Bretton Woods. Harry Dexter White's initial plan, in principle no less far-reaching than Keynes's, proposed two institutions: an international monetary fund, analogous to Keynes's clearing union, and an international bank, which would provide long-term, low-interest loans for reconstruction and development. On both counts, White, like Keynes, hoped to avoid the deflationary shortsightedness of private bankers, who had dominated international credit policy between the wars. But there were two key differences from Keynes's proposal. White, already well to the left of what Congress was likely to accept, imagined a smaller international monetary fund. (The eventual IMF was capitalized at $8.8 billion, a considerable sum but far less than what Keynes wanted.) And unlike Keynes, the Americans did not agree that access to the fund should be unconditional, but argued that the fund's governors would pass on any proposal to draw on its resources, making the fund less a line of credit and more a source of fiscal discipline.

The conference at Bretton Woods was also supposed to address rules for the restoration of trade. Here again, Keynes and White proposed a compromise between the liberal ideal of laissez-faire trade and the imperatives of domestic full employment and planning for high growth. Keynes himself had changed his mind more than once on the desirability of free trade. Beginning as a classical liberal, by the early 1930s he came to believe that free trade was nothing but the international counterpart of the laissez-faire theory that he found so self-defeating in domestic economics. In a famous essay in 1933, Keynes wrote that free trade was expendable.

> There may be some financial calculation which shows it to be advantageous that my savings should be invested in whatever quarter of the habitable globe shows the greatest marginal efficiency of capital or the highest rate of interest. But experience is accumulating that remoteness between ownership and operation is an evil in the relations among men, likely or certain in the long run to set up strains and enmities which will bring to nought the financial calculation.
>
> I sympathize, therefore, with those who would minimize, rather than those who would maximize, economic entanglement among nations. Ideas, knowledge, science, hospitality, travel—these are the things which should of their nature be international. But let goods be homespun whenever it is reasonable and conveniently possible, and, above all, let finance be primarily national.[10]

But the 1930s also demonstrated that one brand of non–free trade was decidedly unattractive. Among the democracies, bilateralism and currency blocs produced economic contraction at best. With the Axis powers, the Nazi economic planner Hjalmar Schacht had used commercial and currency arrangements to create economic satellites of Germany in Southern Europe, while the Japanese had used yen bilateralism to fortify a colonial "co-prosperity sphere." Keynes recognized, however, that the opposite of Schachtian economics was not laissez-faire, and he warned American liberals on more than one occasion that the failure to devise a managed global system friendly to high growth and full employment was precisely what had incubated the Schachtian alternative.[11]

By the time the war had broken out, Keynes had achieved a kind of uneasy synthesis on the trade question. On the one hand, he argued, if one was to avoid gross protection of the kind that had been so deflationary in the interwar years, a transnational system of monetary relations under public rather than private auspices was indispensable; only by creative national and international regimes biased toward high growth and full employment could governments reduce the pressures favoring purely inward-looking protectionism. On the other hand, this very anti-laissez-faire position rendered Keynesian planning somewhat incompatible with traditional liberal trade. In a Keynesian global order, foreign trade needed to be a compromise between more or less open commerce and the imperatives of domestic full employment. Keynes strongly believed that the more the system was biased toward growth and balance, the less this would be a contradiction in practice.[12]

The Bretton Woods concept of commercial (as opposed to monetary) relations can be discerned in the embryonic plans for the International Trade Organization (ITO), which ultimately failed to win ratification. Like the monetary regime, it was a compromise between opposing views within Britain and the United States, further complicated by the diplomatic goals of both nations. On one side, the American liberal internationalists led by Hull saw a chance at long last to enshrine liberal trade. But White and others at the U.S. Treasury, like Keynes, placed stabilization ahead of laissez-faire trade, and White's Bretton Woods plan frankly made room for national economic planning. He viewed opposition to controls on movements of international capital as "hangovers from a nineteenth-century economic creed,"[13] and went so far as to require as a condition of membership in the proposed International Monetary Fund that nations agree "not to accept or permit deposits or investments from any member country except with the permission of the government of that member country."[14] To White, this outright control over the movement of private capital was a necessary concomitant of national economic planning. "The assumption that capital serves a country best by flowing to countries which offer the most attractive terms is valid only under circumstances which are not always present," he wrote.[15]

In meetings between British and American experts in 1943 and early 1944, it had been agreed that some sort of trade convention was necessary that would reconcile the somewhat contradictory goals of relatively open trade and high employment. The Americans were keen to use their leverage to win a British commitment to drop all forms of "discriminatory treatment," including preferential tariffs, which were the centerpiece of the British system of imperial preference, a long-standing abomination to Hull. Beginning with the first Lend-Lease discussions in 1940, Hull had attempted to use the leverage of American financial aid to wean the British away from this legacy of empire, and had compelled the British to sign an article of the Mutual Aid Agreements treaty renouncing preferential arrangements. However, Churchill had no sympathy for this view, being concerned about devising a global alternative to simple laissez-faire and about the practical problems of paying Britain's war debt. He once referred to the proposed ban on any form of trade discrimination as "the lunatic proposals of Mr. Hull."[16] Britain's interest in retaining its sterling bloc, in retiring war debts without unacceptable deflation, and in building a full-employment economy were bound up with its larger vision of a new Keynesian world. From the State Department's perspective, however, the British view represented either intolerable old-fashioned British colonialism or dangerous newfangled collectivism, perhaps both.

In the end, the original bold vision of Bretton Woods was truncated into something rather modest. Although British opinion moved dramatically left in 1945 with the election of Britain's first majority Labour government, American opinion rapidly moved right; with Roosevelt's death and Truman's accession to the presidency, Secretary of the Treasury Fred Vinson replaced Harry White as the chief American negotiator on matters of global finance, and Will Clayton, a Texan who owned 40 percent of the world's largest cotton brokerage house,[17] was now Assistant Secretary of State for Economic Affairs and the dominant American voice on trade policy.

Relations between the United States and Great Britain deteriorated. In June 1945, President Truman announced the abrupt termination of Lend-Lease credits. But Britain had come out of the war far weaker than most British and American planners had anticipated. It depended on imports both for daily necessities and to rebuild its economy, and the war debt had to be segregated from the currency and capital needed for ordinary commerce and reconstruction. Projections assumed a British payments deficit of $3–$4 billion a year for 1946–48, not even counting repayments on the war debt.

In the autumn of 1945, Prime Minister Clement Attlee sent Keynes to Washington to seek additional credits—a grant, or, at worst, an interest-free loan of $6.6 billion. But after testy negotiations, the best Keynes was able to get was a loan of $3.75 billion with strings attached: a promise soon to remove controls on currency and capital movements. Keynes was rightly concerned that an early return to free capital movements and a premature unblocking of sterling accounts representing war debts would lead to a run on the pound, and this is precisely what happened in 1947 when Britain, under American pressure, made the pound convertible; massive sterling outflows and forced devaluation occurred. He was also concerned that in the long run the forces of orthodoxy were orchestrating a return to a laissez-faire system rather than a managed one, and that the constituency for the Bretton Woods policies was vanishing.

Between the Bretton Woods conference of June 1944 and the negotiation of the British loan in the autumn of 1945, the American view had hardened in several respects. The spirit of wartime collaboration was evaporating; Americans who had made sacrifices during the war were in no mood to finance the economies of foreign nations with peculiar ideologies. Britain, now with a Labour government, was viewed less as a faithful ally and more as a nation with dubious collectivist and, simultaneously, colonialist impulses. To those in the U.S. administration who predicated the postwar order on Soviet-American harmony, Britain was the odd man out, a throwback to an imperialist age. At the founding meeting of the IMF and the World Bank, in Savannah, Georgia, in February 1946, the administration made it clear that the United States would enjoy an effective veto over IMF operations. White was passed over for the post of managing director, and IMF headquarters was located in Washington, D.C., under the watchful eye of the U.S. Treasury. Keynes suffered a massive heart attack on the train out of Savannah. He died six weeks later, bitterly disappointed that his bold vision was not to be realized.

Deeper cleavages became evident during 1946 and early 1947: between both the traditional and the radical conceptions of global finance, and between British and American national interests. The Americans viewed the IMF as an agency to be activated only after postwar commercial and financial relations were normalized. But Europe was still struggling with the effects of the war; its economy was devastated. Strict controls remained on currencies. Trade flows had not substantially resumed. The Continent was desperately short of the dollars it needed to buy imports. Yet the United States was unwilling to let either the IMF or the World Bank spend serious money on postwar stabilization, apparently for fear that the resources of these fledgling institutions would quickly be dissipated. Nor was

American public opinion willing to have the United States be the world's banker.

In early meetings in 1943 and 1944 a joint Anglo-American planning committee had agreed on the need for a multilateral convention on commercial policy; it also agreed that individual nations should pursue policies of high growth and full employment within a world system of plentiful credit, anchored by the new supranational financial organizations. In this Keynesian context of high growth, quantitative restrictions on imports should be prohibited except for the purpose of safeguarding a nation's balance of payments, and any such temporary restrictions were to be subject to the approval of the new ITO. The Americans were especially eager for the British to phase out their system of "imperial preferences," a move that the British insisted was feasible only in the context of across-the-board tariff reductions.

The plain contradiction between national high-employment policies, which involved a degree of domestic planning, and the international aspiration to restore laissez-faire was never quite acknowledged, nor was the political difficulty of getting the major powers to subordinate their domestic interests to the principle of global free trade. Nor did the negotiators realistically appreciate that public support for transfers of real authority to supranational institutions was rapidly dwindling.

These contradictions came back to haunt the negotiators when a draft agreement for the International Trade Organization was finally designed at a series of meetings beginning in Geneva in the spring of 1947. In the United States, Republicans, who had won control of Congress in the November 1946 elections, were determined that U.S. tariff concessions be made only in return for British elimination of imperial preference. But in Britain, the political left and right were equally determined to hang on to the empire as a preferential trading and currency area.[18] Though the Labour government was quite prepared, as Churchill was not, to liquidate the old British Empire, Attlee viewed the sterling area and the preference system, reincarnated in the Commonwealth, as necessary to anchor British economic recovery.

The 1947 Geneva sessions ended with a draft for a General Agreement on Tariffs and Trade, but only modest tariff concessions and no resolution of the imperial-preference question. The thorniest issues were put off until the final negotiations for the ITO charter, which began that autumn in Havana. But as the ITO negotiations progressed, it became clear that most nations wanted latitude to engage in restrictions that a free trader would consider discriminatory, both for postwar reconstruction and for planned economic growth. Several poorer nations took offense at the Anglo-American working draft, which largely ignored the imperatives of economic development, and they added a provision that gave them special treatment, endorsing their right to regulate foreign investment and to place quantitative restrictions on imports. The British themselves inserted a new section permitting quantitative import restrictions in order to combat inflation, as well as a declaration of support for full employment. Even the United States, crusader for a pure free trade, insisted on exemptions allowing preferential tariffs for its own economic wards like Cuba and the Philippines, as well as a general exemption that protected U.S. agriculture.

The ITO charter signed at Havana in March 1948 was an awkward compromise that pleased no one. The poor nations saw it as an overly broad endorsement of laissez-faire—"the imperialism of free trade." The British thought it assaulted imperial preference. And although the State Department endeavored to persuade Americans that the proposed ITO was a remarkable achievement that got fifty-four nations to subscribe to "the United States philosophy of the maximum amount of competition and the minimum amount of government control,"[19] there was little sympathy in the relatively isolationist Republican 80th Congress either for the grand design or for the concessions that the United States was willing to make in order to get other nations to go along. The congressional leaders also bridled at even minimal pooling of national sovereignty and at the support for policies of full employment, which they had just watered down as a domestic goal.

In the bowdlerized Employment Act of 1946, major business groups such as the Chamber of Commerce and the National Association of Manufacturers felt betrayed by even a minimal commitment to economic planning. The ITO was supposed to enshrine the principles of liberal trade and make the world safe for exports of American goods and capital. Instead, it seemed to be legitimizing all manner of restrictions on U.S. exports and sanctioning planning. Representatives of the farm bloc were worried about trade-driven pressure to repeal restrictions on imported agricultural products permitted under the Agricultural Adjustment Act; if foreign farm products could enter U.S. markets freely, the entire system of domestic price supports would be undercut.

Congressional hearings on the proposed charter became a lightning rod for broad opposition. In the end, the administration, knowing that the votes were simply not there, quietly withdrew the ITO charter rather than subject it to a humiliating public defeat. The far more modest General Agreement on Tariffs and Trade became by default the skeleton for the postwar global trade regime. It provided only a framework for future reciprocal trade concessions, some broad general principles, a tiny staff in Geneva, and little more. The deep contradictions that surfaced in the ITO negotiations remained unresolved. Throughout history, America's rare global involvements, when they came, had required a sense of crusade, not calculating *Realpolitik*. The Wilsonian enterprise of making the world safe for democracy had been one such crusade; defeating Hitler, another. Building a world economic order on principles of Keynesian internationalism that involved both expenditure of American resources and retraction of American power was no such crusade.

This brief review of international economic relations immediately after World War II suggests how rapidly both postwar unity and the Anglo-American resolve to rebuild a world economic order along Keynesian lines reverted to traditional impulses of isolation and laissez-faire and to parochial conceptions of national interest. In 1944–45, Roosevelt, remembering Versailles, insisted that postwar planning begin while the war was still being prosecuted and imaginations were still bold; this insistence led to the formation of the IMF, the World Bank, and the United Nations. But by 1947, when the ITO was negotiated, this tide of insistence and urgency had ebbed. The ITO's moment had passed before it could be consummated; the organizations created in 1945 proved far weaker in practice than in theory. This abrupt change was a preview of just how powerful was the system's tendency to revert to political fragmentation and financial orthodoxy once the extraordinary imperatives of war were spent and how little sovereignty the major powers were prepared to give over to international organizations. What rescued international unity and permitted a stunted sort of global Keynesianism was, of course, the Cold War.

At the time of Franklin Roosevelt's death in April 1945, planning for the postwar era had been predicated on political and economic assumptions that now seem at once impressively far-reaching and naïve. Economically, the planners of that era aimed for new institutions to secure a mixed economy biased toward high growth and full employment, institutions that entailed the giving up of a good deal of national authority. Geopolitically, Roosevelt was committed to a regime of universal collective security whose institutional embodiment was to be a United Nations Organization. Roosevelt imagined this as the extension of the wartime Grand Alliance, anchored by the cooperation of Great Britain, the U.S.S.R., the United States, and China, which Roosevelt referred to as the Four Policemen. His administration assumed that the wartime collaboration with the Soviet Union would extend into peacetime and that the main threat to world peace would come from a resurgent Germany or Japan.

Many hard-nosed realists among America's foreign-policy makers felt that Russia, as an ally and a fellow victorious great power, had a legitimate right to its own sphere of influence on its western border, within limits. Charles Bohlen, the State Department's Soviet expert, wrote in a memo to Secretary of State James Byrnes in October 1945: "The U.S. should not acquiesce in the establishment of exclusive spheres of influence in Central and Eastern Europe by means of complete domination," but on the other hand "we should not in any sense attempt to deny to the Soviet Union the legitimate prerogatives of a great power in regard to smaller countries resulting from geographic proximity."[20]

In 1943 and 1944 many planners urged that American reconstruction aid be extended to the Soviet Union after the war. Ambassador Averell Harriman, Treasury Secretary Morgenthau, and Lend-Lease chief Harry Hopkins were all strong advocates of postwar aid to the Russians, though Hopkins preferred to carry out the program through an extension of Lend-Lease, whereas Morgenthau and Harriman favored a separate program of reconstruction credits.[21] Harriman, in particular, thought of aid to Russia as a way to encourage the Russians to "play the international game with us in accordance with our standards."[22] Many Roosevelt administration officials also looked enthusiastically on the prospects of postwar trade with the U.S.S.R., a source of such raw materials as mercury, manganese, and chromium and a natural customer for U.S. manufactured goods. Eric Johnston, the dynamic president of the Chamber of Commerce and something of a missionary for the free-enterprise point of view, returned from an eight-week mission to Moscow in the summer of 1944 convinced that the U.S.S.R. could be America's best customer.

In the closing days of the war, efforts to continue economic aid to the Soviet Union foundered on the obstinacy of both the Soviets and the U.S. Congress. The Soviets, for their part, refused to commit to early reimbursement for Lend-Lease materials used in postwar reconstruction. The administration, at that moment, was in a mood to bargain hard, because it wanted Russia to enter the Pacific war against Japan and it also wanted to appease Congress. But Congress, anticipating the war's end and the taxpayers' desire for relief, and expecting the traditional postwar withdrawal from global entanglement, insisted that no Lend-Lease funds be used for postwar reconstruction anywhere and that any postwar aid be legislated as a separate program, presumably through the Export-Import Bank.

In the end, Western Europe was the recipient of generous reconstruction aid, and the Soviet Union was not among the recipients. Rather, the entire rationale for the aid program became one of restraining the U.S.S.R. in Europe. Early signs of this harder line began to materialize almost as soon as Truman succeeded FDR on April 12, 1945. He had been in office just two weeks when he had a very stormy meeting with Molotov, arguing over reports that the Soviet Union, in flat violation of the February 1945 agreement at Yalta on Polish self-determination, had no intention of broadening the provisional Polish government that Stalin had created or allowing it to hold free elections. At the first meetings of the San Francisco Conference in April, the same sour mood continued. With the Asian war by no means won, this abrupt deterioration in U.S.-Soviet relations disturbed many liberals in Washington.

Truman dispatched Hopkins to Moscow in May to see if some compromise on Poland might be negotiated. Stalin insisted on his friendly Polish government, but did make concessions on respecting the independence of China, and accepted the American plan for the new Security Council of the United Nations, breaking a deadlock that had nearly wrecked the San Francisco Conference. The prospect of the United States giving postwar reconstruction aid was kept alive, and plans were laid for another summit meeting for the following July, to be held in Potsdam. With the war in Europe over and negotiations proceeding over Soviet entry into the still fierce combat in the Pacific, Soviet-American relations took a brief turn for the better. In May, Truman could complain, "I was having as much difficulty with Prime Minister Churchill as I was having with Stalin."[23]

Many in Truman's administration and in Congress were far more concerned with resisting U.S. entanglement in Europe than with resisting Soviet expansion. A good deal of sentiment in Washington supported the idea of Europe as a "third force," a buffer between the Soviet Union and the United States, formally allied with neither. As the historian John Lewis Gaddis has observed, American military planners in 1945–46 "saw the United States more as a mediator between Britain and Russia than as a permanent ally of either of them."[24] Even as late as April 1946, at a press conference Truman referred to the American role as that of an "umpire" between the British and the Soviets.[25] The United States was still wavering between its newfound global power and its traditional reluctance to avoid being drawn into the messy conflicts of the Old World.

But as America's enthusiasm for international economic institutions and global economic entanglements subsided, its sense that the Soviet Union threatened Europe slowly increased. Just in time, this would provide the moral fuel necessary for a resurgence of international engagement. The Red Army was advancing in Eastern Europe, and Stalin showed no interest in the niceties of national self-determination. Cut off from American aid, his government declined to participate in either the World Bank or the International Monetary Fund. At the Potsdam Conference of July 1945, the Soviets showed they would resist great-power collaboration in the reconstruction and normalization of Germany, and were far more interested in consolidating their own territorial advantages. The temporary division of Germany into administrative occupation zones, devised at Potsdam mainly for purposes of allocating reparations, soon hardened into a permanent partition. In September, at a conference of Foreign Ministers in London convened to draw up peace treaties with former German satellites, it became clear that the U.S.S.R. would not abide by the Yalta commitment to free elections in Central and Eastern European territories occupied by the Red Army.

In the fall and winter of 1945–46, one group of American officials was already convinced that further appeasement of Stalin would only embolden his demands. Another group of relative accommodationists, which included Vice President Henry Wallace, Secretary of War Henry Stimson, Bohlen, John J. McCloy, Dean Acheson, Walter Lippmann, and to some extent President Truman himself, was still searching for some formula that would accommodate legitimate Soviet desires for territorial security and economic recovery while at the same time setting limits on American concessions and heading off direct conflict. A new British loan had just been negotiated, and there was still a faint hope that perhaps a new round of economic aid to the U.S.S.R. might soften Stalin's bellicosity.

However, the hard-liners were seeing implacable conflict in every Soviet move, and Stalin gave them plenty of justification. In a widely publicized speech on February 9, 1946, he spoke ominously of "capitalist encirclement" of the Soviet Union, and of the fundamental incompatibility between the two systems which might lead to war. Paul Nitze, then a mid-level State Department official, told Secretary of Defense James Forrestal he considered the speech a "delayed declaration of war on the U.S."[26] William O. Douglas, the liberal Supreme Court justice, termed it "the declaration of World War III."[27] In early 1946, Russia was also probing for territorial advantage in Manchuria, Iran, and Turkey.

The gathering alarm was crystallized in George Kennan's famous "long telegram" of February 22, 1946, a 5,500-word diplomatic dispatch from the U.S. embassy in Moscow to the State Department that virtually defined a new policy, and later became the basis for a celebrated article in *Foreign Affairs* on containment. Official Washington read Kennan's telegram not long before newspapers were reporting on Winston Churchill's "iron curtain" speech given in Fulton, Missouri, offering an even gloomier view of Soviet aims and motives. "The Soviet party line," wrote Kennan, then the top American diplomat in Moscow in Ambassador Harriman's absence, "is not based on any objective analysis of the situation beyond Russia's borders. . . . at the bottom of the Kremlin's neurotic view of world affairs is the traditional and instinctive Russian sense of insecurity." He concluded: "In summary, we have a political force committed fanatically to the belief that with the U.S. there can be no permanent harmony. . . . [The] problem of how to cope with this force is undoubtedly the greatest task our diplomacy has ever faced." Yet, he cautioned, "Soviet power, unlike that of Hitlerite Germany, is neither schematic nor adventuristic. It does not work by fixed plans. It does not take unnecessary risks. . . . thus, if the adversary [i.e., the United States] has sufficient force and makes clear his readiness to use it, he rarely has to do so."

In the end, Kennan counseled what came to be known as a policy of "patience and firmness" rather than bellicosity. The United States did not need to go to war against the Russians; they had only to hold them resolutely at bay against the day of their eventual liberalization (a day that Kennan as an octogenarian lived to see). He also emphasized the importance of offering a positive alternative to the Soviet model.

> Much depends on the health and vigor of our own society. World communism is like a malignant parasite which feeds only on diseased tissue. This is the point at which domestic and foreign policies meet. . . . We must formulate and put forward for other nations a much more positive and constructive picture of the sort of world we would like to see than we have put forward in the past. Many foreign peoples, in Europe at least, are tired and frightened by experiences of the past, and are less interested in abstract freedom than in security. They are seeking guidance rather than responsibilities. We should be better able than the Russians to give them this. And unless we do, the Russians surely will.[28]

With remarkable swiftness, this became the consensus view, defining as it did a middle ground in the range of possible attitudes toward the U.S.S.R., and a new concept: cold war. Concern about the threat of Russia rescued the United States' faltering assertiveness in the world and dramatically altered its character. In official Washington, the U.S.S.R.'s perceived geopolitical threat to Europe fused with an old notion of Bolshevism's ideological threat, and American policy changed accordingly. The British loan, unpopular in Congress and in public opinion, narrowly carried in the House and Senate on a tide of anticommunist rhetoric, but further credits to the Soviet Union were shelved.

In that first winter after the war, 1945–46, the American attitude toward Western European suffering, an object of charity, had been testy if not niggardly. American voters wanted demobilization, normalcy, and tax relief. But a year later European reconstruction was a centerpiece of high politics in a new, cold war. In 1947, after a modest recovery, the British economy went into a tailspin. The U.S.-induced move toward convertibility of sterling in July of that year triggered massive speculation against the pound, consuming what remained of Keynes's hard-won loan and leading to a painful and costly devaluation of the pound. No wonder, then, that under such financial stress, Britain began to pull back from expensive foreign-policy commitments. In February 1947, Attlee abruptly informed the Americans that his government could no longer serve as military protector of Turkey and Greece; the United States moved to fill the void, making the eastern Mediterranean an American protectorate.

The State Department initially tried to promote Truman's $400 million aid package for Greece and Turkey as an expression of humanitarian concern for those nations and of loyalty to Britain—but it was roundly criticized for wishing to spend taxpayers' dollars to pull Britain's chestnuts out of the fire. With a dramatic shift in rhetoric, Secretary of State Dean Acheson, in testimony before the Senate Foreign Relations Committee, declared that the real issue was a Manichaean conflict between U.S.-style democracy and Soviet despotism bent on global conquest. Truman's address was even more pointed, presenting a stark choice between "free institutions" and "terror and oppression, a controlled press and radio, fixed elections and the suppression of personal freedom."[29] In March 1947, the aid package, rebaptized the "Truman Doctrine," was duly approved.

Now the United States had its crusade. For advocates of American assertiveness in the world, the Cold War challenge was potent enough to rouse the most passive isolationist. Within barely a year, the familiar foundations of Cold War rearmament were put in place. The Office of Strategic Services, the wartime intelligence agency, abolished in 1946, was scarcely out of business when it was reborn in 1948 as the Central Intelligence Agency.

Foreign economic policy quickly became an adjunct of the new doctrine of containment. In Europe the harsh winter of 1946–47 created not only severe privation but political instability—precisely the diseased tissue of which Kennan's telegram had spoken, on which Stalinism could feed. As John Ikenberry has written, the postwar Pax Americana was an odd, unprecedented sort of imperium—an "empire by invitation." The permanent American protectorate over Europe that became a fixed assumption in U.S. foreign policy as early as 1950 was not at all what U.S. planners had sought.

Between 1944 and 1950, America's goals for the new international order dramatically changed. They began in 1944–45 with Roosevelt's notion of universal collective security in the geopolitical sphere and Keynesian multilateralism in economics. In 1946, the United States was pursuing normalcy—a more laissez-faire view of economics and a political withdrawal. By 1948, it was promoting a strong Western Europe and accepting a relatively managed economy as a temporary expedient. Finally, after 1949, it became an ongoing political and economic presence in Europe, and evolved into the economic "hegemon" for the global system, providing capital, liquidity, and military protection to a world economic order whose commitment to pure laissez-faire would have to wait.

This new American role gave the world economy an unacknowledged Keynesian cast. The IMF was not strong enough to give the system the liquidity Keynes had envisaged, but the dollar was; the World Bank was too limited to finance European recovery, but the European Recovery Plan did the job. The United States' trade surplus might have been a serious drag on European recovery (the United States had an incredible 48 percent share of world industrial production in 1948; and at the point of peak imbalance, Europe was buying seven times what it was selling to the United States), but America's military spending in Europe provided billions of dollars to offset the dollar shortage even before Marshall Plan aid petered out. And the system's toleration of undervalued European currencies encouraged American industry to set up production facilities in Europe rather than exporting goods there. So the classical liberalism of free trade and capital movements remained a U.S. goal for the long term, but in the first postwar decade, Cold War imperatives put laissez-faire on the back burner.

The initial goal of the European Recovery Plan, popularly known as the Marshall Plan, was to build up the nations of Western Europe to the point where they would not need ongoing protection from the United States. It was not to undertake a permanent alliance. "It should be a cardinal point of our policy," Kennan urged, "to see to it that other elements of independent power are developed on the Eurasian land mass as rapidly as possible *in order to take off our shoulders some of the burden of 'bipolarity'* " (emphasis added).[30] In addition, the recommendations of the State Department's Policy Planning Staff, now headed by Kennan, presented to Secretary of State Marshall in May 1947, emphasized "not combating communism as such but the restoration of the economic health and vigor of European society."[31] Yet it was the imperative of combating communism that gave America's newfound generosity its force and political practicality. With the communists as the largest or second-largest parties in the parliaments of several Western European nations, there was a real possibility that both France and Italy would fall under communist sway. When Marshall unveiled his proposals in a speech at the Harvard commencement of June 1947, he was widely applauded for finding a way to avoid a Hobson's choice of either letting the Russians control the Eurasian landmass or going to war.

Yet in 1947–48 the goal was still to promote Western European independence and regional cooperation, not to treat Europe as a ward or sphere of influence. And even in early 1949 there was no assumption of a permanent military alliance. This strategy had several benefits, some of them not entirely intentional: it headed off direct military conflict with the Soviet Union—the instruments of American policy would be mainly economic; and it offered inducements to the nations of Central Europe, not all of which had entirely hardened into Soviet satellites. (Czechoslovakia, a parliamentary democracy until the coup of February 1948, was initially eager to receive Marshall Plan aid.) Regional economic cooperation and pan-Europeanism also neatly obviated the problem of Franco-German enmity, submerging the nationalism of each into a larger European whole. That whole would now be conveniently under an American protectorate, ostensibly vis-à-vis the East but also checking intra-European hostilities.

The developing antagonism with the Soviet Union made it impossible to conclude peace treaties ending the war or permanently to resolve such issues as the redrawing of secure, defensible national frontiers or German rearmament. The American protectorate resolved these knotty issues in a face-saving and seemingly provisional way. It was, for example, much easier for France to tolerate West German rearmament so long as Germany was divided and West Germany and France were both junior members of an Atlantic alliance. (This temporary expedient lasted nearly a half century. As the French say, *"C'est la provisoire qui dure."*)

The United States found itself imposing on the Continent an idealistic conception of European unity, conceived out of pragmatic concern for containing Russia but tempered by a faith in Madisonian federalism. This comported beautifully with the postwar aspirations of the most farsighted pan-Europeans—Jean Monnet, Robert Schuman, Konrad Adenauer, Paul-Henri Spaak, Alcide de Gasperi, among others, who in one way or another believed that European federalism was the only long-term solution to rival mercantilisms, national enmities, and periodic fratricidal wars. All of this put the United States in the paradoxical position of supporting rather more of a managed economy than it quite bargained for. Spending the $13 billion in Marshall Plan aid given between 1948 and 1952 required economic planning. The recipient nations of Marshall Plan aid were encouraged to create the Organization for European Economic Cooperation; its first director was the Frenchman Robert Marjolin, a Yale-educated diplomat who was close both to Monnet and to the officials of the Economic Cooperation Administration.

The first steps to liberalize monetary relations within Europe were accomplished by a U.S.-sponsored European Payments Union that allowed accounts to be settled multilaterally rather than nation by nation. Yet because of the continuing weakness of most of Europe's national economies, the EPU required that the United States accept several features it did not like, including the continuation of strict capital controls and limitations on the convertibility of currencies.

Momentum rapidly built for a regional military alliance. In June 1948, the Senate passed the Vandenberg Resolution, requiring that the United States associate itself with a collective security arrangement in Western Europe. In 1949, when the North Atlantic Treaty Organization agreement was signed, the Truman administration still hoped that Germany would remain demilitarized and that the United States would not need to make a permanent commitment of American troops on European soil. But with the explosion of the first Soviet atomic bomb in 1949 and the outbreak of the Korean War in 1950, sentiment shifted toward a stronger conception of NATO, and this was economically unimaginable without West German rearmament. Monnet's design for an all-European defense force (EDF) proved politically impossible for the French Chamber of Deputies to swallow, and it soon became clear that West German rearmamant was possible only in the context of the American protectorate and of a permanent American military presence in Western Europe. This conception of Atlanticism—Western European political, military, and economic union under the protectorate of the United States—took more than half a decade to jell. But once in place, any alternative became hard to imagine, and it soon became the political orthodoxy on both sides of the Atlantic.

If a permanent military protectorate was more interventionist than the United States had expected, the logic of European economic union was also not quite according to American desires. The first moves toward economic integration, via the European Coal and Steel Community, entailed a blend of state ownership and negotiated shares of European steel and coal capacity that looked more like benign cartelization than like the economics of Adam Smith. For Monnet, who in 1952 became the first president of the ECSC, economic unity was the back-door route to political unity. His purpose, he wrote, was "to make a breach in the ramparts of national sovereignty which will be narrow enough to secure consent, but deep enough to open the way toward the unity which is essential to peace."[32] The Marshall Plan itself became a refuge for American New Dealers who were fleeing the laissez-faire mood of domestic American politics for the more hospitable pro-planning ambience of Western Europe. Albert O. Hirschman, Raymond Vernon, and Charles Kindleberger, among others, all did stints in the Marshall Plan.

In short, the new American policy of engagement required an awkward compromise on cherished principles of economic doctrine. Europe was too weak to tolerate convertible currencies, free movements of capital, and open trade; this would have led to massive outflows of capital, horrendous trade deficits, monetary instability, and even higher unemployment. Also, few European leaders subscribed to the American view of how economies were supposed to operate: whether the politics were Social Democratic, Christian Democratic, or Marxist, Europe was definitely in an anti-laissez-faire mood after the war. There is thus a direct lineage between the Marshall Plan and the pan-Europeanism that eventually matured into a full-blown European Community nearly half a century later: both were rather more statist than most Americans are comfortable with. Yet the Common Market, for its first three decades, was largely the creature of center-right politicians, and though it was an institution of relative economic liberalism, submerging national mercantilist tendencies within a Continent-wide free market, it created a stable regional zone whose financial, monetary, industrial, and social policies were a far cry from the American model of laissez-faire.

The historians David Calleo and Benjamin Rowland discern the antecedents of this European middle way in the prewar pan-Europeanist writings of such diverse thinkers as Richard Coudenhouve and Charles de Gaulle.[33] These statesmen, like Monnet and Schuman later, assumed that European economic union would require a departure from free-market economics, in several respects. Europeans have always been more comfortable than Americans with state intervention in the economy and with partial cartelization of private industry. In France, where private capital was always far weaker than in Britain, both left and right had accepted state-led entrepreneurship for centuries. Moreover a customs union by definition gives preferential treatment to the manufacturers of its member nations. This advances the free flow of commerce within the trade bloc, at the expense of outsiders, and falls far short of free trade. Labor unions and the left had more influence in postwar Europe than in the United States, and they gave European federalism a social democratic flavor that offset the ideology of free markets. Finally, the Marshall Plan itself required step-by-step national bargains over what got produced where, as well as a comprehensive strategy of Community-wide farm price supports. Both of these were necessary if European economic integration was to develop at a socially and nationally bearable pace—a prime rationale for all strategies of mixed, rather than laissez-faire, economics—and both violated pure free trade.

In the 1950s and 1960s, it became conventional to juxtapose the Gaullists, with their mercantilist and neutralist leanings, against the "good" Atlanticist Europeans like Monnet and Schuman. Yet even the European Community of "good" Europeans was far from Cordell Hull's ideal world. As was periodically rediscovered during rounds of trade negotiations, most European statesmen placed the goal of European unity well ahead of the ideal of abstract free markets; this irritated two generations of U.S. diplomats and puzzled American conservatives. Moreover, the anticommunist economic statecraft also required the United States to support leaders of the European democratic left whose policies it did not entirely endorse. Indeed, the labor and social democratic parties of Western Europe were particularly cherished as bulwarks of anti-Bolshevism. But it was hard to find European leaders who did not embrace the idea of a substantial welfare state and a degree of state involvement in the economy.

American policy thus underwrote managed economics almost in spite of itself. The stabilizers built in to temper the anarchy of global capitalism were the responsibility of one hegemonic nation rather than the work of the new supranational institutions. The Keynesian issues remained, but they were obscured by the de facto Keynesianism of the Cold War and by the American military protectorate over mercantilist allies in Western Europe and Japan. This confusion between the ideology of what was supposed to be and the logic of what actually was made it ever harder to define clear goals for the structure of the world economy or for the American national interest within it. The confusion came back to haunt American policy planners when the United States ceased being the sole hegemonic power in the early 1970s and even more painfully when the Cold War petered out in the late 1980s.

# two

# ATLAS ENFEEBLED: THE COSTS
# OF AMERICAN HEGEMONY

By 1950, the architecture of the postwar world was largely framed. Both sides reluctantly accepted the de facto division of Europe. Western Europe was firmly an American geopolitical and geo-economic protectorate, and Eastern Europe was in thrall to Moscow. An armed truce between the two camps quickly came to seem normal. Among the Western powers, the ideal of universal collective security was narrowed to a more manageable ideal of cooperative Atlanticism. On both sides of the ocean, a generation of fervent Atlanticists held power: Europeans who found multiple benefits in alliance with the United States—fratricidal and revanchist impulses within Europe were tempered; economic recovery and commercial union accelerated; and Soviet expansionism was resisted—and American liberals who believed that NATO and West European union would be the means of finally overcoming American isolationism and projecting American ideals and influence onto the global stage.

During the 1950s, two developments occurred that are noteworthy for our discussion here. First, the paramount goal of American geo-economic policy became the creation of an ever more classically liberal commercial, financial, and trading world order. This is precisely what hegemonic powers are expected to do, for their manufacturers and bankers are best positioned to reap the advantage of porous national frontiers. The shift in American thinking intensified as the radical New Deal yielded to the moderate Fair Deal and thence to free-market Republicanism in the 1950s. Second, the strains of America's hegemonic role began to show, though given the immense U.S. lead on so many economic fronts and the imperatives of the Cold War, the strains were considered bearable. Some of the costs, like inflation, could be indirectly shared with allies, without having to share the hegemony; other costs, such as America's disproportionate military spending, were deemed the natural burden of leadership and they produced useful diplomatic leverage in dealings with balky allies as well as certain commercial benefits. Enormous U.S. spending on military aircraft, for example, gave American producers an immense advantage in exports of civilian airliners. For a quarter century, few Americans doubted that the benefits of hegemony justified the costs.

In the 1950s, the main U.S. goal for global monetary relations was the restoration of full currency convertibility, for that was the precondition to free flows of capital and commerce. But laissez-faire finance, for a time, was constrained. To begin with, Europe's economies were not yet strong enough for free currency convertibility. For example, had Italians been permitted freely to exchange lire for dollars, far too many would have moved their funds to the stronger currency, leading to a run on the lira and a depletion of the Bank of Italy's gold and dollar reserves as the Italian government made a futile attempt to defend the prevailing exchange rate. The same was true of francs, drachmas, guilders, and even pounds and marks. Since exchange rates were fixed under the Bretton Woods accord, the system did not allow money to flow wherever people wanted it to go, nor did it let forces of private supply and demand set daily exchange rates. Currencies were subject to an array of controls as a bulwark against an international twist on Gresham's law, in which the stronger currency threatened to drive out the weaker.

Second, most countries still retained controls on capital as well. Just as Europe's domestic economies were still too weak to allow currencies to be freely exchanged, they were also too weak to permit savings to flow abroad. Here again, far too much money needed for capital investment and recovery would have gone to the United States or perhaps Switzerland.

Third, tariffs remained high throughout Europe, and other forms of protectionism persisted from the autarkic 1930s or from necessary wartime economic controls. As a result, each European economy was insulated from the others, and neither goods nor capital flowed freely.

American officials were eager to encourage Western Europe to enact rapid *multilateral* liberalization, in which the flow of capital and goods would be freed of regulatory and tariff constraints not only within Europe but between Europe and the rest of the world. The Europeans, however, thought that liberalization should be more gradual and more regional, both for ideological reasons—they were less devoted to absolute laissez-faire— and for reasons of self-interest. Multilateral liberalization would have disproportionately benefited the hegemon, the United States, at Europe's expense, since the United States had the far more competitive economy and the disproportionate share of the global financial capital and productive resources.

There was thus set into play a subtle but profound difference in the conception of how postwar capitalism was supposed to operate. To the American architects of the system, the seeds of suspicion were sown early on that Europe was a nest of closet mercantilists who never quite shared their vision of a multilateral, liberal, universal economic order. They tended to believe that Europeans, with their history of statism, preferred to hide behind the exigencies of a protracted "recovery" period, long past the point when they could have withstood more open commerce. Echoes of the early debates continued to resound in the late 1980s when people argued over whether the EC of 1992 was really a cover for a "Fortress Europe."

In the event, Americans had to settle for what they hoped would be a temporary regional solution. This took several forms: a European Payments Union to restore multilateral settlement of trade accounts; the continuation of currency and capital controls; continued discrimination against "dollar goods" (American exports). Grudgingly the United States recognized that reciprocal tariff reduction and currency convertibility would have to come first within Europe, and only later between Europe and the rest of the world.

In 1945 and 1946, the U.S. Treasury and State departments had pressed hard for a stabilization plan based on principles of classical economic liberalism. The idea was that Western European nations should quickly remove currency and capital controls and simultaneously devalue the major currencies in order to encourage investment flows of private U.S. capital that would offset their payments deficit with the United States and allow increased European purchases of dollar-denominated goods. The devaluation would also make it more attractive for Americans to buy European products, which would further contribute to industrial recovery and a normalization of commerce. But European production was at such a low level that there was a severe danger that these moves would have triggered massive inflation and a decline in living standards due to outflows of savings and scarcity of goods. Britain had bowed to American pressure to make the pound convertible, in 1947, only to suffer a massive drain of its reserves: controls were quickly restored. In 1949, Britain capitulated to pressure from the U.S. Treasury for a devaluation, which reduced the value of the pound from $4.00 to $2.80.

At the same time, with the particular backing of the Marshall Plan administrator, Paul Hoffman, U.S. policy shifted toward strong support for European integration. The State Department and the Economic Cooperation Administration blocked Treasury pressure on Britain to restore convertibility and called instead for rapid European integration. The benefits of integration were multiple: an expanded market would increase the opportunities for European industry and make Europe more attractive for American capital investment; the realization of economies of scale would make European industry more productive and competitive. If multilateral liberalization was not possible, liberalization within the Common Market (France, West Germany, Italy, Belgium, the Netherlands, and Luxembourg) was the next-best thing.

The first manifestation of this strategy was the Marshall Plan itself, which set in motion an eclectic blend of planning and freer markets. In 1949–50, the United States and the major Western European nations also agreed to a regional clearing union to revive multilateral trade within Europe. Trade, by its very nature, is triangular rather than bilateral. Every country has multiple buyers and suppliers and it is plainly unrealistic to expect the accounts of two trading partners to balance precisely; to require this would be drastically to restrict the total flow of commerce. Europe's postwar strict controls on currencies and capital meant that France, for example, could only buy from Belgium to the extent that France sold to Belgium. The European Payments Union established in September 1950 allowed multilateral settlement of accounts within Europe and the restoration of triangular trade. In addition, the United States pressed through the OEEC for early removal of intra-European import quotas and for tariff reductions. This comported with the Cold War strategy of submerging Franco-German enmity within a larger European whole to make Western European rearmament politically acceptable. This may have required a departure from the ideal principles of economic liberalism, but at least it bound Europe to the West geopolitically. As economically liberal habits took root within Europe, ideological support for classical economics would increase, it was hoped, and eventually Western Europe would see the wisdom of global liberalism as well.

There was thus invented a regionalist and quasi-mercantilist middle way for capitalist Western Europe. Despite the towering dominance of the United States, the Cold War constrained the United States to go along with a Western European political economy of which it did not entirely approve. At the virtual zenith of its geopolitical and geo-economic power, the United States had to make profound concessions with respect to how its lesser allies organized their economies. The historian John Lewis Gaddis termed this paradox "the impotence of omnipotence." The result was a Western European political economy with substantial public ownership, fairly high tariffs, "welfare state" laws passed under relatively conservative auspices which by 1955 were already spending upward of 40 percent of the gross national product, tightly regulated capital markets, and cartelization.

By laissez-faire lights, there was an appalling degree of regulation. Banking was very tightly controlled. For the most part, capital controls meant that citizens could not really invest money in financial instruments outside their own borders. Americans could not put money into foreign treasury securities, nor could Europeans invest financial capital in the United States (though both could and did establish transatlantic subsidiaries). Certain key industries, like telecommunications, were either government monopolies or regulated private monopolies. France, for example, was sharply restricted on purchasing American-made communications equipment, and vice versa. Civil aviation was cartelized. Insurance could not be sold across borders. Government procurement, whether military or civilian, was largely restricted to domestic products. Agriculture was subject to an array of import restrictions and price supports. Moreover, most products were subject to fairly stringent quota or tariff limitations, or both. And to the extent that Europeans were willing gradually to liberalize many of these controls, they insisted on doing so on a reciprocal basis within Europe. Japan was an even more controlled and regulated economy.

Yet, strangely enough, this turned out to be an era of sustained prosperity, growth, and peace—albeit armed—unique in the history of the world. In one generation after 1950, per capita real income in Western Europe rose as much as it had in the previous 150 years.[1] The United States provided much of the fuel for this economic expansion, while the very controls that Americans so disliked served as a rudder. U.S. military goods, domestic purchasing power, and capital exports supported accelerating demand; European demand gradually kicked in as the economies recovered, and ignited a second stage. Between 1950 and 1969, the book value of direct American private investment in Western Europe increased from $1.7 billion to $21.5 billion.[2] The world economy appeared to be in an equilibrium in which American surplus in the export of products was balanced by American export of capital; the two phenomena added up to American domination of the world's capital and product markets.

Yet hegemony had its costs. And the more the world economy recovered strength, the greater those costs became. Historians such as Paul Kennedy have made clear the economic costs of "military overstretch," but in truth the costs of hegemony were paid on many other fronts as well: in the monetary system and in the trading system, in the tendency of the hegemon to subordinate its own economic interests to alliance politics.

The decade of the 1950s began with a concern on both sides of the Atlantic that a permanent scarcity of U.S. dollars in Europe was strangling European recovery; it ended with a worry that a dollar glut in Europe was undermining the U.S. balance of payments and wrecking the entire monetary system. Both concerns were symptoms of a common problem—the attempt by a single dominant nation to be banker to the world.

In 1950, Europe desperately needed dollars to pay for imported American products and capital equipment, but European industry was far too weak to earn enough dollars from export. Between 1948 and 1952, the Marshall Plan provided $13 billion, but everyone worried that when Marshall Plan aid ended, Europe could not earn enough hard currency from its exports to import the dollar goods it needed. But by 1952 American military spending was providing a nice substitute for Marshall Plan aid. Soon Europe's own productive capacity was recovering and transatlantic payments came roughly into balance. In fact, the United States actually ran a slight payments deficit because its outflows of military spending, capital exports, foreign aid, and tourist spending together exceeded its net import earnings and repatriation of profits. By 1958 most Western European countries were at last strong enough economically to allow their currencies to be freely convertible, and the European Payments Union was disbanded in favor of general convertibility. This had taken thirteen years—far longer than the United States had wanted—and despite convertibility for commercial transactions, tight European controls were kept on exports of capital. Meanwhile, Western European economic integration was proceeding apace, beginning with the European Coal and Steel Community and picking up steam when the 1957 Treaty of Rome established a customs union among the six original members of the Common Market, a process strongly supported by the United States.

Yet on the monetary front, a new problem arose. As the hegemonic currency, dollars were in demand for many purposes. During this heyday of the Bretton Woods system, gold could be freely purchased from the United States at $35 an ounce. This meant that dollars were literally as good as gold, and gold and dollars were effectively interchangeable as the reserve currency of most nations. Dollars, by definition the hardest currency, were preferred for commercial transactions. As a growing world economy required an ever increasing supply of dollars, the American payments deficit was effectively the source of the new liquidity necessary to accommodate global economic growth.

By allowing the dollar to be the global currency, the United States risked losing control of its domestic monetary policy and exposed itself and the world to inflationary pressure. The conundrum boiled down to this: if the Federal Reserve Bank held to a monetary policy appropriate to the domestic economic situation, it risked starving the world economy of monetary liquidity; if, on the other hand, it accommodated the world's dollar needs, it invited domestic inflation and gradually undermined international confidence that the dollar would retain its value. That in turn created an irresistible pressure to convert dollars to gold and a crisis for the whole gold exchange system. The more the economies of other nations grew, the more this became a problem for the United States.

Professor Robert Triffin, a Belgian economist who spent part of his career at Yale University, is generally credited with the earliest understanding of this problem, which came to be known as the Triffin dilemma.[3] In the spirit of Keynes, reformers like Triffin urged that the world's monetary base be expanded by creating a genuinely international reserve currency; this would provide the growing world economy with adequate resources and take pressure off the dollar. The U.S. Treasury and the Federal Reserve resisted the idea, however, for America enjoyed the perquisites that went with providing dollars, however difficult the inconveniences, and Americans were unwilling to increase the autonomous power of the IMF as a rival monetary power.

This U.S. position reduced the IMF's ability to provide liquidity. After more than a century of isolation and a brief flirtation with universalist institution building, the United States liked its new hegemony. Americans regularly opposed expansion of IMF resources, not only to resist expansion of a rival locus of monetary power but because the debtor nations who occupied seats on the IMF board were seen as advocates of cheap money. The United States insisted on a high degree of "conditionality" in the deployment of IMF reserves: nations could draw on IMF funds only insofar as this was part of an IMF-approved "stabilization" program, which usually meant a deflationary one that conformed to orthodox American views. In this way, the IMF was quickly transformed into almost the opposite sort of creature from the one imagined by Keynes—an ally and enforcer of fiscal and commercial orthodoxy and a force for economic contraction.

During the 1950s, the United States rejected a series of proposals from several quarters for increasing the world's supply of monetary liquidity. These included a plan backed by Commonwealth nations to increase the dollar value of gold, which would have instantly raised the money supply and also created incentives to extract more gold; this the United States dismissed as inflationary. Others proposed increases in the IMF's own resources, but these, too, were rejected by the United States. As Fred L. Block[4] suggests, the American veto had an underlying logic: keeping liquidity scarce reinforced the traditional discipline of the gold standard, and it increased the leverage of U.S. aid programs, as well as the desirability of U.S. private capital. American policy was to promote overseas investment of U.S. capital through the Export-Import Bank, insurance against loan default and exchange-rate risk, and tax incentives. As long as private capital offered adequate liquidity, the system would have the money it needed without resorting to utopian internationalist schemes, and the capital would be reliably American. It was just the behavior one might have expected of a hegemonic nation, and of course the United States had not only the role of economic guardianship over the trading system but the further geopolitical imperative of the Cold War. The dominance of the dollar served both needs well.

It took a full decade before the pressure on the dollar became intolerable. By the late 1950s, Europe's economies had continued to strengthen, and the United States was running an external payments deficit of $3–$4 billion a year. This was annoying, but entirely different from the chronic trade deficits of the 1980s, for the United States still had an immense trade surplus, both in goods and in what economists call "invisibles"—notably income from foreign investments; the deficit resulted from the offsetting effect of American military spending, foreign aid, tourism, and capital exports. Even so, the imbalance created a monetary problem. Foreign governments were free to exchange their dollar reserves for gold, and as their surpluses increased, many chose to exercise that privilege: gold holdings were more prestigious than dollars, and foreigners (correctly) suspected that the dollar would eventually have to be devalued. By 1960, the dollars held abroad already exceeded the U.S. gold stock by some $19 billion.[5] France began a deliberate policy of converting dollars to gold in 1963 at the rate of about thirty tons of gold per month.[6] If one took the gold-exchange standard literally, the United States as hegemon was technically insolvent.

Yet other than France, which was applying pressure against the dollar mainly to promote a more truly multilateral system, none of the Western European nations was eager to push the system to the breaking point. Increasingly desperate efforts were made to shore up the Bretton Woods dollar-exchange system. During the 1960 American presidential election, a casual response to a reporter's question by the Democratic candidate, John F. Kennedy, seemed to imply that the Democrats might consider devaluation of the dollar. Intense speculation on the London gold market bid up the value of gold to $40 an ounce, far above the $35 rate that the United States was pledged to maintain, and it took concerted purchase of dollars by the world's central bankers to maintain the official parities. As other nations, notably West Germany and Japan, became export powerhouses, the U.S. export surplus in goods and services gradually declined, leaving a smaller trade surplus with which to balance the deficit in capital shipments and military outlays. The Vietnam War, another hegemonic enterprise, only accelerated U.S. foreign spending and increased the U.S. payments deficit. The war, and President Lyndon Johnson's refusal to pay for it by increasing taxes, also spiked the U.S. inflation rate and further undermined international confidence in the dollar. If the dollar lost value, that meant that foreigners holding dollars were losing money. In order for the central banks of Europe and Japan to keep the fixed-rate currency system stable, they were obliged to buy up dollars. To do so, they had to print more of their own currency. Thus did the United States export its inflation and compel its allies to bear its cost.

Despite joint efforts to prop up the dollar, over time there was in fact a good deal of conversion of dollars to gold. The immense stock of gold at Fort Knox gradually dwindled. Almost as soon as the Kennedy administration took office, Robert Roosa, the new Treasury under secretary for international monetary matters, organized a "gold pool" made up of the six Common Market nations plus Britain and Switzerland. Whenever speculators sold dollars and bought gold, the central bankers of these eight nations would intervene on the opposite side of the market to drive the price of gold back down. The New York Federal Reserve Bank, as the Treasury's agent, initiated reciprocal lines of credit ("swap lines") with foreign central banks for purposes of leaning against the wind in global exchange markets, which typically meant intervening to buy dollars. Treasury, for the first time in the Bretton Woods era, sold bonds denominated in foreign currencies that could be purchased only by foreign central banks. These "Roosa bonds" shifted to the United States the risk of a future dollar devaluation and soaked up some of the dollar overhang by converting it to long-term foreign debt.

All of this served only to buy time. In the short run, it discouraged speculation against the dollar, but in the long run, the dollar was overvalued because the United States, as hegemonic supplier of the world's currency, was printing too many of them. The United States repeatedly rejected European suggestions to multilateralize the system along the lines suggested by Triffin and the Keynesians. In 1961, the Kennedy administration agreed to a new $6 billion currency pool, but this was subject to vetoes by any of the ten member nations that supplied the reserves. In 1964, at the behest of the administration, Congress enacted an "interest equalization tax," which taxed away any advantage an American investor gained from purchasing foreign bonds. This was precisely the sort of capital control that American doctrine discouraged on the part of foreigners, but now it was deemed necessary to save the system. Japan, a docile geopolitical ally, was granted a special exemption and could borrow in the New York capital market with no tax penalty, as could Canada. Ironically, the new tax only stimulated expansion of the Eurodollar market, as a place to borrow dollars without paying the tax—and the attempt to rein in the dollar spurred the dollar glut. The Federal Reserve also cajoled its member banks into a voluntary credit restriction program intended to limit capital outflows; this was another covert form of capital controls, which succeeded in reducing the 1965 U.S. payments deficit by about $1 billion.[7]

This brand of solution had its limits. Just as America's special responsibility as world banker made for powerful strictures against its mercantilism, so it also had a unique obligation to keep its capital and product markets relatively open; if the United States were to raise significant barriers on capital and product flows, it would cease being the agent of classical liberalism, and the entire rationale for cooperating with the system it sponsored would collapse. By the mid-1960s the strains had worsened and the Johnson administration was prepared to accept something more far-reaching.

Initially, the Americans pressed for a simple increase in IMF quotas. The European powers, led by France, demanded a new international unit that would effectively replace the dollar as a reserve currency, but the U.S. representatives would not accept this. Eventually, in 1967, an agreement was reached to create a minimalist version of Keynes's proposed international currency, which would be known as Special Drawing Rights. Triffin and others, in the spirit of Keynes, saw SDRs as the eventual replacement for the gold-exchange system, but in practice, only meager quantities of SDRs were created and they failed to be more than a token augmentation of the existing system. Besides, SDRs were not even a genuine currency, since they could be held only by central banks. As long as the system depended on U.S. payments deficits for its liquidity, and those deficits were coupled with a fixed exchange value of gold at $35 an ounce, the dollar was more and more overvalued and the efforts to prop it up were a house of credit cards.

In 1968, the United States moved to a two-tier price for gold—$35 for official settlements and a floating price on the open market. That bought some time but intensified the speculative pressure for a devaluation. Even in 1967, the dollar in effect was international fiat money and not truly redeemable for gold. Under pressure from the U.S. Treasury, West Germany agreed explicitly to forgo its right to exchange dollars for gold; in March of that year, Karl Blessing, president of the Bundesbank, wrote a confidential letter assuring the Federal Reserve that his country, already the West's second financial power, would consider the dollar inconvertible. According to Fred Bergsten,[8] the same letter referred to U.S. troop commitments in Europe. This sort of deal, so typical of postwar economic diplomacy, neatly captures the complex connection between the two faces of American hegemony. As economic hegemon, the United States maintained the dollar as an anchor currency; as military hegemon, it kept troops in Europe. West Germany, a growing economic power but politically a client nation, refrained from exercising perquisites it was otherwise entitled to in the monetary system; instead of exchanging unwanted dollars, it simply accumulated them. This was expensive, but far less expensive than exposing its own currency to global pressures or carrying its defense burden single-handedly. In sum, a key client state was "solving" the American balance-of-payments problem in the short run—by permitting the United States to crawl further and further out on an unsustainable limb. This was costly in the short term to West Germany's finance, but strengthened its "real" economy, for the deutsche mark remained undervalued, thereby helping exports; having the mark not be a key currency kept down German inflation; West Germany also avoided escalating military expenses.

When a new U.S. administration took office in January 1969, it had several alternative ways to rescue the Bretton Woods system and take pressure off the dollar. As Joanne Gowa observed in her study *Closing the Gold Window,*[9] Nixon might have intensified Johnson's antiliberal program of capital controls, reduced the payments deficit by deliberately deflating the domestic economy, trimmed America's costly global commitments, or pressed for a truly multilateral monetary system. But initially his administration did none of these. Instead, it temporized, first deflating the overheated war economy and then trying to prop up the dollar. For several years, the system teetered on the edge of crisis. Every further tactical move the United States made to defend the dollar only certified its weakness and convinced speculators that it would eventually be devalued.

By 1970, it was clear that something had to give. A strategic reform would have tried to multilateralize the world's currency system: this the Americans did not want. A tactical expedient would have been simply to devalue the dollar, but the Europeans did not want to suffer the balance-of-payments consequences of a cheaper dollar, while the Americans resisted the loss of prestige. Though an overvalued dollar was bad for American exports (still only a trivial fraction of GNP), it was good for American multinational corporations and banks that shipped capital abroad. The managing director of the IMF, Pierre-Paul Schweitzer, proposed a cooperative 8 percent devaluation of the dollar, but neither the Americans nor the Europeans were disposed to go along. The crunch finally came in August 1971.

In 1969–70, the U.S. economy had been in recession, thanks to a tight money policy pursued by the Federal Reserve as an antidote to the inflation caused by the Vietnam War. The recession indeed reduced the Americans' appetite for imports and improved the payments deficit. But President

Nixon, with a newly appointed ally in Arthur Burns as chairman of the Fed, anticipated the 1972 election and for political reasons he wanted the recession ended. Burns complied, loosening the monetary policy just two weeks after his January 31, 1970, appointment.[10] Fiscal policy was also loosened, leading to a $23 billion federal budget deficit in fiscal year 1971. This generated the recovery that Nixon wanted, but, perversely, this economic recovery was the last straw for the Bretton Woods system; the dollar as the basic international medium of exchange based on fixed exchange rates had had its day.

The U.S. payments position had been consistently in deficit for twenty years, thanks to the overwhelming outflow of military outlays, foreign aid, private capital, tourist spending, and, as Europe and Japan became more competitive, thanks to escalating imports into the United States. The typical deficit was on the order of $3 billion annually—enough for Western Europe to accumulate several tens of billions of Eurodollars by 1968, but still a manageable sum as long as central bankers cooperated in the various gimmicks devised to reconcile that deficit with a fixed gold-dollar exchange rate. But in 1969, the annual payments deficit hit about $6 billion and, after shrinking in the 1970 recession, soared to an astronomical $29.8 billion in 1971. By early August, America's gold stock fell below the symbolically important level of $10 billion.

Facing reelection, President Nixon and his aggressive Treasury Secretary, John Connally, the former governor of Texas, were not about to hold the U.S. economy hostage to the balance of payments (as nonhegemonic nations must do routinely). In mid-August, Nixon and Connally repaired to Camp David, where they were joined by Burns, Treasury under secretary Paul Volcker, and Herbert Stein, who would shortly become chairman of the President's Council of Economic Advisers. After two days of deliberation, they embraced a program that was largely Connally's invention, with technical guidance from Volcker. It was given the unfortunate name of the New Economic Policy, a phrase once used by Lenin.

Domestically, the policy is best remembered for its temporary freeze on wages and prices, an almost unthinkable turnabout for a Republican President whose detestation of government controls had been acquired while the young Nixon served as a low-level bureaucrat in John Kenneth Galbraith's wartime Office of Price Administration. But the international turnabout was all the more remarkable. The policy was a startling departure from the obligations of hegemony in several respects. It slapped a 10 percent tax on imports and announced the suspension of the convertibility of dollars to gold. Nor would the United States intervene any longer to defend the value of the dollar. Exchange rates would be set by markets or by the intervention of other governments if they chose. Letting the dollar float was, of course, a violation of IMF rules, just as the 10 percent tariff surcharge was a contravention of the GATT.

Even more remarkably, this was all done unilaterally. Other heads of state and central bankers were informed after the decisions had been made and only shortly before President Nixon publicly announced them. The IMF's managing director, Pierre-Paul Schweitzer, suffered the indignity of watching the announcement at the U.S. Treasury on John Connally's television set. Connally and Nixon gambled, correctly, on the proposition that the rest of the world was not ready for a true regime of floating rates. If markets were allowed to set the value of the dollar, other nations would face currency appreciations, weaker export markets, and balance-of-payments crises. Other nations did indeed intervene to prop the dollar up. Once again, America's trading partners were importing inflation, and indirectly sharing the hegemonic burden, while the United States retained some of its key perquisites.

Yet, despite dire warnings that Nixon's new economic nationalism risked setting off a 1930s-style trade war, the ploy seemed to work. After four months of allowing markets to test the "real" value of the dollar, the world's central bankers, including the Federal Reserve, decided to stop the roller coaster. In December, the major nations attempted to resuscitate the fixed exchange system. At the Smithsonian Institution in Washington, agreement was reached to devalue the dollar by an average of 8.57 percent against other major currencies—almost exactly what Schweitzer had recommended months before. But far from being a cooperative decision, this devaluation was extracted by a unilateral maneuver that other nations roundly resented. The Japanese would long remember it as the "Nixon Shock."

Connally, in true Texas power-broker style, had turned up the heat and forced the allies to cut a deal: the 10 percent import surcharge would be dropped in exchange for the devaluation; the industrial nations would attempt, cooperatively, to hold currencies at the new parities, but within bands of fluctuation of 4.5 percent, substantially wider than the 2.25 percent limit of the Bretton Woods accord. President Nixon described this as "the most significant monetary agreement in the history of the world."[11] But fourteen months later, the Bretton Woods system was in crisis again, and this time the crisis was terminal.

In mid-1972, the British pound came under speculative attack. The British government imitated the American strategy of August 1971; it stopped intervening to defend the pound and let the pound's value float downward. Pressure soon shifted back to the dollar, whose rate was supposedly pegged at its new lower value. This was a graphic preview of the chronic, unacknowledged problem with a pure laissez-faire system of floating exchange rates cut loose from either a national hegemon, or the collective hegemony of central bankers, or a world central bank. With floating rates, governments with deficits in their trade or payments accounts could decide not to defend their currencies via domestically unpopular austerity measures but, rather, to shift the burden of adjustment to their trading partners by letting "the market" devalue their currencies. That would make their goods cheaper and those of their trading partners dearer. This worked well enough as long as it was confined to a handful of free riders, but it tended quickly to degenerate into a generalized round of competitive devaluation, as happened in the interwar period when nobody was in charge.

The pressure against the dollar only intensified after Nixon removed wage and price controls, spiking U.S. inflation. In early 1973, the United States negotiated another dollar devaluation, this time of II percent. West Germany now found itself as the banker of last resort, absorbing several billions of unwanted dollars to defend the value of the deutsche mark. By March, the major economic powers threw in the towel. The Bretton Woods era of fixed exchange rates was definitively over. The dollar would simply float, with its value set by markets, as conservative economists had long been recommending. The Europeans, for their part, would preserve a zone of monetary stability within the European Community, by practicing a joint float against the dollar, but pegging their currencies to each other. The Bundesbank would operate as Western Europe's central banker, intervening in money markets to keep currencies from fluctuating excessively against one another. In 1979, this system was formalized with the creation of a European Monetary System (EMS), which operated as a mini–Bretton Woods.

As classical economists explained it, this new nonsystem presumably offered the virtue of permitting countries to practice divergent macroeconomic policies. These, however, would be continuously reconciled in the usual manner of classical economics, through adjustment in prices—in this case the relative price of currencies. The desirability of avoiding high inflation rates or balance-of-payment crises would exert fiscal and monetary discipline, though via the preferred mechanism of the invisible hand, rather than through the visible hands of central bankers. As we shall see, the system had fatal flaws. But at the time it seemed the only alternative that was both politically viable and ideologically correct.

It was, in effect, a double defeat for the Keynesian perspective. Ideologically, monetary management was shelved in favor of market forces, an idea that the arch anti-Keynesian Milton Friedman had been commending since 1953.[12] The principal Keynesian institution, the Bretton Woods system of fixed rates, was dismantled in favor of something much like the classical gold standard, only this time with no explicit link to gold or management by central bankers; currency values would be set by supply and demand for various currencies. Yet, despite the shift away from Keynesian remedies, the problems identified by Keynes would not disappear. Absent a world central bank to create reserves, the pressure for "discipline" would place the adjustment burdens on the deficit countries and bias the whole system toward slow growth. And absent an official hegemon, there would remain the systemic tendencies to dangerous instability, identified by Kindleberger.

Surprisingly enough, a third dilemma endured as well—the Triffin dilemma. Despite the shift to floating rates, the U.S. dollar retained its position as hegemonic currency. And despite Nixon's brief flirtation with economic nationalism, the United States quickly reverted to behaving as hegemonic nation, propagating the virtues of economic liberalism and bearing disproportionate costs. Neither West Germany nor Japan was prepared to bear hegemonic burdens, both being geopolitically vulnerable, stigmatized as the aggressor nations of World War II, and pleased to emphasize economics in their national aspirations rather than politics. With several hundred billion dollars freely flowing through the world's money markets, and dollars continuing as the principal reserve currency as well as the favored currency for commercial transactions, there was simply no alternative to a hegemonic dollar so long as nobody was serious about more fundamental statecraft to rebuild a multilateral monetary order.

In the years after the breakdown of the Bretton Woods fixed-rate system, the IMF created a blue-ribbon Committee of Twenty. The committee offered several recommendations, the most far-reaching of which was gradually to replace gold and national currencies as the principal reserve asset with the Special Drawing Right. At a meeting of the IMF's governing Interim Committee held in Kingston, Jamaica, in February 1976, a number of seemingly far-reaching reforms were agreed upon, abolishing the official price of gold, increasing Fund resources, and making other technical changes. Like so many earlier ones, this agreement was hailed as the inauguration of a new monetary era. In fact, little had changed fundamentally. Though currencies were now officially denominated in SDRs rather than in dollars or gold, nothing was actually done to make SDRs a significant global reserve currency, and they were permitted only the most narrow of functions in settling official accounts. Though much was said about the plight of non-oil-exporting poor countries, only about $3 billion in additional IMF resources were placed at their disposal.

Thus, the major powers continued to accept a floating dollar as fiat money. And, burdened with a stake in its value, they did their best to prop it up. This continued the artificial prolongation of the United States' hegemony—and the cost to the American economy. As Robert Keohane observed in a slightly different context: "The United States contracted a disease of the strong: refusal to adjust. Small states do not have the luxury of deciding whether or how fast to adjust to external change. They do not seek adjustment; it is thrust upon them. Powerful countries can postpone adjustment. The stronger they are, and the less responsive they have to be to other countries, the longer it can be postponed."[13] That observation might serve as the epitaph of the American Century.

It was, of course, not just the dominance of the dollar that continued American monetary hegemony. The persistence of the Cold War as the central geopolitical fact of life also extended America's hegemony past the point of economic prudence. Although the United States belatedly extricated itself from Southeast Asia, and thought twice about prolonged anticommunist adventures outside Europe and the Western Hemisphere, it was still very much the leader of the Western alliance. In fact, the centrality of the Cold War in strategic thinking led the United States to a posture of astonishing weakness when confronted with a new genuine threat to its economic well-being, in the form of the OPEC oil-price increase.

The story of the oil shock has been often recounted and does not require lengthy discussion here. The bare facts are these: With American attention turned elsewhere, the Arab nations took advantage of the 1973 Yom Kippur War between Israel and its neighbors to curtail their oil exports. An explicit boycott was aimed at the United States and at Holland, which had continued to supply Israel with oil, but output was restricted generally. In November and December, OPEC succeeded in reducing world oil production by about 10 percent.[14] Oil is hardly a discretionary purchase. The world is not able abruptly to cut off its appetite for petroleum and does not respond to price increases by decreasing usage proportionately. As economists say, the demand for oil is relatively "price-inelastic." This 10 percent cut in output put significant upward pressure on spot oil prices, which quickly rose from about $3 a barrel to over $11. OPEC did not create an oil cartel. Rather, the OPEC nations adroitly seized control of a long-standing oil cartel, which had been previously used to the advantage of oil-consuming nations, to keep oil prices stable and low.

The stage was long set for this move. If the 1973 war had not triggered it, some other event surely would have. Politically, the United States and Britain had gradually lost their historic leverage in the Arab world. In 1956, the United States, in retaliation against Egyptian President Nasser's nationalism, had withdrawn financing for Egypt's Aswan High Dam; Egypt had then nationalized the Suez Canal. A combined invasion by Israeli, British, and French forces was opposed by the United States, leading to a schism among the Western allies but not restoring U.S. influence in the Arab world. In the two subsequent Arab-Israeli wars, the United States had tilted to the Israeli side, and Arab nationalists turned against the West. Libya had broken away from the Western oil cartel in 1969, and this did not escape the attention of more conservative Arab nations. Economically, the inflationary climate and the belated official devaluation of the dollar meant that the oil-exporting nations had suffered a real decline in earnings, since oil prices were denominated in dollars.

When OPEC began squeezing the West's oil supplies, the United States, preoccupied with Vietnam and Watergate and worried about increased Soviet influence in the Arab world, responded with uncharacteristic timidity. Rather than frontally opposing OPEC, which was led by its key anticommunist Arab ally, Saudi Arabia, the United States first tried to organize a sort of counter-cartel of oil-consuming nations, misnamed the International Energy Agency. This body of Western nations, notably not including France, intended to reduce dependence on imported oil and to share petroleum products in the event of shortage. But as everyone knew, the United States itself produced far more oil than its allies and was far less serious about conservation. Moreover, U.S. multinational companies were on both sides, since they benefited immensely from the windfall increase in oil prices generated by OPEC. By the time it was clear that America's allies had little enthusiasm for IEA, the moment for a decisive political response to OPEC had passed, and the initiative went to the oil-exporting nations, now in firm control of the cartel.

In 1973, the price of oil was between $3 and $4 per barrel, or about half its real (inflation-adjusted) price a quarter century earlier. The first round of price increases in 1973 raised that to more than $11. When high inflation rates in the late 1970s reduced the real earnings, the oil-exporting nations simply raised prices again, from under $14 in early 1978 to more than $35 in mid-1980; remarkably, they made the higher prices stick. This was, of course, yet another demonstration of the decline in American hegemony.

Thus, two seemingly disparate inflationary pressures—in fact connected by their common relation to American hegemonic decline—combined to set off the famous "stagflation" of the late 1970s and the recession of the early 1980s. The first was the stalled monetary revolution of 1971–73. The gold-dollar exchange system of Bretton Woods may have been dethroned by the new regime of floating rates, but in the absence of a world currency or an explicit basket of reserve currencies, and in the presence of half a trillion Eurodollars located outside the United States, there was more pressure on the dollar than ever. The Triffin dilemma continued, in disguised form. The excess Eurodollars, the inflationary fiscal legacy of the Vietnam War, and the attempts to buy social peace throughout the industrial West via inflation-indexed wages and high social spending, all created a context of high embedded inflation.

Then OPEC produced a second wave of inflationary pressure. If dollars did not hold their value in real terms, oil did. And unlike monetary gold, oil was a product with real uses and an abrupt increase in its price imposed real costs. The industrialized nations tried to limit the inflationary effects of the oil price shock in 1974 with the traditional cold bath of restrictive fiscal and monetary policy. This set in motion something that supposedly couldn't happen: inflation and recession at the same time. We have seen what created the inflation—to which an orthodox response created the recession. Even more destructive was the manner in which the West tried to reconcile OPEC's windfall oil profits with the stability of global finance.

Western nations no longer controlled oil flows and oil prices, but at least they could still try to control financial flows and to influence where the petro-profits were invested. Western governments, as good capitalists, did not want direct responsibility for this. They were happy to let commercial banks do the job. What was windfall for OPEC was abrupt hardship for non-oil-exporting Third World nations. The industrial First World could endure a mild recession and adjust to higher oil prices. Indeed, for nimble exporting nations like West Germany and Japan, the oil-price increase was actually a tonic, for it induced conservation measures and, eventually, higher productivity. But for the have-not nations of the Third World, chronically short of hard currencies and facing balance-of-payments crises, the OPEC shock was cataclysmic. Their oil import costs rose by $335 billion between 1973 and 1982, which consumed about two-thirds of their total new debt.[15]

The solution was "recycling." Western banks would accept the swollen oil profits. Between 1974 and 1977, oil-exporting nations generated surpluses of $173 billion, nearly all of which was deposited in grateful Western banks. This new money, it was argued, would in turn be happily lent to needy Third World countries at no apparent risk. Commercial bankers had grown comfortable lending large amounts for development loans in nations such as Brazil, which had grown at prodigious rates in the 1950s and 1960s. These loans tended to be more profitable than ordinary commercial loans because they were made in jumbo amounts to governments or quasi-public development agencies, which in turn parceled them out. The banks were substituting the underwriting judgment of the Argentine Minister of Finance or the Brazilian Minister of Development for their own underwriting chores. Unlike the great investment bankers of the nineteenth and early twentieth centuries, who underwrote bonds in Argentine railroads or Peruvian canals but quickly resold them at a markup to private investors, the commercial banks kept most of these Third World loans on their own books, and as long as Third World growth rates held up, they made a good return. After all, the loans were less expensive to administer than small domestic commercial loans, and they carried premium interest rates.

But when the OPEC shock hit, the bankers failed to recognize that something fundamental had changed. The loans were no longer going to finance commercial projects that would generate income to pay off the loan. Rather, they were going to finance consumption, or balance-of-payments adjustment, and in a new era of slower growth. Yet the bankers took refuge in the concept that "sovereign" loans guaranteed by governments could not go into default. Instead of limiting their exposure, they rushed headlong to expand Third World lending, compensating for the added risk by boosting interest rates and hence profits. The idea that international lending agencies such as the World Bank or the IMF should take responsibility for providing additional liquidity to OPEC-damaged developing nations was a Keynesian notion that did not comport with the vogue for private market solutions and instruments. After all, commercial banks, subject to the discipline of the marketplace, had to be more efficient than public ones, didn't they?

By 1979, the debt of the oil-importing less developed countries had soared to nearly $400 billion, as global interest rates rose sharply and the steepest recession of the postwar period hit; commodity prices softened and the market for Third World commodity exports was seriously depressed. By 1982, when it first became obvious that many Third World debtor nations were on the verge of insolvency, the six largest U.S. banks had more than 200 percent of their own capital tied up in loans to them. If the debtor nations were insolvent, so were the banks. But this is getting ahead of our story.

The stagflation of the 1970s set the stage not only for the slow growth of the 1980s but also for a wrenching move away from mixed economies to pure laissez-faire. Economic distress tends to discredit the regime currently in power, and at this time center-left governments held sway in the principal Atlantic nations. Jimmy Carter was President of the United States. James Callaghan's Labour government was running Britain, and the SPD of Willy Brandt and later Helmut Schmidt was leading West Germany. Socialists also governed Sweden and Austria, countries that weathered the stagflation better than most. Only France had a relatively conservative government, though a fairly *dirigiste* one, and this would soon be ejected in favor of a socialist one.

In 1978, these center-left governments attempted a mildly Keynesian response to the stagflation, known as the "locomotive" strategy. The idea, first conceived by OECD staff economists,[16] was a coordinated program of economic stimulus, which economists like to call "reflation." The word is unfortunate, since it sounds too much like inflation. Reflation means not stimulating higher prices but, rather, restoring economic growth.

When Jimmy Carter had taken office the year before, Europe and America were still suffering the effects of the fall of Bretton Woods and the rise of OPEC. Unemployment was on the increase in most of the OECD countries, and while the new Democratic administration was eager for a reflationary program, Carter and his officials believed that the United States was bearing too large a share of the burden. With a $30 billion trade deficit looming, they believed the United States was serving alone as the engine of global recovery and at an escalating cost. After the twin shock of the collapse of fixed exchange rates and the OPEC price hike, the Western leaders had held annual economic summit conferences, beginning at Rambouillet Castle in November 1975; at the London economic summit session in May 1978, Carter pressed Chancellor Schmidt and Prime Minister Fukuda to join the United States in a coordinated reflation by running bigger German and Japanese budget deficits and by raising the value of their own currencies to take pressure off the dollar and help balance U.S. trade accounts. As a triple locomotive, the world's three most powerful economies together would pull the world out of recession.

But this American overture was rebuffed. West Germany and Japan had grown accustomed to the convenient dual role of geopolitical client and geo-economic free rider. As economically productive nations with high savings rates and deliberately undervalued currencies, they enjoyed the best of all worlds: low real interest rates (which meant low capital costs for their industries) and export surpluses. Export surpluses meant that they could have steady growth and full employment, but without the high fiscal deficits that generate inflation and trigger high interest rates. They grew faster than everyone else, capturing the benefits of the global trading system while bearing few of its burdens. In effect, they were exporting their austerity to the rest of the world, while enjoying domestic prosperity.

It was hardly accidental that these were also America's top two allies, and the most docile ones. They handled their geographic vulnerabilities not by being unusually bellicose toward the U.S.S.R., but by being unusually deferential on matters of high politics to the leader of the Western alliance. Not surprisingly, they tended to be the State Department's favorite client nations. Both the State Department and the Pentagon tended to view their economic free riding as an acceptable price and resisted efforts to pressure them on economic issues.

By 1977, however, the economic asymmetry was seen as intolerable. When Carter's initiatives were rebuffed, Treasury Secretary Michael Blumenthal chose the June 24 session of the OECD, in Paris, to increase the pressure. In an unusually blunt speech, he warned the allied capitalist nations that they could not exist as "islands of prosperity in a sea of economic troubles,"[17] and demanded again that they contribute to a joint strategy of reflation. This time, the United States was prepared to drop a small bomb. It would, Blumenthal hinted broadly, campaign to drive down the value of the dollar. To the Europeans and the Japanese, this was a replay of 1971 only with far higher stakes, given the now perilous condition of the world economy. Within six months, the dollar had dropped 20 percent against the yen and 7 percent against the mark. In order to keep the dollar from dropping further, foreign central banks bought some $35 billion worth of dollars—almost precisely the amount of the U.S. balance-of-payments deficit for 1977.

There was a dreadful irony, it turned out, in the logic of coupling floating rates with continuing dollar hegemony. Dollars, as the Triffin dilemma teaches, were destined to keep losing value over time, because there were simply too many of them. Foreign governments roundly resented this, yet their central banks kept having to absorb ever more dollars to stem the spiral of devaluation. The more they did this, the more they increased the global glut of Eurodollars and other stateless dollars, which only intensified the pressure against the dollar. The Americans, for their part, continued to have a creditor mentality and went on viewing themselves as sound money conservatives—yet the ultimate cheap, fiat money that conservatives supposedly feared was becoming the dollar itself.

The dollar continued to plummet, a trend intensified by the new reality of rates set by markets. In a world with no systematic central-bank intervention to maintain official parities, speculators were free to "ride the trend" and bet against the dollar—which only pushed it down further. This global game of monetary chicken went on for a distressing year. Finally, at the June 1978 summit session, West Germany reluctantly agreed to the locomotive strategy: it would lead the European Community nations in an ambitious program of fiscal stimulus and public spending; this would increase world demand and draw in more American exports, which in turn would allow the United States to stop battering down the dollar.

But the deal was easier struck than done. The embedded inflationary forces overwhelmed the mild elixir of stimulus in Europe and tighter monetary policy in America. The dollar continued its free fall. By the end of 1978, it had lost more than half its value against the yen and over a third of its value against the deutsche mark. Whatever free markets were good for, they were evidently not very good at setting precise exchange rates with any connection to real economic forces, day to day or even month to month. The annual surplus of the OPEC nations had dwindled from a high of some $40 billion to almost nothing. Annoyed that a cheaper dollar had eroded its profits once again, OPEC increased oil prices a second time. West Germany, usually obsessed with the importance of sound money, had gamely agreed to Carter's locomotive strategy—and was rewarded for its pains only with higher inflation.

The world's money markets, faced with escalating inflation, were near panic. In West Germany, there was barely concealed fury at what Schmidt termed the U.S. policy of "malign neglect." Despite the Americans' change of heart, the shift to a tighter money policy, and the emergency creation of a $30 billion foreign-currency pool to support the dollar, the dollar continued to fall and global inflation continued to rise. Exchange rates were floating, but the interest rates on many investments are fixed. Suddenly, interest rates on home mortgages, bonds, and other long-term investments were lower than the inflation rate. That meant that the real cost of borrowing, for creditors, was less than zero percent, and the real return on investment for owners of capital was a loss of their capital stock. In this disastrous and deteriorating climate, Carter's first Federal Reserve chairman, G. William Miller, was widely considered a man with no global financial experience and hopelessly out of his depth. At length, in July 1979, Carter turned to Paul Volcker, well known to other central bankers, Wall Street, and official Washington as a paragon of financial orthodoxy and shrewd ingenuity. Miller was moved to the Treasury, and Volcker named chairman of the Federal Reserve. Carter hoped that Volcker would somehow find a solution to the stagflationary crisis and rescue his own faltering prospects for reelection. He was right only on the first count.

The Federal Reserve Board is carefully structured to be independent of political pressures, yet the Federal Reserve chairman is a thoroughly political creature, ordinarily highly responsive to the President who appoints him. In a famous study, Professor Edward Tufte[18] discerned a "political business cycle" in which money mysteriously loosens in election years, just in time to stimulate recoveries of economic growth and political fortune. This certainly described the behavior of the Fed under Nixon's chairman, Arthur Burns, and Tufte demonstrated to general statistical satisfaction that it described most Fed chairmen. But the luckless Carter got himself the rare Fed chairman who was splendidly oblivious to his sponsor's political fortunes. Volcker's loyalty was to the financial system.

Volcker's very first international meeting as Fed chairman was a near-debacle. At the fall 1979 conference of the IMF, in Belgrade, the first such session ever held in a Marxist country, Volcker faced dire warnings from his fellow central bankers and from commercial bankers that the global financial system was on the verge of collapse. There was mounting anger that the United States under Carter and Miller no longer understood its international obligations or took them seriously.

Volcker sized up the situation, returned early to Washington, and devised a devilishly shrewd ploy. For years, an odd coalition made up of liberal congressmen annoyed at the Fed's lack of accountability and conservative economists eager to make monetary policy more automatic had been urging the Fed to change its operating strategy. The Fed conducted monetary policy by manipulating interest rates. If, for example, the governors of the Fed thought the economy was at risk of inflation, they tried to drive interest rates up to cool the economy down. The Fed did this both by raising the rate at which it lent money to banks and by buying bonds on the open market for its own account, which soaked up some of the national money supply, made money dearer, and bid up prevailing interest rates.

The Fed, not wanting to fuel speculation, never quite announced its goals, which irritated liberal members of Congress. The approach also bothered conservative economists of the monetarist school, whose leader and hero was Milton Friedman. Monetarists believed, with Friedman, that "inflation is always and everywhere a monetary phenomenon"—that is, whatever the presenting causes or secondary influences, the real cause of rising prices is monetary authority bowing to political pressure and printing more money than real economic activity warrants; too much money chases too few goods, and inflation results. Monetarists, therefore, proposed that as long as the Fed attempted to target interest rates, it was in danger of both undershooting—setting rates too low—and occasionally overshooting and setting them too high, in much the same way a novice sailor oversteers. Typically, it succumbed to the political pressure expressed in Congress's chronic annoyance and permitted the stock of money to grow too fast.

Though the Fed set interest rates somewhat indirectly and tended to be coy about its intentions, there was no mistaking when the Fed was attempting to tighten money. Tight money predictably enraged congressmen, who were electorally accountable to families facing higher mortgages and businessmen buffeted by steeper credit costs. Despite the monetarist critique, the Fed, it seemed, was beholden largely to bankers and bondholders, not to the borrowing public.

So at the time Volcker took office, a proposal was floating around economic circles, sponsored by monetarists but with the incongruous support of some populists as well, to have the Fed target the total money supply rather than interest rates. In the view of the Friedman monetarists, this had the virtue of eliminating the temptation to oversteer. The target money supply, over the long term, would be tied to the real rate of economic growth, but in the short run the Fed would lash itself to the mast and put the tiller on automatic pilot. The waves of market forces would toss interest rates back and forth, but over the long term the course would be true. Ironically, the Fed's populist critics, in Congress and elsewhere, were attracted to the money-supply proposal for precisely the opposite reason: if the Fed announced its intention by specifying a long-term target for growth of the money supply, it could be held politically accountable for overshooting or undershooting the goal or for setting one that was too stingy.

For Volcker the idea of monetary targeting was attractive for neither the monetarist reason nor the populist one. In his long history as a financial economist and public official, Volcker had had little sympathy either for Friedman's theories or for populist demands for easy money. But monetary targeting was irresistible to him in October 1979, because it provided an exquisite camouflage for the austerity program that he believed was the only solution to the twin problems of stagflation and the dollar's free fall.

On the evening of October 6, Volcker made a dramatic announcement that ostensibly represented his conversion to the monetarist philosophy. No longer would the Fed target interest rates; rather, it would set long-term targets for growth of the money supply and leave interest rates to be set by the market. This was, of course, stunningly disingenuous, for the Fed could back into whatever interest rates it wanted to by braking money growth. It was presented to Carter as a mere technical change, though it effectively transferred ultimate economic power from the President to the Federal Reserve chairman. By coincidence, the political backlash that brought Margaret Thatcher to power just about the time Volcker made this announcement brought monetarists to power in Britain as well.

It soon became clear that Volcker was bent on strengthening the dollar, breaking the stagflationary cycle, and reassuring the community of creditors mainly via one device: astronomically high interest rates. When Congress and the White House bitterly protested, Volcker shrugged and insisted with an absolutely straight face that the Fed was merely targeting the money supply; if interest rates were soaring to 14 and 16 percent, and finally to a peak of 21.5 percent, that was merely the work of the free market. By the time the politicians grasped what the Fed's game really was, the economy was suffering its bout of tightest credit since the Civil War, and Carter, not Volcker, had suffered the political consequences.

In the short run, the rest of Volcker's anti-inflationary measures seemed to backfire. His controls on credit drove borrowers offshore; with inflation still embedded in the economy for structural, monetary, and sectoral reasons (higher energy, food, and medical costs), very high interest rates became their own independent source of inflation. If your auto loan cost 20 percent rather than 10 percent, that portion of the cost-of-living index was that much higher. As prices rose, wages and social transfers followed. The economy was in a classic inflationary cycle, which could not be broken overnight even by astronomical interest rates. The case of Brazil proved that even interest rates in excess of 100 percent would not deter borrowing so long as inflationary expectations persisted. Throughout 1979 and well into 1980, the real interest rate stayed negative. If inflation was at 17 percent, a loan with a nominal interest rate of 16 percent was still a bargain, with a real rate of minus 1 percent. Expecting even higher prices next year, people kept borrowing, whatever the cost of money. Capital poured out of productive investments into housing, fine art, gold, and any other hard commodities that seemed likely to hold value.

The effect on the real economy was predictably devastating. Speculative investment drove out real investment. People's effective purchasing power plummeted. As prices of existing homes in hot markets were bid up out of sight, developers could not get financing to build new housing elsewhere. Ordinary businesses that depend on bank credit for day-to-day operations faced crushing credit costs. Unemployment rose from 5.8 percent in 1979 to a peak of over 10.7 percent in late 1982. Inflation kept roaring along—prices rose 17 percent in the first quarter of 1980—while the economy sank into recession. The price of gold kept rising, a sign that the dollar's real value was continuing to fall. Foreign-policy concerns—the festering crisis in Iran, the Soviet invasion of Afghanistan—added to nervousness in the money markets and drove gold still higher, to $875 an ounce by January 1980, more than double its October level. Also, the price effects of the second OPEC price hike were still being felt. Tight money by itself having failed to do the trick, Volcker added mandatory controls on credit in March 1980. Soon, the economy was in the worst recession since World War II.

At last, however, the dollar began a belated recovery, rising from a low of 177 yen and 1.7 deutsche marks in January 1980 to over 210 yen and 2 marks by January 20, 1981, the day of Ronald Reagan's inauguration. In an open global economy, high interest rates attract capital investment from abroad. As Walter Bagehot observed in his classic work on the nineteenth-century money markets, *Lombard Street,* a 7 percent interest rate would bring money to London from the North Pole and 10 percent would bring it from the moon.[19] In an economy of floating exchange rates, this effect reinforces itself by the expectation of future appreciation of a tight-money currency. If for example, the dollar is weak and dollar interest rates are abruptly raised, investors in London or Riyadh will find dollar investments highly attractive, not just because of the premium rates but because of the likelihood that the higher rates will lure in other investors—and bid the value of the dollar up even further. That way, the investor stands to make money not just from high returns but from capital appreciation of the dollar as well.

In the case of nonhegemonic currencies, such as the mark, the yen, or the lira, which are more subject to genuine market forces, the interest-rate appeal and the exchange-rate risk usually cut in opposite directions. Investments in yen- or mark-denominated bonds, for example, may earn low interest rates as befits "hard" currencies, but they are nonetheless attractive because hard currencies are likely to appreciate against other currencies over time. If you buy yen bonds for a year, your "coupon" rate of interest may be only 3 percent, but by year's end the yen will have appreciated by 5 percent, leading to a healthy net return of 8 percent. Conversely, if you invest in lira-denominated bonds, the coupon rate may be an attractive 15 percent, but in a year the lira may lose 7 percent of its value, so the net yield on lira bonds and yen bonds is roughly equal. In a perfectly free market, this outcome must occur, since perfectly free markets equilibrate. Speculators make their money because the yields are not perfectly equal or perfectly predictable. In the short run, all markets tend to overshoot or undershoot their "true" equilibrium value.

But the dollar, as the hegemonic currency, is partially immune to this equilibrating logic. And a decade ago, driven by Volcker's policy of extremely tight money, the dollar's interest-rate allure and its exchange-rate allure cut in the same direction. Not only did foreign investors stand to reap astronomical rates of return; they stood to gain from the dollar's strengthening as well. A "weak" currency, with very high interest rates, was behaving anomalously like a "hard" currency. No other currency could have pulled off this simultaneous trick, of course. Not surprisingly, investors operating in a global market newly freed of currency and capital controls poured money into dollars, which bid up the value of the dollar even further.

This had the side effect of pulling the rest of the world deeper into stagflation. Western Europe could not stand by and allow capital to be sucked out into dollar investments. Defensively, it began tightening money, too. The Volcker recession depressing American purchasing power began depressing worldwide purchasing power as well. For the Third World, already reeling from the OPEC price shock, Volcker's policy was a catastrophe coming on top of a disaster. Every additional point of interest added an estimated $2.5 billion to the interest bill of Third World debtor nations. And since their debts were denominated in dollars, every 20 percent increase in the value of the hardening dollar added 20 percent to the principal they owed.

The conservatives who came to power in the late 1970s believed that the cause of the economic crisis was not the collapse of the international monetary system or the OPEC price increase but, rather, excesses of the mixed economy: regulation, welfare-state laws, trade unions, public spending, and other economic stabilizers that had been installed throughout the industrial West during the long postwar boom. If markets were in turmoil, the cure was simply more deregulation and more free market. The policies of Reagan and Thatcher, coupled with those of Volcker and monetarism, all but obliterated the political logic of the postwar mixed economy, the hallmark of which had been a series of barriers, both overt and covert, to absolutely free flows of capital; things had tended to stay put—which enabled center-left parties to broker and defend social contracts that benefitted their constituencies. Social democratic and labor parties had been the natural custodians of these social contracts, and the voters reciprocated by returning them to office. As long as the Keynesian welfare-state social contract delivered economic growth and security to citizens, even center-right parties had dared not dismantle it, but only slowed its consolidation.

The globalization of commerce, without any globalization of political institutions, put this system in jeopardy. A political crisis was deferred as long as economic growth continued, but the arrival of stagflation and monetary upheaval in mid-decade created a very serious electoral and ideological crisis for the parties of the center-left. A politics of high taxation and redistribution could work only so long as employment was relatively full (so that the dependent poor would claim only a small fraction of total spending) and growth was fairly reliable, meaning that wage earners' real income kept growing and they retained confidence in the system and its high taxes. While there is some evidence that by the 1970s the size of the public sector was reaching its natural limits in a mixed economy (35 to 50 percent of gross national product), there is no convincing evidence that its size killed economic growth. As early as 1955, Western Europe had levels of public spending (30 percent of GNP) that, when U.S. public spending reached such levels twenty years later, were said to have killed prosperity. Yet Europe's high public spending occurred on the *eve* of a twenty-year boom![20]

Nonetheless, the stagflation produced an ideological and electoral windfall for conservatives. It seemed easy to claim that excessive redistribution and taxation had killed the golden goose. A whole generation of political analysis focused on the claim that political democracy coupled with a welfare state eventually creates fiscal overload. Interestingly, this analysis was attractive both to the political right, which saw redistribution as the enemy of growth, and to the Marxian left, which saw the Keynesian compromise as a fatally flawed bargain that would eventually succumb to the inevitable contradictions of capitalism. And as a practical matter, slow growth and rising unemployment meant that available public resources had to be diverted from popular universal programs in health, education, pensions, and public services to the unemployed and the new poor. This drove a political wedge between the poor and the working middle class—the essential class coalition of a center-left political alliance. Fiscally, the crisis required bigger deficits and higher taxes, at precisely a moment when citizens were feeling poor and economies were under inflationary stress. All of this ushered in a period of ideological and political confusion on the center-left—and a period of conservative rule.

Yet Ronald Reagan and Margaret Thatcher were not ordinary conservatives. Unlike traditional conservatives, Thatcher had little concern for conserving the social fabric. Tories who worried about the effect of austerity policies on ordinary life or who defended social outlays she sneeringly dismissed as "wets"—a schoolboy term of derision for weak-kneed younger lads who wept or peed in their pants. Reagan was a strong nationalist who, seeing American global power erode, wanted to restore American military hegemony regardless of the cost. Unlike traditional conservatives, he gave only lip service to fiscal prudence and in practice had no fear of budget deficits. The combination of Reaganism and Volckerism set up the worst possible sort of policy collision, and prolonged the imperial overstretch of American hegemonic pretension for yet another decade, at dreadful cost.

three

# REAGANISM: THE GREAT DEFERRAL

The Reagan presidency created a politics of collective denial and deferred an overdue revision of U.S. strategic goals in the world. Rather than recognizing that Europe and Japan had long since become mature economic competitors, able to share security burdens, Reagan's program renewed American imperial pretensions. Rather than grasping that most Western nations relied on a managed form of capitalism, his government intensified America's commitment to one-sided laissez-faire, at the expense of the nation's own economic well-being. At a time when America's economic weight was dramatically reduced, Reagan's programs for a military buildup, tax reduction, and debt drew heavily on what remained of America's hegemonic legacy. In order to continue the "exorbitant privilege" of borrowing from abroad in our own currency, we had to keep the dollar king. In order to retain the allegiance of skeptical allies to newly ambitious foreign-policy goals, we had to defer to other nations' commercial goals; and we had to continue bearing a disproportionate share of military costs. In short, the more the burdens of hegemony became unsustainable, the more it was necessary to maintain the hegemonic pretense. Even when the Cold War finally ended and, with it, the assumptions of the postwar era, the Bush administration was slow to revise the inherited conception of U.S. goals for our own economy or for the global system.

The politics of Reagan's administration were in some respects a reaction to his predecessor. Jimmy Carter's presidency had emphasized global and domestic retrenchment. In his first two years, he had cut defense spending as a fraction of GNP to a postwar low of 6.7 percent. He had engineered the "giveaway" of the Panama Canal. He had made "human rights" an idealistic foreign-policy priority. He had been credulous about the Sandinistas' good intentions in Nicaragua and belatedly indignant about the bad intentions of the Soviet Union in Afghanistan. He had negotiated a second strategic arms treaty with the U.S.S.R., which aroused such skepticism in Congress that it was never submitted for formal ratification. Despite some astonishing diplomatic breakthroughs, such as the Camp David accord with Egypt and Israel, Carter seemed to many European leaders a bumpkin. His nation's dwindling power was seen not as a graceful strategic sharing of global responsibility with allies but as a chaotic and ignominious retreat. His was a presidency marked by gas lines, moralist lectures, chilly rooms, sweaters, high interest rates, and lowered national expectations. All too symbolically, it ended with Americans being held hostage by a third-rate power. At least, this was how the Republicans painted it, and the image was convincing to enough voters to propel Reagan into the White House by a large majority.

Reagan evoked echoes in the national memory of special destiny and effortless possibility—a sense that it was once again Morning in America. After a roller-coaster first term, his popularity recovered with the economy. His reelection campaign declared that America was "back and standing tall." In defiance of the changed global realities, the Reagan presidency reasserted U.S. military and ideological ambitions. The increases in military spending were due not to an increase in actual threats to military security—if anything, the rising threat was economic. Rather, it was due to the new political influence of hard-liners eager to intensify the arms race. Ideologically, the fierce propagation of market economics became synonymous with the reassertion of America's global influence.

The apparent success of this initiative caused immense self-congratulation in conservative circles about both economic philosophy and economic performance. It was certainly true that the 1980s were a decade of worldwide disillusion with statism—whether state-run steel mills in Brazil, state telecommunications monopolies in Western Europe, or the truly deadening state socialism of Eastern Europe. But outside the United States and Britain, the opposite of statism was hardly laissez-faire. The great economic success of the 1980s, Japanese capitalism, was a complex amalgam of fierce competition, cartelization, administered capital flows, selective mercantilism, and an almost feudal conception of reciprocal social obligation. The European Community, likewise, relied on an activist state sector. Successful developing nations were mainly imitating Japan, not the United States. Though American ideas about the genius of markets and the virtue of deregulation were enjoying something of a vogue, American management, whether of corporate enterprises or the public budget, was in well-justified disrepute.

Reagan, like Roosevelt, presided over a diverse band of supposed soul mates, many of whom agreed only that government was bad and the free market good, and disagreed profoundly on many key policy issues. Characteristically, Reagan compromised by letting each faction have its way: thus, his administration included officials whose main priority was military buildup and geopolitical assertiveness (Haig, Weinberger, Perle), others who were traditional fiscal conservatives (Regan, Martin Feldstein, Stockman, Volcker), monetarists (Beryl Sprinkel), and a new breed of radical free marketeer known as the supply-sider (Norman Ture, Paul Craig Roberts). The supply-siders preached an odd mixture—an almost Keynesian gospel of growth stimulated by lower taxes, along with an extreme faith in the genius of unregulated markets. Their prescriptions and those of the traditional fiscal conservatives were totally at odds. But under Reagan all factions prevailed. So high was Reagan's self-confidence, so powerful did he believe his mandate to be, and so shell-shocked was the Democratic opposition, that the Cold Warriors got their military buildup, the fiscal conservatives their declared goal of budget balance, the monetarists their targeting of the money supply, and the free marketeers their deregulation and massive tax cut.

Reagan's economists predicted that supply-side magic would produce a balanced budget by 1984. But instead the effect of a tax cut along with increased military expenditure was a 1984 deficit of $185 billion—more than double Carter's worst. In an ordinary country (France, for example), a policy of deepening deficits would lead people to expect a devaluation of the currency and investor flight from it. This is precisely what happened to François Mitterrand's first government in 1981–83. As the lone socialist among a throng of statesmen influenced by monetarist conservatives, Mitterrand tried to reflate France's economy unilaterally, but in a permeable global economy this had the unfortunate effect of sucking imports into France, increasing France's trade deficit as well as its budget deficit, and creating a balance-of-payments crisis. Eventually, he was forced to accept the devaluation of the franc and to replace his program of Keynesian stimulation with "austerity with a human face."

But the United States could have it both ways—temporarily at least. The deficit was increasing, rates of domestic savings declining, and real economic competitiveness waning. Yet as long as interest rates were very high and the dollar the reigning currency, global financial markets favored dollars. This had the handy side effect of encouraging foreign sources to provide the capital that the administration needed to finance the budget deficit, as well as the capital that private industry needed to make up for diminishing domestic savings (which were being depleted by public borrowing). When Volcker decided in mid-1982 that the United States had had enough of extremely tight money and let interest rates subside somewhat (to a level still high by historical standards), the enormous budget deficit had the Keynesian effect of stimulating a consumption-led boom. Given the high interest rates and the open capital markets, domestic investment could increase too—though financed by foreign borrowing. The supply-siders insisted that their tonic was working, even if half the investment was coming from abroad. Despite tax reductions legislated to favor American investors who aided in "capital formation," domestic savings rates continued to sink to historical lows.

The high dollar, however, gradually priced made-in-America products out of world markets, and the trade deficit worsened. American manufacturers and trade unionists, already suffering from the worst recession since World War II, complained bitterly about the perverse effects of the high-flying dollar. But with its ideology of anti-intervention, the administration took the position that the money markets, by definition, had to be assessing the value of the dollar accurately. This was a nonsensical view, for the inflated status of the dollar conferred by "markets" was directly traceable not to the invisible hand of Adam Smith but to the nimble hand of America's central banker, Paul Volcker. By November 1982, the dollar reached an astonishing level of 278 yen, close to what it had been thirty years earlier, when Japan was a far weaker country. The dollar subsided only slightly over the next two years despite Volcker's gradual lowering of interest rates. Then, in early 1985, the dollar reached a new peak against other major currencies; according to the Federal Reserve, it nearly doubled in value between 1980 and February 1985. The administration found it convenient to point to the high dollar as a badge of global confidence in its policies, but in truth, the dollar was grotesquely out of alignment. It was now well above its level of a decade before, though inflation had been higher and productivity growth lower in the United States than in West Germany or Japan, which should have meant that the dollar would continue to *decline* against the yen and the mark. The Treasury, under Donald Regan, insisting tautologically that the dollar's value had to be "correct," stoutly refused to intervene in the currency markets to drive the dollar down to a more reasonable level.[1]

The convergence of tight money, recession, escalating budget deficit, and globalization of commerce produced further political windfalls for the right. Trade unions, always weaker during periods of high unemployment, were suddenly all but defenseless; it was management that now made "demands" at the bargaining table for concessions. A friendly National Labor Relations Board gave management wide latitude in pursuing tactics that would have been judged illegal in earlier times. Unions lost their solidarity as factories began closing all over the country, forcing union workers in different plants of the same company to bid against one another to determine whose jobs would be saved. Older workers, desperate to retain their past gains, voted to subject new employees to reduced pay scales. These desperation measures wrecked labor solidarity and the industry-wide master contracts, with their bedrock principle that the same work should command the same pay. American workers, once a celebrated blue-collar middle class, were now told they were overpaid drones, selfishly retarding the opportunities of their brethren in Mexico, Taiwan, and the lower-wage backwaters of nonunion America.

The American trade-union rank and file, often socially conservative, had never been very ideological about the labor movement, but they had backed trade unionism and vaguely social democratic policies as long as these delivered economic benefits. Now, the unions could no longer deliver "more"; nearly a majority of union families voted in 1984 for Reagan, as the more optimistic and patriotic candidate. Labor leaders, meanwhile, circled their wagons and became more assertive in the one forum where they still had substantial influence—the institutional Democratic Party. But this only made them seem like a self-serving special-interest group and roused the ire of others in the Democratic coalition and the ridicule of the press.

The federal deficit produced fiscal gridlock in domestic budget politics and thus further demolished the Keynesian center-left coalition and confused American liberals. Nearly all professional economists, except supply-siders, soon appreciated that the Reagan-Volcker combination of high deficits and a strong dollar was lethal for the real American economy. American products were being priced out of world markets; high interest rates meant high capital costs for U.S. industry; high deficits depressed the already anemic savings rate and more than wiped out any incentive for capital formation that the supply-side tax cuts might otherwise have provided. But the Reagan administration had three strong reasons to stay the course: ideologically, the supply-siders kept insisting that their program was good for entrepreneurship; politically, the voters supported tax cuts, especially as real wages fell; and fiscally, the deficit turned out to be a superb device for battering down social domestic programs, a central goal of the Reagan philosophy.

In June 1982, Mexico nearly defaulted on its bank loans, and Volcker, finally concluding that the tight-money medicine had gone on long enough, announced that the Fed would no longer rigidly target money supply. Interest rates magically subsided, and the economy began to recover. However, the strong dollar persisted, now driven by the economy's improved prospects and helped by foreign central bankers who, as always, found it convenient to let their own currencies be slightly undervalued. The budget deficit, given the continuing effects of the 1981 tax cut, also persisted. Indeed, by 1983–84, concern about the deficit crowded out virtually all other domestic economic issues. The hapless Democrats—like generals still fighting the last war and remembering their loss in 1980, when they had been tagged with the "big spender" label—were determined to be more fiscally responsible than the Republicans. In the 1984 election, Walter Mondale ran as the candidate of the economics establishment. Reagan might be fiscally irresponsible, but Mondale would be brave: "We are living on borrowed money and borrowed time," he cried in his speech accepting the Democratic nomination. "Whoever is inaugurated in January will pay Mr. Reagan's bills. The budget will be squeezed. Taxes will go up. And anyone who says they won't is not telling the truth. Mr. Reagan will raise taxes, and so will I. He won't tell you. I just did."

But this stance, seemingly admirable for its candor and willingness to accept pain, left the Democrats in the worst of all worlds. Ever since the New Deal, the Democratic strategy for activist government had been "tax and tax, spend and spend." The taxing was progressive, the spending redistributive. As long as voters believed that they gained from this bargain, they supported Democrats. But the policies of the supply-side era had cut taxes while shifting the tax burden downward during a period of economic hardship. Income and capital-gains taxes for the well-to-do were cut dramatically while payroll taxes increased. Government spending was shifted from well-known domestic programs that helped ordinary people to military ones which produced nothing tangible for the pocketbook. By 1984, tax-and-spend was in disrepute. The taxes on wage earners were more onerous and the tax receipts purchased fewer visible benefits.

For almost half a century, the Keynesian toleration of mild deficits in order to finance spending and stimulate growth had been a winning formula for Democrats. The Republicans had worn the green eyeshade of fiscal responsibility, and wondered why they lost elections. Now, suddenly, the two parties had switched camps. The alchemy of supply-side economics imbued deficit spending with Republican virtue, since these deficits were intended not to increase spending but to put more money in the pockets of entrepreneurs. The Democrats, in a pathetic trade, were the new skinflints—and reaped the appropriate political reward.

In the years of slow growth after 1973, especially during the deep recessions of 1974–75 and 1981–83, the average voter had suffered economically. For 80 percent of American families—the base Democratic constituency of the New Deal coalition—real income peaked in 1973. Mondale's proposed program of fiscal austerity a decade later offered nothing to these hard-pressed voters but higher taxes. Revenues from those taxes paid for nothing tangible—only a sounder budget that satisfied economists and accountants. This was political suicide.

After 1984, the domestic fiscal crisis intensified. Many liberal Democrats in desperation voted for the 1985 Gramm-Rudman-Hollings bill, which mandated a step-by-step program of automatic deficit reduction, extending into the 1990s. The Democrats who supported Gramm-Rudman calculated that, if nothing else, the law would force the Republicans to choose between decreasing the defense budget and honoring their pledge not to raise taxes. The Gramm-Rudman pressure did moderate Reagan's military buildup, but after Mondale's defeat, the Democrats decided that any call for higher taxes had to come from the White House. The fiscal arithmetic was relentless. If the prime objective of fiscal politics is deficit reduction and taxes cannot be increased, all domestic politics boil down to deciding what to cut. This was a politics that hopelessly fragmented the center-left coalition.

Some Democrats tried to hold the line, defending expensive universal programs such as social security and medicare as essential to their cross-class coalition. Others put fiscal prudence first, advocating politically unpopular tax increases and spending cuts. Still others tried to rebuild a populist program of taxing the well-off and expanding the welfare state. But Reagan's own mismanagement had only intensified the very distrust of government that had helped elect him; even many Democrats had come to accept much of the conservative claim that government was unreliable and in any case unavailable. Fiscal deadlock and ideological paralysis reinforced each other, and crippled an opposition politics.

By the mid-1980s, a second deficit—the trade deficit—was also reaching critical proportions. The United States had had a surplus of merchandise trade as late as 1975. Despite the cheap dollar during the Carter years, this had become a deficit of $28.8 billion by 1978, as other nations became competitively stronger. Then in the 1980s, as the United States' competitiveness continued to erode and its markets remained more porous than many foreign ones, the high dollar supercharged this trade imbalance: the deficit in merchandise trade soared to $65.2 billion in 1983 and a peak of $158.2 billion in 1987, when the United States imported nearly twice what it exported. In addition, as the United States became a net borrower rather than a net investor, its balance of capital flows turned negative also: global dividend and interest flows no longer offset the trade deficit but only added to it.[2]

In such crucial industries as automobiles, steel, consumer electronics, and even advanced technologies that had long accounted for lopsided American trade surpluses, American producers were losing major shares of both domestic and global markets. The cause of this shift has been hotly debated. Most orthodox economists, who insist that industrial or trade policy is powerless to change comparative advantage for the better, hold that deteriorating American competitiveness in the 1980s was entirely the result of macroeconomic factors—the high dollar and the low U.S. savings rate. The high dollar put imports on sale and overpriced American-made goods; the low savings rate depressed domestic investment and hence productivity growth. Dissenting economists, economic historians, and students of public policy have argued that, beyond these factors, U.S. industry was already becoming less competitive as a result of complex historical and structural forces and that a cheaper dollar, by itself or in combination with higher domestic savings, could not solve the trade imbalance. But everyone concurred on one point—the high dollar was doing serious damage.

Moreover, America's trading partners were now getting weary of the overvalued dollar. On the one hand, the high dollar generated cost advantages and hence nice trade surpluses, but on the other hand, it drained capital, drove up worldwide interest rates, pushed Third World nations into prolonged depression, and risked the abrupt "hard landing" when markets finally decided that the dollar had peaked.

Shortly after Reagan's second term began, the White House chief of staff, James Baker, and Treasury Secretary Donald Regan startled official Washington by abruptly switching jobs. The idea had been Regan's, but both men had grown frustrated with their old positions. Baker was weary of the White House infighting and wanted to sink his teeth into something more substantive. Regan, feeling somewhat isolated at Treasury, hoped that a move to the White House would bring him closer to real power. He had been the chairman of the brokerage house Merrill Lynch, and was a pure free-market man, Wall Street style. Baker, a onetime Texas business-man, was a far more political creature and a swashbuckling pragmatist. He brought with him to the Treasury his protégé and close working partner, Richard Darman, another ideological pragmatist and infighter of Machia-vellian subtlety.

Baker and Darman arrived at the Treasury in mid-January to find profound concern about the trade deficit, the protectionist pressures it was generating, and the prospect of a crash of the dollar. Baker is no liberal, but he is temperamentally activist; letting the invisible hand do everything leaves no room for activism. At Treasury, he found a dormant institution of potential global economic management, the Group of Five (or G-5), which had sunk into formalistic disuse. The Finance Ministers of the five leading economic powers—the United States, Japan, Great Britain, France, and West Germany—met biannually, often with their respective central bankers, but did little more than issue formal pronouncements urging cooperation. Lately, these pronouncements had resolved that the United States needed to reduce its fiscal deficit so that all countries could loosen the monetary spigots. But thanks to Reagan's determination to avoid a tax increase and the impasse in Congress over what government spending to cut, this could not occur.

Attending their very first G-5 meeting in January 1985, Baker and Darman quietly abandoned the dogma that the value of exchange rates was best left to the market. They and their counterparts soon agreed to coordinated intervention in foreign-exchange markets to drive down the value of the dollar. Over the next year, Baker and Darman worked to turn the G-5 into a real diplomatic mechanism and set in motion a coordinated program of exchange-rate management, as well as closer macroeconomic coordination, which would gradually push the dollar down to more realistic levels. The high value of the dollar, they believed, had become a classic speculative bubble, in which markets were setting an unrealistic exchange rate not for any fundamental economic reason but only because they expected the dollar to soar still higher. The higher it soared, the greater the risk of a crash. The overvalued dollar was killing American exports, and irresistible pressures were growing for protectionism.

To execute their plan, they needed the cooperation not only of foreign central bankers and governors but of their own Federal Reserve. Paul Volcker, as Jimmy Carter had learned the hard way, paid no particular deference to Presidents. But, as it happened, Volcker did need something from the White House. Federal Reserve governors are appointed for fourteen-year terms, but the chairman serves only four years before he must be redesignated chairman. Reagan, against the advice of some of his supply-siders, had reappointed Volcker in 1983: he served as an important global symbol of America's resolve to brake inflation at whatever cost. By 1985, however, Volcker was under fire from some of the Reagan appointees at the Fed, including the vice chairman, Preston Martin, and he needed the support of the White House to retain a working majority. He was also hoping to be offered a third term as chairman in 1987.

In this climate, Baker and Volcker fashioned a close alliance. Baker, Darman, and Assistant Treasury Secretary David Mulford persuaded allied nations to shift to a strategy of active and coordinated exchange-rate management, to drive down the value of the dollar in the short run and to temper speculative currency swings over the longer term. In principle, this was not particularly hard to do. France had long favored "target zones" for exchange-rate parities and greater monetary intervention. West Germany, as de facto central banker of the European Monetary System, had been practicing a form of monetary management within Europe since 1979 and favored greater monetary stability. The Japanese Finance Ministry, home of discreet "administrative guidance," was also not wedded to laissez-faire and had found the previous stance of Donald Regan doctrinaire and unrealistic. Besides, a cheaper dollar would restore greater balance to the trading accounts, in theory at least, and this would brake the drive for U.S. protectionism. Only Mrs. Thatcher's government, made up of even more devout believers in laissez-faire than Reagan's, had qualms.

Still, the shift to managed rates presented a very tricky diplomacy. In a series of conversations in the spring and summer of 1985 with their foreign counterparts, Baker, Darman, and Mulford pressed hard:[3] a cheaper dollar and the ensuing moderation of the U.S. trade deficit, they contended, would depress worldwide purchasing power; to prevent this from triggering a worldwide recession, and from diminishing the ability of Third World nations to service their debts, Japan and West Germany, notorious for running tight fiscal policies, should compensate by shifting to more expansionary policies. But West Germany and Japan balked. Germany had already had one disastrous experience with a badly designed made-in-the-U.S.A. locomotive. The Japanese were also skeptical; they already felt pressure from the United States to open import markets, liberalize capital markets, and reduce taxes. Despite having hurtled onto the global stage as the world's second most powerful economy, and enjoying a chronic trade surplus, Japan was still very conscious of its dependence on exports and very nervous that an excessive increase in the yen's value would price Japanese products out of world markets. Both the West Germans and the Japanese believed that the real source of the trade imbalance was America's failure to reduce its budget deficit, which forced the Federal Reserve to keep interest rates high, and the resulting high dollar caused the trade imbalance; only if the United States reduced its budget deficit, they believed, would a program of coordinated exchange-rate intervention work. They were unwilling to make domestic economic sacrifices just because the United States lacked the political will to achieve the fiscal discipline that even Baker and Darman acknowledged was necessary.

The necessary agreement, therefore, could not be simply that the United States would drop its opposition to managed currency interventions in exchange for foreign economic stimulus. It had to be more venturesome, coordinating macroeconomic policies as well as managing exchange rates. Of course, Baker and Darman could not guarantee this, because they could not ensure that the White House and Congress would agree on a deficit-reduction strategy—particularly with Reagan still determined both to continue military spending and to resist new taxes. Discussions dragged on throughout most of 1985.

An initial breakthrough came in June, in a series of conversations between Baker and top Japanese officials. With Japan now willing to accept a cheaper dollar (which, of course, meant a higher yen), the United States and Japan jointly worked to persuade the Western Europeans at the OECD meetings in July. Several issues were closely linked. Could the major powers really harmonize macroeconomic policies, which involved the most politically sensitive domestic issues of taxing and spending policy? Would politicians, especially independent legislators, make sacrifices at home in order to keep commitments to foreign governments? Since capital flowed freely across national boundaries, could exchange-rate stabilization work in the absence of complementary macroeconomic coordination? How explicit should the target ranges for currencies be, and how should the responsibility for market intervention be shared? At this point, the Gramm-Rudman bill appeared as a splendid *deus ex machina.* Initially, the Reagan people had resisted it, but now the President's belated acceptance of it was offered as proof that the United States was taking deficit reduction seriously.

All of this was sharply contrasted with policy during the first Reagan administration. It portended an era of significantly closer coordinated intervention than even the last two years under Carter, when the United States had agreed to ad hoc interventions in response to bitter European criticisms of "malign neglect." For it was the first time since the collapse of the Bretton Woods system in 1971–73 that the United States was prepared to act systematically to stabilize the value of world currencies and to share authority for this task with its trading partners. But by now, this was a far more daunting exercise than in the Bretton Woods era. Money markets, deregulated and linked electronically, were now trading currencies twenty-four hours a day, an estimated $100–$150 billion, far more money than central bankers could spend on intervention. One government's misperception or miscalculation risked leading to a futile fight with market forces and the squandering of vast sums of government reserves.

This startling turnabout had occurred under an ultraconservative administration. Baker and Darman were recognizing that the United States was inextricably dependent on the cooperation of other capitalist nations and unable to set its own fiscal and monetary policy alone without serious financial consequences for itself and the world economy. Even more surprisingly, they were acknowledging that the "free market" was not capable of making the necessary decisions. Governments had to become intimately involved even in the most "marketlike" transaction of all—the determination of the relative value of national currencies. Paradoxically, the very program of financial deregulation their administration championed necessitated this new form of financial interventionism—which, of course, would not have surprised Keynes.

This impending shift in strategy was a well-kept secret during the summer and early fall of 1985. Throughout, official administration pronouncements continued to insist that markets were reading the value of the dollar correctly, and the intervention was ideologically incorrect and economically unsound. "As an economist," sniffed supply-sider Paul Craig Roberts, "it is very hard to understand the concept of an overvalued dollar."[4]

Then, at a London conference of September 15, 1985, a highly secret working document was circulated. Although the public announcement a week later did not mention targeting exchange rates or amounts of currency intervention, and the press was led to believe the Group of Five had merely negotiated an arrangement to pursue a generally cheaper dollar,[5] in fact all the details had been subject to the most precise negotiation. According to one of Japan's most astute financial journalists, Yoichi Funabashi, who obtained a copy of the secret document, the G-5 ministers agreed to an initial reduction of 10–12 percent in the value of the dollar. They agreed also that $18 billion would be committed for market operations, with roughly 30 percent coming from the United States, 30 percent from Japan, 35 percent from the European countries collectively, led by West Germany, and the remaining 5 percent from Britain (not a member of the European Monetary System).

The policy reversal was announced dramatically on Sunday, September 22, at the Plaza Hotel in New York, after money markets had closed for the weekend. In dramatic contrast to President Nixon's announcement of August 1971, discussed intensely among senior American officials but sprung unilaterally on unsuspecting allies, the Plaza agreement had taken more than six months of painstaking secret diplomacy and was a genuine multilateral undertaking. This time, those kept in the dark were the rest of the U.S. administration. Baker, the supreme quiet infighter, had isolated all his potential opponents. Beryl Sprinkel, the monetarist chairman of the Council of Economic Advisers, was ignorant of the negotiations, as was the laissez-faire Allen Wallis, the State Department's under secretary in charge of international economics, and even White House chief of staff Donald Regan.

Though the official Plaza communiqué did not mention target ranges for the dollar or even the word "intervention," it left little doubt that the era of pure monetary floating was over and that the G-5 nations would do all that was necessary to bring the dollar down to mutually agreed levels. According to the communique,

> The Ministers and Governors agreed that . . . exchange rates should better reflect fundamental economic conditions than has been the case. They believe that agreed policy actions must be implemented and reinforced to improve the fundamentals further, and that in view of the present and prospective changes in fundamentals, some further

orderly appreciation of the main non-dollar currencies against the
dollar is desirable. They stand ready to cooperate more closely to
encourage this when to do so would be helpful.[6]

The money markets did not need an engraved invitation. On Monday,
September 23, the yen appreciated nearly 5 percent against the dollar, a
one-day record.

The accord marked not only an ideological and diplomatic shift but a
shift of power from the State Department, bogged down in a variety of
Cold War and regional disputes, to the Treasury—and a concomitant
acknowledgment that monetary geopolitics were once again as important
to the American national interest as the traditional high politics of war and
peace. Monetary interventionism was cleverly painted by Baker, not as a
retreat from laissez-faire, but as an activist financial counterpart to the
Reagan doctrine of military interventionism. The dollar might be headed
downward, but American leadership was back and standing tall. And in
a way, it was. The concepts were surprisingly French and Japanese. The
scheme was pure Jim Baker.

At first, the Plaza accord seemed to work. In its first six months,
coordinated interventions by finance ministries and central banks spent
almost all of the committed $18 billion and did succeed in driving the dollar
down from 240 yen in September to 200 yen by year's end and 180 yen in
March 1986. In addition, the United States, Japan, and West Germany
made coordinated cuts in their interest rates, relieving some of the interest
burden on the economies of the Third World.

The Plaza system also involved not only an accord among the five
leading industrial capitalist governments, but also a concordat between
their central bankers and finance ministries of those nations, two of
which—the United States and West Germany—possessed fiercely independent central banks. Karl-Otto Poehl, head of the Bundesbank, and to some
extent Paul Volcker, had been reluctant converts to coordinated currency
management. Volcker worried that markets would overreact, letting the
dollar plunge too rapidly, and Poehl had the added concern that coordinated intervention against the dollar complicated his job of managing
parities within the EMS.[7] Gradually, it became clear that ad hoc coordinated intervention had severe limits; it was not, after all, a process of
fundamental global economic statecraft or a pooling of sovereignty into a
new international institution. To a great extent, the limitations of this
collaboration helped trigger the October 1987 stock market crash.

Baker and Darman had hoped to broaden the Plaza regime. If money
markets were to respect the targeted exchange rates, one had to manage
carefully the gap between interest rates in Tokyo, Frankfurt, and New

York. Otherwise, capital would flow to whichever money center had excessive interest rates, bidding up that currency.[8] So they wanted the central bankers to coordinate interest-rate changes as well. This would have the beneficial effect of lowering interest rates worldwide. Initially, this strategy worked. In early March 1986, on three successive days, West Germany, Japan, France, and the United States all lowered their discount rates,[9] and other coordinated rate cuts followed in 1986 and early 1987. However, skeptics had warned all along that domestic monetary policy (interest rates) could not realistically be set in isolation from domestic fiscal policy (budget deficits). If a particular government was running a large deficit, you couldn't expect its central bank to lower the interest rate without risking inflation, notwithstanding an international commitment to do so. The Plaza system logically led to a much more ambitious imperative: budget policies had to be coordinated, too. This did not require identical policies, for in an integrated global market economy one country's deficit might offset another's surplus. But budget policies had to be moving toward a general convergence. Obviously, this was a matter for domestic as well as diplomatic bargaining. The whole thing had to be delicately balanced, politically and economically, like a Calder mobile.

In 1986, at the annual economic summit and at other meetings, Baker and Darman advocated policy coordination and gradual convergence. They fashioned a device that seemed promising—"objective statistical indicators": seemingly technical indices, of growth rates, savings rates, inflation rates, productivity, and so forth, would take the measure of the major economies and automatically indicate appropriate policy shifts. But although the heads of state meeting at Tokyo in May 1986 paid lip service to these indicators in their joint communiqué, nobody seriously believed in such a mechanism. Baker, despite his ingenuity, could not deliver the most important indicator of all, Ronald Reagan, who remained off in his own fiscal world, where deficits didn't matter because of the genius of supply-side economics. Reagan, wedded to tax cuts and a military buildup, also remained in a deadlock with Congress over budget discipline. As long as Baker could not convincingly show that the U.S. budget deficit was being reduced, the whole idea of indicators and closer coordination was a fantasy. Intervention in exchange-rate markets would remain ad hoc, subject to limited success and the episodic temptations of free riding. In fact, several nasty episodes occurred during the next few years, in which one central bank or another was caught intervening on the wrong side of the market, riding a trend in order to make quick money, when it was supposed to be fighting market forces as part of a joint intervention.

The West Germans were especially suspicious of Baker's indicator project. They saw it as a pseudo-technical device to pressure the Federal

Republic, yet again, to play locomotive. Once more, America's failure to put its own house in order was generating a demand that West Germany, a model of fiscal probity, take inflationary risks—*nein, danke*. West Germany already exercised monetary hegemony within the European Monetary System and was performing that task rather better than the United States was playing its own role globally. In addition, Bundesbank president Poehl, the senior statesman among central bankers, had contempt for indicators, which he thought were a reversion to the primitive monetarism of Milton Friedman that so many Americans had a weakness for—a naïve, laissez-faire conceit that policy could be put on some kind of automatic pilot. In an influential article titled "You Can't Robotize Policy Making," Poehl wrote:

> Those who wish to replace persons and ad hoc decisions by regulatory mechanisms and indicators apparently have no perfectly clear idea about the nature of monetary policy decisions or the difficulty of reaching them. The crucial factor in an internationally coordinated economic and monetary policy is the willingness of each individual country to take into account the implications of its own economic policy for the rest of the world. This willingness cannot be decreed from outside. Not even the gold standard managed to bring this about. No system—no matter how sophisticated it may be—can help when this political willingness is lacking. In the event of a conflict, the system collapses.
>
> Willingness to cooperate and accept rules of behavior in economic and monetary policy is a political decision. In democratic states, therefore, there cannot be any automatic mechanisms governing political decisionmaking processes. It would, for instance, never occur to anybody to depersonalize decisions in the field of foreign policy and to pre-program them by means of objective indicators.[10]

In private, Poehl was far less polite.

Had it been unanimously embraced by the allies, the policy of indicators and convergence might have forced the United States to break the deadlock over its own budget. Many economists, and such Democratic leaders as New Jersey Senator Bill Bradley, saw the outlines of a superb agreement here: Baker would negotiate a deal with the West Germans and the Japanese to stimulate their economies—to be activated only when the United States achieved serious deficit reduction. This would give Reagan the face-saving excuse he needed to change his position on taxes. The economist Fred Bergsten described the indicator project as a kind of "international Gramm-Rudman" that would give elected officials political cover.

Perhaps Baker had this in mind, too, but neither he nor Volcker could persuade Reagan. In retrospect, it would seem that Poehl and the Europeans assessed Reagan more astutely than did Baker.[11]

In effect, the United States still wanted things both ways. On the one hand, free-market rhetoric, ideology, and programs were rapidly turning the capitalist world into one big economy with ever freer flows of capital and goods, a world with little room for policy autonomy. This turned out to be a fine way to get rid of regulatory and welfare-state impediments to free commerce, not to mention trade unions. After all, what capitalist power wants its entrepreneurs to be hobbled competitively by burdensome taxes, excess wage costs, recalcitrant unions, or regulatory red tape? On the other hand, the United States of America was not about to have its economic program dictated by other nations or by the imperatives of the very free-market system the policymakers were so intent on creating. A global market might moot the role of policy, but the Reaganites anomalously demanded national sovereignty. If supply-side economics called for enormous deficits, who was Karl-Otto Poehl to say otherwise?

In the spring and summer of 1986, coordination began to unravel. To start with, the yen was appreciating faster than Japanese politicians liked. Finance Minister (and later Prime Minister) Noboru Takeshita had talked about making a major sacrifice and allowing the yen to strengthen to 200 to the dollar, joking about the political liability of his onetime nickname, Minister Endaka (Minister High Yen).[12] Now the yen was trading at 165 and still strengthening, to the dismay of many Japanese and of money markets, which suspected (with some justification) that the intervention program either had lost its consensus on desired exchange-rate targets or lacked the power to bring them about.

In February and March, the problem was less division among the major nations than division within the Federal Reserve itself. By February, a majority of the governors were Reagan appointees. Thanks to the gospel of supply-side economics which they preached, it was permissible, even obligatory, to be advocates of easy money. Volcker found himself in the minority that opposed cheaper money. He urged that the Fed hold off cutting U.S. interest rates, so as to induce other central banks to cut their rates, in line with Baker's Plaza system. However, Preston Martin, the vice chairman and the leader of the easy-money bloc, a former savings-and-loan executive with little international experience, rallied his forces and outvoted the chairman. Volcker then threatened to resign. Eventually, in a testy compromise, Volcker was given two weeks' grace to negotiate a coordinated cut, which he successfully did. Baker strongly backed Volcker—and it was Martin who subsequently quit.

These internal conflicts were mirrored in similar disputes within Japan, with its cabinet system that features a weak Prime Minister and strong rival ministries; and in West Germany, with a coalition government and an independent central bank. In addition, the West Germans were torn between their responsibilities to the G-5 system and their regional obligations to the rather more manageable EMS, which became paramount after 1986, when the EC intensified its plans for a single market.

Between the summit of May 1986 and the stock market crash of 1987, the Plaza system came under increasing strain. In September 1986, Baker and the new Japanese Finance Minister, Kiichi Miyazawa, made a bilateral agreement to keep the dollar, then at a record low of 160 yen, from depreciating further; the Japanese, in turn, pledged to stimulate their economy domestically, which would contribute to global demand and, it was hoped, increase Japan's imports, thereby moderating its still swollen trade surplus and America's trade deficit.

But the dollar continued its free fall, and both academic observers and financial players now warned direly that the dollar would crash. Stephen Marris, the influential former chief economist of the OECD, in a bleak monograph, made the danger of a "crash landing" well known.[13] In January 1987, Baker negotiated yet another major accord, at the Louvre conference in Paris, with an even more precise set of agreements for intervention and an even narrower target range. According to Funabashi, the central bankers and finance ministers agreed to interventions to hold the dollar at the then current levels of 153 yen and 1.82 deutsche marks; a deviation of 2.5 percent from those parities would trigger intervention, and a deviation of 5 percent would trigger high-level policy consultations and more intervention. But the dollar kept falling. As it fell below the psychologically significant level of 150 yen, Japanese financial institutions began selling off dollars and dollar-denominated investments, in rare defiance of the administrative guidance of their Finance Ministry. The United States had been pressing *dirigiste* Japan to abandon its bureaucratic management of capital markets; now the newly liberated Japanese financiers complied with a vengeance. America got its ideological wish with unsuspected results.

In August, Volcker's second term as Federal Reserve chairman expired. The supply-siders had never liked Volcker. His policies were too close to the traditional austerity economics they associated with central bankers. Despite Volcker's close working arrangement with Baker, Reagan decided that he wanted his own man. The new chairman was Alan Greenspan, an experienced economist but something of an unknown quantity in matters of global money management. Greenspan's first act was precisely what newly installed central bankers do to reassure money markets of their anti-inflation zeal: he tightened interest rates. Much to Baker's consternation, Japan and then West Germany followed suit. This, of course, was precisely the opposite of the Plaza system. Rather than coordinated intervention, it was uncoordinated retaliation—and in the wrong direction. Tighter money only slowed world growth and increased the cost of financing the U.S. budget deficit. When West German and Japanese interest rates rose, any favorable international effect of the U.S. monetary tightening on the defense of the dollar was negated; it just left everybody with higher interest rates. But Greenspan, lacking a practiced international hand, had put domestic considerations first. Worst of all, it sent the disastrous signal that the Plaza system of careful money management had broken down.

An annoyed Baker publicly criticized the Bundesbank for raising its interest rates and hinted that the United States was not going to get into an interest-rate war with its allies, even if this meant letting the dollar tumble further. To the badly overvalued stock market, this meant that the great bull market of the 1980s was over. A broad wave of stock dumping turned into panic selling. On October 17, in one day, the Dow Jones lost 508 points, and other stock markets followed. In one sense, the optimists were right that this was merely a "correction," albeit extreme. Throughout the inflationary 1970s, the stock market had lagged behind real economic growth, because returns were higher on bonds. Now, as inflation receded and higher returns were available in stocks, money poured back into equities and bid up the value of stocks far beyond a sustainable level, in a classic case of "overshoot."

In this financial emergency, the new fabric of global monetary cooperation, even if only ad hoc, turned out to furnish an effective emergency safety net. The finance ministers and central bankers, benefiting from two years' experience coordinating interventions, quickly put aside their squabbles and together turned to the urgent business of heading off a world depression. At home, Greenspan opened the money spigots wide and pumped in whatever was necessary to keep the brokerage houses solvent. In Tokyo, the Finance Ministry had not abandoned administrative guidance entirely, and with marvelous discipline, Japanese investors resisted the epidemic of panic selling. Not surprisingly, it was the Tokyo stock market that recovered first and within a year was again setting new records. In several carefully limited respects, Japan was quietly beginning to share hegemonic responsibility with the United States—but without undermining its own industrial might.

After the stock market crash, and several months of frantic collaboration among central banks and finance ministers, the Plaza system settled down to one of tactical intervention and strategic default. The prospect of serious policy coordination was dead. None of the world's leading nations cared to pay the political price of subordinating domestic economic policy to global imperatives, and none wanted to cede sovereignty to new global financial institutions. In January 1989, Secretary Baker moved to the State Department and left international economic policy in the hands of Greenspan and Treasury under secretary David Mulford, a temperamental man with little of Baker's diplomatic finesse. Day-to-day intervention to stabilize interest rates continued to work well enough, though it was far from the lockstep coordination Baker and Darman had envisioned in 1985. The dollar, after hitting a low of about 120 yen, mysteriously rebounded to a level slightly higher than the Finance Ministers were said to want—about 150 yen in mid-1990. It was a level high enough to restore confidence in the dollar, but too high to solve the U.S. trade deficit. The stock market crash did not become a generalized panic. The Dow Jones briefly regained its 1987 high, and a second bad day turned out to be only a hiccup. Ostensibly, the system stabilized. In fact, it was stable only to the extent that the U.S. economy had become a ward of foreign capital.

By the fall of 1990, the perils of this course had become clear. The Japanese financial system was itself shaky, and no longer so free with loans to the United States. According to the Japanese Finance Ministry, Japan actually withdrew a net $8.9 billion from U.S. capital markets during the first half of 1990, after having infused some $180.1 billion into it during the previous five years. Germany, likewise, having committed some $100 billion to its new eastern zone in 1990 and 1991, could no longer be counted on to finance the U.S. capital shortage. All told, a net outflow of more than $20 billion in foreign capital was projected for 1990, after an inflow of $90 billion in 1989, according to the *Wall Street Journal.*

All of this made a mockery of the claims of supply-side economics. In theory, supply-side incentives would create a new tide of capital formation. In practice, they created a new dependence on foreign borrowing, which proved unsustainable. To add insult to injury, in the new globalized economy even American investors were deserting their own country, whose industry had been plainly weakened during the 1980s. In 1990, despite America's capital shortage, U.S. citizens invested a net $62 billion in foreign stocks, bonds, real estate, and corporate plant outside the United States. At the September 1990 meeting of the IMF, the subject on everyone's lips was global capital shortage—and the principal malefactor was the United States.

In 1984 and 1985, orthodox opinion had held that the American trade deficit was entirely the result of an overvalued dollar. Obviously, if the dollar was up 88 percent against currencies of America's major trading partners, this was an immense disadvantage for U.S. producers. As economists were wont to observe, it was the equivalent of a huge tax on U.S.-made products in home and overseas markets—or the equivalent of putting foreign products on sale. Logically, if the dollar reverted to its appropriate level, then American products would again have realistic prices and trade fairly.

The matter of the dollar's "correct" parity level is, of course, a matter of some dispute among different schools of economists. One approach looks at the issue historically. If you pick a period when the U.S. trade accounts were roughly balanced—say, 1970—and then adjust for differentials in subsequent rates of inflation and productivity growth between the United States and other countries, you can roughly calculate what the dollar ought to be today relative to other currencies. Another approach attempts to calculate "purchasing power parities" in different countries. It ought to cost roughly the same sum to buy the same pair of shoes, or the same hotel room, in major world capitals. You can then determine roughly what exchange rates should be from the cost of real products in local currencies. The third approach is simply to let money markets set the value of the dollar. Whatever they determine on any given day is by definition the dollar's "true" value. The trouble with this approach, as we have seen, is that daily value of currencies does not reflect merely the hand of the market; given the terrible instabilities wrought by pure market forces, central bankers' hands manipulate interest rates and turn the heads of innocent markets.[14]

In the early and middle 1980s, the dollar was grossly overvalued by almost any measure. Because of its odd hegemonic role, it had been overvalued for most of the postwar period. Although their calculations varied, most economists in 1984 and 1985 were writing that the dollar had to keep dropping, to 150 yen and perhaps even to 100 yen, in order to return it to the "equilibrium path" that it should have been following since the early 1970s.[15] At that level, in theory at least, American products would be priced competitively in world markets and the trade accounts would roughly balance. The dollar's proper value was, of course, a moving target. Even if the "correct" parity was reached, as long as U.S. inflation continued to be higher and productivity growth lower, then the dollar would have to keep depreciating against the yen and the mark, though at only a few percent a year.

Beginning in 1985, the dollar started falling like a stone. By mid-1987 it was below 150 yen and had lost something like half its value against both the yen and the mark. But by then it was clear that something was seriously wrong with the theory and the policy. The U.S. trade deficit was not improving by anything like what this devaluation should have accomplished. In fact, it kept growing, from $122 billion in 1984 to $134 billion in 1985, to $156 billion in 1986, and then declined only slightly to $146 billion in 1987. By 1990 it had more or less reached a plateau at close to $100 billion a year.

At first, most economists said that this was simply a time lag. They call this lag the "J curve" because deficit statistics can be plotted on a graph shaped like the letter J, illustrating how a cheaper dollar makes the trade deficit get worse before it gets better. This occurs because when the dollar buys less, the "terms of trade" initially worsen. That is, with a cheaper dollar, it takes more bushels of exported American wheat to pay for fewer imported Toyotas. Changing the exchange rate will adjust relative prices instantly, but consumers change their buying habits in response to the new prices only over time. In theory, the lower-priced U.S. goods gradually produce a real competitive advantage as American goods increase their market share at home and abroad, and the picture supposedly improves.

But apparently something more fundamental had changed. Foreign producers managed to hold down their export prices, despite enormous changes in currency values. And if relative prices of imports and domestic products fail to change, then the predicted benefits of a cheaper dollar do not materialize. The persistent failure of the cheaper dollar to improve the U.S. trade balance became a puzzle—and an embarrassment—for economists who had predicted almost unanimously that a cheap dollar would bring far more dramatic trade improvement than it actually did.

At a 1987 conference of prominent international economists, titled "The Economics of the Dollar Cycle," MIT economist Paul Krugman lamented: "The U.S. trade balance has shown less turnaround than anyone expected, or than any of the models predicted." In standard economic theory, if the yen appreciates by 50 percent against the dollar, that shift should be largely "passed through" in the form of a 50 percent price increase on Japanese products. In the American market, that should increase the sales of American products, now cheaper, and depress sales of Japanese imports. By the same token, a cheaper dollar also ought to make U.S. products more attractively priced in foreign markets. During the last phase of the dollar cycle, when the dollar was undervalued in the late 1970s and then overvalued in the early 1980s, prices had responded pretty much in this way. According to Catherine Mann, a World Bank economist who has done extensive research on how actual prices respond to currency swings, historically virtually all of the exchange-rate changes had translated into price changes within two years. But now the anticipated price shift was not happening. A strong dollar in the early 1980s had caused prices of U.S. products to rise steeply and priced many of them out of world markets: now a cheap dollar failed to reverse the damage. And far less of the higher yen or deutsche mark rate was passed through to U.S. consumer markets in the form of higher prices on imports. So Americans went on buying imports, and the trade deficit only worsened.

According to Krugman, formerly a trade specialist on Reagan's Council of Economic Advisers staff, foreign firms, notably (but not exclusively) Japanese firms, are adept at "pricing to market": they trim their prices to fit competitive conditions in the market they are selling in. American firms, on the other hand, characteristically base their prices on their costs plus an anticipated profit. "Pricing to market is not symmetric," Krugman wrote. "The U.S. is a market that is priced to, but U.S. firms do not correspondingly price to other markets."

What the standard theory had failed to anticipate was that neither foreign firms nor foreign governments would respond passively to exchange-rate shifts. More than many American firms, or the U.S. government, foreign firms and some foreign governments work aggressively to defend market share. They were able to do this in a variety of ways, for a variety of reasons.

Most raw materials, such as petroleum, are priced in dollars. In Japan, a 70 percent decline in the value of the dollar means a 70 percent drop in the cost of oil, iron ore, chemical feedstocks, and so on, and this substantially offsets the effect of the higher exchange rate on the price of the finished product. In 1986 and 1987, the Japanese index of wholesale prices actually fell. That translates into a low rate of Japanese inflation, which allows Japanese investors to settle for low nominal rates of return, which in turn gives Japanese industry low capital costs—which continues the virtuous circle of rising productivity and maintains Japan's striking competitive lead, despite the higher yen. The fact that oil and other raw materials are priced in dollars is one more legacy of dollar hegemony.

Notwithstanding the publicity given the dollar's drop against the yen and the West German mark, all currencies did not appreciate against the dollar. Many newly industrializing countries, following a well-worn path, kept their currencies artificially cheap even as their productivity improved, in order to gain price advantage and greater market share. Dozens of Third World nations keep their currencies more or less pegged to the dollar—yet another legacy of the dollar's hegemonic role. Many high-inflation currencies actually fell against the dollar. A cheaper dollar against the yen and the mark did nothing to solve America's trade imbalance with Taiwan or the Philippines. And both U.S. and Japanese firms more and more have moved production to nations with cheap currencies and low wages.

Foreign producers did not pass along the full savings to U.S. customers when the dollar was expensive, so they had a substantial cushion to absorb anticipated price increases as the dollar got cheaper. In a world of floating exchange rates, neither producers nor retailers adjust posted prices in lockstep with currency fluctuations. Wholesalers of imported products suggest that one way they adjust to fluctuating currencies is by absorbing some of the fluctuations—in both directions. They assume they are going to lose some of their normal profit margins when the dollar is cheap, so they maintain posted prices and make extra profits when the dollar is high. An importer of German cutlery doesn't cut his catalogue prices 30 percent when the mark loses 30 percent of its value against the dollar and doesn't raise them 30 percent when the dollar makes a 30 percent gain. Customers don't like that kind of price swing.

Further, many American producers of highly competitive products shortsightedly failed to take advantage of the higher yen and mark to price their products significantly below those of competing imports. The auto industry nicely encapsulates the whole story. Incredibly, though the dollar lost roughly half its value against the yen in 1985–88, the price of American cars sold in the United States actually rose slightly faster than the price of Japanese cars during this period. There were several reasons for this. On the American side, the big automakers had posted losses in three consecutive years during the recession of the early 1980s. The years of the cheap dollar gave Detroit a chance to make up for those bad years by reaping supernormal profits. Pursuing unit profits rather than market share, U.S. automakers matched virtually every price increase of their foreign competitors. Meanwhile, the Japanese held their price increases to about half of what was indicated by the currency fluctuations—by shifting some production to the United States and other cheap-currency countries and by redoubling productivity improvements.

Moreover, many so-called American products are actually not made in the United States. If Japanese producers monopolize production of VCRs, computer disk drives, or much of consumer electronics, the cheap dollar does not bring any of this production home. Every time a Japanese manufacturer introduces a new "must buy" electronics product—fax machines, Nintendo games, CD players, high-definition television—the U.S.-Japan trade deficit increases, and this will not be rectified by adjustment in yen-dollar parities. One statistic gives sobering pause: Nintendo video games alone were responsible for $2 billion in the 1989 U.S.-Japan trade deficit.

A large share of imports is marketed in the United States by retailers or wholesalers who share the foreign producers' interest in holding down the price. Big retailers like Sears, Roebuck, which attach their own brand names to imported products, or designers who license the use of their labels to foreign producers, can buy their goods in lower-wage, cheaper-currency countries if they encounter price increases from Japanese sources; that, in turn, intensifies the pressure on Japan to hold the line on U.S. prices. For example, the Tandy Corporation, makers of Radio Shack electronics products, gets about 50 percent of its product from the Orient, much of it from Japan, including disk drives, laptop computers, and printers. Yet despite the dramatic decline in the dollar, only 4 percent of Tandy products posted price increases in the company's 1988 catalogue. According to Bernard Appel, Tandy's president, both Radio Shack and some of its Japanese suppliers simply held down price increases by moving some production to lower-cost producers.[16]

Japan's trade surplus with the United States in manufactured goods did not decline in 1987 and decreased only slightly in 1988 and 1989. When the surplus did begin to diminish, in 1990, the numbers looked odd to some economists: the statistics on Japanese imports of U.S. manufactured goods seemed to be spiking, but selectively. To old Japan hands, it looked as if MITI was resorting to the old practice of "administrative guidance," to bring the overall accounts into somewhat more presentable balance but without harming the profits of domestic industries and technologies Japan wished to defend. A growing consensus of Japanese economists believe that, for a variety of deeply embedded reasons, the trade surplus is unlikely to shrink significantly, unless fundamental policy and social changes are adopted to alter what has become a structural bias. In response to the high yen, Japan did increase its imports from other Asian nations by about 30 percent, much of it in component parts for reexport. (Interestingly, this shift is not captured in the official U.S. trade statistics, which are compiled on the basis of customs receipts stating a product's apparent country of origin. If a computer using chips made in Korea is imported into the United States from Japan, 100 percent of the cost shows up in the trade accounts as an import from Japan.) In other cases, Japanese producers held the line on prices by trimming profit margins on their sales to the United States, though this factor is often exaggerated. Recent research indicates that Japan's ability to hold down prices has more to do with a decline in raw-material prices, improvements in productivity, and Japan's own selective relocation of production offshore. Overall, major companies traded on the Tokyo stock exchange have reported only a slight loss in their earnings per share since 1985, which suggests that profit margins did not suffer.

Some U.S. firms, like Ford and IBM, have been very successful at operating overseas. But to a greater degree than their Japanese competitors, much of their production for world markets is also located abroad. This interferes with the intended trade effects of a cheaper dollar. If Fords sold in Europe are produced primarily in Europe, the cheaper dollar does not boost exports of made-in-the-U.S.A. cars and does not help the trade balance. Because capital investments are expensive and intended for the long term, major manufacturing firms do not suddenly relocate billion-dollar facilities in response to short-term currency swings. Over the long haul, a cheaper dollar may induce U.S. producers to move some production back to the United States (this has already begun to happen in some industries like electronics), but not nearly enough to change the overall trade imbalance.

According to some students of economic history, this phenomenon of overseas production (which is to say capital exports) substituting for export of products made in the mother country is yet another characteristic cost borne by hegemonic nations. As the British political economist Stuart Holland has demonstrated, one of the hallmarks of Britain's long-term industrial decline after 1890 was its habit of letting capital exports substitute for product exports.[17] As we have seen, a hegemonic nation tends to export capital rather than goods, both to extend its own financial power and to fulfill its function of providing liquidity to other nations in its orbit. Over time, however, this creates a chronic trade imbalance and financial strength at the expense of weak industry. In the case of Britain, the City (London's counterpart of Wall Street) continued to flourish as the industrial Midlands went into eclipse.

The United States has recently followed an almost identical trajectory for virtually the same reasons—but with the added destructive ingredient of capital *imports.* The West Germans and Japanese, in contrast, have stressed product exports rather than capital exports and have enjoyed immense trade surpluses. The West Germans have begun to export substantial capital and they now have something of a financial hegemony in Europe. Japan, exporting some of its immense capital surplus, is careful to tailor its capital-export strategy to the more fundamental goal of maintaining industrial dominance.

Most economists think the dollar needs to continue falling, since the trade accounts have not improved. A minority believe that the dangers of imported inflation outweigh the dangers of the trade deficit and want the dollar to stabilize at somewhere in the range of 100–140 yen. But neither group has examined in detail the dynamics of how, precisely, foreign firms manage to hold down their export prices despite the fact that the dollars they get are now worth up to 70 percent less than they were in early 1985, and why U.S. firms apparently are less tenacious at pricing to hold market share. "That question," according to Catherine Mann, "is viewed by most economists as a black box."

Instead, most economists have investigated what went wrong with the predictive power of their equations. The equations haven't held up, says Harvard's Jeffrey Sachs, in part because U.S. policy chose to drive down the value of the dollar by lowering U.S. interest rates rather than cutting the U.S. deficit. The current mixture of relatively low interest rates and a big public-sector deficit has perpetuated a consumer boom that continues to favor imports. But he admits that still doesn't tell the whole story. Even economists like Sachs are beginning to look harder at "structural" issues of competitiveness that modern macroeconomic analysis avoided as old-fashioned. "We need more industry-by-industry examination of why American producers are failing to compete despite the cheaper dollar, and that has to be integrated with the macoeconomic analysis," says Sachs.

Modern economics has on the whole disdained this task as hopelessly "anecdotal" and imprecise. There is no significant literature on how individual foreign industries or firms have altered their marketing strategies to compensate for exchange-rate shifts or on how their behavior differs from that of their American counterparts. Whatever studies that do exist infer corporate strategies from aggregate statistics rather than examining them directly. One such study, by the Japanese economist Ruyhei Wakasugi of Shinshu University, found that the cost of raw materials, capital, and labor fell in many Japanese industries, allowing prices to stay low with only a moderate decline in profits. According to research by Federal Reserve Board economists Bonnie Lupescoo and Robert Johnson, increases in Japanese export prices have varied dramatically among industries. In the chemicals business, where competition is fierce, Japanese producers took advantage of the drop in the yen price of oil and held price increases to an estimated 9 percent; in precision instruments, where some specialized products are made only in Japan, dollar export prices rose about as much as the value of the yen, without hurting sales.

Economists baffled by the failure of trade balances to follow predictions have borrowed a term from physics, "hysteresis," to express their puzzlement. Hysteresis is the failure of an object to return to its previous equilibrium path once a disturbance is removed. In economic terms, hysteresis means that if the dollar rises by 50 percent and then drops by 50 percent, the world does not return to the way it was, because industries evolve dynamically. The period of the overvalued dollar led to a possibly irreversible structural change, such as an American producer being pushed out of the market for color television sets, while a foreign competitor gains a commanding position; a reversal of currency misalignments won't undo the damage. Hysteresis would seem to be a normal condition of modern industrial life.

But in general, macroeconomists, who have dominated the debate about trade and the dollar, have been extremely skeptical about the effect of structural factors in creating the trade deficit. On the whole, the economics profession is inclined to the view that if the cheaper dollar has not reversed the trade imbalance, it must be because the dollar simply hasn't fallen far enough, or because the United States needs not just a cheap dollar but a cheap dollar plus a higher domestic savings rate, which would reduce the need for imported capital. In the standard analysis, markets are assumed to equilibrate on the basis of price, and structural change is a puzzling and untrustworthy special factor. Moreover, as Jeffrey Sachs points out: "Most economic analyses do not allow for it mathematically." As the saying goes, if your only tool is a hammer, everything looks like a nail.

Even with a much cheaper dollar, the factors that have allowed America's competitors to adjust in the past to a cheapening dollar will continue to operate—the decline in input prices, the ability to outsource, to innovate, to price to market, and the fact that some products just aren't made in the United States. To a few economists who emphasize structural factors, the danger is that an ever-cheaper dollar will only make the United States a poorer country, without making its products fully competitive. Even at 100 yen to the dollar, how many American-made Chevrolets will be sold in Japan and how many VCRs will be made in the U.S.A.?

In short, the academic debate about the dollar continues to be cast primarily in terms of whether the dollar should be allowed to fall even more, or whether it should be stabilized, and not whether currency manipulation is sufficient to repair U.S. competitiveness. But because most economists still focus on statistical aggregates rather than observing what business firms actually do, the debate fails to shed light on why foreign producers seem to operate more adaptively than American ones, despite swings in exchange rates. The Harvard economist Lawrence Summers, arguing for a cheaper dollar rather than a "competitiveness agenda," has written: "A ten percent decline in the dollar exchange rate is equivalent to a ten percent tariff on all imported goods and a ten percent subsidy on all exported goods. Its short run impact on the trade balance dwarfs anything that can be done to improve productivity."[18] But events have overtaken such standard assumptions. Since 1985, a 10 percent decline in the dollar exchange rate in fact hasn't produced a 10 percent increase in the price of imports. Germany and Japan have continued to enjoy both strong currencies and trade surpluses precisely because they continue to show impressive gains in productivity. In both countries a strong currency is the accurate measure of high real wages and a strong economy; in the United States a steadily weakening currency is the measure of a steadily weakening economy.

By the late 1980s, Japan was making up for its trade surplus by shipping to America, on a highly selective basis, some of its capital surplus, as well as more and more Japanese tourists. This balanced the short-run accounts, but led to a crude popular backlash against the Japanese purchase of American factories, hotels, brokerage houses, and national symbols like Rockefeller Center. Even American liberals found themselves patriotically fulminating against the Japanese purchase of Rockefeller Center. Why, the laissez-faire conservatives gibed, should leftists defend the Rockefellers? Why hold one's own capitalists in higher regard than foreign ones, particularly since American capitalists had lately fallen down on the job of managing a competitive national economy? Was the left saying that Charlie Wilson had been right after all: what was good for General Motors was good for the country? Maybe Japanese capitalists *could* do the job better. What if Honda really made better cars and was a nicer company to work for? And European and Canadian capitalists had been buying American companies for years. Many popular brand names which American consumers thought of as local products—Nestlé, Bayer, Electrolux—were foreign-owned. Were the critics perhaps racist?

Did Japanese capital in fact represent net new capital (good) or merely replace one set of owners with another (presumably bad)? Defenders pointed out that the Japanese were, after all, providing new jobs, and by one account the average job created by Japanese capital paid a higher wage than the job it replaced.[19] And Japanese industrial investment was said to benefit Americans by transplanting Japanese technology and management skills. If American automakers had been bad managers, why not welcome the Honda plants springing up in Ohio and Tennessee?

But the issue was not so simple. Unlike European multinational corporations, which operated according to essentially the same rules as their American counterparts, Japanese corporations were renowned for manipulating prices to gain market share. It was clear that Japanese industry as a whole had a mercantilist view about capturing advantage for the mother nation, and they showed a remarkable capacity to function like a cartel when that served their interests, yet fiercely competed among themselves to promote innovation. Capital is supposedly global and stateless. But somehow Japanese capital was more nationalistic than other capital. Americans were extremely confused about how to respond.

All of this confusion was the consequence of viewing the world through a laissez-faire lens. In fact, other nations do care whether their nationally owned firms are able to compete at the leading edge of technology. Because they don't believe in laissez-faire either as a reasonable domestic policy or as a prescription for trade, they are also willing to negotiate social contracts, explicit or implicit, between leading industries and the rest of society, so that what is good for Toyota is indeed good for Japan. Until American policymakers embrace a more realistic ideology, they will continue to view the decline of American economic strength as the result of natural forces, or of fiscal misdeeds, rather than as the long-term consequence of a failure to shift course when circumstances changed.

Because of the devotion to laissez-faire, both economists and policymakers have also failed to address the connections between several sets of seemingly disparate issues—one involving debt, another involving trade, a third involving macroeconomic imbalance, and a fourth involving currency arrangements. Each of these issues belongs to a different diplomatic arena, and the imperatives of different negotiations have often been at odds with each other. For example, in the ongoing negotiations among Third World debtor nations, creditor banks, and the International Monetary Fund, the debtors were put under relentless pressure to initiate domestic austerity programs and produce large export surpluses, in order to generate foreign-exchange earnings with which to service their debt. Yet simultaneously, in the trade liberalization talks at Geneva, the very same nations were told to open their consumer markets to freer imports. If Japan had been judged by GATT standards in the 1950s, its entire development strategy would have been ruled illegitimate. In the 1980s India and Brazil, the bad boys of the trading system, who enjoyed less geopolitical prominence and less economic power than Japan, were the system's identified mercantilist culprits.

What held these seemingly contradictory institutions and impulses together was the logic of laissez-faire. If one believed that the best market was the least regulated one, then all of this made sense, however self-defeating the particulars. If markets were the rule, then all moves toward a freer flow of commerce were to be welcomed. The purgative discipline of free markets, over time, would burn away inefficiency and lead to the optimal allocation of the world's resources. Episodic instability, likewise, was both an acceptable and a necessary price to pay. The ruthless accountability of markets also required a merciless treatment of debtors. If scofflaws were rewarded with debt relief, the whole system would degenerate into endless moral hazard. And if the drive toward ever purer laissez-faire led to commercial disadvantage for the United States, this was simply the market speaking. We had to take the consequences of the gospel we were preaching to the world, however unpleasant. In the orthodox view, America's decline was mainly the just desert of its macroeconomic profligacy—not of some flaw in either its philosophy, its institutions of industrial organization, or its geopolitical or geo-economic priorities.

There is, of course, another, entirely different view of global political economy, of the relation between ideology, geo-economics, and geopolitics. It is the view of this book, one which orthodox opinion tends to dismiss as merely nationalist or mercantilist. In truth, it represents a different form of internationalism, liberal but not laissez-faire, in the spirit of the internationalism of Roosevelt and Keynes.

As noted, this dissenting view, however plausible economically, was a difficult case to make politically as long as the Soviet Union was a convincing military threat. For if the Cold War was central, then it was essential not to offend key allies over commercial conflicts that "the market" should settle in any event.

However, just as the beginning of the Cold War in 1947 and 1948 abruptly altered our strategic assumptions and tactical moves, the end of the Cold War in 1989–91 permits—and demands—a fundamental redefinition of the American national interest. Before we can attempt that, we must appreciate in greater detail just how the hegemonic imperatives we have claimed for our country have crippled our economic goals, at home and abroad. Unfortunately, these imperatives have shaped not just recent history but the assumptions that continue to underlie current policy. We need to look at the way policy is made, and by what lights, in the key realms of trade, U.S.-Japan relations, national security, and finance, and finally to consider some alternatives. It is to these areas that I now turn.

# four

# TRADE: THE NEW ERA AND THE NATIONAL INTEREST

A few short years ago, after the 1986 Gorbachev-Reagan summit at Reyk-javík, we could have imagined one possible avenue toward a pluralist world. Despite the continuing Cold War, this might have begun with a gradual and mutual build-down of arms spending by both great power blocs. It would have included the maturing of the European Community as a regional power; increased sharing of global economic leadership among the United States, the EC, and Japan; a gentle shift in American priorities from geopolitical to geo-economic ones; a more charitable and expansionist approach to the Third World debt crisis—but all in the reassuringly familiar context of a still stable if less fearsome East-West divide. This had been the assumption of such French pan-Europeanists as Mitterrand and Jacques Delors, the EC President, as well as the German architects of *Ostpolitik:* Willy Brandt, Egon Bahr, Helmut Schmidt in the SDP, and many liberal Free Democrats, most notably Foreign Minister Hans-Dietrich Genscher. It depended only on restraint and moderate liberalization within the Eastern bloc and shifting priorities in the United States.

This path, of course, was not taken. The Cold War ended far more abruptly than anyone foresaw, depriving the United States of a chance to get used to a new posture and new goals gradually. And far from seizing the opportunity, the Republican administrations of Ronald Reagan and George Bush preferred to maintain American responsibility for a global trading system which was supposed to become ever more laissez-faire; they were slow to reduce high levels of arms spending. Even as Gorbachev let Eastern Europe go, to U.S. policymakers the East-West strategic balance remained the central geopolitical fact. Well into the Gorbachev era, the Reagan administration had used American economic leverage to push the

NATO allies into a fiercer stance vis-à-vis the Warsaw Pact, offering to trade the fruits of "Star Wars" research for its political support by America's allies. Strategic economic goals for the United States remained not just a low priority but a heresy.

Economically, the Reagan and subsequently the Bush administration pursued the course of least resistance: leave the American conception of grand strategy and national interest intact and borrow enough money from abroad to sustain the pretense. To the German and Japanese creditors, this remained a satisfactory bargain: they could continue to focus on their own economic strength and leave the United States with prime responsibilities for the system, perhaps increasing their own foreign-aid outlays as would befit nouveau riche cousins. As creditor nations, they had the further pleasure of acquiring new leverage over American policies—though, of course, this had to be exercised with the greatest discretion, lest the Americans rudely awaken to the discovery that they were no longer in charge and the whole system come tumbling down. Hegemonic nations, after all, can maintain a rather long trajectory of slow decline without realizing that anything is seriously amiss, so long as overt conflict is deferred. It took Great Britain half a century from the pinnacle of its economic and financial power in the 1870s through two world wars and another generation before its decline became manifest and it began to view itself as a second-rate economic and political power. The American decline from its economic and financial pinnacle has been going on for barely twenty years—and we remain a much larger and more resilient country.

The nonpolicy of deferral, denial, and pretense might have continued for decades—or for as long as Tokyo and Frankfurt kept lending the United States money—were it not for the events of 1989 and 1990. Now, it is undeniable that the postwar era is at last over, and its governing assumptions, long since dead, can now be properly buried. And it is high time to think seriously about the design of a new post-hegemonic world system, to consider what arrangements would be both efficient and durable, where sovereignty should be reclaimed from private institutions and where it should be pooled with new supranational institutions; what rules for the trading system are equitable; and what new strategic goals this suggests for the United States.

For the believers in laissez-faire, this exercise presents neither an institutional nor an intellectual problem. Each government must simply practice a responsible macroeconomics, and the market will take care of the rest. But as we have seen, this view denies many realities: the stubborn historical truth that laissez-faire is systemically unstable, and all the more so across international frontiers. Governments have foreign-policy goals that are inextricably intertwined with economic ones; governments can and do devise strategic trade policies intended to assist their national industries; social contracts require political mediation that cannot be left to markets. And the United States can no longer function as the hegemonic power in a supposed laissez-faire world without incalculable costs to its own well-being and to the larger global system.

My argument in this book is that orthodox American perception of national self-interest in a globalized economy is confused by the interplay of ideology and presumed hegemonic responsibility. Both take for granted the virtue and the necessity of laissez-faire trade; both assume a geopolitical rather than a geo-economic conception of national security. In this view, the freest possible movement of goods and services is seen as a handy perquisite to offer America's allies, as well as something virtuous per se. Moreover, it is taken for granted that in a world of liberal trade the United States as a producer and consumer nation would do just fine. The only task of trade policy, therefore, is to persuade our trading partners to shed their own forms of mercantilism and to use the imperative of reciprocal liberalization to batter down the forces of protectionism at home.

This formulation has ceased to be a useful guide to policy analysis, for several reasons. First, the United States no longer dominates key industries, and the economic sacrifices that go with the hegemonic role have an escalating price. Second, because the United States gives priority to the military rather than the economic aspects of its protectorate, it fails in practice to persuade other nations to play by free-trade rules. Third, most governments—including ours—are thoroughly entangled in the private economy. Most nations do not want simplistic laissez-faire; they want to pursue policies that advantage their own industries and then to have products made in their countries compete relatively freely in world markets. The goal should be a balanced system that makes room for a prosperous America—not laissez-faire.

Self-styled free traders have no good working definition of the concept of protectionism, except in the extreme case of overt market barriers to imports, such as tariffs or quotas. However, a subsidy to exporters, a specific industrial policy using government purchases or research assistance, or a commercial advantage gained from a defense contract is as much an interference with laissez-faire trade as a tariff or a quota. Ideally, a laissez-faire world would be one in which governments had no influence over economic activity. But this is inconceivable, even to economists. Most orthodox ones, with the exception of Milton Friedman-style monetarists, generally admit that government involvement in *macroeconomics* is inevitable and even desirable: making budgets, manipulating public deficits, shaping tax and monetary policy. In a modern economy, however, governments are also involved in dozens of other structural policies that influence the private economy: everything from regulations to tax and savings incentives, public infrastructure investments, apprenticeship programs, research, development, and purchase of material for national defense, or policies explicitly subsidizing national producers in order to capture leadership in advanced production technologies. The standard American view has been tolerant of macroeconomic intervention, intermittently tolerant of regulatory, tax, and infrastructure interventions, and largely intolerant of sectoral intervention aimed at strengthening specific industries or technologies, except under military cover. But most other national governments practice the full gamut of economic interventions. As we shall see, orthodox American opinion has no good criteria for sorting out good interventions from bad ones.

Given all this, whatever global flows of commerce now exist are not the product of classic economic liberalism. Free trade in the textbook sense does not and cannot exist. Even open price competition among products that themselves are the fruits of subsidized research and other government interventions is something other than free trade. Yet the United States has been avoiding policies that are common throughout the industrial world because official opinion conflates and confuses government-industry connections (which are ubiquitous) with the dreaded "protectionism." Because of a fierce ideological commitment to laissez-faire, our departures from it, though frequent, are poorly thought out, lacking in long-term goals, and generally not helpful either to the trading system or to America's own economic self-interest. Indeed, orthodox economists such as Charles Schultze have often argued that the general incoherence of America's departures from laissez-faire is probably desirable, because more coherent intervention would only do more damage.

Free trade as a policy goal is supposed to offer two benefits, logically separate but seldom seen apart in the usual debates. The first benefit is an allocative efficiency: if nothing interferes with the invisible hand of the marketplace, the most efficient producers anywhere in the world get to make and sell what they do best. This idea is profoundly misleading, as both description and prescription. The second benefit of free trade is supposed to be that if such a system were ever agreed to, all trading nations and firms would be playing by the same rules: nobody would subsidize, regulate, or attempt to capture advantage for national producers. Even if one is extremely skeptical of the efficiency claims of free trade, one must admit that a trading system needs common rules. *Yet these need not be laissez-faire rules.* Indeed, they *cannot* be, given the ubiquity of state involvement in the "private" economy.

The system we have today is a far cry from either free trade or common rules. And the de facto rules we live with profoundly disadvantage the United States economy. Different operating assumptions and rules could, however, produce more symmetry in the global trading system *and* greater benefit for the American economy. They would be a hybrid, with elements of managed trade and elements of liberal trade. They would acknowledge that governments wish to be involved in national economic strategy. The result, not "free trade" in the textbook sense, nonetheless would be freer, fairer, and more efficient than what we now have, and it would allow the United States to be more clear-sighted about its own national interest.

The doctrine of free trade rests on the classical economic theory of comparative advantage, originally promulgated in the work of David Ricardo in 1817.[1] This theory assumes that trade occurs because of specialization; there are certain commodities that each nation can produce relatively more efficiently, given its natural resources, labor force, and technological capabilities. If all countries specialize in the commodities in which they possess comparative advantages, exporting these goods and importing others, an optimal allocation of world resources would result. The welfare of each individual country, as well as of the world as a whole, would be maximized with perfectly free trade. It follows that any effort to protect a domestic economy necessarily involves sacrifices in the aggregate to national and international efficiency, although some groups in society (e.g., English landlords in Ricardo's time or Japanese computer producers) may benefit at the expense of others.

The Ricardian approach to international trade originated as a liberal critique of aristocratic privilege in early-nineteenth-century England, where the landed gentry wanted to protect English agriculture while emerging industrial capitalists wanted freedom to exploit trade opportunities. The doctrine served Britain well in the mid-nineteenth century, at the height of British hegemony. In the United States, however, industrial interests were more protectionist from the beginning, as early American manufacturers realized that they could not initially compete with cheaper British imports (this is the famous "infant industry" argument). So, paradoxically, the United States industrialized behind tariff walls in the nineteenth and early twentieth centuries; and the early Republic, which had a small central government (measured in terms of government spending as a fraction of GNP), had an extensive range of what today would be called industrial policies. As noted, both Jefferson and Hamilton used federal power to expand agricultural science and the manufacturing arts, to subsidize the building of canals, roads, and land-grant colleges. The young

American economy also relied on the tariff. As American industry grew stronger, the doctrine of free trade gradually gained converts, and hardened from self-interest into high principle.

Despite retrospective mythology about the nineteenth-century golden age of free trade—which was also an age of substantial mercantilism and colonialism—the era since 1945 is really the only period in which one major power, the United States, truly attempted to propagate and administer a system of free trade worldwide. (In the last century, Britain was as devoted to imperialism as it was to liberal trade among the metropolitan powers, and in this century it retreated, practicing liberal trade only within its own preferential imperial bloc.) In reality, free trade has coexisted with various forms of managed trade ever since the dawn of organized commerce. Yet in the American diplomatic corps today, as well as among influential economists, you find an almost universal devotion to the theory of comparative advantage as politically and scientifically essential. The devotion requires that the United States not only reject industrial policies at home but also wink at them abroad, for standard theory holds that if other nations are so foolish as to subsidize their industries, consumers in other nations should accept the "gift." Though the United States itself was relatively mercantilist in the nineteenth century, the Ricardian view has been internalized and treated as gospel since 1945 precisely *because it is so congruent with the logic of American hegemony.*

In the orthodox idiom, all departures from free trade are protectionist, opportunistic, politically motivated, and self-defeating. Protectionism, in this view, is any government interference with the private market; it alienates our friends and allies, sacrifices economic efficiency, harms domestic consumers, and causes protected industries to stagnate. According to one characteristic paper expressing the standard view: "If a country's trading partners embrace free trade, so much the better, but unilateral free trade serves each country's own self-interest even if the trading partners choose to protect their own markets. This proposition is particularly evident in the case of raw materials. For example, it makes no sense for the United States to restrict imports of coffee, even if Brazil forbids imports of automobiles."[2] Of course, if every other country restricted imports, one wonders where the virtuous free trader would get the foreign exchange with which to buy the coffee. Note that the argument presumes some hypothetical absolute barrier rather than the subtle mix of state-led development and price competition that characterizes actual markets.

But the rhetoric of free trade is chronically littered with misleading metaphors. Free trade, it is often said, is "like a bicycle"—you have to pedal ever faster or you tip over. Whoever argues that has never ridden a bicycle. It is also said, after an aphorism first attributed to the French philosopher Frédéric Bastiat, that even if other nations are stupid enough to "throw rocks into their harbors"—barricading themselves against commerce—it doesn't mean we should do likewise.

Interestingly enough, American doctrine and policy is embracing a purer devotion to free-trade principles at precisely a moment when some orthodox economists are having serious second thoughts about whether the traditional theory is valid, either as a description of how trade really works or as a norm for optimal policy. This "New View" has emerged in the work of Paul Krugman, an eminently respected neoclassical economist at the Massachusetts Institute of Technology and once the staff trade specialist on the Reagan Council of Economic Advisers; and in related work by Avinash Dixit, James Brander, Barbara Spencer, and numerous others.[3]

According to the classical view, countries have *inherent* comparative advantages in particular products due to intrinsic national characteristics. Ricardo assumed that differences in resources and technology would give each nation comparative advantages in certain goods that it could produce with lower labor costs. Later, the Swedish economists Eli Heckscher and Bertil Ohlin argued that comparative advantages were due to differences in "factor proportions": the relative abundance of land, labor, and capital in a given country compared with the relative intensities with which these factors were used in producing various commodities. Later, this theory was formalized by the American economist Paul Samuelson.[4] In what textbooks call the Heckscher-Ohlin-Samuelson (HOS) theory, identical technology in all countries and perfect competition in all markets are assumed. Given these and other, more technical conditions, each country will export those goods that incorporate relatively more of its relatively abundant factor(s).

Whether in the traditional Ricardian or more modern HOS variant, the Old View implies powerfully that *there is a naturally ordained pattern of trade.* The location of industries is not arbitrary; with free trade, industries will automatically be located where they can be most efficiently operated. There is a unique allocation of industries among countries, economically efficient at any point in time, and it can only be achieved through free trade. (There are some subtle differences between the two variants. The Ricardian emphasis on nations' different technological capabilities implicitly acknowledges that social institutions and public policies can potentially affect a nation's "inherent" comparative advantages. The HOS theory, on the other hand, suggests a more extreme bias against intervention, since it holds technology constant and assumes that only natural and immutable "endowments" of productive factors matter to trade. The HOS theory is more sophisticated in its methodology but more primitive in its assumptions about how real economies work.)

The New View acknowledges that the location of manufacturing production in the world comes about not because of inherent comparative advantages in the traditionally understood sense but partly because of historical accidents, partly because of cumulative learning and "niche" positions, and partly because of deliberate policies. The indeterminacy of industrial location reflects the characteristics of the advanced global economy: rapid technological change, economies of scale, and the ability of firms to "slide down the learning curve," as they learn by doing and produce more efficiently. Thus, innovators actually compete on the basis of entrepreneurial and technological prowess rather than factor endowments, using products and processes that can be produced almost anywhere, given capital and skilled managers and workers. Technological leadership can sometimes flow from such arguably "natural" endowments as a skilled labor force (which itself reflects the influence of interventionist education and training policies), but it can also be the deliberate result or fortuitous by-product of an explicit national policy to promote technology. In the New View, competitive advantage is cumulative: learning breeds more learning; technological advantage leads to more advantage.

The truth of the New View is borne out by, among other things, the large amount of intra-industry trade, in which trading partners both export and import similar products—a phenomenon that is not predicted by the Ricardian old view. For example, the United States, Japan, and Germany sell machine tools and computers to each other. If trade worked in Ricardian fashion, each nation would specialize in particular products or components. As Klaus Stegemann has observed in studying intra-industry specialization in the context of European integration: "Which country makes which products within any manufacturing industry cannot be explained exclusively on the basis of differences in natural ability or factor proportions. Variables such as entrepreneurial initiative, investment in human capital, research and development, product design, economies of scale, and learning by doing were recognized to be crucial for the expansion of intra-industry trade."[5] These, in turn, are subject to policy intervention, which, if it leads to technological breakthroughs, may produce positive-sum benefits.

One strand of the New View holds that much international trade can be understood as a form of imperfect competition, in which some producers enjoy supernormal profits, which economists call monopoly "rents." Contrary to the standard theory, such rents are not instantly competed away, but persist, as innovators gain niches in the market and hang on to them. A nation whose firms capture these niches gains an advantage, both in profits and in the continuation of technological dominance. Certain trade policies (tariffs, subsidies, import restraints, etc.) can, under certain circumstances, raise national income by extracting more of these rents at the expense of foreign interests. The deliberate use of such instruments is called "strategic trade policy."

Brander and Spencer, a husband-and-wife team now at the University of British Columbia, term the process of capturing such rents "profit shifting." Work by Lawrence Katz and Lawrence Summers adds the idea that since most of industry's costs are ultimately labor costs, capturing industries that enjoy supernormal profits also benefits the country's work force (a.k.a. its citizens). Workers can capture a share of the profit in the form of wage premiums, or "labor rents," and over time may earn these rents by becoming more knowledgeable and hence more productive. A highly skilled work force, in turn, enables its nation to stay ahead competitively. A nation that succeeds in capturing advanced ("high-value-added") production achieves more output per worker and becomes wealthier.[6]

Krugman, in the introduction to his most recent book, writes:

> In the new theory an important element of arbitrariness is added to [the standard] story. Why are aircraft manufactured in Seattle? It is hard to argue that there is some unique attribute of the city's location that fully explains this. The point is, instead, that the logic of increasing returns [that is, economies of scale and expertise] mandates that aircraft production had to be concentrated *somewhere,* and Seattle just happens to be where the roulette wheel came to a stop. In many of the new models of trade, the actual location of production is to some degree indeterminate. Yet what the example of Seattle suggests, and what is explicit in some of the models, is a critical role for history: Because Seattle (or Detroit or Silicon Valley) was where an industry initially got established, increasing returns keep the industry there.[7]

To a non-economist, this may seem just common sense. But to standard trade economics, this is a revolutionary insight. What Krugman doesn't add here is that the location of Boeing in Seattle, its growing technical expertise, its advantages of scale, were in part the fruits of Air Force contracts, which would not have existed if the Air Force had decided it could get a lower price from, say, Dassault or Mitsubishi. Nor does he point out that the concentration of the semiconductor industry in Silicon Valley reflected the proximity of Berkeley and Stanford, both of which had benefited from targeted spending by military and intelligence agencies, aimed at creating American advantage in computers. The location of the auto industry in Detroit was more historical accident—but keeping it there pays dividends to the national economy and can be affected by national policy.

If the location of production, especially in advanced industries, is substantially arbitrary, then it can be subject to manipulation by a wide range of national policy interventions, whether microeconomic (aimed at helping new industries capture a place in the market, or human capital policies aimed at improving the quality of the work force) or macroeconomic (intended to influence savings rates, capital costs, and so on). Curiously, however, while the New View has blown a big hole in the traditional theory of comparative advantage, on the whole it has stopped short of advocating industrial policies, for two reasons—one ideological and the other technical.

Ideologically, most steadfast neoclassical economists harbor grave doubts about the competence of collective action, especially initiated by politicians responsive to interest groups, to achieve economic policies that might improve on decisions of the market—most especially in the United States, whose political system is believed to be perilously vulnerable to special-interest groups. ("The trouble with picking winners," Delaware senator William Roth recently declared, "is that each congressman would want one for his district."[8]) Also, the technical economics explaining how strategic trade policy enhances overall economic health depends on the assumptions of that particular model. Changing the assumptions changes the recommendation as to whether a policy instrument (e.g., tariff, subsidy, quota) ought to be used and at what level. Since it is very hard to know which model can be applied to any given industry, economists often argue that it is safer to do nothing.

The typical New View scholarly article, especially when written by economists wishing to keep their neoclassical union cards, takes care to include the disclaimer that even if profit shifting or other benign interventions are possible in theory, they are often implausible in practice. According to Krugman, most economists who subscribe to the New View are uneasy about giving aid and comfort to mercantilists. Threading his way between contradictory opinions, he concluded a rueful 1987 essay entitled "Is Free Trade Passé?" thus: "To abandon the free trade principle in pursuit of the gains from sophisticated intervention could open the door to adverse political consequences that would outweigh the potential gains. It is possible, then, both to believe that comparative advantage is an incomplete model of trade and to believe that free trade is the right policy."[9]

Nonetheless, the New View radically alters the debate, for it removes the presumption that nations like Japan, which practices strategic trade, cannot, by definition, be improving their welfare. Orthodox economists must now concede that advocates of industrial policy are not economic illiterates after all. And all of this invites a far more subtle debate on the instruments and purposes of departing from Ricardian trade, which is no longer necessarily optimal. Orthodox economists long criticized advocates of industrial policy for practicing economics without a license, but in their retreat to the claim that strategic trade can work but not here, they now practice political science without a license.

The question of whether it is possible to "capture advantage" is all but settled. Japan and South Korea demonstrate its reality, and even standard economics can now produce models to explain why this is so. Instead of an outworn debate about how to attain idealized laissez-faire, the practical policy questions ought to be these:

• Why do some nations succeed in using a blend of public policies and market institutions to increase their real wealth and capture advantage for their national industries? Is there such a thing as a comparative advantage in economic planning, and how does a nation acquire it?

• Where should industrial and technology policy rank in the hierarchy of foreign-policy goals for the United States? Traditionally, they don't rank at all, on the grounds that if an economic activity is worth doing, the free market will find the capital to do it.

• How can the United States improve its capacity to capture advantage for its key industries without setting off a trade war?

• How can the desire of all nations to maximize their welfare be reconciled with a coherent system of rules for the trading system, even if those rules are not the rules of laissez-faire? What should those rules be?

In the United States, the debate about the appropriate goals for trade policy has been mixed up with a remarkably sterile debate about "industrial policy." Americans are not sure how much the state should interfere with the private economy domestically, but the confusion about the appropriate roles for the state and the market is most muddled in thinking about the desirable norms for the international trading system. For when goods are traded across national frontiers, the power of the state is weakest and that of private capital strongest. The confusion is worst in the United States, because the United States, as guarantor of the global system and purveyor of the ideal of liberal trade, is unsure how to reconcile those goals with its own national interest as an economy.

Many other nations have demonstrated, in actions if not words, that they are not interested in a system of pure Ricardian trade. More than half of international trade today operates by some other standard. Yet, curiously enough, the volume of trade continues to increase faster than total world GNP does. The sins against liberal trade range from economic development initiatives undertaken in poor countries, which might be justified as variations on the traditional "infant industry" loophole, to industrial policies cloaked as national-defense ones, to covert market-closing measures undertaken by the rich and successful trade-surplus nations like Japan. But whatever "distortions" are introduced by the arsenal of subsidies, quotas, tariffs, and other instruments of state-led development, the result is to shift but not necessarily to retard the overall flow of commerce.

During the Carter administration, a debate ensued about whether the nation needed an industrial policy. At the time, several domestic industries were losing their share of domestic and global markets, because of the combined effect of recession and import pressure from newly competitive foreign rivals. The major injured industries—autos, steel, textiles, and consumer electronics—clamored for relief. However, an industrial policy meant different things to different people. To some, it simply meant limiting imports; to others, it was a synonym (or perhaps euphemism) for the old idea of national economic planning, in which the federal government, working with industry and labor, would determine whether it was desirable to retain a national industry in a given case, how much capacity the country needed, and what instruments of public aid (loans, subsidies, quotas, contracts, antitrust relief) the industry needed to develop technologies and markets. Public policy could also help an industry phase out excess capacity and modernize the remaining capacity, and help to broker social contracts between industry and labor so that the benefits and hardships would be shared. This was what the Europeans and the Japanese seemed to be doing. As a by-product, imports in targeted industries would have to be limited, at least for a time, since otherwise vulnerable domestic producers might disappear altogether. This was generally the position of left-of-center economists such as Barry Bluestone and Bennett Harrison, of the labor movement, and of its allies in the Carter administration. The labor movement and the political left like national industrial policies, in part because the nation-state is perforce where social contracts must be negotiated; a pure global free market leaves no room for social bargains among industry, government, and labor.

Others, mainly the leaders of injured industries, had no use for "tripartite" bargains with labor or for government subsidies. Mainly they wanted relief from imports, which they alleged were being "dumped" (sold below the cost of production so as to capture market share and drive out domestic competitors). Virtually every respectable economist argued that these were illegitimate protectionist demands, coming from inefficient producers who belonged on the industrial scrap heap and from their overpaid trade-union allies. Protectionist policies were deemed an abomination; industrial policy was identified as the same creature using a different name. Under the

American system—the system the United States was attempting to impose upon the world—picking winners and losers was the business of the free market. How could a government bureaucrat presume to outguess the market? Moreover, the world's richest nation and the sponsor of trade liberalization had no business fencing out the products of catch-up nations that were its allies. If foreigners could produce cars or television sets more efficiently, more power to them (and to the lucky American consumer). If the United States had trouble competing, that was because American managers were lazy, its workers overpaid, its savings rates too low, and its macroeconomic policy topsy-turvy. Protectionism, by wrongly scapegoating foreigners when the weaknesses were our own, risked setting off trade war and distracted attention from real problems of competition, which were mainly macroeconomic.

The economists seemed to win the debate in theory and persuaded most editorial writers of the virtue of their position. But the Carter administration was deeply split. On one side, the Council of Economic Advisers, representing the economic priesthood, certified the sinfulness of industrial policy. The Treasury, desiring open capital markets and needing the cooperation of other central bankers, sided with the Council, and so did the State Department, for the usual hegemonic reasons. On the other side, key subcabinet officials in the Commerce Department such as Frank Weil, Sidney Harman, and others, believed that the government had to help modernize and salvage key industries. Harman sponsored a successful small-scale program for modernizing the domestic shoe industry, as well as a pilot effort to automate production of garments. It was a minimalist version of what MITI did on a large scale. The Labor Department, under Secretary Ray Marshall, also supported industrial policy, and the Office of the U.S. Trade Representative, a close observer of actual trade practices, was sympathetic as well, for it was clear that foreign nations did indeed frequently price their products below cost and erect barriers to U.S. exports—practices that would be illegal under American antitrust law and that were often impossible to reach under existing trade law.

One other agency of government weighed in on the side of industrial policy: the Pentagon. Indeed, the Pentagon has long been America's substitute for a commercial technology policy, military doctrine having it that America must have domestic production capability to meet "surge" or "mobilization" conditions as well as peacetime weaponry needs. The military establishment operates or underwrites some six hundred national laboratories and contract research centers at a cost of $40 billion a year. NASA and the Department of Energy also spend tens of billions of dollars annually to develop advanced technologies, produce materials with military applications, and make sure that defense-related products are produced in the United States. Obviously, if the United States lost its steel industry or its capacity to manufacture motor vehicles or microprocessors, this would have national-defense implications.

Yet at the same time the Pentagon was a big part of the problem. While the generals and admirals wanted to maintain U.S. production capacity in everything from missile technology to mess kits, they also wanted a closely integrated Allied defense. In practice, this meant an immense amount of technology sharing with industries in Asia and Europe who were also America's commercial rivals. In making technology-transfer deals, the Pentagon seldom considered the implications for American commercial competitiveness, while foreign governments took full advantage of U.S. confusion and negotiated all the technology transfer they could get. This contradictory behavior of the Pentagon, as de facto repository of technological nationalism and as the central agency of technological diffusion to America's commercial rivals, epitomizes the hegemonic dilemma. (See Chapter 7.)

Then an interesting thing happened. The economists and their laissez-faire allies in the State Department and the Treasury won the ideological debate: free trade remained official American dogma. However, the industrial nationalists at Commerce, Labor, USTR, Pentagon, and CIA won at least half a loaf when it came to actual policies. Unfortunately, because of the ideological dissembling, it was the worse half of the loaf.

Given its predilection for free markets, the administration could not stipulate that it wanted to retain an automobile or steel industry of such and such a size, and tailor trade and investment policy accordingly. Instead, the government fell back on purely defensive measures that it disguised as temporary. In order to keep to the letter of the GATT, it asked allies to offer "voluntary" restraints on exports as an alternative to U.S. import quotas. In the case of autos, for example, imports by 1979 accounted for 20 percent of the domestic auto market. The government refused to slap either a quota or a domestic-content requirement on foreign manufacturers, and instead resorted to an entirely disingenuous regime, disguised as voluntary restraints. The Japanese "unilaterally" limited their auto exports to the United States to 1.85 million cars a year, which allowed the government to pretend it was honoring free trade as usual—and allowed Japan to determine just what it exported to the United States. (It also allowed Japanese companies to charge more for their cars than would have been charged in a free market, since the demand exceeded the permitted supply; economists call these supernormal profits "quota rents.") And, of course, it also exposed the U.S. authorities as perfect hypocrites.

Essentially the same thing occurred in the steel industry. As the combined effect of world recession and the sudden entry of lower-cost steel battered the American industry, the Carter administration resorted to a pretend regime of "voluntary" restraints by exporting nations. Since we disdained economic planning, we could not use this relief (as Europeans and Japanese did) to project the reasonable size or efficient shape for a domestic steel industry ten years hence. Rather, American trade negotiators apologized for their hypocrisy and their capitulation to domestic pressure groups, and promised to abolish the import restraints as soon as possible. And in 1982, when the Harley-Davidson motorcycle company demonstrated that its Japanese competitors were causing it grave harm, the United States backed into an "industrial policy" for motorcycles (!), not because the U.S. government particularly cared about motorcycles, but because a trade-relief petition forced the issue. Yet, at the same time, the government disdained to formulate anything like an industrial policy for more consequential industries such as semiconductors, machine tools, optical-fiber technology, or high-definition television, except where an explicit "national defense" angle could be demonstrated.

The United States has long had a highly protectionist regime for agriculture, despite the plain contradiction with the orthodox view of trade. Dissenting economists have long argued that agriculture is a prime candidate for a regime of price supports, because individual farmers are vulnerable to the weather and to mutually ruinous price competition. In agriculture, the price signals of the "free market" are perverse. When overproduction occurs, the price falls. But because of the lag between the planting and the harvest, a farmer unloads his bumper crop at whatever the market offers, at a time when all his neighbors are likely to have bumper crops, too—which depresses the price further. Only if there is some guaranteed price is the individual farmer able to invest in mechanization, fertilizers, irrigation, and the other sources of dynamic increases in productivity. In this century, prior to the era of American hegemony, farm policy was guided by the anti-laissez-faire view. Lately, the United States has preached that even agriculture should follow the laws of laissez-faire. Administration officials, however, do not know how to withdraw from the current structure of farm price supports, except by having all other nations forswear price regulation for farm products—a diplomatic posture that other countries consider unrealistic and probably cynical. During the Reagan administration, for all its professed ideological devotion to free trade, these absurd inconsistencies only increased.

In the meantime, official American policy goals for the trading system remained unchanged. The General Agreement on Tariffs and Trade (GATT) by default had become the international body of rules and practices governing trade, as well as the arena in which the United States acted to encourage ever increasing liberalization. Every few years, the United States sponsored another "round" of GATT trade talks, an extended series of bilateral and multilateral negotiations in which nations traded off concessions on multiple fronts; at the end one grand deal was struck. The Kennedy Round (1963–67), for example, reduced tariffs an average of 36–39 percent.

Yet the GATT itself, and the related body of international trade law, remains weak and riddled with contradictions. Ideologically, it is ostensibly committed to trade liberalization, but its assumptions are mercantilist. The Ricardian doctrine of free trade holds that even unilateral free trade will benefit nations that relax their barriers. However, the GATT realistically assumes that most nations will believe that to remove their own barriers unilaterally is to provide not so much opportunity for consumers but concessions to be suffered by producers, and that concessions must be negotiated reciprocally. Thus a GATT round is not an exercise in unilateral disarmament but a series of carefully staged tit-for-tats. You lower your tariffs in cars, and I'll lower mine in machine tools. You open your markets to my banks, and I'll open mine to your insurance companies. And the system is riddled with loopholes.

Article 6 of the GATT Charter allows nations to levy antidumping duties when foreign products are found to have been sold at a price below that charged in the producer nation's home market. This finding is made not by the GATT but under the domestic law of the importing nation. Article 12 allows nations with balance-of-payments difficulties to discriminate against imports. Virtually all developing nations have awarded themselves a blanket right to protect under this general waiver, and the GATT has accepted their need for what is termed "special and differential treatment." Article 19, the all-purpose "escape clause," permits unilateral discriminatory responses if imports threaten domestic industries with "serious injury." Taken together, these provisions leave the GATT system relying on the self-restraint and fear of retaliation on the part of major trading nations as the driving force for liberal trade, rather than on a coherent or consistent body of world law.

Constitutionally, the GATT has almost no independent power. It is merely a standing diplomatic conference with a small technical secretariat. In cases of complaints, it can convene fact-finding panels, but it has no power to resolve definitively trade disputes. Remedies for unfair trade practices have to be imposed unilaterally or negotiated bilaterally. In U.S. law, Section 201 of the 1974 Trade Act corresponds to the escape clause of the GATT. An industry may file complaints with the U.S. International Trade Commission alleging damage due to imports, and if the commission finds that the complaint has merit, it is up to the President to fashion a remedy. Often, foreign-policy concerns take priority and no remedy is found. Section 301 of the Trade Act corresponds to the GATT prohibition against dumping. Here again, it is the responsibility of the President to negotiate relief or to impose retaliations, and Presidents often decide that foreign-policy considerations override commercial ones.

Nor is there even a common set of rules on what constitutes predatory commercial practices. The issue of what constitutes predatory commercial practices or "dumping" is worth a whole treatise in itself. In domestic U.S. law, selling below cost in order to drive out a competitor is a well-defined violation of antitrust law. However, in countries such as Japan and South Korea, where banking-industrial combines (*keiretsu* in Japan, *chaebol* in Korea) often develop new products by providing capital at very low interest rates and absorb heavy losses for several years, selling below cost is an accepted business practice. Indeed, many economists hold that selling below cost for a time is the essence of entrepreneurship and that the antidumping petition is just another form of protection. Yet when wielded by a nation systematically devoted to the practice of strategic trade, selective pricing can indeed be highly predatory, even if it is not subject to the GATT.

Many other modern mercantilist practices are simply beyond the reach of the GATT. For example, in America anybody who cares to open a retail establishment is free to do so, but binding relationships between retailers and suppliers that discriminate against competing suppliers violate antitrust laws. However, in Japan, retailing is tightly regulated, entry is not free, and department stores have long-standing relationships with distributors who in turn have close relationships with producers. If a Japanese department store were to permit U.S.-made products with price advantages to compete openly against Japanese products favored by the wholesalers, they would put at risk their entire relationship with the distribution network. As a result, price-competitive U.S. products are subjected to high markups in Japanese department stores so that they don't undercut their Japanese rivals. This practice, like many other selective pricing practices, is not reachable under existing trade law, yet it so profoundly violates a key presumption of competitive markets (free entry) as to render the entire Japanese system protectionist.

Dumping[10] was first recognized as a concept in U.S. law in the Antidumping Act of 1916, which defines dumping as price discrimination between purchasers in different national markets, more or less on the model of "predatory pricing" in domestic antitrust law. The act was passed during World War I, because domestic industries feared that the war's end and the restoration of commerce would bring with it a flood of cheap imports. Characteristically, like other failed remedies, it was enacted to head off outright "protectionism." However, unlike antitrust law, the body of antidumping laws does not usually allow the aggrieved party to sue; rather, an industry alleging injury must petition the U.S. government for relief. The government, via its International Trade Commission, makes a finding of fact, and then a recommendation to the President, which the President is free to accept or reject. This, of course, reflects the fact that foreign policy is intimately involved in trade disputes. A President who accords trade a low priority is free to reject many ITC recommendations, as President Reagan often did. To add insult to injury, the remedy imposed under antidumping law is a "countervailing duty"—a special tariff which supposedly raises the U.S. price of a dumped product to a fair market price. But the revenues from this duty go to the U.S. Treasury, not to the injured industry.

Antidumping—as a concept and as a remedy—has been justifiably criticized as both too weak and too blunt an instrument of redress. At one extreme, free trade advocates have contended that some antidumping cases unfairly punish foreign producers that have a genuine competitive advantage. Usually, however, antidumping fails as either deterrent or as recompense in the case of genuinely unfair practices, because the law is too weak. The filing of a dumping complaint is time-consuming, and there is no guarantee of redress even if the finding of dumping is unequivocal. In addition, many genuinely anticompetitive practices, such as Japan's distribution and retailing system and its business-government "targeting" of emerging industries, are virtually unreachable. The process is so attenuated that by the time it has been confirmed that dumping or predatory pricing occurred and a remedy is applied (countervailing duties), irreparable damage has often been done and the American industry is out of business. A good example is color television, where complaints about dumping and price fixing worked their way through the U.S. administrative process and the courts for several years and never provided relief adequate to save the U.S. producers. All but one U.S. producer (Zenith) was driven from the market.

When a major color television case finally reached the U.S. Supreme Court in 1986, twelve years after the initial suit, the lower court rulings had been substantially influenced by the free-market Chicago school of law and economics. This school essentially held that, evidence aside, the Japanese exporters could not have been dumping—by definition—because firms that price products below their true cost will lose money and go broke. Hence, dumping did not occur because it could not occur. Courts have traditionally held that price discrimination does not occur when products are substantially different from one another, even when they compete in the marketplace as effective substitutes. In the color TV case, Zenith alleged that twenty-one Japanese firms had conspired to drive U.S. producers out of the market by charging artificially high prices for imports into Japan, while setting artificially low prices for their own TV exports to the United States. The Supreme Court held that even though it was entirely possible that Japanese producers were using excess profits earned by price fixing in Japan to undercut their American competitors in the U.S. market, "American antitrust laws do not regulate the competitive competitions of other nations' economies."[11] The Court favorably cited Judge Frank Easterbrook of the Appeals Court, a leading exponent of the conservative law and economics group, to the effect that predatory pricing schemes run contrary to economic theory. "For this reason, there is a consensus among commentators that predatory pricing schemes are rarely tried, and [are] even more rarely successful."[12]

This is, of course, arguable even within a domestic economy. But it is entirely reasonable in a nation such as Japan, where industrial targeting is the norm, that firms often behave just as the color TV manufacturers were said to have done. The point is not that this behavior is good or bad; the point is that its effect on U.S. producers is not reached by any common body of law, international or domestic, that U.S. officials influenced by laissez-faire doctrine do not consider this a high priority, and that conservative American judges, influenced by the same theory, deny American firms redress in the courts. Some critics have suggested amending the laws to make Japanese-style price discrimination a clearer violation of U.S. antitrust law.[13]

U.S. administrations don't like antidumping remedies, because friendly allied nations tend to see these as hostile acts; and the federal government has often interceded with American producers to discourage them from pressing their cases to completion. As a substitute, successive administrations have resorted to clumsy and flawed accords on "voluntary" restraints, by which foreign nations agree to restrain their exports of shoes, textiles, steel, semiconductors, autos, or whatever—an even more grotesque violation of the free-trade doctrine. And because of the prevailing laissez-faire ideology, they make these trade-restraint deals without establishing complementary domestic industrial or technological goals. This, in turn, makes the administration defensive, and open to the charge of mere protectionism.

For GATT's first thirty years, its trade liberalization talks, under American sponsorship, succeeded in reducing overt barriers to free trade, such as tariffs. By the Tokyo Round (1973–79), the United States began to advocate the abolition of "nontariff barriers" such as government subsidies, technical standards, and preferential procurement. One man's nontariff barrier, however, is another man's economic development program. Although the Tokyo Round did produce a series of minimalist codes of conduct about subsidies, technical standards, government procurement, customs procedures, licensing, and other policies that might be "trade-distorting," it did not establish clear criteria for determining just what was a "trade-distorting subsidy," or any remedy other than the traditional unilateral right to apply countervailing duties if another nation resorted to subsidies or more covert measures favoring its producers. For in the past decade, free traders have lamented that as tariff barriers have fallen, non-tariff interventionism has increased—in industrial policies in other countries that include subsidies, market closings, recession cartels, and preferential capital allocation schemes, and in subterfuges in the United States like orderly marketing agreements and voluntary export restraints demanded of trading partners.

The most recent series of negotiations, the Uruguay Round (named for its initial meeting at Punta del Este), began in late 1986 under the auspices of the GATT. The United States, which had been pressing for a new round since 1981, played its familiar hegemonic role: once again, the goal of the trade round, seen by other nations as mainly an American one, was ever-greater liberalization of the world trading system. The Uruguay Round witnessed for the first time a serious effort to get nations to decontrol price supports and subsidies in agriculture and to increase the administrative strength of the GATT system, which remains powerless to enforce its decisions. The United States proposed a grandiose series of objectives intended to root out "nontariff barriers," to strengthen the dispute-settlement machinery of the GATT, and to bring the GATT norms of liberal trade to areas currently outside the GATT, such as trade in services.

"Services" was a grab-bag category that included everything from banking, accountancy, travel brokerage, and insurance underwriting to "labor" services such as construction crews. The U.S. administration convinced itself that a natural U.S. comparative advantage in services might offset the escalating trade deficit in product exports. Politically, the Reagan administration tried to build support for trade liberalization as a counterweight for the forces of "protection," appealing to those segments of American business with an interest in liberalized markets—notably multinational corporations, financial service businesses, and industries hoping for expanded opportunities in export and/or direct foreign investment. As the Uruguay Round continued, it was clear to many observers that this was an agenda appropriate to the economic self-interest of the United States circa 1955 and oddly out of sync with the nation America had become by the 1990s and with many of the world's practical trade issues.

For example, the U.S. eagerness for liberalization in services had been predicated on three notions: that the United States, with its substantial competitive advantage in banking, insurance, etc., had much to gain if nations opened these areas of commerce to foreign competition; that a domestic constituency supporting export of services could help to counterbalance the increasingly protectionist constituency among manufacturers; and that the logic of trade liberalization as a whole required that it be extended from trade in goods to trade in services, the fastest-growing sector. But the United States has become a major capital importer, and all of the world's ten largest banks are Japanese. An American campaign to force nations to open their borders to greater foreign banking penetration benefits Japan more than America.

By the same token, free traders thought that liberalization of trade in farm products would have both national and systemic benefits. Agriculture had a long-standing exemption from the GATT system, thanks in large part to the American farm lobby. Europe emulated American price-support policies, stabilized farmer earnings, and was awash in surplus farm products and costly subsidies. Much of the world had benefited from the U.S.-inspired "Green Revolution," and even countries like India have become net exporters of food. A liberal regime in farm trade, like more liberal trade in services, is an American goal that is partly nationalist and partly ideological—but woefully misconceived on both counts. In the 1970s, when GATT enthusiasts first began seriously to explore how to open up trade in farm products, it seemed that the United States had much to gain. A decade later, however, total decontrol of agricultural trade would not necessarily help American farmers. The famous negotiations with Japan to persuade it to open its markets to beef and oranges were more likely to advantage Brazilian citrus plantations and beef ranches in Australia; freer trade in grain stood to benefit Canada and Argentina. This might or might not be good for the efficiency of the entire system. In the short run it would shift production to the lowest-cost producer (good), but in the long run it would encourage ruinous overproduction and depressed producer income (bad). What is needed is a more sophisticated and equitable system of farm stabilization, not laissez-faire trade. Like other dilemmas created by economic stabilization outrunning national sovereignties, this is hard to solve, harder still to administer, and hardest of all if one wears doctrinaire blinders.

Yet in these and other areas the United States remained stuck in the groove it designed for itself back in the 1950s, which reflected its geo-economic position then. Newer problems, as well as the new realities of the American situation, were oddly absent from the GATT talks. Japan's chronic surplus position and its structural causes were not discussed. The EC, in 1983, had put forward a broad, generic complaint against Japan's entire economic system as biased toward exports and against imports, but this was fiercely resisted by U.S. officials as an unseemly "ganging up on Japan."

In one area, the protection of "intellectual property," America's ideological goals did converge with its national economic self-interest. One of the United States' genuine comparative advantages—technological prowess—is continually eroded as other nations get to commercialize American inventions, but the administration fails to make protection of U.S. patents and proprietary technologies a top priority. Many countries, especially developing nations but also Japan, tolerate a great deal of industrial piracy as an informal brand of technology transfer. Brazilians conclude that if American banks are squeezing them dry, why should they give top priority to protecting American firms against the Brazilians copying their technology—especially since Brazilian exports are needed to earn foreign exchange in order to pay back the same banks? Other Third World countries take U.S. liberalization rhetoric at its word and refuse to enforce tighter patent laws until the United States gives them concessions they want and the United States professes to support: free entry of cheap labor as part of construction contracts, free entry of textile exports, and liberalization of farm exports. So in the Uruguay Round, the United States made scant headway in gaining concessions that would have truly produced fairer as well as freer trade.

Concurrently with its intensified rush toward ever freer trade, the free-market Reagan administration enacted some halting and rather guilt-ridden measures that were, by its own definition, protectionist: agricultural legislation gave the government enhanced ability to subsidize farm exports; a 1986 semiconductor agreement with Japan, after failed earlier agreements, resorted to a market-share target for U.S. exports to Japan (which has not been reached), as well as a halfhearted domestic industrial policy to maintain U.S. competitiveness in chips. After almost a decade of failing to stabilize the steel industry, the administration imposed quantitative Voluntary Export Restraints (VER) on steel imports. Textiles continue to be subject to a managed trade regime, under the Multi-Fibre Arrangement (MFA), and in the Uruguay Round, the United States argued for extending MFA and making it permissible under the GATT. The Japanese auto quota continued. Railing against bilateral trading blocs as an affront to the GATT's fundamental multilateral logic, the administration nonetheless negotiated bilateral free-trade agreements with Israel and Canada and a regional Caribbean Basin trade pact, and made grandiose noises about similar arrangements with Mexico and even Japan.

The administration was never clear, either with itself or with U.S. allies, about which of these were expedient temporary adjustments, which were tactical maneuvers intended to be bargained away for reciprocal liberalizations, which were adjuncts of domestic industrial policies, which were craven capitulations to domestic pressure groups, and which were necessary long-term solutions in industries that simply don't lend themselves to Ricardian trade. And as this creeping protectionism burgeoned, the administration, like an intermittent alcoholic, intensified its crusade to persuade its trading partners to abandon all forms of mercantilism in one grand pledge of mutual temperance.

Viewed casually, these opposite thrusts of trade policy seem hypocritical if not incoherent. But understood as expressing the logic of the United States' hegemony, they make a certain amount of sense. Quotas are an instructive case in point. As neoclassical economists constantly point out, an allocated quota is probably the most inefficient form of protection: it gives the foreign exporting nation the power to rig the market, and if that nation is a mercantilist country like Japan, this is a formidable power indeed; and it raises prices for one's own consumers while delivering the quota rents to the exporter partner. Unless it is coupled with a careful program to restructure the protected domestic industry (which is ideologically anathema to conservatives), the latter is very likely simply to raise its own prices but not its productivity. If the quota is a quantity of units rather than a sum of money, it also encourages the exporting nation to move up and capture a richer segment of the protected market (as the Japanese did in the case of autos).

Economists urge that if one must have a spell of protection, tariffs (which are at least transparent and marketlike) are always preferable to quotas; and if one must resort to quotas they should be auctioned—so that the lowest-cost foreign producer eventually winds up with the right to export while we capture the quota rents. This is all clear enough and the logic is seemingly irrefutable. Why, then, would a nation devoted to a free-trade system and to free-market principles resort to allocated quotas, of all things? The answer, once again, lies in the logic of geopolitical hegemony.

As a form of protection, a multilateral tariff or an auctioned quota leaves you with nothing to bestow selectively on your friends. But an allocated quota is a form of geopolitical currency, because it is discretionary. Whenever the United States departs from the principle of treating all nations alike ("multilateral most-favored-nation"), its stated norm for the trading system, as hegemon it likes to do so in ways that provide some bargaining counters. This has been the case with oil, where import quotas were bargained and allocated, with steel, with textiles, and with farm products. If steel quotas were auctioned rather than allocated, this would enrage our high-cost producer friends, which include debtor nations like Brazil. Allocating—and withdrawing—import quotas is a long-standing hegemonic habit. When Fidel Castro became an intolerable thorn in the side of the United States, what did we withdraw? Cuba's sugar quota. Moreover, a quota disguised as a "voluntary restraint" on the part of the exporting nation also complies with the letter of the GATT law, even though it is actually an overt form of bilateralism as well as a departure from free trade which fools no one. In each of these instances, a political objective drowns out competing economic objectives and makes the United States appear foolish and disingenuous.

Much of the debate about free trade, managed trade, industrial policy, and so forth is confused by implied conceptions of the "national interest." From the perspective of traditional economic liberalism, the national interest is defined primarily in terms of geopolitical national security. There is also a supposed abstract and generalized "consumer" interest in liberal trade, which is treated in isolation from the influence of Ricardian trade on domestic productive employment. Insofar as an open trading system wins friends for the United States, liberal trade complements its traditional national security goals. In this conception, there is no room for an economic national interest defined in terms of industrial objectives, nor are there geo-economic goals beyond those that supposedly flow naturally from free markets: the freest possible market yields results that are "natural" and hence optimal. Even if other trading nations violate its norms, the United States still allegedly gains both economic and geopolitical advantage by practicing liberal trade. The possibility of a national interest colliding with Ricardian trading norms is thus neatly excluded by definition.

This perspective begs several questions. In practice, one can identify a number of specific goals for the U.S. economy that cannot necessarily be achieved in a conventional free-trade environment—particularly when that environment is lopsided: these include full employment at decent wages, rapid productivity growth, rising levels of real income distributed equitably, retention of technological leadership in major industries, maintenance of a skilled work force. While it is conventional to argue that "we" must do this or that for the economy to thrive, it is not always clear who "we" is. For example, the interests of American-based banks and multinational corporations, key supporters of the Ricardian view of trade, are not always served by pursuing the goals of high and rising living standards for American citizens and the maintenance of American technological leadership. The merits of different trade policies must be weighed against true national objectives rather than narrow corporate ones, and in the context of other U.S. foreign-policy objectives, with which trade objectives sometimes compete.

. . .

Elsewhere on the global scene, yet another trend has deeply troubled orthodox economists—the move to regionalism. The European Common Market, established with American support early in the Cold War era, matured into the signal success story of the model that had been hoped for in 1944: both a successful mixed economy and an example of "one-worldism," albeit on a regional scale. Yet after the economic shocks of the mid-1970s, most of Europe slid into stagflation, and American conservatives claimed that this fate was all too predictable: Europe was over-regulated, overtaxed, and alarmingly statist; its labor unions enjoyed too much power, and high unemployment and retarded entrepreneurship were the consequences. Its woes were an object lesson in welfare-state excess. This came to be known as "Euro-sclerosis." The early 1980s were a period when enlightened Europeans were supposedly deregulating, privatizing, and making Europe over in the American image. Then in 1985, a French socialist, Jacques Delors, sponsored a little-noticed initiative aiming at complete removal of the barriers to free commerce within Europe by 1992. Slowly, and then with increasing fervor, the very idea of this target date poured new energy into the Western European enterprise. Rates of productivity growth recovered and again surpassed American ones. The EC nations did lower their very high marginal taxes, encouraged entrepreneurship, and reformed regulatory excess, but in a spirit far from that of Anglo-Saxon laissez-faire. As Europe moved to a single market, the exercise included a high degree of national economic planning, strong welfare-state guarantees, and a collective refusal to let Japanese or American competition push them out of key industries simply because the gospel of laissez-faire awarded the entire market to this year's low-cost producer.

Customs unions, of which the EC is a premier example, have long troubled free-trade economists.[14] On the one hand, a customs union, which removes trade barriers among participating nations, obviously enhances liberal trade within its boundaries. On the other hand, it does so at the expense of nonmember nations and threatens to divert preexisting patterns of trade. When, for example, the United States and Canada complete the process of abolishing all tariffs between them, Canada is likely to capture market share that formerly went to, say, New Zealand. Thus a new customs union expands the realm of free trade but contracts the realm of multilateralism. There is no satisfactory theoretical resolution to the customs union question. Most economists resolve it by recourse to an uncharacteristic empiricism: if a particular customs union enhances trade, it is virtuous; otherwise, it is a protectionist abomination. In no event should a new customs union raise preexisting tariffs with third countries, but only lower them among its members. The founding fathers of the GATT permitted customs unions for several practical diplomatic reasons. The British Commonwealth, a preferential trade area, was a fact of life, and the United States also sponsored preferential trade relationships with several of its wards, while some form of Western European economic union was already a gleam in the eye.

American conservatives have been ambivalent about European economic unification, for precisely the reasons that Professor Jacob Viner suggested in his classic work on the subject. On the one hand, the Common Market represents a victory for economic liberalism. For forty years the supporters of free commerce in Western Europe had championed economic integration, while European social democrats had suspected this would be a source of empowerment to international capital at the expense of domestic full employment. Europe's economic liberals wanted to sweep away the tariffs, monopolies, quotas, customs checks, preferential procurements, excessive regulations, and other vestiges of nationalism—this could best be done in the idealistic context of transcending the discredited nation-state and building a unified and liberal Europe. Socialists and labor parties had been dubious, for the usual reason that the market can be tamed only by the polity: give capital the ability to outrun the constraints of national regulation, and no social contract is possible.

Yet as the European Community metamorphosed from a mere customs union into a genuine political confederation, its ideological meaning metamorphosed, too. Once its members had delegated substantial portions of sovereignty to it, the Community became not merely the realm of liberated capital but something akin to a super nation-state. If it could have a common agricultural policy, it could also have a common technology policy and even a common labor policy. As Europe's internal market was completed, attention shifted to the task of building Euro-federalism. In the run toward 1992, the need for a common European social policy also received increasing attention, so that constituent states could not outbid each other, U.S. style, to throw away social benefits in the competition to attract capital and jobs. Whatever sort of hybrid this was turning out to be politically and economically, it wasn't laissez-faire. And it was thriving. As Western Europe's economy continued to grow, energized by the move toward full economic union yet keeping the elements of its mixed economy, people stopped talking of Euro-sclerosis. Europe was doing well indeed, with higher rates of savings, investment, and productivity growth, balanced trade accounts, and fiscal discipline despite a much higher level of taxation. By the late 1980s, even the French socialists were among the most ardent supporters of European union. If Mitterrand-style socialism was not practical within one country because of the fickle velocity of global capital, a mixed economy might be feasible on a continent-wide scale. The British Labour Party, which had long viewed European union as not only suspiciously foreign but suspiciously capitalist, now saw it as a magnificent counterweight to Thatcherism. And Mrs. Thatcher, that paragon of nineteenth-century laissez-faire, found herself on the losing end of 11–1 votes in the EC, and began to look more and more like a nationalist champion of Little England.

American conservatives had the same worries. In the second Reagan administration, U.S.-EC relations markedly deteriorated. Senior American officials gave on-the-record speeches warning against "Fortress Europe." For a moment, it looked as if the EC, as well as Japan, might be singled out as a malefactor under the 1988 Trade Act, which requires the President to identify nations that were not abiding by the canons of liberal trade. But by decade's end, the Bush administration had patched things up and decided that the new EC, despite some mercantilist transgressions, could be lived with. Yet in the closing deliberations of the Uruguay trade round, many of the nastiest disputes were between the United States and the EC.

With the end of the Cold War, Western Europe and the EC were abruptly catapulted into a greater role, both as a geopolitical player and as an economic role model. For the first time since World War II, Germany found itself in the position of a major diplomatic force. Chancellor Kohl's determination to complete German unification in a single year, over the initial objections of the U.S.S.R. and amid unease on the part of several allies, suddenly made Germany the political as well as the economic powerhouse of Central Europe. These events made the other eleven members of the EC all the more determined to accelerate completion of the Community, as a political as well as an economic union. The nations of Western Europe, committed to détente earlier and with more enthusiasm than the United States, became a force for substantial economic aid to both the former satellites and the Soviet Union itself. (The United States, in fiscal straits, was largely out of the aid business.) Finally, as U.S. economists pressed hard for an ultra-free-market transition, Western Europe remained far more sympathetic to a middle way and a managed transition, reminiscent of the Marshall Plan. Thus, one more indication of the erosion of effective American hegemony was the emergence of a newly assertive Europe, offering a rather different economic model.

Let me recapitulate the argument thus far and summarize why Ricardian trade fails as a description, as a systemic norm, or as a strategy that serves the interest of the United States and the world. Trade theory now holds that comparative advantage (the free market) does not necessarily dictate the location of production; in our imperfect world, national policies can and do capture advantage. Substantial amounts of trade, in products where cheap labor, climate, or natural resources significantly affect costs, still proceed along Ricardian lines. But semiconductors, for example, can and will be produced most efficiently wherever the best technology has been developed and applied. And this is true not only for "high-tech" products; West German and U.S. firms have successfully applied advanced production technology to the textile industry and remain competitive in global markets because of efficient capital rather than cheap labor.

Politically, the United States has advocated free trade not because it is necessarily optimal for either the American or the world economy (though we have convinced ourselves that it is) but because liberal trade is a logical imperative if one cares to be the hegemon. This made sense when American industry was dominant and its products were superior. But America's systemic goals as hegemon and its national goals as an economy are no longer identical.

What ought a mixed system look like? It is tricky enough to design a mixed economic system within national borders, where sovereignty is a settled question. It is far more difficult to fashion one across national frontiers, where political sovereignty is dispersed. Obviously a mixed system is far messier than a system of perfectly free trade—though the fairer comparison is with the existing system of trade, which is also very messy. And even if one could design an ideal system to regulate a global mixed economy, there remains the political problem of negotiating one's way from here to there.

In certain sectors, managed trade makes sense because it is stabilizing and enhances productive innovation and because it is needed to get nations to operate according to rules that are at least universal and reciprocal, if not Ricardian. We should not manage trade in, say, semiconductors merely to win concessions that move our entire system toward freer semiconductor trade; for the moment, retaining and restoring U.S. capacity in that crucial sector takes priority over liberalization of markets as a systemic goal—especially if our trading partners insist that they wish to develop and maintain their own semiconductor capacities. We should not disguise that goal as merely a tactic to make Japan "play fair" and open its markets—to products that U.S. firms may no longer make, thanks to earlier episodes of Japanese mercantilism.

On the other hand, in other industries and at other times nations may decide that interventionist subsidies and other market manipulations are imposing costs that exceed benefits, and they may wish to negotiate reciprocal limits on such subsidies and greater mutual market access.

*Pace* economic orthodoxy, there are really two sorts of efficiency. Static, "allocative" efficiency results from market forces responding to price signals. But market forces do not necessarily place exactly the "right" amount of capital investment in particular sectors where risk is high but the potential of technological reward is great. In a free-trade economy, cheap labor in very poor regions may capture markets; yet the presence of such labor deters investment in dynamic technologies that make the world economy more productive as a whole. An agreement to reciprocally limit subsidies (the "managed" solution), rather than banning them (the free-trade solution), may well produce net benefits. One must also be clear about whether having industrial policies and complementary managed trade is a unilateral attempt to capture advantage at the expense of other nations, or whether they can benefit the system as a whole via technological innovation, stabilization, and diffusion of productive wealth. To the extent that the United States wishes to remain an influential and well-behaved citizen of the trading system, though perhaps not its hegemon, we should not emulate Japan-like unilaterialism; we should strive for reciprocal rules.

A look at some actual industries where trade has been conducted along other than classically liberal lines suggests some intriguing lessons and models.

*Textiles.* The Multi-Fibre Arrangement offers a good example of a reasonably successful managed-trade regime. It was gradually imposed on nations with textile- and apparel-exporting industries by nations with established producers, primarily because the latter did not wish to give up these industries entirely. Since in the United States cotton is a protected commodity whose domestic price is held above the world free-market price, free trade in textiles would substantially undermine our internal managed-price regime in cotton. By the same token, since textiles are the primary component of apparel and since textiles used by apparel makers are often purchased locally, a managed-trade regime in textiles logically required managed trade in apparel.

The MFA regime was intended to regulate trade in natural and later in synthetic fibers and apparel, not by allocating rigid quotas, but by limiting the rate of growth of imports and bargaining about shares of that increase. The targeted growth of U.S. imports was held to an annual rate of 6 percent. Significantly, despite this degree of protection, the rate of inflation in textiles and apparel lagged behind the general inflation rate by 7.8 percent during MFA's first decade and by 27.5 percent during its second. And productivity gains in textiles were the second greatest of any U.S. industry, after microelectronics. Here is a case where the doctrine of comparative advantage would have it that the wealthier producer nations in Europe and North America should have simply "let textiles go." Unlike, say, semiconductors, it is not self-evident that textile production and apparel making are key industries with dynamic technological benefits that justify a departure from Ricardian trade on either national security or "learning curve" grounds. Textiles and, even more, apparel are labor-intensive, relatively low-technology industries that can give newly industrializing nations important experience in organizing production and entrepreneurship for world markets. So the presumptive case against managed trade in textiles and apparel is strong indeed. In the current GATT round, relief from the limits of MFA is a high priority for several nations which are under pressure to increase their exports in order to pay their foreign debts and under pressure from the OECD nations to extend intellectual property protections and to liberalize trade in financial services.

The systemic as opposed to the narrow self-interest arguments favoring MFA boil down to two. First, although protection is popularly believed to result in stagnation and excessive wage levels in the protected industry, in fact productivity growth in American and Western European textile production has been about double the industrial average. And wages have remained among the lowest of all manufacturing wages, though this is truer in the United States than in Western Europe because the United States has lower minimum wages and tolerates much greater wage differentials from industry to industry. (Swedish textile workers earn nearly what Swedish auto workers do.) U.S. producers responded to MFA by automating their manufacturing process, since the MFA regime struck a good balance between providing a partially protected market (which made it rational to invest) and allowing some import penetration (which maintained competitive pressure to invest). Import growth occurred both because of MFA and through various leakages, including the proliferation of substitute materials not initially covered by MFA and the entry of new producer nations not party to it. In effect, U.S. producers could figure that they had some competition from imports but were not at risk of being obliterated by them—a climate that recommended a strategy of investing in productivity-enhancing automation. Since 1977, the industry has invested an average of $1.6 billion a year in new capital equipment; today, two-thirds of its production machinery is less than a decade old, making it one of America's most modern industries.[15]

The principal trade unions in textiles and apparel appreciated this logic and cooperated with automation. The restraint on the growth rate in imports gave some assurance that market share could be retained by domestic producers, which in turn made it feasible to invest in automation. The leakage of additional imports, as well as intra-industry competition from OECD competitors (British tailoring and Italian and French fashion are still powerful), kept the competitive pressure high. Significantly, there has been more "leakage" of Third World textile imports into the United States than into Western Europe. The reason is that the United States, with its ideas about hegemonic responsibilities, interprets MFA limits far more liberally than Western European nations.

There is evidence that at least some of the new producing nations are not entirely unhappy with MFA, because it has made an otherwise chronically unstable market more predictable. It has given their producers some ability to forecast what their market share and hence needed capacity could be and therefore has given them some basis for making costly investments. (Without MFA, China could single-handedly make off with much of world apparel production.) Third World textile production and apparel making are now hotbeds of entrepreneurship. Though it is a regime that "regulates" markets, MFA stops well short of cartelization. There is widespread competition, and much of it is price competition. Despite spuriously precise calculation by neoclassical economists computing the cost of textile protection—one study put it at $135,000 per job[16]—or the amount of Third World production that was denied, it is all but impossible to predict what would have ensued in the absence of MFA or something like it.

As the New View of trade suggests, the worldwide division of labor is theoretically indeterminate, even in low-wage industries like textiles and apparel. It is unlikely that the same degree of productivity-enhancing investment would have occurred without some form of managed-trade regime. Rather, production would have migrated all that much faster to low-wage countries with less reason to replace cheap labor with expensive capital. The result might well have been overcapacity, flat wages, overproduction, low profits, less investment in more productive machinery—and pressure for some other, more rigid form of cartelization. This sequence must logically be understood as an integral aspect of the dynamics of trade, not as an alternative to it. This is even more important to appreciate when the major new entrant is a nation with the characteristics of the People's Republic of China, which does not use a price system like the Western one and which measures the production capacity of its knitwear factories by the million dozen.

So it is reasonable to argue that a free-trade regime in textiles and apparel is improbable and that the MFA regime has brought benefits. But this, of course, does not tell us whether the present MFA is more or less "fair" or economically "efficient" than some other theoretically possible system. What it does suggest is that regimes like MFA take into account a factor that is often left out of conventional economic analysis predicated upon a general equilibrium, namely time. Shifting the world's textile and apparel production to lower-wage countries has indeed occurred under the auspices of MFA, but it has occurred gradually, and the OECD nations have retained their share of world textile production and invested in advanced production technology, which is itself soon diffused to the Third World.

Can MFA be defended as encouraging both economic efficiency and the needs of the Third World? If efficiency includes the value of protecting companies against mutually ruinous competition and offering an incentive to increase productivity rather than relying on cheap labor, it probably can. Should MFA-type managed trade be extended to other industries? Not necessarily. Other industries have very different structural characteristics. Is MFA fairer or more efficient than some other possible managed-trade regime for textiles? Quite possibly not. Economic theory does not tell us whether Third World textile imports to the United States should grow at 6 percent a year or 1 percent a year or at some other rate. That is why standard economics is so seductive; it leaves the answers to all such questions to the invisible hand. In a trading system where the benefits are subject to constant negotiation and refinement, and where the United States (or a successor trilateral hegemony of the United States, the EC, and Japan) cares about the stability, growth, and political friendship of the Third World, we can expect sectoral departures from pure free trade, and they will have to be evaluated case by case.

The MFA regime is a relatively flexible one. It could accommodate faster or slower import penetration into OECD countries. In fact, the domestic industry has bitterly complained that the U.S. government has permitted too many loopholes in MFA, and has sponsored legislation (which the administration opposed) to limit growth rates of textile and apparel imports to just 1 percent per year. Alternatively, the OECD nations may decide at some point that their own interest in the health of Third World nations and their own desire for freer exports of financial services or high-technology products and for greater protection of intellectual property require them to concede a greater share of their textile and apparel markets to Third World producers. Or they may conclude that a limit on the rate of import penetration is consistent with productivity, domestic employment needs, and stabilization of the world textile trade. MFA could evolve toward more liberal trade. But a revised MFA is not the same thing as totally laissez-faire free trade in textiles and apparel, and it is likely to be more efficient than the alternative prospect of mutually ruinous competition, diminished investment in productivity, and stagnant wages.

The complex of apparel, textiles, and textile-making machinery is also a good illustration of the "food chain" analogy in trade. Textiles are, of course, an input in clothing. Because other nations are rather more mercantilist than the United States, few apparel producers in the Orient import U.S.-made textiles; they buy locally. As a result, if the United States continues to lose its domestic apparel industry, it could well lose more of its textile industry, too. It has already lost most of its textile machinery industry, to Germany, Austria, and Japan. Significantly, Germany, with the world's highest wage rates, is able to compete effectively in the market for production machinery because its engineering excellence and productivity are even higher than its wages. If an industry like textile machinery production is lost, it is likely to stay lost, because of the high costs of reentry and the Krugman-type cumulative knowledge that existing producers keep refining.

In 1988, one large U.S. textile producer, the Milliken Company, concerned by mounting imports, organized a computerized "quick response" system. The idea was to capitalize on the U.S. lead in computer software by designing a computerized inventory system that would link a retailer, an apparel manufacturer, and the textile producer. This would enable a retailer to avoid carrying expensive inventories. Rather, the textile producer and the apparel maker could keep track of the retailer's inventory and produce to order in fairly small batches. The retailer could order products by style, color, size, etc., with a total production and shipping time as short as two weeks. This strategy would maximize a natural competitive advantage of having the manufacturer close to the end consumer market and persuade retailers to "buy American," since retailers typically buy from low-wage producers in the Orient an entire season in advance; what is gained in low wholesale prices may be lost in unsold merchandise. But consider for a moment this kind of collaboration between American retailers, textile producers, and apparel makers from the perspective of free-trade theory. Is it "mercantilist"? In a sense, it certainly is, for the aim is to retain and expand U.S.-based industry. But the question is nearly meaningless, for the exercise obviously increases efficiency. Mainly, it takes a leaf from the Japanese book, by inventing a U.S. version of Japan's famed "just in time" inventory system and tightening the links between suppliers of components, producers, and end users—all in order to retain a market. "Free trade" and "mercantilism" are just not very helpful concepts in explaining what is going on.

*Steel.* Depending on one's choice of lens, you can see the U.S. steel industry either as suffering from a bungled managed-trade regime or as crying out for more managed trade. Rightly or wrongly, most large nations have decided that a domestic steel industry is a good thing: it creates what economists call "externalities"—in this case, external benefits not captured in the narrow calculus of steel production. These include import substitution savings, advances in production technology, labor rents, and prestige. If completely free markets left to their own devices produce excess capacity, competitive overproduction, falling profits, and a pressure for cartelization, unorganized nation-by-nation mercantilism produces an even more extreme case of the same. What is important to realize is that our present trade regime in steel, such as it is, is the cumulative result of individual national mercantilist strategies and not a deliberate global system of managed trade.

As recently as 1975, world steel production and consumption were roughly in balance. New industrial powers like Japan, South Korea, and Brazil made massive investments in steel capacity. Established steel-producing nations in Western Europe defensively invested in modernizing their plant to meet the new competition. Virtually all this new steel capacity, with the exception of that in the United States, Canada, and West Germany, depended on national market-distorting subsidy programs—cheap loans, grants, wage subsidies, import restraints, recession cartels, and every other known form of mercantilism. At just about the time that some 40 million metric tons of new capacity were coming on line, recession and the twin oil-price shocks sharply reduced the demand for steel. A decade ago, world capacity was nearly double world output.

In Western Europe, which had had a common-market regime in steel since 1952, the European Community has had a common program of plant modernization, rationalization, and politically negotiated closings of outmoded facilities, attempting to spread the pain around. This politically allocated burden sharing meant that the industry did not necessarily migrate to the most efficient producers, even though EC steelmaking as a whole grew more productive. The EC also used price controls, allocation of market shares, and import controls. Between 1980 and 1985, steel subsidies in the EC exceeded $35 billion. These subsidies, which had no counterpart in the U.S. steel industry, forced U.S.-made steel to compete with artificially cheap steel produced overseas. Other steelmaking nations—Japan, Brazil, Korea—typically dealt with their excess capacity by excluding imports, dumping exports, and cartelizing their domestic production.

Domestic overcapacity and cartelization produces pressure to dump excess steel, since the per-unit cost depends heavily on how much capacity is or is not idle. Unlike textiles, steel is "price-inelastic": if one producer lowers his price, that merely shifts his market share; it doesn't increase overall demand. And unlike textiles, steel production requires extremely expensive and long-lived plant and equipment. The market for steel is slower to equilibrate shifts in supply and demand—that old devil time again—and adjusts even more slowly when governments contribute subsidies.

Subsidies in the steel industry are notoriously difficult to measure. Though the United States disdains any kind of industrial policy for steel, or any systematic effort to rationalize steelmaking capacity, it nonetheless has a chaotic assortment of what must be counted as subsidies. These include investment tax credits, worker retraining schemes, as well as pension-fund bailouts by the government and bankruptcy reorganizations with payoffs at so many cents on the dollar that occur when firms go broke.

During the past decades, the only steelmaking nation open to substantial imports was the United States. Its position was perfectly consistent with its hegemonic imperative to confer the benefits of open import markets on its trading partners, however mercantilist their own practices. It also comported with the prevailing American ideology of free trade. In their accounts of the increasingly uncompetitive position of American steel, economists and editorial writers gave attention to the high wages paid to American steelworkers and the poor capital-investment decisions of American managers. Foreign mercantilism and the risks of losing an industry as basic as steel were considered minor issues. The Old View of Ricardian trade theory said that if foreign nations were stupid enough to subsidize their steel shipments to us, we should gratefully accept the gift, regardless of the long-term consequences and costs.

The remedy sanctioned by both GATT law and domestic trade law—antidumping cases—made the American government uneasy for the political reasons we have already examined. This is another aspect of the burdens of hegemony (uneasy lies the head that wears the hegemonic crown): if membership in the U.S.-sponsored GATT system is cajoled rather than coerced, then American administrations will go to great lengths to avoid resorting to remedies that provoke intra-alliance conflict. The European Community, abjuring both hegemonic perquisites and responsibilities, was far more willing to impose antidumping remedies.

Instead, the United States embarked on a series of halfhearted measures attempting to reconcile some import restraint with marketlike principles and respect for the formal norms of the GATT. The first of these was the ill-starred "trigger price mechanism" initiated during the Carter administration, which regulated steel imports according to a pricing formula supposedly based on the unsubsidized Japanese cost of production. This, however, let Western European steelmakers dump steel at the Japanese price, below their own, created a glut on U.S. markets, and failed to slow the accelerating imports. Eventually, after several false starts, it fell to the free-market Reagan administration to impose a quota regime, characteristically disguised as "Voluntary" Export Restraints (VERs).

Prodded by Congress, the administration insisted that the profits earned from the system must go into plant modernization. The domestic industry, underpriced for a decade, turned profitable in 1987 and even more so in 1988. Steel capacity was reduced from about 144 million metric tons in 1977 to about 73 million metric tons in 1987. The remaining capacity is now among the world's most productive. At current exchange rates, the United States can produce cheaper steel than Japan. Yet characteristically this combination of managed-trade regime and minimalist industrial policy was depicted not as something sensible in its own right, or even as a necessary adjustment to the cartelization of the world steel industry, but as a scandalous and GATT-defying capitulation to a special-interest group.

American policy cannot address the success or failure of VERs for steel without candidly considering some nettlesome questions. What is our long-term goal both for our steel industry and for the world trading system as it involves steel? The orthodox view is that the "protectionist" remedy—in this case VERs—never should have been used at all and should now be phased out as quickly as possible. But obviously, as long as immense steel overcapacity exists and most countries are willing to keep dumping their steel, open U.S. markets are not compatible with the goal of retaining a domestic integrated carbon-steel industry, if that is indeed our goal. In advocating unilateral free trade in steel the implicit industrial goal is the ultimate disappearance of much of America's steel industry. The missing policy debate here is not so much about free trade versus managed trade (since managed trade is what most of the world has), but whether or not the United States should maintain and develop the capacity to make basic steel at state-of-the-art productivity.

The claim that we should simply allow subsidized producers to supply our steel ignores the time-tested double-edged nature of cartels. A cartel that can dump can also gouge. A quasi-managed regime has the virtue of protecting domestic steel consumers (and producers) both against cyclical swings in price and against the price gouging that can occur when suppliers are a foreign cartel.

American diplomats have insisted that the VER regime is a regrettable, temporary expedient and that the ideal solution would be a mutual agreement to swear off subsidies and import restraints; in the meantime, the United States should try to set a good example and keep its markets more open than those of other nations—the hegemonic sacrifice. But why, if other nations almost unanimously have "voted with their feet" to have mercantilist policies for steel, should it fall to the United States to purify the world and to begin by giving up much of its own steel industry? Why should the United States expend scarce diplomatic capital—and real capital as well—to propagate laissez-faire steelmaking to a skeptical world?

The real problem with the current trade regime for steel is that, unlike MFA, it is not really a regime at all. Most nations subsidize, protect, and dump excess steel where they can, with no set of norms or rules. If the rest of the world isn't buying America's brand of laissez-faire, perhaps a more coherent and reciprocal managed-trade regime is advisable. The United States VER regime currently allows an import penetration level of about 20 percent. That is sufficient to provide imports to safeguard against domestic bottlenecks; in addition, the government allows "short supply" petitions, by which steel users can circumvent the import quotas when a particular product is unavailable domestically.

One possible alternative regime would require nations that wish to retain domestic steelmaking to concede a share of their domestic market to open import competition and to agree to a common program for the gradual reduction of subsidies and excess capacities. If the import-penetration level were set at 25 percent, say, the quotas could be auctioned by the importing nation and the quota receipts used to subsidize capacity phase-out and worker retraining. A world goal might be to restore steel capacity to its historical level of 125 percent of average production. Each country would be assured of its ability to supply most of its own steel needs and could pursue its own policies for promoting domestic competitiveness. The benchmark world capacity goal would allow enough steelmaking capacity to give each member country the imported steel that it needed. Import competition would keep pressure on domestic firms to keep their facilities modern and productive. Nations wishing a more laissez-faire approach could raise their import quotas whenever domestic supplies grew tight or profits became supernormal. The most productive steelmaking nations would capture the lion's share of the export markets.

Most importantly, all participating nations would have to agree to the common program of 25 percent market opening and the gradual phase-out of subsidies and excess capacity. This program would not be "free trade," of course, but it would be a far more viable, efficient, and balanced system than the current one. It would also express what seems to be the clear preference of most major trading nations—near self-sufficiency in steel—and would enable them to pursue various domestic strategies. It would relieve the United States of its current Atlas-like chore—shouldering the entire burden of the gap between stated ideology and reality in steel.

This general approach also permits and encourages direct cross-border investment. If Japanese capital thinks Japan has the best steelmaking techniques, it can, of course, set up shop in Youngstown, Ohio, alone or in partnership with American firms. This puts the American steel industry under competitive pressure from Japanese technology and Japanese management, but without exporting steelmaking jobs to Japan.

To be sure, this regime would not be perfect. It would need continuous negotiation and refinement and would be complicated by the multiplicity of steel products and development of new ones. It would need to make room for other emerging nations that wish to join the steelmaking club. But if new entrants enjoy low costs and high productivity, then 25 percent of the steel consumption of steelmaking nations plus 75 to 100 percent of their own markets is a good market to compete for. New entrants, like old producers, would have to subscribe to the same rules of 75 percent domestic supply, 25 percent open competition for imports (perhaps poor nations could be permitted 85 or 90 percent domestic supply for a period of ten years).

Steel shows an important problem with the way that most Americans view the trading system. We believe in our hegemonic souls that agreeing to a stated set of norms falling short of pure free trade is sinful. Yet the proposed regime in steel, though a form of managed trade, would be substantially more marketlike than the present one. It would leave plenty of room for domestic competition as long as nations chose to enforce their antitrust laws. And it would benefit the American industry, since we are the only major industrial nation that is now a net importer of steel. Since our steel mills are now among the world's most productive, we could presumably compete for a share of newly opened foreign markets. Since advanced production technology is portable and most trade does not reflect Ricardian comparative advantage, allocative efficiency does not require all nations to import their steel from the "most efficient nation"; what may matter more is that nations keep their seat at the steelmakers' table. This system would even allow Ricardian purists to gamble that Ricardo was right and throw their entire markets open.

The United States could use the familiar diplomatic ploy of offering access to our own market in order to pry other markets open, but stopping well short of trying to reorder the world according to the dictates of Ricardian trade. Here again, as in textiles, the systemic goal is freer trade, but not free trade. The paradox of our quixotic quest for free trade has been that it denied us freer trade. The American goals, for our own nation and also for a stable world system, should be, first, a balance of benefits and obligations, and second, some assurance that domestic industry will remain healthy and under competitive pressure to become ever more productive.

*Semiconductors.* The semiconductor industry offers yet another case—a dynamic industry with a rapidly evolving technology and only a few producer nations—and teaches some important lessons about the relationship between issues of free trade versus managed trade and bilateralism versus multilateralism. Consider the problems of the current bilateral U.S.-Japan semiconductor accord versus some hypothetical multilateral arrangement. U.S. semiconductor manufacturers complained that Japanese ones play by different rules. The Japanese goal is long-term growth, technological supremacy, and a gradual increase in market share. Although there was not much identifiable government subsidy in the traditional sense, there was clearly a coordinated strategy between government and industry. And since Japanese electronics and semiconductor manufacturers are integrated, Japanese firms had a market power not available to their U.S. competitors. U.S. firms argued that Japan was selling below cost both in the United States and in other markets. But dumping, as we have seen, is a phenomenon that must be understood in the dimension of time. Looked at over twenty years, the Japanese semiconductor strategy has been profitable indeed. Japan might have been selling below its cost this month or that year, but over time as its market share and technological leadership increased, the overall strategy allowed the industry to turn a substantial profit.

When earlier approaches failed and the American semiconductor industry suffered to the point where militarily defined national security concerns emerged, the United States at length put aside its ideological qualms about managed trade and negotiated a quasi-carteliztion. The Japanese pledged to cease selling semiconductors below cost in third markets and promised to set a 20 percent market-share target for U.S. exports to Japan. To date, neither promise has been kept. In the summer of 1989, the United States and Japan announced yet another agreement to fulfill previously broken promises. At this writing, the U.S. share of the semiconductor market in Japan is about 12 percent; Japan is still gaining in world market share, and the U.S. semiconductor producers are continuing to lose ground.

In any event, this attempted regime was also a clear violation of the GATT. Western Europe, the world's number-three producer of semiconductors, loudly and justifiably complained that it had been left out of the negotiations and that its semiconductor market was likely to become a virtual prisoner of Japanese industrial policy. Depending on market conditions, semiconductors exported from Japan to Western Europe would sometimes be "too cheap," which would undercut Western Europe's fledgling attempt to develop its own market, and would sometimes be "too expensive," which would disadvantage the users—European electronics manufacturers—by pricing their end products out of the market. Western Europe then defensively negotiated its own semiconductor deal with Japan.

The underlying problem is that one major producer—Japan—is cartelized, while a second, the EC, uses subsidies and managed trade policies to build its industries, but there is no coherent set of ground rules to govern what is plainly other than free trade. Japanese producers have characteristically varied their prices more or less in unison, with guidance from MITI, in order to defend and expand Japan's overall market position. The semiconductor industry is highly cyclical. When the industry has been in glut, Japanese producers, all part of huge industrial groups, have continued to increase production capacity and drop prices, absorbing temporary losses as part of a long-term strategy to gain a commanding position. American producers, usually smaller and more entrepreneurial companies, have not had such deep pockets or such long-range time horizons. (IBM is in a special category, since it produces semiconductors for its own use.) During the phase of the cycle when chips are in scarce supply, Japanese firms have been quick to raise prices at the expense of their U.S. customers. After the 1986 Semiconductor Trade Agreement, committing Japan to buy more U.S.-made chips and to cease dumping in third-country markets, semiconductors suddenly went into short supply in 1987, prompting cries of anguish from U.S. purchasers of semiconductors. This is, of course, the problem when a domestic industry is dependent on a cartelized foreign supplier. As in steel, a cartel can pursue predatory pricing to drive out its competitors—and, once dominant, can turn around and gouge its captive customers.

Computer companies, the principal customers of the semiconductor industry, have been ambivalent about the Japanese. On the one hand, they are eager to maintain cordial relations with an important source of supply and are pleased when Japanese semiconductor makers engage in one of their periodic bouts of price-cutting. On the other hand, whenever the Japanese cartel takes advantage of scarcity and begins price-gouging, they suddenly turn patriotic and begin worrying about the health of the U.S. semiconductor industry. In 1989, the computer industry was on the verge of capitalizing a joint venture called U.S. Memories, intended to put the United States back into the memory-chip business. Mysteriously, the Japanese reverted for a time to price-cutting, and U.S. computer makers decided that they didn't need American-made memory chips after all. Japanese prices subsequently rose yet again.

The general American antipathy toward anything smacking of industrial policy has led to serious confusion with respect to a national strategy on semiconductors. Historically, the large military demand for ever more advanced semiconductors operated as a "demand-side" policy that guaranteed the embryonic industry a market. The armed forces also provided a supply-side industrial policy with their research and development funds. The Sematech consortium was permitted government funds only on national security grounds—not because it could be admitted that the United States needed a commercially viable semiconductor industry, for that would violate conventional views about free trade. The government has had its nose rubbed in these contradictions when it discreetly discouraged a Japanese purchase of Perkin-Elmer's semiconductor fabrication business;

Pentagon and Commerce Department officials concerned with the nation's "defense industrial base" were also dismayed when the Hercules Corporation decided to sell its Semi-gas subsidiary to Nippon Senso of Japan. Semi-gas, a small entrepreneurial firm that had been bought by Hercules only three years before, is the world's largest producer of equipment used to purify the air during the production of silicon chips. It is one of more than one hundred companies that supply the fourteen original members of Sematech, and it benefited from Sematech's research program.

The 1988 Trade Act created a government Committee on Foreign Investment in the U.S. (CFIUS), empowered to block acquisitions deemed to be not in the national interest. But the Bush Administration has refused to use CFIUS as intended. It declined to veto the Semi-gas deal, and, out of more than four hundred cases reviewed since 1988, it has blocked just one purchase—a proposed Chinese acquisition of a Seattle aircraft parts producer—and that was stopped not on grounds of either competitiveness or national security but as a mild sanction against the Tiananmen Square massacre. In all, CFIUS has refused to block some thirty foreign purchases of U.S. semiconductor makers.[17]

Thus, our prevailing ideology paralyzes our ability to determine, let alone act in, the national interest where semiconductors are concerned. On the one hand, public policy supports research and development, ostensibly because the Pentagon deems it necessary to retain U.S. semiconductor capability. The administration even resorted to a managed-trade remedy, because that seemed the only way for Japanese and American business practices to "mesh" in a manner that would in this instance limit the effects of Japan's chronic mercantilism and allow U.S. firms to capture market share that they had earned. Yet, because of its prevailing doctrine of laissez-faire, the administration is unwilling to review foreign purchases, or to take a position on whether it matters when key firms or key technologies pass under foreign control, or even to use its leverage to negotiate equitable technology-transfer agreements. All of this amuses and baffles the Japanese, who do not leave such matters to the invisible hand.

Until the American government (and prevailing economic theory) grasps this nettle, it will be impossible for us to have a coherent trade or technology policy, and our industrial fate will be captive to other nations' industrial policies.

There seems to be a case for a managed-trade arrangement in semiconductors, assuring nations that want to develop semiconductor industries dominance in their own markets, while allowing residual competition domestically and in third markets. But the semiconductor case presents yet another problem. Unlike steel and textiles, which are produced worldwide, there are only two major semiconductor producers—the United States and

Japan—and an emerging third one in the European Community. There-fore, most third-country markets would be 100 percent open to exports, even under a managed-trade regime. However, if Japan has a fundamen-tally different long-term strategy than the United States—relentless price cutting in order to gain market share—it will gradually capture most of these third-country markets in ways that the United States and perhaps the EC consider illegitimate. This effectively gives the latter the choice of either ceding markets or fighting fire with fire, leading to the familiar pattern of subsidy wars, excess capacity, widespread dumping, and staggering losses.

This is a problem whether the rules and the trading system are ostensi-bly liberal or managed; in fact, though the present "management" of semiconductor trade is incoherent and asymmetrical, it is plainly some-thing other than liberal. Again, the problem is surely more soluble if the management is explicit rather than covert and guilt-ridden, since it is easier to enforce accountability multilaterally and with a system of explicit rules. A multilateral semiconductor accord would have to include rules for fair and unfair pricing and subsidy—something akin to a shared understanding of the principles of antitrust. The alternative is to cartelize semiconductor markets worldwide, which is surely a third best, if that. A managed-trade regime in semiconductors, as in steel, might assure each major producing nation a large share of its own market, allow free competition for the remainder, and require a common understanding of antitrust principles and predatory pricing.

This review of three industries suggests that where nations want to retain domestic production capacity and not cede their entire market to foreign suppliers, it is possible to design relatively liberal and balanced managed-trade regimes: not free trade, but freer trade. Several caveats are in order. First, there is not one template that fits all industries. In textiles and apparel, the "threat" to OECD producers is from low-wage, newly industrializing countries; the risk of future worldwide excess capacity is tempered by the fact that "capacity"—a garment shop—is not as expensive or long-lived as a steel mill. Moreover, there is plenty of competition among advanced nations to keep competitive pressure on each other, and no reason to cartelize. A regime based on limiting the total rate of increase of imports has been moderately successful—though it produces far more "leakage" than any domestic industry wants. In steel, on the other hand, the problem is worldwide subsidy and overcapacity, coupled with a near-universal desire to retain domestic steelmaking facilities. The present non-regime is a series of purely tactical expedients, and the remedy may be a more explicit managed regime based on market shares. In semiconductors, though a reciprocal import-share regime would solve problems in the home economies of producer nations, it would require a whole other set of negotiated common principles to establish norms of behavior in third-country markets.

The suitability of managed-trade regimes in some products does not mean that the world needs or wants a generic system of managed trade. Ideally, the norm should be roughly that of the GATT—relatively liberal trade, based on the familiar principles of multilateral most-favored-nation, nondiscrimination, national treatment, with limited tolerance for market-distorting subsidies, quotas, and market-closing devices. The reason that a GATT-like system should be the norm is that it is simpler and cleaner (though, as the long, complex history of dumping disputes attests, it is not nearly so simple or clean as its defenders claim).

Even if a liberal-trade regime is the residual norm, however, it is very clear that some key nations do not want such a regime in some key products. Nor is it clear that a departure from liberal norms concerning those products need harm allocative efficiency. Indeed, it may bring benefits, if overcapacity and glut can be frankly addressed, negotiated, and resolved (as it apparently has been in textiles).

How does one choose which products are candidates for a managed-trade regime? The most logical place to look is those products where nations are currently restraining trade and for one reason or another wish to retain or develop technological and production capacity. If there is widespread reluctance to observe the norms of liberal trade, a frankly acknowledged managed-trade regime, with a balance of benefits as the core principle, is vastly preferable to the current patchwork of subterfuges and imbalance concessions. If at some point the members of the GATT wish to shift their managed-trade regime in, say, wheat to relatively freer trade, that is, of course, their prerogative.

A balance of benefits is also a better way to reconcile the many domestic economic interventions all over the world with equity and comity in the trading system as a whole. Simply countervailing other nations' subsidy or market-closing policies is no solution. In a new industry, say high-definition television, where each major region wishes to acquire production capacity, a balance-of-benefits approach could calculate and negotiate limits on the total amount of subsidy. Nations that wanted their products to be freely marketed would have to abide by those limits. Alternatively, in a sector in which nations had fairly mercantilist goals, they could follow the formula outlined above for steel, where a portion of each domestic market could be reserved for domestic suppliers, the rest available for imports, perhaps with auctioned quotas. If trading nations eventually wearied of ruinous subsidy wars as the industry matured, further reciprocal reductions in subsidies could be negotiated.

The recent U.S. position on farm trade is a splendid illustration of the best being the enemy of the good when it comes to reciprocal reduction of subsidy and oversupply. In the October 1988 Montreal "midterm review" of the GATT round, EC ministers urged the United States to pursue a gradual program of reciprocal reduction of farm subsidies, with some tolerance for supply and price management and a mutual respect for historic regional export markets. The United States took the position that it would agree to this interim approach only if Western Europe joined it in a grandiose commitment to absolutely free trade in agriculture by the year 2000. The Western Europeans rightly saw this as a cynical maneuver which the U.S. delegation contrived in order to seem absolutely devoted to the freest possible trade while winking to domestic farm interests that no capitulation was genuinely contemplated. The predictable result was impasse. Even the nations that are the lowest-cost producers and the most committed to a liberal trade in agriculture, such as Canada and Australia, shared the EC view that partially managed trade in farm products was the only conceivable route toward freer trade. In late 1990, the GATT round was dangerously close to collapsing, thanks to the ultra-laissez-faire position of the United States on agriculture.

The point here is that free traders need to understand that partially managed trade can be the way to have freer and more sustainable trade, as well as a more balanced and sustainable role for the United States in the global system. Note also that this approach would inject more multilateralism into the trading system. At present, the ideal of "multilateralism" is yoked to the ideal of "liberalism," for both historical and ideological reasons. But these two ideals are logically separable. It is possible to have a trading regime that is slightly less liberal (in that it tolerates economic development subsidies and some explicitly managed trade), but more genuinely multilateral than the present system, in which hidden bilateral side deals do real harm both to the multilateral norms and to the flow of commerce.

What about the question of overall balance in the trading system? Here, we must learn to view nations with chronic trade surpluses as free riders. When a nation runs a chronic surplus, it produces more goods than it consumes. That allows it to enjoy the benefits of a rather tight fiscal and monetary policy—low rates of interest and inflation—without suffering from high unemployment, because the unemployment is exported. Domestic industry has lower capital costs than its competitors, and this is likely to lead to more productivity growth, which exacerbates the imbalance. Surplus nations are a source of exported austerity; they force other nations to depress demand to reduce their imbalances.

Keynes had the right answer. Incentives should be structured into the international monetary and trading systems to encourage surplus nations to expand both their economies and their markets for imports. One approach would be to "tax" nations with chronic surpluses and to have the tax capitalize Third World development and refinancing funds. Section 301 of the 1988 Trade Act required the administration to identify nations with unfair trade practices and to negotiate remedies. Although this forced a reluctant administration to make trade reciprocity a higher priority, the skeptics were right to be wary of it, because this approach makes the United States the aggrieved party, when in fact the aggrieved party ought to be the trading system as a whole. Here again, if the United States can let go of the idea that the trading system is its special responsibility and that the only defensible rules for that system are Ricardian ones, then, paradoxically, it will be in a better position to bargain for system-wide reciprocity, based on the principles of roughly balanced benefits and roughly balanced trading accounts. The European Community proposed something like this standard for the Uruguay Round, but the United States rejected it as smacking too much of managed trade.

With a balance-of-benefits approach, there are several tests of whether a given nation is playing fair. Over time, it must have an overall rough balance in its trade accounts. If it is a party to a specific managed-trade arrangement, it must honor it. And its overall pattern of departures from free trade—market closings, subsidies, cartels, etc.—must not exceed some negotiated norm. If this approach were elevated to system-wide accountability rather than nation-by-nation retaliation, that would be a real gain for multilateralism. If, for example, Japan is party to a steel arrangement that requires it to open 25 percent of its markets to steel imports and it fails to comply, there should be some automatic consequence imposed by the GATT and not by the U.S. government. (One logical consequence could be that other nations would close their 25 percent import markets to Japanese steel.) And selectively managed trade would still provide the benefits of fairly open commerce and competition.

What would be the U.S. national interest in such a system? By recognizing that managed trade is sometimes the best available option, the United States would be able to better differentiate short-term tactical maneuvers from long-term strategic economic goals. Because of its devotion to the GATT, the United States typically regards all departures from liberal trade as short-term tactical expedients, to be given up unilaterally as soon as possible. But if managed trade in key industries is legitimate, we become much freer to press our trading partners—not simply to practice laissez-faire in their own economies (our traditional diplomatic goal) but to bring a balance of obligations and benefits to the trading system. We are also freed to define industrial goals for our own domestic economy and strategies for carrying them out. That, incidentally, might or might not dictate targeted industrial policies in any given sector. Under a managed-trade regime for semiconductors, we might choose to subsidize semiconductor research and development via a joint industry-government consortium such as the current Sematech consortium of major semiconductor producers, in which government matches industry research contributions. In the case of steel, we might decide that holding foreign subsidized steel to a 25 percent market share is sufficient to allow a renaissance in American steel through free-market principles, with only a reinvestment quid pro quo and some retraining aid as minimalist industrial policies.

In sum, free trade has been the enemy of freer trade. In a world where most nations recognize that the state needs to be involved in the private economy, the United States is odd man out. An immense amount of trade expansion and efficient wealth-creation has taken place in nations that, by Ricardian lights, are appallingly mercantilist. Our misperception about how their economies actually work, and how to interact with them, has done untold damage to our economy and to the harmony of the world trading system.

In a future GATT round, the United States should bring a wholly different set of goals to the table: ever more laissez-faire trade should not be one of them. Rather, we should work toward a system based on a balance of benefits and responsibilities for the major trading nations; a stronger GATT with real judicial powers; a common, system-wide understanding of what constitutes predatory pricing and dumping; a universal code of intellectual property rights; a tolerance for diverse strategies of economic development, including acceptance of targeted development strategies for developing nations rather than attempting to convert them to laissez-faire; and penalties on rich nations that run chronic trade surpluses. If American diplomats insist that multilateral rules require laissez-faire rules, they are likely to lose both, to the detriment of both the trading system and the well-being of the United States.

Albert O. Hirschman, one of the world's great eclectic economic thinkers, once wrote: "International trade remains a political act whether it takes place under a system of free trade protection, of state trading or private enterprise, of most-favored-nation clause or discriminating treatments."[18] In the absence of a world government, cross-border trade is always subject to rules that must be policitally negotiated among nations that are sovereign in their own realm but not outside their borders. Those who find that reality an affront to an idealized sense of allocative efficiency are obliged to offer a practical case for regional political integration, if not for world government. If world government seems a utopian conceit, a regime of pure Ricardian trade across national frontiers is all the more radically utopian.

# five

# NICHIBEI: THE TRILLION-DOLLAR MISUNDERSTANDING

Nowhere is the American confusion between its goals for the trade system and its military and economic goals as a nation more extreme than in the case of its complex relationship with Japan. The relationship is called *Nichibei* in Japanese, a contraction of the words *Nihon,* Japan, and *Beikoku,* the Japanese word for America, which literally translates as "Rice Country." Beikoku has nothing to do with rice; the word is derived from a kanji character that in Chinese also happens to mean rice, which to the Chinese signals rich country. The pun is unintentionally ironic, since rice is one of many products that Japan refuses to import from the United States. It is also fitting, since wealthy Japanese view America as a vast, cheap, provincial, potentially productive but somewhat confused land to be organized and exploited—a rice country. As I am writing these words, the morning paper brings a report that an official of the Japanese Agriculture Ministry politely but firmly instructed U.S. officials to remove about five pounds of U.S.-grown rice that was on display in an international food exhibition in the Tokyo suburb of Makuhari. Foreign rice, even five pounds of it, violates Japan's Food Control Law.[1] When Japan and the United States at last made headway in negotiations aimed at getting the former to agree to buy more American beef, American cattlemen looked forward to increasing their exports. Instead, Japanese interests began buying American ranches. When Japan needed more lumber, Japanese companies bought entire American forests. The one import that Japan truly needs is land. A rice country indeed.

For forty-five years, the United States has been Japan's biggest customer as well as its military protector, and Nichibei has been a central preoccupation of Japanese foreign policy. To the Japanese, Nichibei is primarily an economic question. But during the Cold War, U.S.-Japan economic relations were an afterthought in America's strategic thinking, and they are still plagued with terrible confusions of ideology and misplaced national priorities. U.S.-Japan relations are the signal manifestation of the American hegemonic disease—the twin assumptions that military concerns outweigh economic ones and that laissez-faire is a reasonable description of or prescription for how economies operate. Given the United States' new financial dependence on Japan, which I shall examine in this chapter, Japan's dependence on trade with the rest of the world, and the new uncertainty about what the shape of post-Cold War international relations will be, there is no more important relationship for world stability than Nichibei. The abruptness of the shift in the relative financial standing of the United States and Japan is unprecedented in the history of the world. In 1980, the value of stocks traded on the New York stock exchange were almost double that of the Tokyo exchange; by 1990, the value of the Tokyo exchange was nearly triple that of Wall Street, and the Tokyo exchange equaled an incredible 60 percent of all the world's listed stocks. This represented not merely paper assets, for it gave Japan the power to buy real assets all over the world; in principle, by pledging collateral and leveraging the other 40 percent, Japan could buy the rest of world's industry and finance outright. That this has not occurred is due to Japan's administered restraint, not to the logic of Western-style market capitalism.

In the first phase of postwar U.S.-Japan relations, economics really didn't matter. The United States was a military superpower and commercial behemoth. Japan was a defeated Axis power, vulnerable geopolitically, stripped of military resources, dependent on the American protectorate and American markets, lacking in raw materials, reduced to exports of cheap textiles and transistors. Its political and economic system had been made over in the American image under the auspices of General MacArthur. Though Japan did have an unfortunate penchant for highly mercantilist and protectionist economic practices, these could be indulged, for Japan, now a loyal client state, was still recovering from the war.

Until the late 1970s, Japan was too poor and the United States too rich for the asymmetry in economic practices to matter much. But then "made in Japan" ceased being a synonym for "shoddy" and instead became a seal of quality in cameras, television sets, compact cars, steel, etc. And instead of demanding that Japan behave like the economic superpower it was becoming, Americans were indulgent. Diplomats continued to put military considerations first. Economists, using the usual deductive method, offered the following logic: We know that state planning and protectionism can only make things worse; it follows that even if Japanese policies appear to be protectionist, they must not be protectionist, for otherwise Japan would not be doing so well. If Japanese products are outselling American ones, they must have been destined to do so based on the law of comparative advantage, which it would be arrogant and futile to resist. Standard economics also insists that the determinants of trade balances are ultimately macroeconomic. If the United States has a public deficit of a certain size, a particular value of the dollar, and a shortage of private savings, it is likely to have a trade deficit, too. Given the disparity between Japanese and U.S. rates of savings and public deficit, if we pressured the Japanese to buy $10 billion worth of U.S. products, American consumers would only buy $10 billion in other imports. So according to standard economics, trade policy is powerless to help the trade imbalance. (This is nonsense when viewed from the perspective of the "New View," which recognizes the dynamic gains of trade.)

But while economists have debated whether mercantilism can produce gains, the Japanese continued to refine their remarkable system of managed capitalism and strategic trade. Entire libraries have been written on the relationship between Japan's economic and social systems. For the purposes of our discussion here, four essentials matter:

*Corporatism.* The Japanese, as Chalmers Johnson observed in his classic 1982 work, *MITI and the Japanese Miracle,*[2] have never believed in Adam Smith. Rather, "Japan can be located precisely in a line of descent from the German Historical School—sometimes labeled economic nationalism, *Handelspolitik,* or neomercantilism." This is, of course, the school of Friedrich List. Chalmers called Japan a "developmental state." The modern Japanese government is the descendant of the powerful ministries of the feudal shogun. Unlike American ones and like French ones, Japanese government agencies enjoy immense prestige and attract top-quality students in each year's graduating university classes. In Japan's very hierarchical system, the ablest students study at the most prestigious faculty of Japan's most prestigious university, namely the Faculty of Law at Tokyo University, and these graduates in turn enter the most prestigious ministries. It is hard for libertarian Americans to grasp that government bureaucrats may be among the most eminent and revered members of society, but this is the Japanese way. Ever since the Meiji Restoration of 1868, Japanese capitalism has been state-led. The Ministry of Agriculture and Commerce, organized in 1881, in the fourteenth year of the Restoration, is the forerunner of today's Ministry of International Trade and Industry; it established the goals, organized the cartels, and helped to assemble the capital. The Japanese government decided to work with and through private corporations, rather than sponsoring state-owned industry. "The government sold them its pilot plants, provided them with exclusive licenses and other privileges, and often provided them with part of their capital funds,"[3]

Johnson writes. Though ownership was private, development was based on cartelization rather than price competition.

Likewise, Japan's recovery from World War II was managed by the Japanese state and conducted along highly mercantilist lines. A voluminous literature recounts how MITI pursued critical technologies, restricted imports, and propelled Japanese industry into the technologies it regarded as critical: steel and autos in the 1960s, consumer electronics and computers in the 1970s, an entire range of advanced technologies in the 1980s. Within thirty years, Japan had ceased to be a catch-up economy, but it still acted like a developmental state. However, MITI is by no means a Soviet-style "Gosplan." It tends to operate with a light touch and helps to manage consensual initiatives of private industry. That state-led capitalism coexists so well with efficient competition is attributable to Japanese cultural values.

*Group loyalty and mutual obligation.* Japan's most tenacious cultural values are rooted in loyalty to the group, whether the corporation, the family, or the nation as a whole. This produces a strong sense of comity and mutual obligation, a deference to hierarchy, as well as an insular sense of differentness. There is an entire genre of Japanese literature, *Nihonjin-ron,* about the uniqueness of Japan. The idea is deeply rooted that the Japanese are unique and in many ways superior—yet vulnerable to undesired foreign influences. In an almost feudal way, deference within the hierarchy is balanced and reinforced by a reciprocal responsibility on the part of the superior toward the subordinate. Much in Japanese society, including its business practices, is built on long-term relationships, which is Japan's way of delivering comity and dealing with its sense of vulnerability. In contrast, relationships with foreigners, who are not part of the social contract, tend to be expedient and contingent. As it turns out, these cultural traits mesh beautifully with the strategies of the developmental state. And the successes of the developmental state, in turn, allow Japanese industry to fulfill its mutual obligations to a complex network of suppliers, customers, and employees. Embracing genuine economic liberalism would undermine much of this logic, and though Japan ritually accepts the forms of laissez-faire, it necessarily resists the content.

*Capital markets and capital formation.* Although Japan is a fiercely capitalist country, it is not a market system in the same sense as the United States. Its capital markets are as different from ours as its product markets. Most corporate stock is never traded but is simply held for the long term by other corporations and banks. Investors live with extremely low rates of return, but the corollary is that Japanese industry has extremely low capital costs and spectacular long-term gains. Land use is heavily regulated, and land prices are astronomical. Japan, a relatively barren archipelago the size of California, is "worth" $14 trillion, or twice the entire United States. This high-priced real estate, in turn, collateralizes stock purchases and helps push up stock prices. Japanese investors, enriched from the stock boom, then bid up land prices even further. In an unregulated system, this would be a disastrous speculative bubble. But Japan is not a country where everything is for sale. There is no such thing as a hostile corporate takeover. Firms, rather than putting everything out for bid, prize long-term relationships with their customers and suppliers. This system, while very different from our own, manages to combine competitive discipline with institutional stability and has led to record rates of economic growth for four decades. Government policy, social structure, and custom have all stimulated prodigious rates of savings, through tax-free postal savings accounts, lump-sum bonus payments to workers, and other means. Japan's rather underdeveloped pension system and the extremely high cost of housing encourage people to save. So does the high price of consumer goods. Throughout the past decades, both GNP and real wages have increased prodigiously, but real wages have lagged behind the increase in output, giving manufacturers a competitive advantage.[4] Most interest rates have been tightly regulated; government bond issues are parceled out to underwriters rather than auctioned, which helps the government to discipline investment houses and hold down rates. Certain speculative maneuvers, such as computerized program and stock options trading, have been prohibited or discouraged. Until very recently, foreign stockbrokers and banks had only limited operations in the Tokyo money market, and there were equally tight controls on the ability of Japanese investors to send yen overseas.

*One-way internationalization.* Ever since 1853, when Commodore Perry attempted to "open" Japan to Western trade on Western terms (and failed), the Japanese have been astute at accepting certain forms of Western economics and fruits of Western technology while retaining their own distinct essence, and autonomy. Between 1951 and 1983, Japanese corporations have skimmed off the cream of Western technology at a total estimated cost of $17 billion in licensing fees.[5] They have done this by refusing to let foreign corporations operate in Japan unless they worked through joint ventures with Japanese partners, or licensed technology to the Japanese, or both. Technology was imported, but products by and large were not. Typically, Japan refused to import products deemed threatening to infant Japanese industries, and instead learned to make their own, importing only what could not be produced domestically or what had to be imported in order to learn the desired technology. This was an explicit national policy but not a centrally administered plan.

This history and cultural tradition has led to a form of capitalism that is radically different from that practiced in the West. The deeply Japanese desire for harmony and reciprocity allows Japan to derive most of the benefits, but bear few of the costs, normally associated with cartelization and management of markets. Cartelization and shared monopoly, in the Japanese cultural context, do not lead to price gouging and inefficiency, as they do in the individualist West. The Japanese adroitly use research cartels to develop new technologies and "recession cartels" to cut back overproduction and maintain prices during periods of slack demand. They tolerate fierce price cutting when an industry is seeking global market share, but MITI tenders "administrative guidance" whenever "market confusion," which is to say cutthroat competition, threatens the harmonious domestic market.

When the American occupation of Japan came to an end in 1949—after ostensibly making Japan into a liberal democracy—many Americans mistakenly assumed that Japan's institutions were now carbon copies of our own. But most American transplants were subtly resisted in the usual Japanese manner. For example, the U.S. occupation exported a body of antitrust law, which was duly enacted—and duly ignored. The occupation broke up Japan's prewar industrial groups, the famed *zaibatsu,* as relics of 1930s corporatist militarism, but after a decent interval Japan's industrial-banking combines regrouped as postwar *keiretsu.*

It is a grave mistake to view Japan as a centrally planned economy. Its coherence is, rather, the result of consensual discussion and bargaining among industry and government; Japanese competitors innovate and compete fiercely with one another—though not on the simple basis of price.

The nature of Japan's "differentness" and the necessary remedy, if any, has been hotly debated in the West. Roughly, the typical debate pits orthodox macroeconomists and the diplomatic establishment against structuralist economists and scholars of Japanese history and society. The second group examines in detail how Japan actually works. The first group derives its notions about Japan from building models and making deductions. It emphasizes that Japan is different in ways that validate standard economics. The country has a virtuously high rate of savings; consumers are paragons of self-denial; workers put in long hours and are meticulously productive; unions are docile and employees are loyal to the firm. If only Americans saved as much and worked as hard! Since the orthodox school assumes that Adam Smith rules of standard Western economic theory apply worldwide, it tends to minimize or ignore the structural, cultural, and policy differences, most of which violate standard Western conceptions of how efficient markets must operate.

The second group, which I find more persuasive, doesn't deny the importance of high savings rates and productive workers, but it insists that these must be understood not as the products of laissez-faire markets but rather as the fruits of a very different social and industrial structure, government, culture, and conception of capitalism. Japan's docile unions, for example, cannot be understood without their reciprocal counterpart— namely, the quasi-feudal corporations, which seldom lay off workers and maintain much narrower pay differentials than their U.S. counterparts. High savings rates and lifelong training reflect deliberate public policy choices.

The debate is also about remedy. If Japan is essentially a market society rather like ours, whose members merely happen to save more and work harder, then the only "Japan problem" is that we are not so diligent as they. If, on the other hand, Japan's system of strategic "tribal bureaucratic capitalism," as the writer Murray Sayle has called it, works well within Japan but turns predatory when applied to Japan's trading partners, then the "Japan problem" is a severe one for the rest of the world.

American-style capitalism rewards entrepreneurship by allowing entrepreneurs to make a lot of money on successful innovation. If a firm takes a new product to market, for a period it enjoys supernormal profits ("rents"). Other firms eventually introduce substitute products, and the supernormal profits are competed away. But in the meantime, they are the source of the capital that finances further innovation. If one large trading partner, in this case Japan, blocks innovators from exploiting their advantage, it short-circuits this process. The Japanese do this in three ways: they deny access to their home market to American products; they use mercantilist means to acquire the most advanced U.S. technologies; and Japanese companies eager to grab market share in the world's largest and freest consumer market, the United States, use price-cutting techniques that are illegal under domestic law to drive away American competitors.

Short of conceding to Japan the entire advanced end of industrial production and gradually becoming its economic colony, there are only two possible remedies: either Japan must agree to make itself over in the Western image and run its economy and society according to principles of classical economic liberalism, or the United States must allow Japan to be Japan internally yet somehow devise a modus vivendi so that Japan ceases to derive lopsided benefit from the global trading system without bearing the proportional burden of maintaining it. The first remedy is wholly implausible; the Japanese have been successfully resisting Westernization for more than a century, and as they become stronger they become better able to resist external pressure. The second remedy is imaginable, though it is not the goal of current U.S. policy. Thus, we have an impasse in which Japan's trade surplus persists, America's deficit persists, Japanese mercantilism continues to push American firms out of manufacturing advanced products, and the capital flow equilibrates only because Japanese interests are acquiring American land, hotels, office buildings, and companies. Bad feelings are festering and the risk of a major Nichibei rift increases.

To be sure, Americans' low savings rate, our spotty educational and training system, our decaying infrastructure, the military bias in our government research and technology expenditures, our speculative capital markets, our dysfunctional system of labor-management relations, our corporate managers' short-run consciousness, and our ideological confusion about national security goals would be serious problems even if Japan did not exist. But the existence of Japan intensifies these problems.


When the American economist Mordechai Kreinin found himself with a sabbatical year in Melbourne, Australia, he realized that Australia was an ideal laboratory in which to compare the behavior of Japanese, European, and American multinational corporations. Here was a "third country" in which foreign industrial firms competed head to head, none of which had the advantage of playing on its home field.

American manufacturers competing in Japan, Kreinin observed, "continuously complain that the market is 'cornered' by their Japanese competitors, through a web of long-standing business relationships, and that it is difficult, if not impossible to penetrate this old boys' network."

> . . . the complaints are centered less on governmental restrictions and more on business and consumer practices, based on the domestic social environment and cultural tradition, that deny entry to foreign-made products. That may be compounded by informal administrative guidance from the government of Japan. Government officials and academics in Japan . . . tend to deny these claims. They maintain that the market is open; that it is the paucity of high-quality, competitively priced American (and other) products, and lack of sales initiative by American (and other) suppliers, that prevents penetration of their markets.[6]

Economists have trouble sorting out these claims and counterclaims. Doing their work in the usual way, by deductive inference, they devise a model specifying how much trade Japan "should have," given its structural characteristics; they then assess how much trade actually occurred, and attribute the discrepancy to some unfathomable discrimination. Unfortunately, this procedure gives divergent and inconclusive results. University of Michigan professor Gary Saxonhouse concludes that Japan's pattern of imports and exports is just about what one should expect. Brookings economist Robert Lawrence, using a different model with different assumptions, finds that Japan's imports of manufactured goods are about 40 percent lower than they "should" be.

In Australia, Kreinin did what few economists do: he got out of the office and began looking at actual commercial behavior. He interviewed executives of twenty Japanese, twenty-two American, and twenty European firms operating in Australia; his particular interest was how and from whom they procured capital machinery and equipment. Several notable differences were immediately evident. First, the American and European firms operated essentially as Australian companies; their senior managers were mostly Australian nationals. The Australian subsidiaries usually submitted annual capital budgets for approval to the parent companies. "Once approved, the subsidiary has complete freedom to operate within the budget," Kreinin found.[7] By contrast, Japan's Australian companies tended to be "tightly controlled by their respective parent company. Only one subsidiary is fully Australian managed." They might have Australian division managers, but invariably Japanese "advisers" with a direct pipeline to top management in Tokyo were in command.

Most interesting were the purchasing practices of Kreinin's sixty-two companies. Of the twenty-two American companies, sixteen bought their supplies from an evenly distributed array of companies of diverse nationality. Of the six who tended to buy mainly from one nation, only two bought exclusively from American suppliers. In other words, the American firms behaved pretty much the way the standard economic model would predict: they maximized their capital budget by purchasing from anybody and everybody on the basis of price and quality. Twenty-one out of twenty-two American companies put their prospective purchases of machinery out for bids. That is, a supplier who got business last year had no expectation of getting repeat business unless he continued to have the best product at the best price. "In no case did the country of origin play any role whatsoever in the purchase decision. Nor was it ever hinted or suggested by the parent company that preference should be given to American equipment."[8] The European firms mostly behaved in the same way. Eighteen of the twenty companies had no pattern in how they bought machinery and equipment. In the case of one West German and one Swedish company, the machines were purchased in, respectively, West Germany and Sweden; in the latter case, the machinery was highly specialized and produced mostly by the parent company. But in the case of the Japanese companies, fifteen out of twenty, including the biggest ones, purchased more than 80 percent of capital equipment and machinery from Japanese firms.

Comparing internal procedures, Kreinin found that where the American and European firms typically put their purchases out for international bids, the Japanese firms typically did not, but, rather, went to Japan, usually through the parent company, and bought Japanese supplies whenever they could. The prices were negotiated rather than arrived at after bids. In the rare case where a non-Japanese supplier tried to break in by offering a product with a lower price, the Japanese supplier usually matched the price to keep the business.

Kreinin's Japanese subjects gave several reasons for their seemingly "irrational" preference for buying Japanese rather than on the basis of price and quality. They cited the superiority of Japanese technology, the convenience of buying through the parent company, and in some cases the explicit provisions of joint-venture agreements (which the parent company had, of course, negotiated when coming to Australia) requiring the Australian subsidiary to buy Japanese. One interviewee told Kreinin that if his company tried to put an order out for bids, Western style, competing suppliers in Japan would simply agree on a negotiated price and divide up the business. The only Western nation whose behavior suggested a faint similarity to Japanese cartelization was, not surprisingly, West Germany.

The purchasing practices of Japanese subsidiaries in Australia make perfect sense in the Japanese culture. Intense consciousness of group loyalty and reciprocity make it natural to prefer to buy Japanese, unless there is literally no alternative. And the desirability of maintaining these cultural norms impels the Japanese to strive for preeminence in the entire range of manufactured goods. The ethos of maintaining long-term relationships suggests the value of doing a favor to a fellow Japanese firm, in the expectation that the favor will be returned. An entire vocabulary in Japanese suggests this social and commercial etiquette.

Where custom and social convention are not sufficient, the structure of Japanese business and banking helps to explain why the practices persist. Most major Japanese firms are part of industrial groups *(keiretsu)* anchored by major banks. These behemoth groups include Mitsui, Mitsubishi, Matsushita, Sumitomo, Sanwa, Fuyo, and Dai-Ichi Kangyo. New groups, organized along roughly similar lines, have emerged around successful industrial firms such as Hitachi and Toshiba. It only seems logical to the Japanese subsidiary of Mitsubishi in Australia to look to Mitsubishi for capital equipment and for parts. If Mitsubishi or one of its affiliates doesn't manufacture the desired product, another Japanese supplier surely does. By arranging to purchase it even if from an ostensible competitor, the parent company does a favor, and the company that gets the business incurs an obligation that will be repaid. Given all of these opportunities to offer favors and incur obligations, it makes little sense to give the business to foreigners so long as there is a Japanese alternative. Unless foreign customers or partners vigorously bargain for a bigger cut as a condition for doing business, this is likely to continue.

It is easy enough to see why this system makes sense to the Japanese. Most economists have a harder time understanding why it leads to an efficient outcome. But an extensive body of literature explains the institutional and structural reasons why an economy based on long-term, rather than contingent, relationships can produce equal or greater efficiency than a price-auction system.[9] If workers know their jobs are secure, it makes sense to be loyal to the firm's welfare for the long term. If firms know that employees have a lifetime commitment, it makes sense to invest heavily in their training. If firms that are part of an industrial/banking group know they are under no pressure to produce profits for the current quarter, they can plan rationally for the long term.

It is even harder for Western economists to grasp that long-term supplier-producer relationships, without constant price-auction bidding, can lead to efficient pricing. One intriguing concept, invented, ironically, by conservative American economists, helps to shed light on this conundrum. The concept, called "contestability theory," is used by conservative economists opposed to antitrust. In antitrust theory (a peculiarly American invention of the progressive era) antitrust laws are necessary to keep companies from using discriminatory pricing to drive out competitors, dominate markets, and then soak consumers. However, the conservative Chicago school has long argued that no monopolist can last very long because eventually a new competitor will come along and underprice him; public policy needn't worry about monopoly, because the free market, with its usual self-regulating genius, will purge the marketplace of monopolists. Contestability theory, in this connection, argues that a price-competitive market does not require an actual competitor, only the threat of a potential one; therefore antitrust laws are unnecessary. For example, if a single airline dominates a route, there is a limit to how much it can raise the price of the fare, because if it gets too greedy another airline will start flying the route with lower fares.

Contestability theory skips lightly over a few crucial details, such as the fact that there are barriers to free market entry for many products and an established monopolist can easily cut prices selectively to deter new entrants. But it does help explain Japan. Suppliers and purchasers with long-term relationships do not behave like American monopolists; they bargain fiercely over prices. The ultimate price may be just as efficient as one set by open bids, because both parties to the transaction have an ultimate recourse of taking their business elsewhere, even if they would rather not. The relationship may be long-term, but if one partner begins behaving greedily, it is contestable. In Kreinin's case study about Australia, "buying Japanese" did not mean buying from a producer charging a monopoly price. Indeed, the parent company had every incentive to negotiate the best price possible, because it was under pressure from its own Japanese competitors.

A study by the British sociologist Ronald Dore[10] looks at the same phenomenon of efficiency within long-term relationships in the Japanese textile industry. Dore distinguishes between "long-term trust relationships" and "arm's-length contractual relationships." His work suggests that Japan benefits from a socioeconomy of what he calls "flexible rigidity." Skeptics often point out that only about a third of Japan's workers have jobs in firms (usually large ones) that offer the security of genuine lifetime employment. Yet the structure of Japanese reciprocity covers other sectors as well. The textile industry suggests how the ethic of reciprocity extends far beyond the primary labor sector of large corporations.

In Dore's case study, the weaving industry is dominated by some 50,000 small enterprises, usually family concerns with only a few paid employees. These subcontractors exist in an almost feudal relationship with Japan's Big Nine spinners. The predictability of the relationships and the sharing of economic loss during slack periods create a network in which technology can be diffused and quality assured. The rigidity is in the long-term relationship, but the security it affords in turn allows flexibility in rapid adaptation and new techniques. This explains how a seemingly archaic cottage industry can manufacture goods so productively. Once again, this almost fanatic group orientation would break down if Japan were opened to free price competition from abroad, and this is why true liberalization has been so fiercely resisted—and why it could come only when Japanese firms dominate virtually every technology worth having.

Another not very well appreciated aspect of Japan's "free riding" on the world trading system is the Japanese policy of patent protection. Japan, generally renowned for efficient government administration, oddly keeps its Patent Office grossly understaffed. As a result, it typically takes six or seven years to win approval for a patent, compared with about eighteen months in the United States. Moreover, the patent application becomes a matter of public record eighteen months after the application is filed, whereas in the United States the application is kept secret until the patent is granted. Thus, filing a patent application in Japan is tantamount to inviting your competitors to examine your trade secrets. Since technology evolves very rapidly, the result is that non-Japanese companies often operate in Japan with virtually no patent protection. This helps persuade them to give up and license their proprietary technology or operate with Japanese partners. The Patent Office, incidentally, is a division of MITI, and the director of the Patent Office serves a two-year term, after which he moves on to another MITI job. Small wonder that patent policy is an adjunct of Japan's overall economic nationalism.

This lack of patent protection puts U.S. firms at a serious competitive disadvantage when they are technologically ahead of their Japanese competitors, such as in biotechnology. There have been cases where Japanese competitors essentially pirated technology from American biotech firms and reexported the products back to the U.S. market. According to Joseph Massey, the Assistant U.S. Trade Representative in charge of Japan policy, testifying before a Senate subcommittee,

> U.S. firms seeking patents in Japan in such high-technology fields as amorphous metals, advanced ceramics, and fiber optics report having had to wait as long as from ten years to more than 13 years for their key patents to be granted. Meanwhile, Japanese firms had developed their own, very similar, products and marketed them not only in Japan but in the United States and in third markets as well. . . . The original inventor of the technology ends up with an abbreviated duration of protection and with competitors who have learned and adapted and sometimes copied his technology and secured a substantial position in the market in it.[11]

Massey also testified that when a foreign firm files for a Japanese patent to protect a new technology, Japanese competitors often flood the Japanese patent office

> with a large number of applications so as to establish so many prior claims that the foreign competitor will be unable to exercise his own patents without having to get licenses from the Japanese competitors. The price for these licenses is usually that the foreign firm cross-license the Japanese competitors [that is, permit them to use the foreigner's new technology]. To do this, of course, is to give over the most important competitive advantage a foreign firm has in Japan, its proprietary technology.[12]

This form of technological nationalism allowed Japanese manufacturers in the late 1970s to gain access to American semiconductor technology, which was then far ahead of its Japanese counterpart. But firms like Motorola were able to operate in Japan only on condition that they license their technology to potential Japanese competitors.

Logically, one might conclude that Japanese producers operate under the same anticompetitive constraints of a weak patent system that invites a free-for-all of industrial piracy. But here the Japanese traditions of cartelization and administrative guidance take over and protect producers from mutually ruinous infringement. It is also noteworthy that the ratio of patents obtained in the United States by Japanese companies to patents obtained in Japan by U.S. companies has been steadily widening, and is now about four to one.[13]

There is an extensive literature on numerous other mechanisms, cultural, institutional, and regulatory, that have enabled Japan to resist manufactured imports. Clyde Prestowitz's 1988 book, *Trading Places,* is an encyclopedia of the subtle techniques, ranging from convoluted product certifications to retail-wholesale cartels to exclusion of foreign products by trade associations. (Oddly, however, some products that the Japanese do not deem strategic enjoy perfectly free entry. I heard the Japanese consul general in Boston give a solemn speech to a university audience boasting about the large U.S. market share in safety razors and fast food.) In 1989 and 1990, after a flush of enthusiasm about American firms being able at last to crack the Japanese market, many longtime U.S. companies in the Japanese market quietly sold out to Japanese partners or rivals. The barriers were simply too high.

In the last ten years, as both the U.S. trade deficit and Japan's financial and economic strength increased, a debate within the Reagan administration proceeded along the usual lines. On one side were the Commerce Department, concerned with helping U.S. industry; the USTR, familiar with Japanese negotiating habits; and some offices within the Pentagon and the National Security Council worried about America's industrial capacity in strategic products. On the opposite side, for the usual reasons, were Treasury, the State Department, the Council of Economic Advisers, and those in the national security establishment who give priority to a smooth military alliance.

In practice, America's Japan diplomacy oscillated between get-tough rhetoric, followed by Japanese promises to liberalize, and lengthy and usually inconclusive negotiations, after which essentially the same problems materialized in new form. The U.S. ambassador in Tokyo, former Senate Majority Leader Mike Mansfield, was warmly disposed toward the Japanese and determined to avoid frictions; he was known as a virtual second Japanese ambassador to the United States. Career experts in his embassy who favored a harder line on trade issues were effectively isolated. Meanwhile, the Japanese mounted a diplomatic and propaganda offensive to convince American public opinion that Japanese markets were really as open as American markets to anyone who cared to compete vigorously, and that most of the complaints boiled down either to American industrial inadequacy, to American failure to compete vigorously in unfamiliar foreign markets, or to racist Japan-bashing.

In the background was Congress, responsive to complaints from injured constituents, both industry and labor, yet uncertain of what was an ideologically appropriate doctrine or a tactically effective response. Democrats, for the most part, considered themselves good free traders; if an American industry was suffering, one had to be sure that the cause was genuine unfair trade practices and not merely its own poor management. In the 1963 Trade Expansion Act, liberal Democrats had been happy to give President Kennedy expanded negotiating authority to liberalize international markets in return for "trade adjustment assistance"—a kind of superunemployment insurance that would compensate displaced workers. (In the absence of long-term planning, most of the displaced workers took the money and ran; none of the multibillion-dollar outlay served to retrain them or to modernize plants. This was a laissez-faire compensatory remedy at its purest: "rational" workers would surely purchase the necessary skills training, the argument ran, and "rational" industry would find the necessary capital.) By 1981, with the Republicans in power, there was no trade adjustment assistance to be had, and the workers' vulnerability to displacement was one more factor in weakening the unions.

Liberals, long accustomed to criticizing corporate excess, were uneasy in supporting America's fattest corporations, and as good internationalists were equally queasy about attacking foreigners. Republicans, likewise, who believed in free markets even more passionately than Democrats, didn't know how to react to good, innovative Republican business leaders with valid complaints about predatory Japanese practices. By 1984, when the trade deficit with Japan approached $50 billion, congressional Democrats filed legislation proposing a 25 percent tariff surcharge against Japan and three other nations with large surpluses if the surpluses were not significantly reduced by 1986. The Reagan White House was appalled, and fought back on two fronts. Domestically, it moved to defeat any such legislation, but internationally, it used the threat of a mad-dog Congress to pry some concessions out of the Japanese, and the hard-liners within the administration were given more latitude to negotiate.

The relative hard-liners among America's trade negotiators seemed to make some modest headway. But as Senator Jack Danforth, the Senate's leading trade expert, was wont to observe: "Behind every door is another door." Opening Japan, as Commodore Perry and General MacArthur had found, was not simply a matter of passing a law. In one set of products where trade was ostensibly free—supercomputers, telecommunications satellites, semiconductors, and even some consumer electronics products such as pagers—the linkages within Japanese *keiretsu* made sure that the market share of foreign products was limited to specialty niches. In the semiconductor industry, U.S. producers managed a global market share of more than 50 percent, but in Japan it remained stuck around 10 percent, whether the yen was trading at 280 to the dollar or at 120. Plainly, something other than ordinary price competition was at work.

In another category of products, where Japan was a highly inefficient producer but Japanese notions of reciprocity required that the business be given to Japanese suppliers—rice, tobacco, beef, citrus products, and milled lumber—markets were simply closed. In other areas, where nations with cheap labor costs and advanced technologies could compete in Japanese markets on the basis of price—say, South Korean steel, autos, and ships—imports were flatly prohibited. Later, as Japan's producer networks expanded outward, Southeast Asia became a handy source of supply for electronics components for its multinational corporations. Cheap electronics products marketed by non-Japanese Asian sources, however, were hard to find in Japanese stores. Hyundai cars could not be bought in Japan. When an independent petroleum importer, Lion Petroleum, tried to sell retail gasoline in Japan, undercutting Japan's informal gas cartel, MITI told it to stop or face shutdown, citing no law or explicit policy, but simply asserting "administrative guidance" intended to prevent "confusion" (unrestrained price competition) in the marketplace.

On the eve of a summit meeting with Japanese Prime Minister Yasuhiro Nakasone in late 1984, Reagan's cabinet considered hardening the American position. Merely conferring rights was not sufficient to change behavior; the exercise required what lawyers call an "effects test." The Commerce Department and the USTR argued that the proof of progress had to be a measured increase in actual American sales in Japan. But the other cabinet departments and the Council of Economic Advisers objected: negotiating a particular market share would be embracing, rather than challenging, Japan's management of its markets. In the guise of promoting laissez-faire, America would be conspiring in a form of economic planning.

Instead, the United States concocted another round of talks aimed at exporting laissez-faire to Japan. It decided to concentrate on four sectors where U.S. products were widely held to be competitive: telecommunications, electronics, pharmaceutical/medical products, and forest products. The United States could press the Japanese to adopt fair rules; the free market would settle the outcomes. (The negotiations came to be known as the MOSS talks, standing for Market-Oriented, Sector-Specific.) The disjunction between Japanese and American commercial practices was paralleled in the negotiations, where issues were never quite engaged. The Americans projected their own national ethos of individualism, legalism, and laissez-faire onto Japan's subtle consensual accommodation, proceeding as if the task were simply one of finding the Japanese equivalent of the Federal Register and making the appropriate changes. The MOSS talks sought out protectionist needles in the Japanese haystack one by one.

But their dislike of any form of economic nationalism left America's negotiators at a profound disadvantage. The Commerce Department, for example, does not keep statistics on the market share of U.S.-based companies in Japan, for that might give aid and comfort to planners. Instead, it relies for this data on MITI! When I visited Japan to report on the MOSS negotiations in mid-1985, I was shocked to find that U.S. documents and cables about the MOSS talks were unclassified. You could simply drop by the U.S. embassy and find out our negotiating strategy, so low was the strategic priority assigned to trade. (Where military security is involved, in contrast, the Pentagon has been known to classify newspaper clippings.)

Cynics at the embassy said that MOSS stood for More Of the Same Stuff. A good illustration is telecommunications. The Nippon Telephone and Telegraph Company, formerly a state monopoly, was deregulated in April 1985. Shortly after, U.S. and Japanese negotiators triumphantly announced a reduction in the number of technical standards and other measures that were keeping U.S. makers of telecommunications out of the Japanese market. But NTT, which has relations dating back nearly a century with its favored suppliers, simply kept on buying Japanese. The MOSS negotiations in telecommunications produced a number of formalistic breakthroughs, and a few token, high-visibility purchases, but scant increase in market share for U.S. producers. Years later, the imbalance in telecommunications trade is as lopsided as ever.

In the spring of 1986, U.S. policy ostensibly changed again. The Cabinet Council on Economic Policy, chaired by Treasury Secretary James Baker, agreed to ask Japan to make specific commitments to become a major importer of manufactured goods. "U.S. to Take Radical Path on Japan Trade," headlined the *Wall Street Journal.*[14] New commitments were made. A blue-ribbon Japanese task force called on MITI to reverse its century-old priority and, instead of pumping out exports, to turn Japan into an "importing superpower." But this also turned out to be more of the same stuff.

Another instructive American initiative was a series of negotiations known as the yen-dollar talks. These talks, sponsored by Treasury Secretary Donald Regan, a former chairman of Merrill Lynch, were the financial counterpart of the MOSS talks. They pressed Japan to open its tightly regulated financial markets and to internationalize the yen. The United States had both ideological and practical reasons for pursuing yen liberalization. Ideologically, the closed Japanese capital markets affronted the doctrine of laissez-faire. As a Wall Street chief executive, Regan knew only too well just how closed was the Tokyo capital market, soon to be the world's largest. American commercial and investment bankers wanted a piece of the action. As I have already suggested, restrictions on the yen put inflationary pressures on the dollar, and some American officials were eager to see the yen become a reserve and transaction currency commensurate with Japan's economy. More practically, the United States needed Japan's surplus to finance its own escalating debt, leaving aside that the rising deficit was in part due to Japan's predation upon America. If the trade accounts had been in balance, there would have been far less need for inflows of Japanese capital.

The Americans thought the negotiations highly successful, but in reality the yen-dollar talks had the character of Br'er Rabbit's "Please don't fling me in the briar patch." The Japanese were not at all reluctant to see yen flow outward. Their immense surpluses had to go somewhere. Investing yen in American business would increase Japan's commercial reach and damp down U.S. protectionist pressures. The more that Japanese joint ventures were commingled with American production outposts, the harder it would be to tell "them" from "us." Likewise, Japan's huge stockbrokerages could become mighty global players overnight, and Japan was all too pleased to establish a presence on Wall Street. (Nomura, Japan's largest stockbrokerage, is bigger than the top eight U.S. firms put together.) The purchase of U.S. Treasury bonds would establish a new dimension of Nichibei co-dependency and make Americans think twice before "getting tough with Japan."

American yen-dollar negotiators convinced themselves that it was their pressure that had induced Japan to do something that it had wanted to do anyway. They couldn't understand why their counterparts negotiating *commercial* liberalization were having such a hard time. However, there was a very different aspect to the story: the Japanese, fully understanding the logic of their own system, were very slow to open the Tokyo capital market to full liberalization; foreign stockbrokers were allowed in, but they got only crumbs, and whole sectors of the Tokyo money market remained off-limits. Despite U.S. pressures, most Japanese government bond issues were allocated, rather than auctioned in the U.S. manner.

Given the relationship between Japan's tightly regulated and highly valued real estate, its inflated stock prices, its low capital costs, and its profound concern for long-term relationships, a Western-style price auction could initiate the collapse of the entire Japanese economy. A free capital market would undermine the deeper logic of Japan's entire system. T. Boone Pickens, the famous corporate raider, found this out when he attempted a hostile takeover of a Japanese auto-parts maker. He bought 28 percent of the shares of the company on the Tokyo stock exchange, and then, as the leading minority stockholder, asked for a seat on the board. Pickens found he couldn't even get access to the company books. To the group-conscious Japanese, a hostile takeover is an absurdity.

As the Tokyo capital market made grudging concessions and offered token liberalizations, the powerful Ministry of Finance worried that it was losing control. In the October 1987 stock market crash, the Tokyo market fell the least and recovered first of all the world markets, in part because of the strength of Japan's economy, but also because the Finance Ministry was able to step in and give big institutional investors—pension funds, mutual funds, and insurance companies—"administrative guidance" to avoid panic selling. If markets were permitted to act in the Western style, as purely speculative creatures, this safety net would disappear. Yet the highly regulated Tokyo stock exchange did permit experimentation with such Western techniques as options markets and computerized program trading, which threatened to turn it into a New York-style capital casino. In February 1990, a wave of selling by Salomon Brothers, signaled by program trades, pushed the thinly capitalized Tokyo exchange into a sickening nosedive; it lost nearly 5 percent of its value in a single day. Though Nomura officials had put out the word that it intended to follow Salomon Brothers into program trading once the trail had been blazed, the Ministry of Finance slammed on the regulatory breaks. Nomura representatives subsequently explained that the home money market in Tokyo would never be as available for speculative plays as New York's.

When I visited Nomura's impressive New York operation, I found a roughly equal number of bright young Americans and bright young Japanese. The Americans spoke English. The Japanese spoke Japanese *and* English. I asked an American whether he planned to learn Japanese. He replied that his Japanese superiors had explained that this would not be necessary, that Nomura, the quintessential internationalized Japanese brokerage house, had no program for encouraging their American employees to learn Japanese, or to ascend to the top rungs of the company ladder. Once again, the uniquely Japanese system of comity and reciprocity was not available to foreigners.

The American policy of encouraging Japan to liberalize has reached an ironic pass. The United States, having spent a decade pressing Japan to make its money markets over in the American image, in the meantime became severely dependent on Japanese credit; but that credit, in turn, depended on managed financial markets. In 1990, Japan's newly liberalized financial system was suddenly vulnerable to speculative excess, leading to an abrupt regulatory clampdown, and suddenly far less Japanese capital flowed to America.

When the cheap dollar failed to solve America's trade imbalance, Japan's economic presence became more visible everywhere in the world, and as the Reagan administration approached its end in late 1987–88, public and congressional opinion favored a harder line on America's Japan policy. The market-opening legislation first proposed in 1984 had become the Gephardt Amendment—a provision proposed by the Missouri Democrat that required chronic trade-surplus nations such as Japan to achieve a rough bilateral trade balance with the United States or face retaliatory sanctions. Gephardt, then a candidate for the Democratic presidential nomination, sought to ride the theme of "economic nationalism" into the White House. The idea that Democrats should champion America's economic as well as its military security seemed to make political sense: socially conservative but economically vulnerable wage-earning voters had been deserting the Democratic Party because it had little to offer them economically, and liberal Democrats seemed somehow less patriotic than Reagan Republicans when it came to facing down hostile foreigners.

Economic nationalism responded to both complaints. It offered the promise of economic redress and a practical patriotism that working-class voters could grasp. In Gephardt's most often quoted speech (and television commercial), he explained how all of South Korea's protectionist devices raised the cost of a $10,000 Chrysler K car to $48,000 in Seoul. "Take off those taxes and tariffs," he warned the South Koreans. "If you don't, you're going to leave the negotiating table wondering how you're going to sell $48,000 Hyundais in America."[15] The appeal initially did well. It was like raw meat tossed to a hungry and fearful wage-earning electorate. In the critical Iowa caucuses, Gephardt gained an impressive victory, getting his votes from precisely those conservative working-class "Reagan Democrats" who had been the first to defect to the Republican Party. Yet seldom has a Democratic front-runner been more relentlessly criticized in the national press. Ideologically, Gephardt is a moderate, associated with the center-right Democratic Leadership Council. Since he was not making a clear ideological shift to embrace managed markets rather than laissez-faire, his program was depicted as simple nativism. Rather than challenging laissez-faire itself, Gephardt seemed to be saying that laissez-faire was indeed the preferred philosophy, but nasty foreigners were abusing it, so they deserved retaliation.

In his proposed amendment, Gephardt also made a serious tactical and conceptual mistake in proposing *bilateral* balance as the test of Japan's good faith. Although it is reasonable and desirable to insist that major nations not run chronic trade surpluses, the appropriate aggrieved party is the trading system as a whole and not individual deficit nations. Trade, by its nature, is "triangular"—nation A runs a deficit with nation B, but a surplus with nation C—which enables nations to buy each other's products without strict bilateral balance. It is truly damaging to trade flows to insist on balance between pairs of nations; that is a throwback to exchange controls and virtual barter. In demanding bilateral balance rather than balance with the system, and cloaking it in jingoistic-sounding rhetoric, Gephardt's remedy invited additional condemnation.

All of this engendered an almost unanimous denunciation from right-thinking editorialists, who may not have followed the nuances of U.S.-Japan trade negotiations but who were schooled to be good free traders. The *Wall Street Journal* began its sneering editorial: "Democrat Richard Gephardt is running for President on a pledge to slash the tires on Korean Hyundais."[16] The moderately liberal *New York Times* declared, in an editorial titled "Reckless Driving": "Mr. Gephardt isn't talking macroeconomics; he's talking revenge."[17] Even the Boston *Globe,* with probably the most liberal editorial page of America's major dailies, warned: "If Gephardt carries the same protectionist pitch to the White House, a bigger bill will be presented to American consumers."[18] Gephardt, who had poured all of his campaign treasury into the Iowa race, found himself on the defensive and out of money, and his campaign soon faded.

In the meantime, the Reagan administration, which needed a 1988 trade bill to get negotiating authority for the Tokyo Round of the GATT talks, tried hard to defeat the Gephardt Amendment, but it narrowly passed the House by four votes. To get rid of its formula, the administration reluctantly accepted a substitute bill with a tough targeting provision, in which the government was required to make an assessment of nations that flouted the canons of liberal trade; to name the malefactors and the malpractices; and to begin a program of concerted negotiations for redress. If the negotiations failed to produce results, sanctions were to be imposed. Gephardt's test of bilateral balance was gone, but as the price for retaining a commitment to multilateral free trade, the law required a new specificity in trade-opening negotiations, to make sure that nations like Japan at least honored the rules of laissez-faire that even liberal Democrats presumed they were supposed to favor.

A review of prices in Tokyo and New York conducted jointly by MITI and the Department of Commerce confirmed what casual observers understood all too well. Japanese electronics products, oddly, could be had more cheaply on Forty-seventh Street in Manhattan than in the Ginza. U.S.

products, on the other hand, seemed to have unaccountably high markups in Tokyo department stores.[19] The details were a staggering indictment of Japanese mercantilism. A made-in-the-U.S.A. electric shaver retailed for $44.95 in New York but $90.14 in Tokyo. A spark plug made in Europe sold for $1.69 in the United States but $7.60 in Japan. A European-made car cost $24,228 in the United States but $29,578 in Japan. A U.S.-made industrial casting machine cost $431 in America but $993 in Japan. Bed linen made in Australia retailed for $20 in the United States but $63.38 in Japan. American golf clubs sold for $340 at home but $659.15 in Japan. An unidentified U.S.-made pharmaceutical product cost $2.59 in America but $5.99 in Japan. On average, comparable capital goods were priced 68.18 percent lower in the United States; auto parts 82 percent lower, electronics products 40 percent lower, cars 71 percent lower, and food 96 percent lower.[20] And this was after a 120 percent devaluation of the dollar was supposed to make U.S. products more competitive in Japan! Against the reality of a simple pricing survey, the deductivism of standard economics, positing an iron "law of one price," melted away.

Supposedly, congressional meddling in trade issues was counterproductive, but the 1988 Trade Act forced a serious stock taking. Compelled by Congress to list nations in violation of free trade, the administration had several possible courses. It could minimize the damage to U.S.-Japan relations by listing almost everybody, since the Western European nations committed various mercantilist sins, too. But this would seem a gratuitous attack on the EC, whose domestic markets were more price-competitive than Japan's and whose multinationals behaved much more like American multinationals. Most Third World nations were extreme free-trade violators, too. But any watering down of the intent of the Trade Act would enrage Congress and lead to an even harder line in the next bill. At length, the USTR listed Japan, India, and Brazil.

Why India and Brazil? Mainly because the free-trade establishment holds India and Brazil in special contempt, not for being more mercantilist than other nations, but because they are informal leaders of a Third World bloc at the GATT that challenges American views and goals, organizing other countries to demand U.S. concessions in exchange for those the United States proposes. For example, if the United States wants "intellectual property" protection, the Brazilians and Indians want it to remove quotas on textiles and farm products, as well as give freer entry for Third World labor. Since Brazil and India are both statist in their own domestic development strategies, they are the identified sinners at the GATT. The 1988 Trade Act offered a spendid chance to settle an old score.

The listing of Japan as a free-trade violator set in motion a yearlong negotiation that came to be known as the Structural Impediments Initiative, or SII. Moving one step beyond the MOSS talks, the SII talks tried to pierce the veil of Japanese formalism and get to the reality of Japanese trade restraint. But little headway could be made: Japan's Prime Minister had no strength to insist on difficult structural changes. In 1990, the Japanese continued to resist altering their retailing and distribution system, and would not allow price competition in products like superconductors, where MITI and their industrialists wanted to surpass the American competition. Eventually, the Bush administration decided not to risk an open break with Japan, and pronounced itself satisfied with a series of relatively vague Japanese promises to try harder in the future. Japan was removed from the list of priority trade offenders—though the bilateral trade imbalance was scarcely changed.

Japan's negotiating strategy had been to take American self-criticism at its word and to suggest a symmetry of misdeeds. Yes, Japan did retain a few barriers to imports, but the United States, on its part, was partly to blame for the trade imbalance, for the well-known reasons that its savings rate was too low, its budget deficit too high, and it had protectionist measures of its own in agriculture, textiles, and military procurement. It was unreasonable to put all the adjustment pressure on Japan, they argued. The observations in late 1989 of the veteran trade negotiator Clyde Prestowitz, predicting the failure of the SII talks, are worth quoting:

This creation of pseudo parity is an old and powerful Japanese tactic. The main U.S. issue is the different nature of the Japanese economic system and how to deal with it and in particular how to achieve reasonable entry into it. Although it is often sloppily discussed in terms of the trade deficit, the issue is not really the size of the trade deficit; that is a symptom. *The question is how to mesh the Japanese and U.S. systems on a basis that is not disadvantageous to the United States* [emphasis added]. By referring to the problem of reducing the deficit and asking for discussion of U.S. structural phenomena, Japan changes the nature of the debate. This new debate is based on the old implicit assumption of the similarity of the two systems. Thus, the U.S. government budget is defined as a structural impediment to trade equivalent to bid rigging, tied distribution, and industrial policy. That a country with a $120 billion trade deficit is unlikely to have effective barriers to entry is lost in the camaraderie of the task of trying to find how both sides can work together to reduce the deficit, as is the fundamental U.S. concern with the different nature of the two systems. The inevitable outcome is that Japan must stimulate its domestic economy while the U.S. reduces its budget deficit—in other words, pure pablum.[21]

Prestowitz was one of a handful of well-informed experts whose books, with their more alarmist view of Japan, have begun to get a grudgingly respectful hearing. These include Prestowitz's own *Trading Places* (1988), Dutch journalist Karel van Wolferen's *The Enigma of Japanese Power* (1988), Daniel Burstein's *Yen!* (1989), journalist James Fallows's several dispatches for *The Atlantic,* and exposés of Japanese influence peddling by critic Pat Choate and others. These writers have all studied Japan in detail, and many of them have great affection for Japanese society, culture, and industrial dynamism. Prestowitz, who has an Asian wife and an adopted Asian son, and van Wolferen are both fluent in Japanese and have between them spent forty years in Japan. In the usual laissez-faire circles, this entire group has been dismissed as jingoist "Japan-bashers."

Ironically, Prestowitz's book was very respectfully reviewed in Japan, for he seemed to be the rare American who grasped how Japan actually worked. The object of his wrath was not Japanese but American policy, which he views as corroding both Nichibei and America's self-interests. To quote him again: Because we assume "that American-style capitalism and laissez-faire international trade are not only good but morally right, [policy] implicitly defines deviations from such a system as 'unfair.' There is no provision for the possibility of a different system or for dealing with problems that arise not out of unfairness but from the grinding of systems that simply do not mesh well. . . . Faced with the profound implications of labeling the whole Japanese system unfair, the administration shied away. . . ."[22]

If Commodore Perry failed with gunboats to make Japan over in the Western image, and General MacArthur failed despite a full-fledged occupation after an unconditional military surrender, it is inconceivable that the United States can succeed now when its economy grows daily more dependent on Japan. The real task of American policy is to devise a coexistence that will allow Japan and the United States, in Prestowitz's term, to "mesh." Clinging to laissez-faire makes the task all the more difficult. Prestowitz, Fallows, van Wolferen, and others have all remarked on the apparent anomaly that the Japanese have little difficulty coming to terms with foreign demands when specific goals are set. This is a form of market management they can deal with, even if they bargain hard over the details. For it permits planning, equitable social bargaining, and sharing of the necessary adjustment. The Japanese government was willing, for example, to restrict auto exports to the United States to 1.85 million cars, a quota that was parceled out among Japanese automakers. They were willing to set and meet domestic-content requirements of 50, 60, or 80 percent for products sold in the European market, or to negotiate content deals with the United States as part of joint development of aircraft. (The

greater the American discomfort with such agreements, the greater the
Japanese ability to win an advantage. This, of course, is our fault, not
theirs.) What the Japanese are evidently not willing to do is to adopt the
Western practice of agreeing to an abstract set of rules and then let the
chips fall where they may. For that would be to invite "confusion" and to
make impossible the honoring of reciprocal obligation. The trick, for West-
erners, is to insist that Japan widen the circle of reciprocity to include
foreigners. That will be difficult enough on an administered basis, and
impossible if the United States insists on laissez-faire as the only criterion.
Here is Fallows on this point:

> The standard complaint about Japanese trading practice is that it's
> hypocritical. Japanese manufactures sell freely in the United States,
> but foreigners must fight their way through public and private cartels
> to compete in Japan. The very idea of hypocrisy, however, assumes
> that there should be one rule of behavior, which should apply to
> everyone at all times. Japan's brand of morality is more "situational,"
> applying rules that seem appropriate to each occasion. . . . My point
> is not to criticize the fundamentals of Japanese morality—on the
> whole they're less troublesome for the world than universal creeds
> that lead one society to try to convert everybody else. But they have
> an effect on Japan's international dealings that other countries, with
> different values, would be foolish to ignore.

Fallows then quotes a British friend, recalling negotiations about seats for
foreign firms on the Tokyo stock exchange. The Japanese wanted to talk
about the number of seats, but the British were fighting for the abstract
principle that all seats be available for sale to anyone, Western style.

> Each time we said that, the Japanese reply was, "How many seats do
> you want?" We would say, "We don't know how many, we want it
> to be available to any qualified applicant." And they would say, "Do
> you want two seats? Do you want three?" Eventually, the British got
> weary of the standoff, and asked for two. The Japanese deliberated
> for a while, and agreed to two. By then, another British stockbroker-
> age wanted in. They were incensed at us for not sticking to our word
> and not knowing what we wanted. I'm sure they thought it was a case
> of Western deception. When foreign negotiators ask Japan to em-
> brace the principle of free trade, they run up against not only Japa-
> nese special interests but also a broader Japanese discomfort with the
> very prospect of abiding by abstract principles.[23]

The stronger Japan grows, and the more vulnerable the United States is to its capital, the more American charges of "unfairness" anger the Japanese. Lately, as they have seemingly acquiesced in the legalistic changes that Americans have demanded, though the economic fundamentals remain unchanged, the Japanese have grown aware of their own new stature and impatient with America's seemingly contradictory demands. The nationalistic best-seller *The Japan That Can Say "No,"* by Sony chairman Akio Morita and Diet member Shintaro Ishihara (intended for Japan-only publication and circulated in bootleg translation in the West), is only the latest in a recent wave of antiforeign books.

Japan is likely to take on the global responsibilities that go with its new financial and commercial might only if the United States does not make demands that are tantamount to undoing Japan's entire domestic system. Burstein and van Wolferen have painted a rather pessimistic picture of Japan's capacity to change in any way. Burstein suggests that by the time Americans wake up, we will be so deeply in debt to Japanese owners and creditors that change will be impossible, short of a total rupture. Van Wolferen's characterization of Japanese society is that of an alarmingly feudal one. His Japan is heavily reliant on the mutual dependence of various claimant groups, based on a cultural and systemic logic rather than a governmental one, which is diffused in many loci of power rather than centralized. Characteristically, the cabinet is headed by a weak Prime Minister, invariably a compromise candidate whose policies are subject to multiple vetoes. Van Wolferen is also worth quoting:

Diplomacy takes a government's ability to make responsible decisions for granted; it would be extremely difficult for foreign governments to proceed without the assumption of a Japanese government that can cope with the external world, as other governments do, simply by changing its policies. Nevertheless . . . statecraft in Japan is quite different from in Europe, the Americas, and most of contemporary Asia. For centuries it has entailed a balance between semiautonomous groups that share in power. . . . All are components of what we may call the System in order to distinguish it from the State. No one is ultimately in charge. These semi-autonomous components, each endowed with discretionary powers that undermine the authority of the state, are not represented by any central body that rules the roost. It is important to distinguish this situation from others where governments are besieged by special interest groups, or are unable to make up their minds because of inter-departmental disputes. We are not dealing with lobbies but with a structural phenomenon unaccounted for in the categories of accepted political theory. . . . There is no supreme institution with ultimate policy-making jurisdiction. Hence, there is no place where, as Harry Truman said, the buck stops. In Japan, the buck keeps circulating.[24]

Foreign trade negotiators often experienced this elusiveness as Japan's equivalent of playing good cop/bad cop. MITI would love to open up Japan to U.S. communications satellites, it says, but it can't get the Ministry of Post and Telecommunications to cooperate. But if van Wolferen is right, the reality is even worse: perhaps MITI *really* can't obtain the consent of its fellow ministries; perhaps the Prime Minister can't keep his word and at the same time remain Prime Minister. (Indeed, van Wolferen blames Japan's entry into World War II on the autonomous power of the Japanese warlords. The Foreign Ministry knew all too well that a war with the United States would be a catastrophe, but it didn't control the Ministry of War.) He adds:

> Barring some great upheaval unforeseen at present, it is unlikely that Japanese institutions will come to mesh more smoothly with the outside world, because this would entail the break-up of the bureaucracy-business partnership that forms the heart of the System. The wonderful alternative of turning the System into a genuine modern state, and Japanese subjects into citizens, would require realignments of power akin to those of a genuine revolution.[25]

Perhaps this conclusion, while accurate about the unlikelihood of radical domestic change in Japan, is too pessimistic about Japan's possible relations with the rest of the world. For it is quite evident that Japan can coexist with the trading system in a balanced way, *as long as the trading system does not demand that Japanese society change.* Here again, the true enemy of mutual accommodation is the U.S. mentality of laissez-faire at all costs.

It is instructive to compare the EC's Japan policy with America's. Relations between Japan and the European Community suggest that the trading system can withstand a surprising degree of management and economic nationalism, even that the latter is compatible with increasing trade. They differ markedly in both style and substance from the relationship the United States has with either. Both Japan and the EC are, of course, more mercantilist than the United States, though in different ways. Neither has the larger diplomatic goals for the Western alliance that dominate American diplomatic thinking and blunt occasional impulses for a more aggressive trade policy. Neither worries so much about its Ricardian good name, and neither has America's fears about retaliation. Both occasionally play a kind of trade hardball that the United States tries to avoid, both to set a good example as a free trader and out of concern for its wider geopolitical goals. Yet, as fellow mercantilists, the Japanese and Western Europeans may well understand each other somewhat better than the United States understands either, and consequently their trading relationship involves rather less pretense and hypocrisy.

Japan sold EC countries $47.9 billion in exports in 1989; in return, Japan took $28.2 billion in European imports, a ratio only slightly less lopsided than the U.S.-Japan imbalance ($93.6 billion in exports; $44.6 billion in imports). Japan's exports to "protectionist" Western Europe have been growing at a faster rate than those to the "liberal" United States. The trade imbalance, wider in the mid-1980s, narrowed slightly at the end of the decade thanks in part to a series of selective European trade and investment policies. (This achievement is rather more impressive than the United States' slight narrowing of its trade deficit with the Japanese, because the Western Europeans did it without cheapening their currencies against the yen.) Western Europe welcomes Japanese direct investment, provided most of the added value is produced in Europe. In certain key industries—such as high-speed rail—Western European governments have insisted that producers be European, as part of a long-term strategy to remain competitive.

The EC resorts to outright protectionism against the Japanese, especially in sectors that are the object of EC technology policy, such as semiconductors, telecommunications, and consumer electronics. It has determined that at least one Western European manufacturer of consumer electronics (Philips, Thomson, or both) shall survive, and it does not mind pursuing trade restraints to assure that outcome. Individual nations likewise have acted to restrict imports, the most flagrant case being France's famous VCR customs slowdown at Poitiers, in which the French government insisted that Japanese videocassette recorders be processed at a remote customs point of entry, one VCR at a time. At present, a "voluntary" quota limits VCR shipments from Japan to the EC to 1.7 million a year.

While the EC moves rapidly to the completion of its single internal market, scheduled for 1992, a number of national and Community barriers still exist. Most EC member nations have strict quantitative restrictions on imported autos, disguised as voluntary restraints; these are as low as virtually zero in Italy, 3 percent of the domestic market in the case of France, and as high as 11 percent for Britain. The revised regime for 1992 will not do away with these; it will merely replace them with some Community-wide "voluntary" restraint, as yet to be determined. In telecommunications, the narrow mercantilism of national procurement will give way to the more liberal mercantilism of Community Preference, to qualify for which a product must be of at least half European content. "Quite clearly, we're not going to open telecom to totally free trade," a senior EC official told me unapologetically. (The EC's top officials will speak with surprising candor about their Japan policy, though mostly not for attribution. One exception is France's Minister for European Affairs, Edith Cresson, who commented on the record to a U.S. reporter: "Japanese sit up all night thinking of ways to screw us both."[26])

The EC has been far more explicit than the United States about tying its trade diplomacy to industrial-policy goals. As 1992 approaches, the process of setting standards for pan-Europe has been seen as a double-edged sword, with both a liberal side and a mercantilist one, useful for the all-European market and at the same time giving Western European manufacturers a competitive advantage within the EC market. Brussels does not worry about whether this approach bothers Japan. It has aggressively encouraged joint ventures among Europe's major manufacturers, so as to take advantage of the emerging continent-wide market. Through the EU-REKA program of high-technology research, funded at about $1.5 billion a year and matched by private company outlays, nineteen European national governments and the EC Commission hope to spur development of competitive industry in several important sectors. EUREKA was sponsored by President Mitterrand of France to compete with the anticipated commercial benefits of "Star Wars" to the United States. Thus, in 1986, when the Japanese persuaded the State Department to back their proposed technical production standard for the fledgling high-definition television (HDTV) industry, EC representatives indignantly vetoed it because Thomson and Philips were developing their own system.

The EC has also been extremely tough about opposing Japanese dumping. Beginning in 1985, it claimed to have caught the Japanese selling many products below cost: notably computer printers, electronic typewriters, and digital scales, and when the Japanese responded with what the Europeans call "screwdriver factories"—plants in Western Europe where the final product assembly was done with mostly Japanese parts—it applied the content regulation requiring that at least 50 percent of "European" products be produced in Europe, and further insisted that Japanese parts be provided to European subsidiaries at a markup, so that a company's internal bookkeeping manipulations couldn't be used to disguise a subsidy. "In Europe," according to a senior EC official, "antidumping is an acceptable, honorable way to pursue your commercial interests. It is fairly low-key and technical. In the United States, the whole thing is political and further complicated by other diplomatic concerns."[27]

Thus far the Eurocrats have not made an issue of contesting which end of the product is produced in Western Europe—the Japanese are famous for producing the more advanced components at home—as long as the European value-added exceeds 50 percent and in some high-priority areas as much as 80 percent. However, in industries where EC-sponsored applied research money has been paid, Japanese firms may participate only if the research has been done in Europe. The major industrial participants in EC-funded joint ventures under the European Strategic Programme for Research and Development in Information Technology (ESPRIT) include a few American ones but virtually no Japanese. "There is a very significant difference in U.S. versus Japanese investment in Europe," according to a senior consultant to the Commission of the EC. "Ford Europe is a European company. American pharmaceutical companies in Europe hire high-priced European professionals; they have a serious European R and D presence. By and large, Japanese companies in Europe are mostly assembly or marketing outposts."[28]

If this strategy is beginning to change, it is largely as the result of deliberate EC actions and not thanks to the invisible hand. Japan would prefer to make products in Japan and ship them to Europe. But Japanese direct capital investment in the EC has recently soared. Britain, with its decaying industry and its failed laissez-faire approach to reindustrialization, is particularly open to Japanese capital investment, and the Japanese have used it as an export platform to the rest of Western Europe. In mid-1989, Toyota announced plans for a $1.2 billion auto plant in the Midlands, the largest Japanese investment in Europe. Nissan is expanding its plant near Newcastle to a capacity of 400,000 cars a year, and Fujitsu has its major European semiconductor plant in northeastern England, subsidized in part with a $50 million British government grant. While the British were willing to waive domestic-content requirements, the EC Commission insisted that their content requirements be applied to Japanese cars and other products made in the United Kingdom, in order that they be treated as made-in-the-EC products and not as mere Japanese imports. This annoyed the Japanese, but they complied.

Technology transfer in general is an explicit policy concern in EC-Japan relations. In joint ventures between Japanese and European firms, Brussels sometimes butts in a way that Washington seldom does except when strategic military technology is involved. Yet EC officials insist their approach is more internationalist than its American counterpart, and they are on the whole right. "IBM-Europe and GE participate in ESPRIT, but the United States keeps European companies out of Sematech," complains a European technology official. "They keep us out so that they can also exclude the Japanese."[29]

The Western Europeans view themselves as, on the whole, free traders, with selective and strategic exceptions for purposes of technological development. "If we didn't, the Japanese would take it all," says a consultant to the EC.[30] They share the view that the Japanese take unfair advantage of the trading system, but unlike the American hard-liners, they make policy and in doing so do not subordinate economic to military concerns. While the United States has attempted patient, sector-by-sector persuasion, the EC has occasionally resorted to broad actions against the entire Japanese system. In March 1982 the Community filed a far-reaching complaint under GATT Article 23, essentially alleging that the entire structure of Japan, Inc., amounts to one grand conspiracy in restraint of trade, and citing the now familiar litany of charges—that Japan uses technical standards, company interlocks, customs runarounds, "administrative guidance," an impenetrable distribution system, and so on to restrict the volume of imports into its markets. As a remedy, the Community requested both sector-by-sector market-opening initiatives and a general policy commitment to throw Japan's planning machinery into reverse and set specific import targets.

This complaint, which the United States refused to join out of deference to its key Pacific ally, was in fact far more faithful to GATT principles than the several that the United States and Japan negotiated. In retrospect, it can be seen that the Community made the mistake of being right too soon. By 1986, Prime Minister Yasuhiro Nakasone was pledging much the same thing, and the United States was pursuing bilateral counterparts of the EC's GATT complaint, through the MOSS and SII talks. Western Europeans, meanwhile, mistrust these bilateral efforts because they suspect that the outcome will be market-sharing deals, in which the Japanese agree to buy a certain amount of non-Japanese telecommunication satellites, supercomputers, medical devices, or whatever, which will, of course, be made in the United States and not in Europe. These fears were realized when the United States and Japan consummated their 1986 semiconductor agreement, aimed explicitly at increasing U.S. market share in Japan and preventing both further price cutting by the Japanese in the United States and Japanese dumping in third markets. Viewed from Brussels, this was a plain cartel of the sort that Americans are wont to lecture people about. For, in effect, it gave MITI control over the price and the quantity of Japanese semiconductors available to Western Europe. (EC officials also complained bitterly that the deal was a complete surprise when it broke in the press. Indeed, as rumors swept about, senior diplomats were unable even to get telephone calls returned from Washington or from American embassies. The EC filed a GATT complaint, which produced a ruling early in 1988 that the arrangement indeed had violated the GATT. A GATT panel found for the EC, but no serious remedial action was taken.)

A core contradiction in the United States stance infuriates the Western Europeans. The United States champions the principle of "multilateralism" as a fundamental of the GATT regime. This principle holds that the products of all nations are to be treated alike in domestic markets. It is a necessary corollary of the most-favored-nation (MFN) doctrine, requiring that tariff concessions given to one trading partner be given to all, and not be undercut by bilateral special deals. Multilateralism and MFN are pillars of free-trade theory.

Yet in its Japan diplomacy, the United States has been thoroughly bilateral, and its remedies have often been bilateral as well. Despite its professed concern for the multilateral trading system and though American and Western European goals for Japanese market opening are similar, the United States has not used the GATT as its principal market-opening mechanism or joined with the Western Europeans to press common complaints. Diplomats say this expresses the wish not to humiliate the Japanese, the tacit tradition that the two powers ought not to "gang up" on the third, and a concern to keep dealings with Japan and with Europe separate. Thus, the United States vetoed the EC proposal to require that major trading nations—i.e., Japan—pursue a "balance of obligations and benefits" from the GATT system. "We felt that the Japanese were deriving too many benefits from the GATT system and not giving enough in return," said an EC official. "The Americans laughed at us."

The Western Europeans backed the American initiative to open Japan's markets for beef and oranges, while the Americans quietly encouraged them in objecting to Japanese taxes on imported wines and liquors. But our ambivalence continues, and it doesn't have the excuse of representing a consensus of twelve sovereign nations, whose policies range from resolutely free-market (Britain) to generally free-market (West Germany) to opportunistically mercantilist (Italy), to doctrinally mercantilist (France). The most striking difference is that we force market-opening measures on Japan while Europe takes a hard line to protect its key industries. Only one recent case comes to mind in which European protectionism was narrowly focused to extract reciprocal concessions from the Japanese. This was in early 1988, when the United Kingdom demanded reciprocal access for its bank branches in Tokyo before Japanese banks would be allowed full privileges in London.

The Japanese have worried, with some justification, about 1992. Thus far, Europe's national quantitative restrictions have been directed mainly against the Orient; American products have had few barriers except in such sectors as agriculture, steel, and textiles, where everyone is protectionist. But when national barriers are converted into explicit EC barriers, will Europe keep out "Japanese" autos made in the U.S.A.? This concern is shared by Japanese and U.S. trade officials. Prime Ministers Takeshita and Kaifu have both gone to Europe to urge the early appointment of a high-level joint working group to sort out what will happen after 1992. At this writing (late 1990), it is widely expected that "voluntary" Japanese restraints on exports to EC countries will continue well into the 1990s and perhaps beyond. Europe intends to keep its auto industry.

The Japanese disdain European protectionism, which they see as a rather pathetic and self-defeating effort by a trading area that is lagging in technology. A good case in point is high-definition television, where the EC is spending some $250 million to launch a European entrant and in the meantime hopes to use technical standards to keep Japanese technology from taking over its markets. "We said flatly to the Japanese that if we get no agreement on standards there will be no access to the market," boasts an EC official.[31] "That position is a typical infant-industry argument," replies a Japanese diplomat. "They have not come up with the technology yet. Japan has. While they develop their own, they want a wall around Europe. Infant industry is fine for developing countries, but OECD member nations should not be using the infant-industry argument."[32] Before Americans become smug over pots calling the kettles black, they ought to consider the implications: this selective mercantilism has not wrecked EC-Japan trade, which in both directions has increased faster than U.S. trade. And both sides recognize the importance of relating technology, industry, and trade policy. Both the Japanese and the European Community have clear goals for the development of HDTV, a market that, it is estimated, will be worth $100 billion a year by 2005, and their position on technical standards and trade is guided by the industrial goals. The United States, running a poor third in the HDTV race, has no such industrial or technological goals, and the official policy on HDTV standards is considered a regulatory matter, a question for the FCC. Not long ago, U.S. trade negotiators found themselves in the awkward position of asking for reciprocal access to telecommunications markets in Europe and Japan, *after* the United States had unilaterally thrown open its market as an accidental by-product of the AT&T breakup.

Economic nationalism, defined as the strategic pursuit of industrial and technological goals, does not seem necessarily destructive of the trading system. Europe and Japan manage to coexist and to sell in each other's markets, though each has industrial policies of its own. One might even argue that the coherence of their policies leads to more coherent trading relations.

Also, the trading system is rather more receptive to national planning than its defenders fear. Lars Anell, Swedish ambassador to the GATT, uses the example of shipbuilding to make the paradoxical point that managed trade can be conducive to freer trade: "Sweden abolished shipbuilding subsidies in the early 1970s. Today we are the happy buyer of foreign subsidized ships. But we phased out of shipbuilding on social terms, and we didn't do it overnight."[33] Freer trade in ships required negotiation about subsidy ratios, market shares, capacity, product lives—the stuff of managed trade. Western Europeans, like the Japanese, are comfortable with this, since they have long been dealing with these issues for steel, agriculture, ships, and autos. As a result of this and the older legacies of French *étatisme* and German cartelization, the EC is not likely to adopt a pure, U.S.-style laissez-faire system.

The United States may wish, for ideological reasons, to disdain government involvement in industrial planning, in the commercialization of new technologies, or in linking research and development subsidies to new industries and established trade goals. But we should not delude ourselves into thinking that by doing so we serve the health and welfare goals of the global trading system. Indeed, the sheer confusion of our national economic goals worsens trade difficulties. Nowhere is this clearer than in America's faltering attempt to reconcile its national security and economic needs.

≈

# six

# SECURITY: MILITARY OR

# ECONOMIC?

In the era of American hegemony coupled with laissez-faire economics, national security has had a narrow meaning to U.S. leaders. The centrality of the Cold War defined security as territorial, military, and geopolitical. The CIA did assess extensively the economic capability of defined enemies, but was not in the business of assessing the economic "threat" of allies—for that contradicted the prevailing ideology. The reigning doctrine of laissez-faire insisted that there was no such thing as "economic security" except in the narrowest sense of ensuring that defense matériel and certain vital supplies like petroleum would be available in time of war, and no such thing as a national interest in the competitive advantage of U.S.-owned companies. In the orthodox view, the only way to assure true economic security was to maximize national wealth and income; economic theory taught that the way to accomplish that was via the freest possible markets, not via economic nationalism.

In 1990, U.S. intelligence agencies began uneasily contemplating a future mission that included intensified analyses of the economic strength of allies. But even this project was defined rather narrowly as a need to anticipate foreign financial or economic instability, and not as an assessment of the commercial strength of capitalist rivals. Characteristically, the intelligence agencies could tiptoe closer to economic nationalism than, say, the Commerce Department or the National Science Foundation, because the CIA and the NSA could link the health of industries to the national defense. "Among both senior intelligence officials and those in Congress who oversee their activities," reported *New York Times* correspondent Michael Wines in mid-1990, "the Soviet military retreat has given rise to a belief that American security now rests more in economic strength than in armed might. The temptation to use espionage as a weapon in the world's trade wars is fast becoming the hottest issue in intelligence circles."[1]

Despite our best efforts to pretend otherwise, the very idea of national security, even defined in purely military terms, has profound economic implications. A defense establishment that consumes between 6 and 11 percent of the gross national product has immense influence on what the private economy manufactures and what technologies it develops. The more the U.S. government has disclaimed and disdained any commercial-technology policy objectives, the larger the Pentagon has loomed, by default, as America's de facto industrial policy.

Exercising its global hegemony, the United States found it convenient to use many economic levers as foreign-policy instruments—foreign aid, foreign military assistance, investment guarantees, low-interest Export-Import Bank loans, embargoes, preferential and restrictive import quotas—all of which interfered mightily with Adam Smith's invisible hand. As a Cold Warrior, laissez-faire America even embraced—of all things—government controls of exports. The symbolic event that signaled technological Cold War was the Soviet Union's test of an atomic bomb only four years behind the first U.S. test. It was widely believed that the secret recipe for the bomb had been stolen by spies; a security-conscious nation had to take steps to make certain that other military technologies would not be leaked to the other side. This conviction introduced a complex, though hardly perceived, regulatory constraint on the exports of American technology and goods. The advent of Sputnik, in 1958, encouraged a new spate of government-financed research, ostensibly for development of space technology, but with far-flung commercial implications.

To reconcile the obvious contradiction between a free-market ideology and a technological nationalism for military purposes, U.S. officials indulged the pretense that defense and commercial life were wholly separate realms. Defense wasn't supposed to count in the civilian economy—and official policy was to make sure that this would be the case. So the United States could berate its allies in one forum for failing to embrace free-trade dogma, while simultaneously criticizing them in another for failing to honor a U.S.-sponsored embargo. U.S. officials could do this with no sense of contradiction, for containing communism and promoting laissez-faire were both irreproachable goals. If this inconsistency confused the allies, it confused the American officials even more. National security exemptions from the doctrine of free trade were not clearly defined, yet the influence of military spending on the economy influenced U.S. industry, sometimes for better, sometimes for worse. The ideological confusion about the relationship between military security and economic security became a serious problem when American industry became uncompetitive in the 1980s.

The connections between military goals, hegemonic responsibility, and U.S. economic performance are complex, and far more subtle than merely the sheer economic drain of defense spending. Here is the central logic: a powerful, hegemonic government with a huge military establishment, which professes a laissez-faire ideology, has to maintain that any commercial benefit derived from work done for the national defense is incidental, not deliberate. Otherwise, allied nations might see the huge U.S. military establishment as an engine of unacceptable mercantilism, threatening their economies rather than protecting their sovereignty.

In the 1970s and 1980s, the unacknowledged interplay of military and commercial goals led to a pattern of truly bizarre policies on issues concerning technology transfer and commercial competition. One set of Pentagon officials repeatedly gave away America's most advanced technologies to military allies as part of the plan to yoke them to a common allied defense—even though these allies were also commercial rivals. At the same moment, another set of Pentagon officials worried that certain American industries on which they depended for vital procurements were no longer viable, and they sponsored industrial policies to save them. Simultaneously, still another set of Pentagon officials tightened controls on the export of certain high-technology products, which made it hard for the firms that produced them, on which the Pentagon depended, to stay in business.

This deep confusion hobbled America's ability to exploit commercially many of its best technologies. Advanced aircraft, semiconductors, optical fibers, machine tools, and supercomputers were deemed vital to the national security only to the extent that they affected our military preparedness; any government efforts to promote them had to be limited to defense-related activities. This self-defeating argument was another logical consequence of the official American devotion to laissez-faire. Instead of our immense military expenditures stimulating commercial innovation and our commitment to liberal trade encouraging entrepreneurship, the military priorities have tied the hands of the entrepreneurs, while the doctrinal loyalty to laissez-faire has thwarted the potential commercial benefits of the huge public outlay for defense technology. *All these contradictions have intensified as America has gradually lost commercial and technological preeminence.*

The long Cold War era did allow a technology policy to be camouflaged in military garb, even as U.S. officials blandly insisted this was not the case. But the Cold War's end produces both shrinking military budgets and confusion about the defense mission. It becomes ever harder to hide America's technology goals in the military closet. In the 1990s, there is a belated opportunity to shift resources into civilian research and technology. But the task of redirecting America's goals and resources is made more difficult by the lingering fealty to an outworn ideology of laissez-faire. In order to achieve a coherent national technology policy, it is first necessary to acknowledge that the United States has economic as well as military interests in the world. It is necessary to grasp that laissez-faire is not the operating principle of most countries. Only with this recognition does it become possible for government policy to decide when technologies should be transferred to allies for the sake of common military objectives, and subject to what quid pro quos, and how commercial interests should be weighed against military interests. Some technologies, certainly, should be assisted by government for commercial rather than military objectives in the first place.

Some writers, including Seymour Melman, Lloyd Dumas, John E. Ullmann, Mary Kaldor, and Paul Kennedy,[2] to mention just a few, have argued that a large defense establishment is bad for a nation's economic well-being per se, by soaking up a disproportionate share of science and engineering talent as well as taxpayers' money for research and development. (In the United States, the military share of government R&D has risen from below 50 percent to about 70 percent over the past ten years.) According to this view, a large military also thwarts investment in civilian infrastructure, which is important to productivity growth. Dumas suggests that the defense sector, both the Pentagon and private military contractors, preempts private civilian capital spending, and calculates that it owns 46 percent of our total capital goods. It is held, further, that as technology has become more rarefied and specialized, fewer easy commercial benefits occur than in the days when an air transport developed by Boeing under contract to the Air Force could be easily made over into the first commercial Boeing 707. There is no commercial market for a Stealth bomber. About 70 percent of the Defense Department's subsidy of semiconductor research and development in the mid-1980s went into the creation of a "hardened" microchip—one which can function in space and can withstand the effects of radiation from a nuclear blast. There is not much of a commercial market for that either. John Ullmann found that fewer than 1 percent of the 8,000 patents stimulated by research sponsored by the Navy available for commercial licensing were actually licensed.[3]

Paul Kennedy has emphasized the sheer economic inefficiency of much military hardware and the economic drain it represents. The costs of high-technology weaponry have escalated geometrically. It now costs more for one plane than the entire U.S. Air Corps spent on aircraft procurement in 1941. Kennedy notes that the Reagan administration in its first term spent 75 percent more on buying aircraft but got only 9 percent more planes. At this rate, by the year 2005 the Air Force will be able to afford one plane.[4] Melman and Kaldor have also argued that a large military budget creates a commercially lazy segment of technologically advanced industry, vulnerable to competition from more commercially oriented nations. In her brilliant history, *The Baroque Arsenal,* Kaldor's case in point is the century-long decline of British industry, which she attributes substantially to its heavy dependence on military contracts. Melman's review of U.S. military contractors demonstrates that productivity growth in the defense sector lags behind its commercial counterpart.

But this view may overstate the case. After all, there is little doubt that the immense military outlay in World War II produced technological advances on which U.S. industry lived for thirty years, as well as a concentrated burst of learning and experience for more than a million engineers and skilled machinists. At that time there was no fear of transgressing liberal trade policies, since a war was on and trade had all but ceased. Self-sufficiency was a necessary wartime goal, and by 1945 the United States was all but autarkic. And there are still many inventions conceived in military laboratories that continue to have commercial applications. Even the Stealth bomber, the ultimate white elephant, required new and very expensive composite materials, and these perhaps could be exploited commercially. Also, while it is probably true that reliance on Pentagon contracts as the main source of business makes a company fat and lazy, military R&D is one of the few areas that encourage long-term planning and thinking in an industrial culture driven by short-term quarterly-profit mania. It is also significant that America's economic standing in the world has declined as the proportion of defense expenditures in relation to GNP has also declined.

My purpose here is not to take issue with Melman and others—on balance I think their perceptions are accurate, if exaggerated. Rather, I want to delve into other dynamics that have been ignored. My own view is that the problem is less a large military establishment per se than the near-religious insistence that commercial benefits are verboten, that civilian counterparts of defense-funded research and technology assistance are not permitted, and that we must be generous with technology transfers to allies but rigidly control them when there is even the slightest risk that they might fall into the wrong hands. These dynamics, rather than the Pentagon itself, are truly lethal; they are the result not simply of having a large military establishment but of a fundamentalist devotion to laissez-faire interacting with military goals.

Obviously, the size of the defense establishment should be determined strictly by America's genuine defense needs, whatever those are deemed to be at a given time—not by the covert prospect of commercial benefits. With the end of outright hostilities with the Soviet Union and Eastern Europe, strictly military needs have obviously lessened. All the more reason, then, to separate the goals and benefits of government support for technology from defense spending and to consider a broader conception of national economic interest.

A good place to start to understand America's confused foreign economic policy goals is with the seldom told story of export controls. But first a bit of distant history. In the Constitutional Convention of 1787, America's founding fathers argued about taxes on exports. They finally concluded that the new federal government should have the power to levy tariffs on imports but that states be prohibited from levying export taxes. The young Republic needed to develop export industries. Only when the United States became a great power did the federal government decide that exports were too sensitive to be left entirely to private commerce: in July 1940, with Europe already at war, Congress authorized the President to prohibit or curtail the export of militarily significant technologies and products. When the United States joined the war, the War Department and the Commerce Department devised an ad hoc system of export licensing to ensure that militarily sensitive technologies would not be exported to, say, Argentina or Sweden, whence they might be reexported to Nazi Germany. This system had no constitutional basis; it was simply launched under the President's emergency war-making powers.

In 1949, Congress enacted a comprehensive export-control regime that empowered the executive branch to determine which categories of products required export licenses, to create a licensing system, and to impose penalties for violations. Remarkably, because of its inclusion under the executive branch's war-making powers, export control is exempt from the usual due process for issuance of federal regulations under the Administrative Procedures Act, which allows public comment, and from judicial review as well. The whole system, in other words, is beyond civil challenge.

The Export Control Act of 1949 was intended to limit the diffusion of both military and what the Pentagon calls "dual-use" technologies, a dual-use product being a commercial product that might have a military application. The basic system works like this: A series of regulations known as ITAR (International Traffic in Arms Regulations) produces a munitions list. If an item is on that list, or a new technology falls into its general category, the exporter must apply to the State Department for a license for each shipment of products. The list itself is classified, and producers often find that an item is on it only when they apply for an export license. The "dual-use" products are subject to regulations issued by the Commerce Department, which acts with the advice and consent of the Pentagon and the intelligence agencies. The current U.S. Control List runs to 128 pages and includes such broad product categories as metalworking machinery, chemical and petroleum equipment, electrical and power generating equipment, transportation equipment, electronics and precision equipment. Exports of "technical data" are also subject to licensing under a similar set of regulations. Since 1985, the Commerce Department has divided products into less sensitive and more highly sensitive items. For less sensitive products, exporters can get a general "G-COM" license, which covers multiple shipments. More sensitive items, which include most high-tech products, require individual licensing. Approximately 200,000 applications are processed for "individual validated licenses" (IVLs) yearly.[5] Most applications are completed within 30 days, but 5 percent take more than 100 days;[6] 1 to 2 percent of license applications are denied.

This entire regime, which now applies to upward of 40 percent of all U.S. manufactured exports as well as technical data, has three tacit presumptions that were more or less correct in 1949 but have been overtaken by events: that the United States is the leader in, and hence controls the diffusion of, most advanced technology; that exports don't matter much to the U.S. economy and hence that the commercial costs of this regime are trivial; that military and "dual-use" technology is something esoteric and easily isolated.

Since this regime was installed, the development and production of manufactured goods using advanced technologies have become key to the wealth of nations. And yesterday's rarefied high technologies have become today's commercial norms. My thirteen-year-old daughter does her book reports on a computer whose counterpart would have been a top military secret in 1970. But to the export-control mentality, virtually every technologically sophisticated item is defined as having a potential military use. Commonplace technologies and high-tech mass commodities are still subjected to export licenses. As high-tech products are "commodified," the grudging liberalization of the export-control regime has not kept pace with technological advance. Personal computers are still deemed sensitive exports. And only in 1989 did the government, over the Pentagon's strenuous objections, agree to move 286-level personal computers from the IVL list to the more general list. More powerful 386-level personal computers, which can be purchased for about $2,000 at your local Radio Shack, still require individual licenses and are highly restricted. The regulations are as thick as a large city telephone directory. Here is a small sample from the letter C in the Commerce Department's Alphabetical Index to the Commodity Control List: "Calcium, high purity; Camera shutters (specified);

Carbon dioxide; Cedar, western red; Communication equipment, airborne; Compasses/gyroscopes/accelerometers (specified); Containers for liquid fluorine."

I am writing these words on a not-very-sophisticated computer. Recently, I purchased a tiny circuit board from a computer retailer for $129, to upgrade the computing capacity by a not-very-impressive 768 kilobytes of random-access memory. On the package was a warning statement that this component was being sold in conformance with export-control laws and was not to be reexported to a third country. According to a former subcabinet official, a dispute between the Departments of Commerce and Defense about exports of recreational scuba-diving gear to an unfriendly country had to be resolved at the assistant secretary level. "There was intense pressure to deny a license," he recalls. "We made a Solomon-like decision. Face masks and wet suits were permitted. Flippers and underwater scooters were not." This suggests the scope of this little-known system, which has become a kind of monstrous MITI-in-reverse, where vast bureaucratic resources are devoted to *restricting U.S. exports.*

Since 1949, when NATO was established, the United States has induced its allies to join an ad hoc Coordinating Committee on Multilateral Export Controls, generally known as CoCom. Logically, if the United States is supposed to have free trade with friendly nations, then they must have essentially the same strategic export-control regime as the United States, in order to create an allied *cordon sanitaire* without loopholes. NATO member nations were required by the United States to enact their own regulations and to maintain comparable enforcement programs. Restrictions on exporting strategic products apply not only to the Warsaw Pact nations but to others outside CoCom discipline that might reexport to the East. CoCom, with its small technical secretariat based in Paris, is supposed to coordinate the export-control policies of all cooperating nations, which include all the NATO countries, Japan, and a few smaller Western European nations. Though nominally a supranational institution, CoCom is mainly an extension of U.S. foreign policy. In CoCom deliberations, the United States is invariably the force for the hardest line and the most restrictive policies.

Moreover, the United States reserves the right to maintain higher export-control standards for its own producers than other CoCom nations. It also requires American exporters to obtain certifications from their customers regarding the product's end use. And uniquely among CoCom members, the United States requires licenses for reexport of products made in America, or by U.S. subsidiaries of foreign companies, or with U.S.-originated technology. In other words, a buyer of an American high-tech product cannot use it freely without U.S. government approval, and the

United States uniquely claims an extraterritorial reach for its export-control laws. Often a foreign product containing a U.S.-made microprocessor, say, is subject to U.S. export-control laws and is denied a license to be shipped either to a Warsaw Pact country or to a nonaligned one that is not party to CoCom and thus lacks reexport controls.

CoCom requires unanimity to change or liberalize its standards. This amounts to an American veto on all proposals, and since 1985 it has conducted annual reviews of products on its proscribed list: virtually every other nation has been pressing for a much more extensive liberalization than the United States has been willing to accept. Because of American policy in recent years of treating China as a relatively friendly nation, China received far more liberal treatment under CoCom than other communist nations, and it was only in mid-1990 that the United States agreed to let the nations of Eastern Europe have access to roughly the same Western technology that China has been getting for over a decade.

The costs of this rigamarole to U.S. industry are immense, and not all of them are obvious. Most clearly, the United States is losing vast trade opportunities with Central and Eastern Europe—and Western Europe begins with a geographic and cultural head start. For example, in 1989 the German firm Siemens concluded a billion-dollar deal to sell personal computers to the Soviet Union. Atari, a U.S. firm, was discouraged by the Commerce Department from even applying for export licenses for a similar deal. More sizable, however, are the losses in the normal trade among the leading capitalist nations. As alternative Japanese or European sources of supply become available, many foreign customers simply reject U.S. suppliers because they don't want the red tape that goes with making an American purchase.

A blue-ribbon commission under the aegis of the National Academy of Sciences documented numerous cases in which the delay in processing an application for an export license cost American firms business. License approvals to non-CoCom nations, such as Austria, take two to three months—long enough to lose a sale. According to one of the papers done for the Academy, "U.S. firms unanimously report that U.S. export license processing requires five to thirty times longer than Japanese licensing procedure, even where no such license has ever been denied in the firm's history."[7] (Where competition with Japanese producers threatens, Japan can't find enough clerks to staff its Patent Office, but somehow, when the purpose is Japanese high-tech exports, MITI spares no expense to expedite the paperwork.) The panel estimated the total annual cost to American industry of some $9.3 billion a year, and this understates the true full cost, since the lost business comes mostly at the frontier of advanced technology.

Many Western European businesses have made a major effort to "de-

Americanize" products that once used U.S.-licensed technology or U.S. components. CoCom gives its European members a handy (and not unreasonable) cloak behind which to hide their emerging technological nationalism. Some U.S. companies with European installations have been kept out of EC-funded research consortia such as BRITE and ESPRIT, for which they otherwise qualify, lest the entire research product be "tainted" and subject to U.S. export controls. The chairman of Philips publicly declared that his company would seek to replace American components wherever possible, so that Philips products would not be subject to extraterritorial U.S. export controls. A senior executive of another European high-tech firm told me that his company recently decided to stop using the semiconductors which it had long purchased from a U.S. supplier. "We knew them, we had a long-standing relationship, and we would have preferred to keep doing business with them. But the export controls made it more trouble than it was worth."[8]

Whole categories of technology are being denied commercial exploitation, either because their development was assisted by companies having Pentagon contracts or because they are deemed too sensitive to export. The latter includes what intelligence experts call encryption—the coding of electronic messages. The National Security Agency operates on the premise that it must be able to listen in on foreign communications, while top-secret communications of the U.S. government must be securely foolproof. If encoding technologies that the NSA could not readily break were in general circulation, this would undermine the NSA's entire logic. So NSA has a gentlemen's agreement with U.S. electronics firms that the industry will produce no encoding technology that the NSA could not break in the event of an emergency. Increasingly, encryption is coming to include much of advanced telecommunications, and it took extensive negotiations and a special waiver before American banks were able to employ encoding technology secure enough to permit the mass use of automated teller machines yet breakable enough to satisfy the NSA.

Especially now that the Cold War is over, the absurdity of this becomes palpable. For example, Hungary wants to redesign its telephone system. Telephone switching involves very advanced computer technology, and a modern telephone grid requires optical-fiber technology. To subject every component of such a project to export licensing is to promote exactly the kind of statist nightmare the Hungarians thought they were escaping when they declared an end to their communist state. Though a small number of products really do require controls, lest they fall into the hands of terrorists, the current U.S. position risks having the entire export-control system evaporate as Western Europeans give up buying American and question our priorities, if not our sanity.

There are countless other Catch-22s. For example, U.S. companies are sometimes denied the right to apply for patents overseas because the Pentagon or the NSA doesn't want the patent offices of even friendly powers to see their specifications. Yet comparable products made overseas are exportable, without equally stringent licensing constraints; as a consequence, made-in-the-U.S.A. technology is denied patent protections overseas, leaving competing foreign firms free to acquire technologies and processes to which U.S. firms should have proprietary rights.

Although countries allied with the United States are supposed to be subject to the same export-control regime, they have wide discretion to enforce their own systems with a lighter hand. Germany has generally allowed its makers of sensitive technology to export to third countries and even to Eastern Europe. When France pulled out of NATO's common command structure in 1966, it briefly stopped cooperating with CoCom, and at about the same time established a French national computer company, Machines Bull, because the United States would not permit American computers to be sold for use in the French nuclear *force de frappe.* Bull sold some computers to Russia, and if you visit the Tass office in Moscow today, you will see a Bull computer, vintage 1967, twenty-five years out of date and still operating. IBM is prohibited from selling Tass a modern model.

American multinational corporations like IBM complain that the red tape also increases their administrative expenses and diminishes their competitiveness. This is not merely the expense of filling out forms. Multinational corporations typically have plants in several countries, some of which are CoCom members and some of which are not; if they want to ship components of sensitive materials from one plant to another, they must get export licenses. Even though these are private firms engaged in purely commercial transactions, some technical data on civilian products are deemed too sensitive to let out of the United States at all. One high-tech producer had to fly in engineers from all over the world to discuss a manufacturing problem, because the technical data could not be disseminated. Export licensing regulations also restrict access to advanced technology by foreign nationals working for firms in the United States. This is not a trivial matter: roughly one-third of new engineering Ph.D.s working in the United States are citizens of other nations.[9] Regulations even require licenses before a U.S. producer can *repair* a piece of high-tech equipment that was previously sold![10]

This system engenders a good deal of ill will among our allies, who ironically view it as a form of the very mercantilism that the United States supposedly eschews. Logically, that seems contradictory, since export controls put U.S.-originated products at a particular disadvantage, and American producers suffer the most damage. However, when an allied nation has a competitive advantage, such as Germany's in machine tools, the effect of the CoCom regulations is to hamper its exploitation. Older generations of machine tools may be traded, under the most general and least onerous licensing strictures, since they are deemed less important militarily (these include some product categories where U.S. manufacturers are still competitive), but the more advanced products, where Germany leads, have the tightest restrictions. The West Germans have accused the Americans of using a national security rationale to keep them from exploiting their lead: would that American policy were so coherent!

In the last few years, the venerable machine-tool industry of industrial lathes, punches, and drill presses became a brand-new, computerized ("numerically controlled") industry. Yet the basic CoCom list of technical specifications for prohibited machine-tool exports was not revised between 1974 and 1990. (As noted, revision of the CoCom list requires unanimous consent, and the United States often vetoes proposed liberalizations.) CoCom specifications for machine-tool exports are based on machining tolerances. For sixteen years, tools that can produce machine parts within plus or minus ten microns were subject to export controls, because the Defense Department in 1974 believed this to be approximately the state of Soviet technology. But since then, five-micron tolerances have gone from state-of-the-art to off-the-shelf, and most machine-tool producers no longer build tools with tolerances as crude as ten microns. Since some of the nations allied to us administer their own export controls with a lighter hand, the Soviet Union is hardly denied all access to sophisticated machine tools: the system merely ensures that Japanese and German rather than U.S. producers get its business. The Soviet Union is the world's third-largest importer of machine tools. (It imported more than $1 billion worth in 1988: West Germany supplied products with a value of $568 million, Japan $122 million, while U.S. producers made sales totaling just $1.3 million.[11]) To bring the story to an ironic full circle, computer-controlled machine tools were invented in the United States, under contract to—who else?—the Air Force! Thus, our self-defeating "industrial policy" for advanced technology, conceived and then constrained by military logic, perfectly cancels itself out.

In a recent machine-tool licensing case, the Moore Special Tool Company of Bridgeport, Connecticut, was denied a license by the Pentagon to ship machinery for making soft-drink cans to Hungary. The Pentagon's reason for the denial was that the stated end use of the machine doesn't require the level of technology that the machine provides. The Moore Company is another poignant example of a firm that is precisely the sort of entrepreneurial creature America needs. Exports account for 40 percent of its total sales. A research lab in Shanghai was recently named for Wayne R. Moore, president of the family-owned company. Moore is also an example of a firm that the military establishment helped to develop technologies some of which are now considered too sensitive to export freely. The Department of Energy is a customer for highly classified Moore mirror-turning machines, with tolerances measured in angstroms, used by Lawrence Livermore and Rocky Flats to fabricate weapons. Once again, the military establishment functions as a technological patron in a fashion that is commercially perverse, almost like one of those novelty boxes which you turn on only to have a hand come out of the box to switch it off. In late 1990, Moore was on the verge of selling 40 percent of its stock to a Japanese company, creating great unease at the Department of Energy.

Japan and the United States have signed a secret agreement committing both nations to the same export-control standards in supercomputer exports. Supercomputers are among the most sensitive of dual-use products, since they can be used to make advanced weapons and are also useful to universities, manufacturing firms, and research laboratories. Here, American manufacturers are competing head to head with their Japanese rivals. But the Japanese give greater leeway to third-country customers, since they consider economic success an essential aspect of their national security. American producers will not be able to exploit competitive advantage. When an American supercomputer maker, for example Cray Research, tries to sell a supercomputer, say to a university in Austria (which is not a CoCom member), Cray must first get enforceable assurances from the university about who will be permitted access to the computer and for what purposes. American law virtually reaches into another sovereign nation, in a purely commercial transaction, to demand the equivalent of a security clearance. If Cray fails to get such assurances, it will be denied the export license. If it obtains the license but the customer fails to keep his promise, Cray can be held responsible. In one celebrated case, Digital Equipment Corporation sold a shipment of personal computers to a West German businessman. The computers were then exported, in violation of CoCom and U.S. strictures, to Bulgaria, which began making counterfeit Digital computers. Digital was subsequently fined several million dollars, on the ground that it *should have known* that the customer, who turned out to be a spy, was untrustworthy. Companies who find themselves in this position seldom appeal because, as noted, the courts have stayed out of challenging the constitutionality or even the due process of export controls and because high-tech producers will need the goodwill of the defense establishment to get their export license next time.

American supercomputer technology was heavily subsidized by the U.S. military, in large part to meet the needs of the government's own weapons design laboratories, at Los Alamos, Sandia, and Lawrence Livermore. The Strategic Defense Initiative (Star Wars), with its reliance on laser and other focused-energy weapons, requires even greater computational power. Needless to say, if supercomputers are the crown jewels of nuclear weapons design, missile design, Star Wars, and so on, it logically follows that they would not be good things for "the other side" to get their hands on. From this premise has flowed the U.S. policy of keeping supercomputer exports very tightly controlled. There are, however, four distinct fallacies in this view. First, supercomputers also have countless civilian applications—everything from banking to biomedical research to weather mapping, to the design of complex nonmilitary systems. Secondly, the very closeness with which the U.S. government has held supercomputers has driven other nations to design their own. Israel, precluded from buying a U.S.-made supercomputer for its national technical university, is now rapidly developing its own machine, as are India and Brazil. (Although "import substitution" as a trade policy is out of fashion among administration economists, export controls have precisely this effect on newly industrializing countries.) Third, although supercomputers are very handy in designing advanced weapons, they are not required for this purpose. Seymour Cray is fond of pointing out that he designed the Cray I on an Apple; for that matter, the mathematics of the very first atomic bomb was worked out on a slide rule. And fourth, the technology is anything but static.

Conventionally, a supercomputer has been defined as a machine that will do a minimum of 100 million floating point operations (calculations) per second, or 100 megaFLOPs, or MFLOPs (1 megaFLOP = 1 million floating point operations). The Cray I, introduced in 1976, operates at one hundred sixty megaFLOPS—slightly above the level proposed by the administration to define supercomputers. (The current administration rule would allow relatively free sales of supercomputers of a capacity below 150 MFLOPs, and would require the usual safeguards for higher levels for non-CoCom countries, and for machines of capacity 300 MFLOPs or higher to CoCom destinations.) However, the Bulgarian Academy of Sciences has demonstrated a machine with a capacity of 500 megaflops. And there is now a wide variety of machines offered by different manufacturers, some with price-tags below a million dollars, that exceed 1,000 megaFLOPs. Intel currently sells a chip, the i860, available at mass-market retailers, which all by itself has a computing capacity of 60 MFLOPs. Inserted in two personal computers operated in harness, the chip creates a supercomputer.

Despite the June 1990 liberalization, the U.S. government still encumbers exports of advanced computers—products invented in large part with help from the U.S. government. Although this technology cannot be kept in a bottle, U.S. industry can. This roadblock to American sales of super-computers is particularly unfortunate, since U.S.-made supercomputers continue to deliver more computing power for less cost than their Japanese rivals. Yet many customers will buy a slightly less desirable Japanese machine, just to purchase a lower level of export-control complications.

There is a paradox in the government's relationship to the supercomputer industry, one that serves as a metaphor for the larger problem. On the one hand, U.S. military interests incubated the industry; the government's military establishment depends on the survival of supercomputer companies like Cray and Control Data. On the other hand, Cray and the others do not exist solely as captive contractors to government—three-fourths of their sales are to nongovernment customers. So if the government squeezes too tightly, it kills this golden technology, even for military, let alone commercial, ends. To put this in perspective, Cray, despite its early links to the military, is a relatively small entrepreneurial company, with some 5,000 employees and sales of about $750 million. Its three main Japanese competitors are Hitachi (sales: $50 billion); NEC (sales: $32 billion); and Fujitsu (sales: $18 billion), each among the world's fifty largest industrial corporations.

At this writing, U.S. trade negotiators are trying to get Japan, which protects its own supercomputer industry, to buy more U.S.-made super-computers—while simultaneously the Pentagon is ferociously resisting efforts by supercomputer companies to sell products to countries outside CoCom, such as India. Japan, of course, has no such reluctance or policy contradiction, because its military goals and its economic goals are complements, not opposites.

Communications satellites, to pick another example of a product where the United States has a big technological lead, are on the Munitions List, which requires the most extensive and restrictive sort of export licensing procedure. Here again, commercial trade negotiators with the Japanese and those at the Pentagon were at cross-purposes. It took congressional action to get the Pentagon to downgrade aircraft inertial navigation systems to a lower category of sensitivity, but the Pentagon was able to keep technical data in connection with such systems at the higher classification level.[12]

This dismal story has the beginning of a happy ending—though the ultimate result will take years to know. In late 1989, other members of CoCom applied concerted pressure on the United States to acknowledge that the Cold War was truly over and to finally liberalize the entire system of export controls. In effect, the United States government had three export-control policies—a different one in each cabinet department: the Commerce Department was eager to liberalize controls in order to help

U.S. producers compete; the State Department was inclined to some liberalization, in order to placate NATO allies and gain greater U.S. commercial influence in Eastern Europe; the Pentagon remained opposed to any significant liberalization. In the wings, Congress was rewriting the Export Administration Act, and was very sympathetic to the complaints of U.S.-based exporters that lingering Cold War objectives were costing them business. If the administration did not agree to some liberalization, it risked a congressional directive to do so.

At a high-level meeting at Paris in June 1990, the administration did agree to an administrative simplification of the entire system, though details remained to be worked out. The phrase widely used was "higher fences around fewer products," meaning that some products would be decontrolled, while a "core list" of truly strategic goods and technologies would be controlled more tightly. The negotiations focused on three strategic dual-use sectors where disagreements among the allies were particularly contentious: machine tools, computers, and telecommunications. The Germans, newly influential in world politics, flatly threatened to pull out of CoCom unless standards were significantly liberalized for exports of machine tools and computers. The British argued that it was absurd to insist on one set of liberalized standards for Eastern Europe and another for the U.S.S.R., since it was now in the interest of the West that the economic reforms of Mikhail Gorbachev succeed, and the Soviet Union desperately needed Western technology.

At the Paris meeting, the United States agreed that Eastern Europe and the Soviet Union could have access to computer technology at a slightly lower level of sophistication than that allowed China—moderately advanced personal computers and relatively low-level "mainframes." The United States capitulated to German demands and allowed the export of more advanced machine tools. However, in some cases products could go to Eastern Europe that would not be permitted to the U.S.S.R., and in each case the "end use" of the product would have to be certified by the importer, lest a machine tool ostensibly destined for a bicycle shop in Prague be diverted to a missile factory in Minsk. The Pentagon agency in charge of export controls, the Defense Technology Security Administration (DTSA), resisted even this compromise. A high-ranking official of DTSA, reminded by members of the subcabinet interagency group working out details of the agreement that it had been personally approved by President Bush, snapped, "He doesn't speak for DTSA!"[13]

In the crucial area of telecommunications, the National Security Agency got its way. Tight controls would remain on optical-fiber technology, digital switching, and the other elements of an advanced telephone system that several nations of Eastern Europe were eager to buy. And the

United States, unilaterally, insisted on controlling exports of U.S. products more stringently than the controls enforced by, say, Germany. The result of this was predictable. European companies like France's Alcatel and Germany's Siemens would be in a better position to do business with Eastern Europe than their U.S.-based competitors. This was particularly ironic, for the United States is the one great power that comes to Eastern Europe with relatively clean hands. The Eastern Europeans are particularly eager for a strong American commercial presence; they do not want political liberation from the Soviet bloc only to become commercial satellites of Germany.

The telephone systems of Eastern Europe are about fifty years behind those of the West technically. In the region, there are long waiting lists for telephone service, ranging from eight to fourteen years. Hungary has entered into agreements with Alcatel (French), SEL (German), and Northern Telecom (Canadian) to provide various aspects of its new network. U.S. West and L. M. Ericsson of Sweden have entered into an agreement with Magyar Posta to provide cellular radio service, although U.S. West is not permitted to expand beyond a single-cell site in Budapest. Since Sweden is not a CoCom member, Ericsson is permitted more latitude than U.S. West; Ericsson, for example, can train the Hungarians in the use of certain technologies, whereas U.S. West cannot. In Czechoslovakia, the present telephone system was installed by Siemens in the 1930s, and the government, seeking manufacturing technology for local production to modernize the system, is negotiating with a number of Western suppliers, including Siemens, Alcatel, Northern Telecom, and Ericsson. U.S. West and Bell Atlantic have both been involved in joint venture discussions with the Czech Post and Telecommunications ministry, but the Prague press has reported government concerns about whether U.S. firms would be "reliable suppliers," given U.S. export-control constraints.

AT&T, along with several former Bell system operating companies, has begun to explore joint ventures in Eastern Europe and in the U.S.S.R. But current export-control standards do not permit the U.S. firms to sell technology at the level the Eastern Europeans want; and for such a once-in-a-generation investment, they are not likely to be satisfied with 1970s technology when 1990s technology is available.

Perhaps the most far-reaching denial to date was the veto in June 1990 of a proposed joint venture involving U.S. West in the installation of a long-distance trans-Siberian optical fiber line in the Soviet Union. (U.S. West is the "Baby Bell" company serving the Rocky Mountain States.) A British firm, Cable & Wireless, was also interested in the deal, and the final decision to withhold both U.S. and British participation was made by President Bush and Prime Minister Thatcher personally on June 5, the day after Soviet President Gorbachev concluded his U.S. goodwill tour. According to very well placed sources, the National Security Agency wants to delay Soviet achievement of optical fiber capability: optical fiber cables are installed underground, and are far more difficult to tap than the microwave communications which are the current basis for much of the world's telephone traffic. (According to U.S. Congressman Amory Houghton, former chairman of Corning Glass, optical fiber systems can be intercepted—but it is more expensive to do so.) At this writing, the Koreans, who have a growing capability in fiber optics, have reportedly begun negotiations with the Soviets.

U.S. telephone companies, of course, have long cooperated with the Pentagon and intelligence agencies. Many in the industry have argued that one way or another the U.S.S.R. is bound to get up-to-date optical fiber and digital switching technology eventually, and that it would make more sense for the intelligence community to allow American companies to be the ones installing and servicing it. But so far this argument has fallen on deaf ears.

It is also clear that low-level Pentagon officials retain immense power to thwart liberalizations that have been agreed to in principle by their superiors. Only a week after the Paris conference of June 8, a U.S.-German-Hungarian consortium building a factory to make plastic and rubber injection molding for consumer products applied to the Defense Department to import U.S.-made machine tools well within the tolerances agreed to at Paris. The application was rejected. Conceptions of national security that were built up over half a century will not vanish overnight.

Although American corporate executives had been pressing for a liberalization of export controls for decades, the Reagan administration tightened them, in line with its general policy of getting tough with the Russians. This was not without irony, since most of those same executives had voted for Reagan because he had promised to get the government off the backs of American entrepreneurs. The Reagan administration also persuaded NATO allies to allow whole new product categories to be added to the CoCom list. The architects of the hardening line included Secretary of Defense Caspar Weinberger, Assistant Secretary of Defense Richard Perle, and National Security Adviser William Clark. They had allies in the Pentagon's career force of export-control bureaucrats, who have a near-paranoid fear of technological espionage.

Beyond controlling strategic materials and technologies to keep them out of Russian hands, the Reagan administration pursued a more general policy of squeezing the Soviet Union economically. The huge defense buildup was intended not just to keep the United States dominant in strategic weaponry but also to force the Soviet Union into economic hardship in trying to keep up. Then, after the Solidarity movement in Poland had been repressed and martial law imposed in mid-December 1981, in his Christmas Day message Reagan announced a series of economic sanctions against the Soviet Union, including suspension of all Aeroflot service between the U.S.S.R. and the United States and denial of export licenses for electronic equipment and other high-technology materials. The administration also decided to interfere with a pending project that had been troubling Weinberger and Perle all year—a grand scheme to enable the Russians to sell natural gas to Western Europe.

Several years before, the Soviets had entered negotiations with a consortium of Western European governments, banks, utility companies, and manufacturers to help develop the extensive natural-gas fields of western Siberia. A group led by the Deutsche Bank agreed to lend the Soviets $10–$15 billion to purchase gas-drilling equipment and lay two 3,000-mile pipelines. In return, the Western Europeans would get a reliable source of cheap energy, the equivalent of roughly a million barrels a day of crude oil. The Soviet Union may not have been the ideal supplier, but at the time Western Europe's principal source of gas was an even shadier supplier— Libya. The proposed pipeline would supply an estimated 6 percent of Europe's total energy needs. A series of contracts were signed in the fall of 1981.

Reagan officials had been extremely wary of the pipeline deal. They objected that this would leave Europe partly reliant on the Soviets for a crucial product, and hence vulnerable to Soviet pressure in the event of a crisis, and more likely to curry Soviet favor generally. They also objected that the Soviets would have a new source of hard Western currency—over $10 billion yearly—which contradicted the general American policy of intensified economic pressure. Interestingly, the administration did not contend that the Western Europeans were shipping the Russians militarily sensitive technology, only that they were undercutting a policy of what amounted to economic warfare.

Western Europe was then in the trough of the worst recession since World War II. The pipeline was the biggest trade deal ever with the U.S.S.R., and it was expected to provide Western Europe not only with cheap energy but also with a new source of orders for its depressed steel industry and several hundred thousand badly needed skilled jobs. When the Europeans refused to heed Washington's wishes, the administration tried to use the export-control machinery to bring their recalcitrant NATO allies to heel. At the time, U.S. companies, then also reeling under the twin impact of recession and Japanese competition, had chances to make sales to the pipeline project totaling an estimated $300–$600 million. Caterpillar Tractor, which had developed advanced pipe-laying and gas-compressor technology for the trans-Alaska pipeline, was set to provide two hundred pipe-laying machines at a cost of $90 million. Another U.S. company, General Electric, had contracts to supply $175 million in rotors and nozzles for gas-field turbine compressors to John Brown of England, AEG-Telefunken in Germany, and Nuovo Pignone in Italy, prime contractors for the pipeline. But pursuant to the President's new policy, the Department of Commerce announced on December 29 that Caterpillar's export license was revoked and that no new licenses in connection with the pipeline project would be issued.

It was exactly this sort of stricture, and Washington's episodic Cold War caprices, that gave American companies the reputation for being less than reliable business partners. Unlike Reagan, most European leaders in the early 1980s were not pursuing a policy of economic warfare against the Russians. This time our NATO allies told the United States government to go to hell. On January 4, the ten Foreign Ministers of the Common Market countries signed a declaration indicating they would make their own decision about whether to proceed with the pipeline. In late January, France became the first EC nation to sign a long-term contract to buy Soviet natural gas.

Perle and Weinberger convinced Reagan to extend U.S. pipeline sanctions to foreign subsidiaries of U.S. firms and even to U.S. technology already under license to foreign concerns. This decision was made while Secretary of State Haig was away, trying to negotiate a compromise with the Europeans. According to Haig's memoirs, at the National Security Council, where the decision was made, only the hard line was proposed. This new policy was a flagrant attempt to extend U.S. law to Europe, extraterritorially, and to compel private companies to violate contracts. EC Foreign Ministers, again unanimously, condemned the action. The French government instructed French companies to proceed with the work, and the Foreign Minister declared publicly, "This day, June 18, 1982, could well go down as the beginning of the end of the Atlantic alliance."[14] Reagan's closest ideological ally, Mrs. Thatcher's government in England, went so far as to issue an order prohibiting any U.K. company from complying with U.S. extraterritorial law. (So the John Brown engineering firm would be in violation of American law if it ignored the U.S. directive and in violation of British law if it obeyed.) Haig resigned, and his successor, George Shultz, has told associates that he spent virtually his first year as Secretary of State cleaning up the damage.

In the end, the pipeline was built ahead of schedule. U.S. companies lost hundreds of millions of dollars' worth of orders, and the nations of the

European Community learned that if they stuck together they could pursue an independent foreign policy despite intense American pressure. In the mid-1970s, Caterpillar Tractor had had 85 percent of the Soviet market for pipe-laying machinery, while its arch Japanese rival, Komatsu, had 15 percent. Ten years later, that ratio had reversed. GE has long been known as the world's premier manufacturer of turbines, but since the pipeline dispute, the European manufacturers and the EC Commission have embarked on a program to free themselves from dependence on an American supplier.

Anthony Blinken's history of the pipeline case quotes Horst Kerlen, vice president of AEG's compressor subsidiary: "There is a doubt, a lack of trust, a feeling against the United States. . . . We have to be very cautious now about any new contracts that would bind us so totally to the U.S." Though the pipeline affair was a far more dramatic imbroglio than the typical dispute over export controls, it suggests precisely what happens hundreds of times daily, when American producers lose business and customers or governments of allied nations lose confidence in America.

The bizarre world of export controls illustrates one aspect of the dangers we run in emphasizing military, as opposed to economic, security and in ignoring our usual fealty to laissez-faire where national security is concerned. Yet, simultaneously, our very commitment to laissez-faire creates serious distortions in another major area where government profoundly influences the development of commercial technology—Pentagon procurement. Every few days, the *Wall Street Journal* publishes a brief list of major Pentagon contracts awarded during the previous week. Here is the item for Monday, April 16, 1990, in its entirety:

> Washington — International Business Machines Corporation received a $238.7 million Air Force contract for aircraft electronics. Ten companies received $10 million from the Air Force for hazardous waste research. They were: Roy F. Weston, Inc.; Earth Technology Corp. Engineering Science; ICF Technology, Inc.; NUS Group; O'Brien and Gere Engineers, Inc.; Radian Corp.; and Tetra Tech, Inc.
>
> McDonnell Douglas Corp. got a $25.5 million Air Force contract for F-15/e aircraft.
>
> Raytheon Co. received a $21.7 million Army contract for Stinger missiles.
>
> Martin Marietta Corp. was awarded a $14.9 million Army contract for mortar ammunition.

Strikingly, these awards run from purely military (mortar ammunition) to dual use (aircraft electronics) to technologies with broad commercial applications (hazardous waste research).

The Pentagon is an immense force in the private-sector economy. Through the Defense Department and other agencies whose research and technology programs are guided and limited by national security concerns (NASA, the Department of Energy, the CIA, and the code-breaking National Security Agency), the government spends something like $60 billion a year on technological innovation. Roughly $40 billion in R&D money is expended directly by the Pentagon, through the Pentagon's own research labs ($6 billion yearly, employing some 38,000 people[15]), through labs operated by defense contractors and paid for by the Pentagon, in Pentagon-sponsored university research, or as research related to weapons procurement. The "national laboratories" run by the Department of Energy, like Oak Ridge, Argonne, Los Alamos, Brookhaven, Lawrence Livermore, whose names are household words, are essentially arms of U.S. military policy. Some of the financing for the world-renowned Bell Labs was generated by long-term contracts underwritten by the Pentagon. The first defense laboratory, the Naval Observatory, was founded in 1842. Today, the military-industrial complex directly employs about 30 percent of all the scientists, technicians, and engineers in America.[16]

Under the rubric of defense preparedness, the Pentagon finances broad-spectrum research on technologies and industrial processes that are only minimally related to narrowly defined military goals. It spends close to a billion dollars a year on biomedical R&D, for example, much of which spills over into innovations that become commercialized. The Pentagon has also been the principal backer of dual-use technologies. It spent about a billion dollars subsidizing the development of very-high-speed integrated circuits (VHSICs), which have many military and commercial uses. In the 1950s and 1960s, when the integrated-circuit and semiconductor industry was in its infancy, roughly one-third of all integrated circuits made in the United States were produced for either the Defense Department or the space program, and most of private industry's research and development for integrated circuits was funded by those two agencies.[17]

The Pentagon's "independent" R&D program, budgeted at about $8 billion a year, includes exploratory research conducted by corporations that have long-term relations with the Pentagon but also serve civilian markets, such as General Electric and Pratt & Whitney. Countless dual-use technologies for use in aviation, such as advanced composite materials used in turbine blades, were developed in part with Pentagon funding. The Defense Department also finances research and development on advanced manufacturing technology generally, often organizing consortia of university researchers and private companies. Pentagon officials, with their penchant for terse jargon, dub this "Man-Tech." Military subsidies provide industry with about $170 million a year for various manufacturing-technology applications, ranging from automated engine production to ship design and weaving techniques for the manufacture of military uniforms.

The Navy is currently sponsoring a $93 million fully computerized "factory of the future" to improve the efficiency of ship maintenance. When a ship is brought in for repair or overhaul, crucial parts are sometimes missing; the Navy has to cannibalize other ships or wait months to have the parts made. Now America's leading manufacturing firms have set up shop near the Charleston, South Carolina, airport to design a system in which everything from the soliciting of bids, the design of blueprints, and the acquisition of parts to the final production and shipping will be accomplished by computer. This is the counterpart of Japan's famous "just in time" production system. The Navy calls it RAMP, for Rapid Acquisition of Manufactured Parts. But obviously the firms involved—Westinghouse, General Motors, McDonnell Douglas, Grumman, and Battelle, among others—are interested in far more than repairing ships.[18]

Since most defense contractors are also commercial producers, much of this technological learning cannot help spilling over into the civilian economy. At Hughes Aircraft, for example, the same team of engineers designs and builds the structure, the solar-energy panels, and the telecommunications package for military and commercial satellites. According to Lewis Branscomb, former chief scientist of IBM and currently director of a three-year study on dual-use technologies, Hughes has roughly 30 percent of the military satellite market and 70–80 percent of the global commercial market for communications satellites. There is little doubt that the military subsidies helped Hughes gain its commercial niche. Sometimes, a long-term relationship between a contractor and the armed forces produces benefits in unexpected ways. Boeing's C-147 Air Force transport plane was reborn as the first 707 in the 1950s. In the following decade, Boeing spent hundreds of millions of dollars of its own and the government's money preparing a (losing) bid to supply the Air Force with a new generation of wide-body transports; when Lockheed won the bid with its C-5A (a project plagued with cost overruns), Boeing used many of its own innovations to make what became the 747.

The appropriately futuristic-sounding DARPA (the Defense Advanced Research Projects Agency) is a $1.3 billion-a-year investment bank for high-tech R&D projects with military potential. DARPA originated in 1958 after Sputnik. According to Pentagon literature, its purpose is to "maintain U.S. technological superiority over potential adversaries" and to this end "pursue imaginative and innovative research and development projects offering significant military utility that exploits scientific break-throughs and demonstrates the feasibility of revolutionary approaches."[19] Note that in standard American economics, and in economic policymak-ing, the very concept of "U.S. technological superiority" is an impermissi-ble assault on the prevailing doctrine of free trade, and the very idea of technological superiority is considered a nationalistic anachronism.

Note also that this assumption is not shared by America's trading partners. We have already referred to Japan's techno-nationalism. Like-wise, the European Community is explicit about the pursuit of nationalist technological goals for commercial purposes. The 1989 report of ESPRIT states baldly:

The European Information Technology Industry in the early 1980s was characterized by decreasing market share, leading to lack of critical mass, low R&D, and reduced capital investments. Something substantial needed to be done to reverse this trend. European compa-nies have considerably increased their market share from 33% in 1983 to 48% in 1987. U.S. companies lost market share in the European market during this period. However these improvements do not mean the situation is satisfactory, far from it.[20]

Unlike the United States, Western Europe and Japan do not feel the ideological need to cloak national technology goals in military dress. DARPA has been forced to embrace a concept of "defense" that takes it far from narrowly military products and technologies. In spite of the prevailing free-market dogma, DARPA funding over the years has contributed to an extraordinary range of commercial and military breakthroughs. These include such purely military projects as stealth (radar-evading) technology, "smart" weapons, laser weapons, surveillance systems, submarines, but also many dual-use technologies valuable to civilian industry: superconduc-tivity, gallium arsenide for advanced semiconductors, ceramics, robotics, X-ray lithography, and high-definition display systems for manufacturing technology. According to a 1990 case study of DARPA published by the Harvard Business School:

In computers, in particular, DARPA's contribution was nothing short of dazzling. The agency funded research that developed the concept of the personal computer and the menu- and icon-driven software that went into the first Apple Macintosh. It supplied grants, and later, the venture capital, to fund development of artificial intelli-gence and parallel processing computers. In fact, in the late 1960s, it designated four research institutions—Stanford, Berkeley, Carnegie-Mellon, and MIT—as academic centers for the study of computers and computing; using agency seed money, DARPA virtually single-handedly created the United States' position of world leadership in computer sciences. (The four DARPA-funded centers would train, directly or indirectly, nearly every [early] computer sciences expert in the nation.)[21]

In the 1960s, when DARPA got serious about computers, most academic computing involved cumbersome systems of punch cards that ran one at a time. Different machines in different universities were incompatible. DARPA pushed hard to standardize computer parameters and languages and virtually invented what became modern computer time-sharing and networking. In 1971, DARPA began operating the first "packet switching" network, allowing users at different research locations to communicate. According to the *Wall Street Journal,* this technology became the international standard.[22]

Because of its willingness to commit capital for the long term in a society driven by short-term profitability, DARPA's priorities significantly influence which new technologies may command private venture-capital funding. *Barron's* has termed DARPA "the biggest venture capital fund in the world." In some cases, DARPA has even become the principal investor of equity capital as well as research funding. According to Harvard Business School professor George Lodge: "When DARPA invests, it is a signal to the private venture-capital community that a technology is taking off."[23]

Senator Jeff Bingaman, a young, politically moderate Democrat from New Mexico, currently chairs the Armed Services Committee's Subcommittee on Defense Industry and Technology. Bingaman appreciates the absurdity of pretending that the United States operates a laissez-faire economy with no common interests or relations between defense spending and commercial prowess in industry. If he had his druthers, Bingaman would prefer to have a civilian agency, such as the Commerce Department, sponsor development in technologies and industrial processes that are in the national commercial interest. But as a political pragmatist, he recognizes that "industrial policy" is an ideological lightning rod. So instead, he has used his chairmanship to develop the logic of the Pentagon's interest in maintaining long-term industrial competitiveness for America's manufacturing base. His committee hearings offer an encyclopedic tour of the contradictions in America's technology nonpolicy.

According to Bingaman and people close to him, his eventual goal, perhaps in the next Democratic administration, is to have an official policy that recognizes the absurdity of the current situation and that embraces a national technology policy straightforwardly. In the meantime, he is using the Pentagon as a stalking horse, and the Pentagon is happy to cooperate. In 1988, Bingaman succeeded in getting Congress to pass a bill requiring the Defense Department to identify "critical technologies" essential to the national defense. The Pentagon earnestly pursued the task, and in a May 1989 report came up with twenty-two:

Microelectronic circuits and their fabrication
Gallium arsenide and other semiconductor compounds
Software producibility
Parallel computer architectures
Machine intelligence/robotics
Simulation and modeling
Integrated optics
Fiber optics
Sensitive radars
Passive sensors
Automatic target recognition
Phased arrays
Data fusion
Signature control
Computational fluid dynamics
Air-breathing propulsion (i.e., jet engines)
High-power microwaves
Pulsed power
Hypervelocity missiles
Advanced composite materials
Superconductivity
Biotechnology materials and processing[24]

What we have here, of course, is a broad range of technologies appropriate to a diversified, advanced economy. Unlike the other government agencies that affect the civilian economy, the Pentagon has no aversion to industrial planning. On the contrary, it recognizes that the availability of militarily critical technologies (which also happen to be commercially critical) cannot be left to chance—or to other people's industrial policies. By default, the closest thing to an American industrial-planning czar is a soft-spoken scientist named Dr. David Milburn, whose title is Deputy Director, Defense Research and Engineering. Dr. Milburn is in charge of identifying which technologies are critical to the national defense and of coordinating Pentagon-sponsored research with the R&D underwritten by other agencies. However, the rules of the ideological game do not allow the government to admit openly that it encourages American commercial leadership in advanced technologies.

It is a top priority of the Pentagon to integrate allied military forces into a consolidated national security structure. The Pentagon would like NATO countries and Japan to purchase U.S. military hardware—everything from carbines to advanced F-16 jet fighters. But our allies recognize their own commercial as well as military national interests, and from their viewpoint, the purchase of U.S. military hardware is a splendid opportunity both to obtain jobs for their high-skilled workers and engineers and to absorb U.S. technology. How do they do this? By negotiating for "content" and "offset" agreements that require a share of the actual production of the weapon to be located in the country purchasing the weapon. The Pentagon usually complies.

When the United States and an allied nation adopt a common weapon system, a Memorandum of Understanding (MOU, in military jargon) is negotiated describing in precise detail what technology is to be transferred and what part of the product is to be manufactured where. Over the years, America's military allies and Japan have successfully demanded that a very high fraction of the "content" of the product be produced locally. An F-16 engineered by General Dynamics is likely to be produced in large part by Mitsubishi in Japan or by an ad hoc consortium of European companies in Holland. An "offset" deal specifies the percentage of the total production outlay that must be made outside the United States. Recent administrations have been so eager to have allies committed to a common defense that many such deals had "offsets" exceeding 100 percent; that is, the United States agreed to contract out to foreign producers an amount of business equal to more than the entire cost of the deal, either in components of that product or in some other product. In the sale of the AWACS flying radar system to Great Britain, the offset was 125 percent.[25] (Even Mrs. Thatcher had no qualms about taking advantage of America's conception of military hegemony to obtain economic benefits for her country.)

This generosity with allies has consequences for American industry. Essentially, it breaks the links between defense contractors like Boeing, General Electric, or General Dynamics and their web of American subcontractors who specialize in everything from machining to specialty metals to software. It also means the U.S. taxpayer is subsidizing overseas production. This would be fine if there were symmetry in the way different nations approached this issue, but there is not. Other nations give priority to economic benefit; the United States, in line with the ostensible purpose of the endeavor, gives priority to the military. Alone among the allied nations, the United States lacks a coherent co-production, domestic-content, or offset policy of its own. Although it routinely agrees to the most lavish offsets when it is diffusing technology and production, it usually disdains U.S. domestic-content requirements as mercantilist.

A recent vivid illustration of this policy confusion is the FSX deal with Japan, which became popular knowledge only at the eleventh hour of negotiation. Because of Japan's low military budget, and because of the intimate relations between defense spending and technological leadership in aerospace, aircraft production is the one major industry where Japan has little presence and the United States remains the world leader. (Our trade surplus in aircraft in 1989 was $11.5 billion.) Japan is immensely ahead in other high-tech exports and is eager to capture leadership in aircraft as well. MITI's "Vision of Japan in the 1980s" called for technological autonomy in aerospace.

Some five years ago, the Japanese government looked for a way to build a new fighter plane for its "self-defense forces" in Japan to replace the fleet of aging American F-1s. At the time, the most advanced and successful fighter aircraft in the world was the American F-16. With Japan's trade surplus approaching $50 billion, the simplest solution—indeed the one signaled by the free market—would have been for Japan to buy F-16s outright from the United States, with the purchase perhaps sweetened with some Japanese co-production terms. This would have gotten Japan the best buy for its money and would have been a nice Japanese "offset" against America's trade deficit. But the Japanese convinced the Pentagon and the State Department that a simple purchase of U.S. planes was politically out of the question. They wanted their own plane, or at a minimum they wanted a new plane jointly developed with the United States. So, in 1986 and 1987, the issue became how much technology would have to be transferred and how much content would have to be located in Japan for a new, joint U.S.-Japan aircraft, the FSX, that would preserve the all-important principle of an integrated defense. U.S. policymakers never seriously considered taking a hard line on *economic* grounds and insisting that Japan buy the American F-16 or using the ample leverage the United States had on trade issues of great importance to the Japanese. "Linkage" of trade and defense issues was explicitly rejected. Nor did they consider the competitive effect of the sale on America's one remaining high-tech export champion, the aircraft industry. In the end, the administration simply gave away the store.

As these negotiations proceeded, the Japanese adopted the tactic of insisting on a combination of specifications for their proposed aircraft that no off-the-shelf U.S. plane could meet. According to Clyde Prestowitz's authoritative account,[26] the Japanese insisted that the plane had to meet sixty-four "design parameters," including two engines (which eliminated the single-engine F-16) and extra-long range (which excluded the other U.S.-produced candidate, the F-18). What struck the U.S. diplomats as remarkable throughout these negotiations was the lack of reference to the plane's actual military mission. There was "no real discussion of the Soviet threat, of coordination with U.S. forces, or the desirability of inoperability with U.S. aircraft . . . For Japan, in contrast to the United States, defense appears to have been a minor consideration compared with building a Japanese airplane and industry,"[27] Prestowitz reports.

In October 1987, after more and more testy negotiations, the Japanese went through the motions of giving in. With great fanfare, they agreed that the FSX could be a jointly developed plane after all, based on a modified F-16. Then, as follow-up discussions proceeded, it became clear that they were intent on building a wholly new plane, borrowing what technology they could from the F-16. In late November, the U.S. government agreed to a Memorandum of Understanding permitting unlimited transfer of F-16 technology to Japan for a token fee of $500,000 per plane and construction of at least 60 percent of the plane in Japan. The project was described as "joint development," but the Japanese retained total control over design decisions. In effect, the United States turned over proprietary aviation technology worth several billion dollars and subsidized the birth of a rival commercial aircraft industry.

Under the terms of the 1988 Defense Authorization Act, Congress has to be notified of such arrangements and has the power to veto them. The FSX deal provoked a storm of criticism in Congress and became the first foreign-policy crisis of the new Bush administration. While the CIA, the Commerce Department, the National Security Council, and the U.S. Trade Representative all expressed grave misgivings, the Pentagon and the State Department were eager to have the plan go forward. Much of the debate turned on questions about technology transfer. Would the terms produce a net gain or loss for U.S. aircraft technology? But because of the administration's ideological opposition to having an industrial policy, it was precisely the sort of question it was ill equipped to assess. Other debates turned on whether the United States or Japan was "ahead" in composite materials or phased-array radars—questions that were in principle inadmissible when speaking of an ally. The Japanese, in contrast, viewed technology transfer as the essence of the deal.

Eventually, President Bush endorsed the FSX, with only slight modifications. Though trade negotiations with the Japanese in a separate arena had reached one of their periodic impasses, the President agreed with State and Defense that trade and defense should be treated as wholly separate realms. Then the administration mobilized all of its political clout to avoid an embarrassing defeat in Congress. A Senate resolution to scrap the entire deal was defeated 52–47; a second resolution demanding tighter terms passed but was vetoed by the President. As usual, much of the press treated the congressional opposition as Japan-bashing. Japan is now well on its way to developing a commercial aviation industry, with a technological subsidy estimated at $4–$8 billion courtesy of the U.S. taxpayers.


It is ironic that the Defense Department is the only government agency which feels able to state a goal of maintaining America's "technology base." But national security alone overrides our national ideological commitment to the propagation of laissez-faire. The Pentagon is also painfully aware that it cannot pay for the entire American industrial establishment single-handedly, yet its ability to procure the advanced technologies and production processes needed for sophisticated weapons depends on the general good health of American industry. Most of what the Pentagon buys ultimately rests on what Pentagon jargon calls COTS—"civilian off-the-shelf technology."

Until recently, the ideological paradox of the Pentagon's implicit techno-nationalism was not a serious problem. American firms remained competitive in virtually all the commercial technologies the Pentagon cared about. With full confidence that the U.S. manufacturing base itself was intact, DARPA could concentrate on developing new esoteric technologies, the national laboratories could subsidize basic research, and procurement contracts could generate commercial benefits. But as American-owned firms were driven out of technologies that are key to the national defense—semiconductors, advanced machine tools, advanced electronics, composite materials—the Pentagon's implicit nationalism became explicit. And it became controversial.

Some Pentagon officials have argued that the logic of national security requires an intensified commitment to *civilian* manufacturing technology. In a report to the Secretary of Defense entitled "Technology Base Management," a blue-ribbon panel chaired by MIT provost John Deutsch expressed alarm that federal investment in civilian R&D for industrial growth was just 0.2 percent of total federal outlays, far below what was being spent by other industrial nations.[28] Even Defense Secretary Richard Cheney has declared, in the Pentagon's 1989 report assessing Soviet military power, that "although the Soviet Union constitutes the greatest threat to U.S. security, the greatest challenge to U.S. technology and industrial base will almost certainly come from the United States' own allies. Thus, the United States must succeed in this 'friendly competition' with advanced Western industrial states if its economic power, and the West's system of collective security, is to endure."[29]

If U.S. producers are no longer making what the military needs, the Pentagon has only three choices: to buy the products from foreign suppliers (which creates military vulnerability), to maintain a captive industry just for itself (which is prohibitively expensive), or to spend money revitalizing American industry (which is tantamount to a broad national industrial policy). Ideologically, industrial policy would be impermissible unless justified as connected to military imperatives; an October 1988 report to the Defense Science Board, by a panel chaired by Robert Fuhrman, president of Lockheed, took this absurd logic to its natural conclusion and recommended putting the Pentagon directly in charge of U.S. industrial policy.[30]

Another Defense Science Board report, in October 1989 in the wake of the FSX affair, soberly assessed the costs and benefits of technology-sharing policy dominated by geopolitical goals. The report, "Defense Industrial Cooperation with Pacific Rim Nations," was prepared by a distinguished panel chaired by Dr. Malcolm R. Currie, former chief executive of the Hughes Aircraft Company, and included Thomas Murrin, now Under Secretary of Commerce. "National security," the authors concluded, "can no longer be viewed only in military terms, but must include economic well-being as a key component. Therefore, we must explicitly line cooperative defense technology-sharing issues with economic issues, including trade balance and market access."[31] American policy, the panel concluded, was badly fragmented and "torn between pursuing defense industrial cooperation to help military posture and strengthen the fabric of security cooperation" on the one hand and "limiting defense industrial cooperation to avoid damage to U.S. industrial/technology competitive health" on the other.[32] The panel's conclusion—that national economic and technology goals should be an explicit part of diplomatic bargaining— was plain heresy. Increasing numbers of officials with hands-on experience dealing with technology, in the Commerce Department, the USTR, the Pentagon, and the intelligence community, were challenging the prevailing dogma, but it remained official policy.

Still another report, released in November 1989 by the National Advisory Committee on Semiconductors, was ominously titled "A Strategic Industry at Risk." Just in case anybody missed the point, the report's glossy cover juxtaposed a set of American red and white stripes over a Japanese red rising sun. The committee was chaired by Ian Ross, president of Bell Labs, and its membership read like a Who's Who of the leaders of America's high-technology industry. The report's opening paragraph contradicts the philosophy of laissez-faire in several distinct respects:

The semiconductor industry is strategic to America. The industry is the foundation of the information age, playing a crucial role in the consumer electronics industry, and other industries that have a high electronic content in their products. America's national security also depends on the semiconductor industry. United States and NATO forces rely on the technological advantage of advanced semiconductors to offset the numerical superiority of potential adversaries.[33]

The report gave the statistics on the abrupt decline in American semiconductors and semiconductor manufacturing machinery and explained how the industry was in danger of collapsing altogether. Japanese producers now hold over 80 percent of the world market for memory chips (D-RAMs). As they gain more market share, they can afford to spend more on R&D, which propels them further ahead. As the costs of research have increased, so has Japan's lead in capital spending. In 1988, Japanese "merchant" semiconductor firms (those supplying the world market) outspent their American counterparts by about five to one. In specialized semiconductor products, Japan has also been outstripping American rivals. In MOS (metal oxide semiconductor) devices, the fastest-growing segment of the semiconductor market, five of the six top firms are now Japanese. In 1990, the world's sixth-largest firm, the U.S.-based Intel, which holds about 20 percent of world market share in specialized programmable chips known as E-PROMs, could not raise the $300 million capital to build a new manufacturing plant and in effect ceded much of its market share to Japan. In 1988, the American semiconductor industry spent about $3 billion on pure R&D and another $3.5 billion on capital equipment. But obviously, as its market share erodes, its ability to raise capital erodes, too.

As the U.S. market position in semiconductors has declined, so has its position in equipment used to fabricate chips. In 1983, five of the top six makers of semiconductor equipment were American; by 1988, four of the top six were Japanese, and one major American firm, Perkin-Elmer, was on the verge of selling its X-ray lithography business to Sony. (At the eleventh hour, IBM stepped in.) The fact that more than 80 percent of the most advanced semiconductor manufacturing is now located in the Far East gives the Asian makers an advantage and correspondingly disadvantages U.S. producers. According to the report, 70 percent of the next generation of semiconductor manufacturing equipment purchased by U.S. companies will be supplied by Japan.

The report uses a "food chain" analogy. As markets decline, capital spending declines apace, and the entire U.S. industry, including "upstream" makers of semiconductor manufacturing equipment, the semiconductor chips themselves, and end-use products in electronics and manufacturing, ceases to be able to compete. The semiconductor manufacturing industry "advances manufacturing disciplines as diverse as machine tools, vacuum control, automated controls, and computer aided design."[34] Likewise, "today's $50 billion world chip industry leverages a $750 billion global market in electronics."[35]

Several arguments in this report are noteworthy and emblematic of the new industrial-policy debate. On the one hand, the committee argues that there *is* an American national economic interest, independent of its national security interest narrowly defined. If "we" lose semiconductors, we lose manufacturing technologies and consumer product markets, too. Standard economics and reigning U.S. policy question the very idea of "we." In the orthodox dogma, there is no such thing as we: in the global free marketplace, where nationality and location of production are of no consequence, American citizens should buy the best products from the lowest-cost producer. What this ignores, of course, is that "our" ability to buy these products depends on our purchasing power, and this purchasing power depends on the productivity of our economy. If American producers are driven out of the most advanced end of manufacturing, then American consumers will gradually lose the wealth with which to buy the splendid foreign products. And if our trade deficit is such that we can pay for imports only by selling off American companies and American real estate rather than American products, then our economy remains competitive only by becoming someone else's colony.

Though they essentially accept this logic, the authors of quasi-official studies like the semiconductor report continue to face a dilemma. The thrust of their argument assaults the assumptions of laissez-faire, but it never quite takes on laissez-faire itself, since that would be to declare oneself outside the national consensus. Instead, the argument is cloaked in the language of military security. The clear message is the warning about "the technical edge we depend on for national security."[36] The message about civilian economic competitiveness is more muted.

This game of cloaking civilian interventionist policies in national security dates back at least to the Eisenhower administration, when big spending programs with a liberal Democratic flavor were rendered ideologically acceptable to Republicans by tacking on the magic words "national defense." This gave respectability to the National Defense Education Act, which provided federal aid to education, as well as the National Defense Highway Act, allowing motorists to tag along on highways built ostensibly for tanks.

It is time to stop kidding ourselves. But the Bush administration shows no sign of doing so, and even Democrats such as Bingaman are a little shy about attacking the prevailing dogma head-on, lest they be criticized as statists. Advocates of civilian technology have made some tactical gains, but they are still on the losing side of an ideological consensus which allows exceptions only for the armed forces.

The industrial-policy debate of the 1990s is different from the one of the late 1970s. Industrial-policy advocates in the Carter era did not believe in laissez-faire either, but they were attacked as opportunistic representatives of "loser" industries, industries that deserved to suffer the verdict of the marketplace. "Engine Charlie" Wilson's dictum—what's good for General Motors is good for the country—was remembered with scorn, and liberals had long attacked the auto industry as lazy, oligopolistic, and slow to meet changing consumer tastes. Going to bat for Detroit seemed little more than a tactic to defend inflated UAW wages. This was exactly the sort of protectionism that economists warned against. Much the same could be said of those who wanted to save the steel industry, an industry that epitomized the arrogance of executives and the consequences of periodically agreeing to wage increases in excess of productivity gains. It was easy to claim then that the apparent decline of American autos and steel was in part the temporary result of recession. In fact, that was the official finding of the U.S. International Trade Commission in response to a petition for trade relief by the auto industry. The United States still enjoyed an overall trade surplus in manufactured goods and an overwhelming lead in the "sunrise" industries incorporating advanced technology. Letting new manufacturing nations move into medium-tech consumer products like autos and steel was just what markets were supposed to do. Holding back this process was considered as futile as ordering the tides to halt.

As a result, when the U.S. government did bow to political pressure to offer "temporary" trade relief to autos and steel, they did so with a very guilty conscience and refused to define an affirmative set of industrial or technological goals. Eventually, the American industries would have to adjust to a smaller market share or lose out entirely to imports.

But the current debate is altogether different. The United States now has a massive trade deficit which was not remedied by a cheaper dollar. The affected industries are not unionized, high-wage, "declining" rust-belt producers but the gems of America's most advanced technology. Yet the underlying ideological issue is the same: should government help U.S. industry remain competitive if governments of other trading nations are helping foreign producers to capture advantage?

The semiconductor report offers a set of frankly interventionist remedies, beginning with the blunt goal of expanding the global market share of the U.S. semiconductor industry. To this end, it proposes doubling DARPA's current $100 million annual contribution to the Sematech research consortium and creating a counterpart Consumer Electronics Capital Corporation (CECC) to set up a billion-dollar pool of long-term "patient capital" aimed at rebuilding the consumer electronics industry. It also called for more "market-oriented" reforms to lower the cost of private capital, as well as liberalization of antitrust laws to promote more joint ventures. These recommendations were rebuffed by the Bush administration, whose economic and budget officials viewed them as a special-interest raid on the U.S. Treasury as well as an ideologically illegitimate brand of state planning.

There have been other such initiatives, but virtually all have run into the same ideological wall. Senator Ernest Hollings of South Carolina succeeded in inserting into the 1988 Trade Act a provision setting up an embryonic "civilian DARPA" at the Commerce Department. He seized on the National Bureau of Standards, which has long performed the industrial-policy task of helping industry to harmonize technical specifications, and upgraded it to a National Institute of Standards and Technology. But the administration kept funding limited to a token $10 million. Other pending legislation sponsored by Senator John Glenn and several other Democrats would convert the Commerce Department into a Department of Industry and Technology, one of whose agencies would be a more substantial civilian DARPA, known as the Advanced Civilian Technology Agency. This was also opposed by the Bush administration.

Still another incursion that Bush cut off involves high-definition television (HDTV), which was pioneered by the Japanese, using the combined power of their national television network, NHK, MITI, and the cartel of electronics suppliers. The Japanese were positioning themselves to dominate the next generation of consumer television receivers, as well as to lead in a technology with significant industrial applications. DARPA has been financing innovations in flat-screen, high-definition monitors that are useful in computer-aided design and manufacturing, as well as in sophisticated radar. The idea of an HDTV project attracted Commerce Secretary Robert Mosbacher and Under Secretary Thomas Murrin, a former Westinghouse senior executive and scientist at Carnegie-Mellon University, a onetime Pentagon adviser, and a well-respected veteran in the Pentagon/high-tech world. Mosbacher, during 1989, publicized plans for a big American initiative to challenge Japan's dominance and recapture a domestic television industry with HDTV. DARPA's chief, Craig Fields, supported this, and the American Electronics Association did so as well, sponsoring a report by the Boston Consulting Group calculating its benefits. A bipartisan group called Rebuild America tried to give the plan an ideologically permissible new name. This wasn't industrial policy; it was, in the words of Rebuild America, "industry-led policy."

The White House was not fooled. The "Gang of Four"—White House chief of staff John Sununu, budget director Richard Darman, chief economist Michael Boskin, and domestic-policy chief Roger Porter blocked the proposal, just as they blocked increased funding for Sematech and other initiatives. Mosbacher, despite his personal friendship with President Bush, found himself isolated, and he quietly retreated. Fields was hard pressed to defend his existing budget, without mounting risky incursions into civilian territory. As pressure was brought on the overall Pentagon budget, administration budget officials tried to divert $20 million of the $30 million DARPA subsidy to HDTV and to end DARPA's funding for Sematech. In early 1990, Fields was fired and Murrin was warned not to buck official policy. Another high-ranking advocate of military-industrial collaboration, Assistant Secretary of Defense Robert Costello, quietly departed for the Hudson Institute.

If the forces of orthodoxy are firmly in control of the Bush administration, the debate is at least far richer and less one-sided than it was a decade ago. It is not just a few loser industries who support a national technology, but most high-tech industries. Prominent Republicans such as Clyde Prestowitz and Kevin Phillips have joined forces with Democratic liberals to call for a benign form of economic nationalism. Even mainstream trade economists such as Paul Krugman are expressing second thoughts.

The issue is also forced by the realities of a pluralist world. The Bush administration's policy is in sharp contrast to that of our allies and trading partners. The Japanese have long made technological supremacy their number-one foreign-policy goal. The European Community, with a smaller military establishment and with little antipathy to state intervention, explicitly aims to recapture industrial leadership in many areas.

Scholars have debated whether our militarized high-tech policy has on balance been good or bad for our industry. The only reasonable answer must be that it has been both. On the one hand, the trillions spent by the Pentagon on arms since the end of World War II have produced spectacular technological breakthroughs. On the other hand, the national security emphasis has limited the form of this technology and its freedom to be applied. As long as U.S. government technology spending must justify itself in narrowly military terms, this will continue to be the case. And the budget squeeze makes the outlays harder to defend.

The days when "national security" permitted an enormous amount of government subsidy for advanced technology, in defiance of official doctrine, are over. Just as the eclipse of a Soviet military threat demands a radical redefinition of American military security, it calls for a clarification of our conception of economic security and an honest acknowledgment of the government's role in the private, peacetime economy.

In sum, the hegemonic dilemma harms the United States not just by imposing the cost of military outlays on the U.S. economy but in multiple ways. The common element in all of this is a utopian conception of the virtue of laissez-faire that was never entirely appropriate even when the United States stood alone as the great economic power. It is certainly not appropriate today, either for the United States or for the world economic system, when the world has become more pluralist and the U.S. economy is diminished. To complete the discussion of the costs of hegemony yoked to laissez-faire, we must return to the realm where planning for the postwar era began—finance.

# seven

# GLOBAL FINANCE: SLOUCHING
# TOWARD PLURALISM

The world monetary system since the breakup of Bretton Woods in 1971–73 has been a series of ad hoc arrangements based on muddled views about whether markets can be trusted to set the value of national currencies. The system lurched from fixed exchange rates until 1973, to floating rates between 1973 and 1985, to an uneasy attempt to manage parities within rough target zones under the Plaza accord after 1985. But the institutional machinery and the theoretical understanding of the exercise has lagged far behind the practice. This, too, is a consequence of the U.S. attempt to maintain political dominance while it propagates laissez-faire as doctrine.

In practice, the Plaza system is heavily dependent on the cooperation of the three great monetary powers—the United States, Japan, and Germany—and the role of Germany will soon give way to an EC that is likely to have a common currency and a common central bank early in the next century. Yet because of the residual dominant role of the dollar and the reluctance of U.S. policymakers to cede greater influence either to other nations or to a new set of transnational institutions, the United States continues to bear burdens that no longer produce commensurate benefits. As a matter of ideology, the United States continues to stand for the proposition that global finance, to the maximum extent possible, should be privatized and left to commercial banks, money markets, and corporations. This stance—the dominance of the dollar, the resistance to new public institutions, the romanticization of the free market—invites instability that damages the entire system.

Given that the events of 1989 and 1990 have irrevocably altered the postwar system, what alternative structures and relationships are possible—in monetary arrangements, debt management, and development policy? What kinds of institutions will be required? What sharing of sovereignty? What relative new roles for great and small powers? What division of responsibility between private actors and public ones?

Consider first the organization of money. Within national boundaries, the state monopolizes the printing of money, but as economics students know, this is not as simple as it seems, since banks also "create" money whenever they extend credit. Allowing banks to create enough credit to finance a growing economy without triggering inflation or excessively risky lending requires governments to conduct prudent monetary, fiscal, and regulatory policies. Governments control the standards by which credit is granted by regulating what multiple of their own capital banks may lend and by varying the rate at which the central banks lend to commercial banks. They manipulate the volume of the circulating money supply by selling or purchasing government securities to create or soak up currency. Prudent governments attempt to tie money growth approximately to the real rate of economic growth, to avoid inflation. They supervise banks, limit entry of competing banks, and insure deposits. There is no way that this exercise can be apolitical, for these decisions determine creditors' and debtors' gains and losses and the soundness of the entire banking system. Across national frontiers, where dozens of national currencies are in circulation, where reserve requirements can be evaded, and where there is no sovereign government, the exercise becomes far more complex.

In the laissez-faire view, there are essentially two ways of organizing a global money system. One is a classical gold standard; the other is a system of pure floating rates. The virtue of both, from a laissez-faire perspective, is that they are supposedly self-regulating. One uses an "objective," universally valued commodity—gold—as the yardstick; the other lets market forces dictate the value of money itself. But, of course, governments being intimately implicated in the creation of money and the maintenance of its value, neither of these "self-regulating" approaches works very well in practice. As we have seen, a pure gold standard has many problems: for one, as Benjamin J. Cohen observed in his fine 1977 study, *Organizing the World's Money,* [1] a gold standard is politically naïve. It assumes that democratically elected governments will tolerate the austerities imposed by external forces without responding defensively. It ignores the political risk of competitive deflations and holds the real economy hostage to the vagaries of gold discoveries. None of this has stopped many conservative theorists (and nationalists) from longing for the simplicity, automaticity, and universality of a simple gold standard. General de Gaulle favored it not because he believed in laissez-faire but as a means of ending Anglo-Saxon monetary hegemony. In his first administration, when monetary eccentrics had influence on policy, President Reagan yielded to pressure from right-wing Republican gold bugs such as Lewis Lehrman and Jack Kemp and appointed a commission to investigate the pros and cons of returning to a simple gold standard. Its report was inconclusive, and the project was quietly shelved.

Other conservative economists argue for a system of floating rates. The last two decades provided a pretty fair test of the proposition that pure floating exchange rates are economically efficient and politically bearable. Evidently they are not. As the Bretton Woods system was coming under stress, it was Milton Friedman who argued most emphatically for the multiple virtues of floating rates. According to Friedman, floating rates would allow money markets to set the "true" value of currencies. Money would become just like any other commodity, with its correct price and quantity determined by the marketplace. It would help this process if, on the domestic front, central bankers would put the money supply on automatic pilot rather than meddling, announcing a rate of growth for the money supply and not deviating from it. According to Friedman, floating rates not only would allow markets to set currency values accurately but would allow nations autonomy to carry out divergent economic policies. For example, if a nation chose to tolerate slightly higher inflation than its neighbors, markets would compensate by proportionally devaluing its currency. Floating rates, Friedman contended, "are a means of permitting each country to seek monetary stability according to its own lights, without either imposing its mistakes on its neighbors or having their mistakes imposed on it."[2]

Among its other liabilities, this view was splendidly indifferent to the realities of high politics—the plain fact that the United States had strategic reasons for wishing the dollar to be special. It was also indifferent to the consequences of dollar hegemony—the fact that the dollar, as the world's key currency, could stay out of alignment for long periods of time. Further, the floating-exchange-rate school ignored the risk that central bankers and finance ministries of other nations might find it convenient to use their own monetary policies to undervalue their currencies slightly, as a form of neomercantilism to help their exports. Nonhegemonic nations also had regulatory devices at their disposal to discourage the use of their money as reserve or transaction currencies. Like the gold standard, the idea of pure floating rates left out politics. Moreover, it understated the speculative damage that floating rates could wreak upon the real economy by sending mixed signals to investors and businesses. Friedman, characteristically, solved the problem of speculative instability with tautology. He argued that "destabilizing" speculators, by definition, would lose money and be driven out of business; only constructive speculators who nudged exchange rates in the direction of their true equilibrium path would prosper; hence, speculation could not be a problem. But, of course, the long run is made up of countless short runs in which destructive speculators make a lot of money and ordinary producers become cautious. All markets tend to overshoot; world economic history is a history of speculative bubbles followed by panics. Money is a particularly volatile commodity, because it can be borrowed and the "leveraging" then exaggerates speculative swings in its value. When a market in something as basic as the coin of the realm— which denominates the value of all other goods and services—is cut loose to overshoot wildly and repeatedly, harm to the real economy results.

True, buyers and sellers of real goods can protect themselves against currency swings with "hedging" techniques. But short-term hedging against, say, a ninety-day adverse swing in the dollar value of German marks offers no guarantees for the investor deciding whether to locate a billion-dollar manufacturing facility with a ten-year useful life in Düsseldorf or Taipei. Alexandre Lamfalussy, the canny Swiss who heads the Bank for International Settlements (the central bankers' central bank), observed in 1981, following a decade of floating rates:

> No optimum allocation [of economic activity] can take place unless market participants know with some degree of certainty the direction in which relative prices will move. But how could they have made any reasonable guesses about exchange rate movements with the kind of experience we have had since 1973? The real cost of the present situation [pure floating rates] is, I fear, that decision-makers in the field of trade and investment have to concentrate an excessively large proportion of their energy on trying to guess exchange rate movements rather than on improving production processes, inventing new products and seeking out new markets.[3]

Even worse, the floating-rate regime had flunked Friedman's most elementary claim: far from promoting automatic adjustment and equilibration, it encouraged greater volatility and instability. By 1978, after five years of floating rates, as the economist Susan Strange calculated, the countries with the biggest surpluses—Japan, West Germany, Switzerland, the Netherlands, and Belgium—had surpluses twice as big as before, while the major deficit countries—the United States, Britain, France, Canada, and Italy—had deficits three times as great.[4] Floating rates tended to exaggerate differences rather than equilibrate them.

In practice, the non-utopian alternative ways of organizing a viable world monetary order boil down to four: a system of fairly stable rates with a single hegemon; a "managed float," in which markets set parities but the world's central bankers intervene to temper the ups and downs; a shared hegemony of a few key currencies; or a world central bank. None of these systems is ideal; all are departures from simple laissez-faire. With the first, a single powerful nation is the central banker, as Great Britain and the United States have been, and allows its currency to anchor the system. An essentially hegemonic system can have either fixed exchange rates that are periodically adjusted, as in the heyday of both the gold standard and the Bretton Woods system, or flexible rates, as was attempted in the 1970s and early 1980s. In either case, as we have seen, the system is quite stable so long as the hegemon keeps doing its duty—but the hegemonic nation eventually pays a price.

A system of fixed rates, departing from pure laissez-faire, is easier to sustain when there are limits on free capital movements as well. Otherwise money gravitates to harder currencies, and speculative pressures against weak currencies build up, forcing devaluations. The Bretton Woods system of fixed rates worked as long as it did mainly for two reasons: the dominance of the U.S. economy, which permitted a long-term outflow of overvalued American dollars to lubricate the system; and the temporary limits on other transnational capital flows. The deregulation of capital movements and the deterioration of a fixed-rate system went hand in hand, for as capital was freed to seek its highest rate of return, speculative movements overwhelmed the official parities. Alternatively, for fixed exchange rates to endure without capital controls, there needs to be either a coordination or a convergence of rates of economic growth—in short, a convergence of macroeconomic policy, so that the world is truly one big economy and the world's several currencies might as well be one currency. (In the 1950s, when a British pound equaled $2.80 seemingly for all eternity, exchange-rate speculation was futile, and it didn't matter whether you held dollars or pounds.)

In the unlikely event of a genuine convergence of world rates of economic growth, inflation, and macroeconomic policies, fixed exchange rates could endure and periodic revaluations would be unnecessary. Though there might still be a hundred different currencies, in effect there would be one. But the precondition for this state of affairs—a single macroeconomic policy—is tantamount to a single world government, at least in the realm of economics. And this seems highly unrealistic, except perhaps regionally as with the EC. A hegemonic system based on a single key currency becomes harder and harder to sustain.

For the last few years, the system has evolved in the direction of the second alternative—a "managed float." In the idiom of the dismal science, which has a weakness for mixing metaphors, this is a variation on an even more barbarous linguistic muddle, known as the "crawling peg." The idea is that major nations "peg" their exchange rates either to an explicit parity (e.g., one dollar equals 125 yen) or to a narrow range (a dollar fluctuating between, say, 120 and 130 yen). The parities or ranges can gradually shift, though at a sluggish rate controlled by central bank intervention. They "crawl" rather than surge. Hence, the crawling peg. At the Plaza, the world's financial leaders acknowledged that a pure system of floating rates was dangerously unstable. Without quite admitting it publicly, they set target ranges for each key currency, as well as embracing more systematic intervention. But there were two rather divergent views of what the system was really supposed to do. The conservatives, like West Germany's Karl-Otto Poehl, wanted the official money managers more or less to follow the market, with periodic revisions of parity benchmarks—a "crawling peg" precisely. Monetary intervention, in this minimalist view, was intended mainly to smooth out day-to-day instabilities, not to fight market forces. The more aggressive interventionists, notably the French, wanted the managed float to behave more like the Bretton Woods system and to maintain parities within fairly narrow ranges, over long periods of time, by aggressive central bank intervention. The task of maintaining parities, in turn, would generate political pressure for greater convergence of economic fundamentals. Only as an exercise in muddle-through has the Plaza system been a short-term success, and it has intensified strains on the United States.


The current nonsystem of managed floating has been further complicated by the existence of a more explicitly managed subsystem in its midst, namely the European Monetary System (EMS). The EMS functions like a mini–Bretton Woods; it is a system of fairly stable exchange rates within Europe, anchored by the German Bundesbank. EMS originated in the mid-1970s, as a response to the United States' retreat from effective monetary stewardship. In December 1969, when the dollar was coming under intolerable pressure, the German Chancellor, Willy Brandt, had proposed the beginnings of a European Monetary Union in two stages. At the time, the wide disparities in growth rates and inflation rates were thwarting European economic union and monetary stability, and the instability, in turn, was generating national protectionist pressures, which further set back the cause of economic integration. At the European summit of December 1–2, 1969, at The Hague, Brandt won the agreement of other leaders: first to make a concerted effort to harmonize short-term economic policies and subsequently to create a common European Reserve Fund, to which member nations would transfer some of their foreign-exchange reserves. This quasi-central bank would be Keynes's clearing union—on one continent. A real European central bank was not seriously discussed for another two decades.

The Western European countries did attempt to narrow the range of fluctuations of their currencies vis-à-vis each other. This narrow band of permissible variation, also modeled on the original Bretton Woods system, was called a "tunnel," and the narrow fluctuations in currency values came to be known as the "snake in the tunnel," or simply the snake. At the first Western economic conference, at Rambouillet castle in 1975, the Americans gave their cautious blessing to the European currency snake; the IMF Articles of Agreement were amended to permit it, and U.S. officials agreed to occasional interventions to steady dollar fluctuations which would help make the snake viable.[5] But economic turbulence and the incompletion of European commercial integration made the enterprise very difficult. Moreover, the snake had no head. Eventually, in the spring of 1978, Chancellor Helmut Schmidt and President Valéry Giscard d'Estaing agreed on a more formal European Monetary System, whose effective head would be the Deutsche Bundesbank. The plan was conceived over the initial strenuous objection of the Bundesbank itself, whose governors viewed the idea as a source of imported inflation. But the EMS has worked better than almost anyone anticipated. It has provided a zone of monetary stability within Europe.

The EMS uses a European Currency Unit (ECU) as a denominator of value. The ECU's value is based on a weighted average of Western European currency values. Currencies are supposed to fluctuate within very narrow bands of plus or minus 2.25 percent. When a currency approaches the top or bottom of its allowable range, governments and/or their central bankers intervene in the money markets to push the exchange rate back where it belongs. Periodic revisions in parities are permitted on a consensus basis. All central bankers commit reserves to the stabilization process, but the Bundesbank is the system's effective central banker, lending other central banks money at short term to finance interventions.

Though this sounds very much like Bretton Woods, the EMS goes well beyond what Bretton Woods could accomplish, because of the context of European regional economic integration and European political federalism. Maintaining exchange-rate parities has had the effect of making member nations run convergent macroeconomic policies. Obviously, if France is operating a high-inflation economy and West Germany a low-inflation one, their exchange-rate parities cannot long be maintained, notwithstanding all the central-bank intervention imaginable. As the Western European economies have become more integrated with each other, the EMS has added a stimulus to further integration. And the rates—of economic growth, inflation, unemployment, etc.—among the EMS members indeed converged. Other aspects of economic integration, such as a common agricultural policy and the increasing importance of intra-European trade, also created complementary pressures, for a single market dictates a single price. If, for example, French and West German wheat fetch the same price (which they do under the Common Market's farm regime), then it won't do to have competitive devaluations causing agricultural price wars. The yearly variability of Western European currencies against the ECU gradually subsided during the 1980s, from well over 15 percentage points to just a few, expressing both the convergence of real economies and the efficacy of the monetary system.[6] By 1990, remarkably, France's rate of inflation was below West Germany's. In the meantime, the ECU gradually gained credibility as a global unit of account, and by 1989, over $150 billion worth of ECU-denominated bonds issued by governments and private borrowers was outstanding.[7]

The more venturesome European federalists have long argued that the EMS needs to evolve into a true European central bank with a single circulating currency. This idea of a common European currency, once proposed by Jean Monnet and seconded repeatedly by Robert Triffin, got an important practical boost at the Strasbourg European summit meeting in December 1989 when Jacques Delors's design for a European central bank and common currency, to be gradually phased in over more than a decade, was accepted. The idea is to create a central bank roughly modeled on the U.S. Federal Reserve, called "Euro-fed"; then to establish permanent fixed parities, which would operate for a while in parallel with the ECU; and finally to convert all national currencies to the ECU. Several obstacles remain, of course, including Britain's nonmembership in the EMS, as well as Germany's awkward divided loyalties between the imperatives of European union on the one hand and the completion of German economic unification on the other. Yet at Strasbourg, the French insisted that progress on the money question would be the test of Germany's continuing good faith as an active European power, and in the end Germany embraced the French position. The French, in turn, implicitly accepted that the dominance of the Bundesbank pulls the rest of Europe toward a German-style macroeconomics—low inflation, slow but steady growth, and monetary discipline. At the same time, the more that the DM or the successor ECU comes to be used as a global currency, the greater is the risk of imported inflation.

The convergence in the late 1980s of the thinking of French socialists and German conservatives puzzled many observers. But it shouldn't have. The French, after their disastrous attempt at unilateral reflation in 1981–82, came around to the German view of the virtue of price stability. The French also recognized that they had a better chance of imposing their views within a pan-European whole. As long as the Bundesbank is Europe's de facto central bank, the French have no votes; they would have at least one vote in a new Euro-fed. The Germans, for their part, appreciated that the DM would carry less of a hegemonic burden if a Europe-wide currency were substituted. Most important, the convergence of policy reflected a growing ideological convergence. On the left, Western European Marxism is all but dead. On the right, the only utopian free-market conservative at this writing is Mrs. Thatcher, and she is isolated. European center-right and center-left, whether labeled Christian Democrat or Social Democrat, share a common philosophy of what Germans call a social market economy—a capitalist economy tempered substantially by public intervention. Thus, the final integration of the European commercial market had to be complemented by an integration of European public financial institutions, and eventually by a more robust European political federalism—otherwise the delicate balance between market and polity would be hopelessly tilted in favor of the market. On this point, French socialists and German central bankers are in full agreement.[8]

It is very likely that within a decade or so the preconditions could exist for a global monetary system of the third variety—namely, a system based on a few key currencies, in this case the dollar, the yen, and the mark or ECU. Yet evolution in this direction is complicated by several factors. One is the American reluctance to give up the perquisites of dollar domination; the other is the divided responsibilities of the new Germany. Thus far, German policy has given priority first to domestic monetary stability of the enlarged deutsche mark area, second to stability within the EMS, and only third to its still limited role as one of the global money managers. For the next several years, Germany will have its hands full reconciling its absorption of the former German Democratic Republic with its continental role as monetary hegemon for the EC. However, as European integration proceeds, the EC will increasingly become a single unit with economic and monetary strength equal to or greater than the United States.

The EMS is sometimes held up as a model of an embryonic global central banking system, not unlike Keynes's original conception of a currency union. But if there are political obstacles to the creation of a single central bank and currency within Western Europe, which for forty years has been gradually moving toward political federation and economic union, there are obviously profound obstacles to the creation of a global central bank, the fourth alternative. A worldwide central bank modeled on the Federal Reserve would require nations to give up a significant degree of sovereignty in their monetary policies and hence substantial political sovereignty as well. In practice, a regime of more or less free trade has this effect in any event. If a nation has an irresponsibly inflationary monetary policy, its currency loses value and it suffers a balance-of-payments crisis. From a conservative perspective, this form of discipline has the virtue of seeming "objective" rather than deliberate. It is one thing to yield sovereignty, discreetly, to global market forces. It is quite something else to yield it to an explicit political institution or federation, which might have policies counterbalancing market imperatives. This was, of course, Keynes's insight at Bretton Woods. The world's financial markets would be unlikely to look kindly on a politically accountable genuine world central bank.

Moreover, a world central bank would require far greater power-sharing between rich and poor nations. Under the present system, the world's smaller and less developed countries are subject to deliberate and explicit constraints under the aegis of the IMF and the World Bank. A generation of IMF "stabilization" programs has imposed austerity remedies on developing nations that wish to be certified as sound candidates for investment. The United States, one of the macroeconomic malefactors, has never been subject to the discipline of an IMF stabilization program. That would be an unthinkable affront, no matter how irresponsible the U.S. deficit. As the Romans said, *quod licet Jovi, non licet bovi:* what is permitted the gods is not allowed to cattle. For the most part, it is the world's smaller and poorer nations that have had to submit to the economic pain and political indignity of carrying out IMF-imposed "stabilization" schemes. When Britain—Britain!—had to succumb to an IMF plan in the mid-1970s, nothing could have been a surer signal that it had fallen from the ranks of the world's financial great powers.

Any plan for a world central bank would founder on the same rock that wrecked the Keynes-White concept of the original IMF—a refusal by the great powers, particularly the United States, to cede sovereignty. Still, it is imaginable that within a decade or two the financial system will be something of a hybrid—a system based on three key currencies with a strengthened global bank. Politically, it will come clear by the year 2000 that the dollar is no longer hegemonic, especially if Europe continues its progress toward monetary union. Japan is already a significantly greater financial power than we, and Europe will soon pass the United States in gross national product. Japan and Europe are also net creditors, which the United States is not.

When the United States is no longer dominant financially and the dollar gradually gives ground to the yen and the DM/ECU as a reserve and transaction currency, the U.S. will no longer be able to cling to the idea that it actually exercises hegemony. Monetary sovereignty with two other major powers would already be shared, and there would far less reason to resist sharing it with a global central bank as well. Of course, a "global central bank" would not be a true central bank on the model of the Federal Reserve or the Bundesbank—that is, it would not issue circulating currency—but it might well be a significantly expanded version of the current

IMF, with far more liquidity. And a far greater share of global reserves could be held in the form of the IMF's "currency," whether Special Drawing Rights or some successor.

It is important to realize that the main obstacle to a stronger, larger, and more expansionary IMF has been the United States, as long as dollar hegemony prevailed—actually well beyond that point. But once the dollar is roughly coequal with the ECU and the yen, the political and economic logic for that resistance evaporates. Indeed, the IMF itself then becomes an attractive counterweight to ECU or yen hegemony. Moreover, as we have seen, the official U.S. position resisted a Keynes-style IMF almost subliminally, because America as the major creditor nation disdained a global central bank favoring cheap credit. As the United States becomes increasingly a debtor, plentiful credit looks better and better.

A more robust version of an IMF would require not only an expansion of monetary resources and mission, but an expansive rather than austere conception of its own function in the world economy. Here, Europe's progress toward monetary union offers a very important model. By the year 2000, twelve important industrial nations will have had two decades' experience subordinating and coordinating monetary policy and may well have a single currency. A regional central bank will likely be a practical reality. The EMS experience will be instructive about the practical sharing of sovereignty and the building of transnational public institutions to help channel, stabilize, and civilize brute market forces.

There remains the troubling question of the Third World debt, as well as the closely related question of economic health among the world's poorer nations. Here again, the United States, itself a debtor, has behaved like the most shortsighted of creditors, resisting expansionary solutions to Third World debt. In brief, it has done this for four reasons: its creditor mentality, the shakiness of its big banks, its hegemonic imperative, and the ideological conceits of laissez-faire *redux*.

Let us consider first the lingering creditor mentality itself. Although the United States as a whole is a net debtor nation, American banks are net creditors of Third World nations. Republican administrations have fallen into the fallacy of mistaking American national interest and the interest of the world financial system for the interests of particular U.S. banks. Providing wholesale relief to the Third World debtors is said to reward the profligate and punish the thrifty, creating a "moral hazard" that would tempt improvident nations to incur unproductive debts all over again. What bankruptcy laws permit millionaire entrepreneurs, who are celebrated as "risk takers," is denied to Third World debtors, who are expected to tighten their belts until they cough up every last nickel. *Quod licet Jovi . . .*

Nations have defaulted on external debts throughout history, and after a decent interval have been permitted back into the world's credit markets. New revolutionary governments have often repudiated the debts of their predecessor regimes. The American South may rise again economically, but nobody is likely to redeem your Confederate bonds. Indeed, if Southern economic development had been held hostage to the redemption of Confederate bonds, its economic recovery would have been much slower. This seems only commonsensical when applied to one's own nation, but as creditors Americans have far less sympathy for the plight of other debtor countries.

"The fiscal history of Latin America is replete with instances of government defaults," wrote Max Winkler in 1933. "Borrowing and default follow one another with almost perfect regularity. When payment is resumed, the past is easily forgotten and a new borrowing orgy ensues."[9] In fact, payment is sometimes written off—as about $5 billion of Latin American debt was in the 1930s—and lending resumes anyway. Investors and creditors would prefer that no default ever occurred, but they keep investing money in places like Latin America because the payoffs are so high so much of the time. A cold-eyed view of capitalism would hold that creditors knew what they were doing and that the higher rates precisely reflected the risk of defaults. The American commission in charge of the annexation of Cuba in 1898 wrote of the previous Cuban government's obligations: "The creditors, from the beginning, took the chances of the investment. The very pledge of the national credit, while on the one hand demonstrates the national character of the debt, on the other hand proclaims the notorious risk."[10] There is still a committee of the heirs of British creditors attempting to collect on nineteenth-century bonds issued by several American states that went into default around the time of the Civil War. These, of course, have long been written off as practically uncollectible. But there is no such realism when it comes to the current crop of Third World debtors. In the case of recent bad debts, creditors cling to the illusion that the debts are collectible.

At one time or another, defaulters have included most of the world's developing nations and most of Europe as well after World War I. Historians blame much of the economic turmoil and the nationalistic political strife leading to World War II on the failure of the great powers to broker a satisfactory solution to the World War I debt. The Treaty of Versailles required Germany to pay war reparations of some $31 billion to the victorious European allies. They, in turn, owed about $20 billion to the United

States, which they could not pay unless Germany paid them. Keynes, writing in 1919, foresaw a disaster in the making and called for a drastic scaling down of German reparations, as well as a cancellation of inter-allied debts.[11] The 1920s were a decade of laissez-faire and muddle-through, the creditor mentality firmly in control. Debts were sacrosanct. New money was lent, not to finance recovery, but to assure payment of old debt. Under the 1924 Dawes Plan, the United States lent Germany money so that it could keep on paying back France and England. The Young Plan of 1929 stretched out Germany's repayment terms. Finally, after the onset of the Great Depression, Germany stopped paying reparations entirely, and at the 1932 Lausanne conference, France and Britain agreed to cancel German debts; shortly thereafter, they defaulted on their debts to the United States. (Finland was fondly remembered by a generation of Americans as the one nation that paid America back in full.) In 1931 and 1932, a total of about $80 billion of uncollectible sovereign debt was simply renegotiated or written off—but it was too late to undo the economic and political damage. Less than a year after the Lausanne conference, Hitler took power in Berlin.

The statesmen of Bretton Woods recognized that debt forgiveness is sometimes the better part of prudence. But in the 1980s, the Third World debtors did not include any great powers capable of starting a world war. Half-measures—the Baker Plan, the Brady Plan—bore an uncanny similarity to the Dawes Plan and the Young Plan. They offered too little relief too late, and just enough forbearance to prevent total collapse—a slow bleed. The policy cost some of the world's poorest countries ten years of what might have been economic growth.

The second, related motive for perpetuating the debt crisis of the 1980s had to do with the balance sheets of the creditor banks. These were already shaky, thanks to another gift of the laissez-faire era—deregulation. In the decade before, in line with the then prevailing wisdom, American banks had been freed to spawn bank holding companies, to undertake risky investments in real estate, to bid up interest rates in competing for short-term deposits, and to escape a variety of regulatory strictures. The prudent barrier between finance and commerce was in many ways breached. Since the bitter lessons of the 1930s, regulatory doctrine had held that banks were no ordinary enterprises: they used other people's money, which gave them extraordinary reach and extraordinary responsibility; the systemic costs of their bank failures were higher for the economy and society than the occasional failure of a business financed by somebody's own equity capital. The new, deregulatory doctrine held that banks should be entrepreneurial like everyone else. Congress was on the verge of repealing the Glass-

Steagall Act, which keeps banks out of stock underwriting and brokerage, when the savings-and-loan debacle finally dampened this deregulatory ardor.

The orgy of Third World debt was only the most visible and costly casualty of go-go banking, and one of the earliest. Bankers had found to their delight that huge loans could be booked at a fraction of the usual administrative cost and at premium rates, by dealing with Third World governments rather than pursuing the humdrum, unglamorous business of ordinary commercial lending. By the late 1970s, the biggest American banks were making more than half their profits from Third World lending. By 1982, nine of them had more than 200 percent of their equity capital tied up in such loans. If the loans—even a portion of them—stopped paying interest, the banks' earnings would suffer, and then the value of their stock; if the loans were written off, they would be instantly insolvent. European banks, less directly exposed, suffered from a different problem: thanks to the Eurodollar market, most of their Third World lending had been in dollars, too; but the European central banks had limited dollar resources, and, unlike the Federal Reserve, they could not print dollars in case of an emergency.

Two other developments occurred that made the big banks even more dependent on this stream of profits from the Third World. Extremely high inflation meant that many domestic borrowers, such as homeowners with 7 percent mortgages, were paying banks interest rates that in real terms were negative. It was a debtor's holiday and a creditor's nightmare. A bank paying 15 percent on certificates of deposit to finance a 7 percent mortgage was losing fortunes. As ordinary banking became unprofitable, bankers turned to higher-risk lending. But gradually many of the speculative investments that had been so fashionable only a few years before began to turn sour. So balance sheets didn't look very good, even before the Third World debt bubble showed signs of bursting. As it became evident that Third World debtors could not repay, it was extremely impolitic for regulators to require the banks to "write down" the book value of their loans to the actual value that markets (in their sublime and unerring wisdom) were placing on them. By the mid-1980s, Mexican or Brazilian debt, if you cared to buy it in the secondary market, was trading at about fifty cents on the dollar.

But what markets knew, regulators could not admit—lest a full-blown banking panic occur. Once again, the invisible hand was too fickle, too volatile, too heedless of secondary consequences, to trust fully. (Might there be a larger lesson here?) Banks were permitted to carry loans at book value rather than the depressed market value, and in return, they were encouraged to keep rolling over the loans, making new ones to finance interest payments on old loans at market rates of interest, pushing debtor nations deeper into debt rather than offering genuine relief. This slow bleed meant that an ever higher fraction of export earnings of poor countries in the Third World had to be paid out to service prior debt. Normally, capital flows from rich regions to poorer ones. For much of the 1980s, the capital flow to Latin America was negative.

Third, the balance-sheet mentality was once again reinforced by the United States' hegemonic imperative. Given the meager state of America's global financial resources, a truly expansionary solution to the Third World debt crisis would entail substantially more power-sharing with other nations than the United States has been prepared to consider. It would also entail either an increase in the financial resources of public global banks and regional development banks or an increase in the practical power of other creditor nations like Japan and West Germany—and probably both, with a concomitant decline in official American influence. Because of Japan's and West Germany's deference to American leadership, there has been a remarkable lag in the relative influence of nations within the councils of the IMF and the World Bank. It is as if the clock had stopped and the degree of financial weight had frozen in the 1960s. The United States still controls enough voting weight within the Bank and the Fund to veto decisions, and likes it that way. It has resisted or diluted most efforts to increase Fund and Bank resources because that would mean more power-sharing. Only in 1990 was Japan belatedly moved up from fifth to second place (which it shares with Germany) in voting rights at the Bank. Nor are Japan and West Germany entirely unhappy with this remarkable time lag: letting the United States take the lead makes the Third World debt more an American problem and allows them to continue their long-standing and highly rewarding practice of putting their own domestic economic objectives first. The United States would do well to share these burdens.

The fourth cause of debt stalemate is ideological. The Third World debt was hardly incurred under laissez-faire auspices. Indeed, banks lent far too much money under the convenient fiction that these were "sovereign" loans implicitly guaranteed by host governments—a transaction precisely immune from market consequences; they further believed their own governments would help them in a true liquidity crisis, as indeed they did. Moreover, the debt crisis itself was triggered by two government-inspired events—the price gouging of the oil cartel and the tight-money response of the Federal Reserve, neither of which expressed the workings of the invisible hand. So governments were intimately implicated on both sides of the loan transactions, in many ways. Yet though the debt was not a result of market forces, the resulting predicament of the Third World debtor nations offered the ideological conservatives of the Republican administrations in power since 1980 a splendid opportunity to inflict laissez-faire economics on needy nations.

In the prevailing ideological cant, the debtor nations were said to have gotten into financial difficulty because of sins of statism. To get out of their (allegedly self-inflicted) difficulty, they needed not infusions of cheap credit but lessons in Friedman-style economics, and they needed to win back the confidence of private investors and bankers of the First World. Rather than solve the Third World debt with infusions of new, cheap development capital, as farsighted Americans did after World War II, the architects of debt "relief" in the 1980s practiced a stringent austerity economics more reminiscent of the medicine administered to Germany after Versailles. Whereas Germany was punished as the presumed aggressor in World War I, the Third World debtors were punished for presumed sins against the reigning doctrine of laissez-faire. "Capitalist" success stories of East Asia were held up as alternative free-market models—never mind that Japanese and South Korean development strategies in their takeoff phase were at least as far from laissez-faire economies as Brazil or Argentina. The Asians simply practiced a far more effective brand of mercantilism, embedded in different cultures and histories. They generated high domestic rates of savings, had plenty of government planning, and fiercely resisted the entry of foreign bankers and Western investment capital and Western products. They channeled very-low-interest loans to export industries, and their economies prospered. As a consequence, they had the good fortune not to fall afoul of the IMF.[12]

In one key respect the Latin American debtor nations practiced a strategy of development radically different and less shrewd than the Asian brand. Where the Asians geared up to compete in world markets, the Latin Americans embraced the idea of "import substitution": they would break free of their dependence on American and European manufactured goods by restricting their imports and developing domestic substitutes instead. This ideology, known as *dependencia* theory, developed after World War II when Latin American economies feared that their dependence on exports of primary products and imports of manufactured goods dictated ever worsening terms of trade, in which it would take more and more tons of sugar or coffee to buy fewer and fewer Chevrolets. It was also believed that this economic dependence created local political elites with scant commitment to their own nations' development, stunted the maturation of durable and competent institutions of democratic government, and contributed to cycles of chronic political and economic instability. Reliance on foreign capital not only crowded out local firms and distorted labor markets but also encouraged the perpetuation of authoritarian governments, the sort that foreign capitalists favored because they guaranteed "stability." Only by a crash program of state-tutored industrialization could Latin America break out of this trap.[13]

In some of its incarnations, this view had a Marxian tinge, but it was mainly nationalist—both resentful of the heavy influence of North American and British capital and fearful of a banana-republic economic future. The impulse was like Alexander Hamilton's, or Lincoln's, or List's or Bismarck's, or Jacques Delors's, or that of the Japanese industrialists of the Meiji Restoration—to nurture the development of national industry, using import restraint and government assistance to increase national wealth and avoid political and economic dependence on foreign powers. In fact, with the exception of the oil-driven commodities inflation of the 1970s, real raw materials prices indeed underwent a long slow decline after World War II.[14] Import substitution became the gospel of the World Bank and the regional public development banks. During the period of worldwide boom, it seemed to work. Notwithstanding chronic political instability, authoritarianism, inflation, and other ills, Latin American growth rates in the 1950s and 1960s were prodigious—often upward of 5 percent a year in real terms. In the fifteen years between 1965 and 1980, the economy of Brazil, a "statist" nemesis of laissez-faire advocates, trebled; per capita gross national product doubled. Industry was developed under the aegis of what international bankers call the "Bras brothers"—state-owned combines like Petrobras, Electrobras, Siderbras, Telebras, Nuclebras, and many others, which had each borrowed billions from major foreign banks.[15] As late as 1979, Brazil could persuade the international lending community to invest immense sums in state-led projects, such as Delfim Neto's gasahol scheme, to which a banking consortium lent $1.2 billion, whose repayment was guaranteed by the Brazilian government itself. And Mexico banked on inflated oil prices to collateralize huge increases in its sovereign debt.

Unfortunately, most of the Latin American nations became textbook examples of what befalls protected economies when the protection is not offset by vigorous competition either within domestic markets or in the world economy. Many Latin American enterprises, like the Bras brothers, were either state-owned or "parastatal" (a word that instructively looks close to the word "parasitic") and heavily dependent on state subsidies. Import substitution by itself is a losing economic strategy. Unlike their East Asian counterparts, which used a period of domestic protection to prepare to vigorously compete in global markets, many of the sheltered Latin American industries became steadily less efficient. As their real productivity declined, the nations tried to maintain living standards by borrowing. Where the Asians generated prodigious levels of domestic savings, the Latinos with private wealth sent much of it to Zurich or Miami rather than plowing it back into the local economy. Though the precise balance can never be known, most studies have suggested that as the banks poured in new loans, the money poured out in the form of "flight capital" even faster. According to a study by Occidental College economist Manuel Pastor, using World Bank data, capital flight in the 1973–87 period equaled 61 percent of new foreign lending to Argentina, 64 percent in the case of Mexico, and an incredible 132 percent in the case of Venezuela; that is, for every dollar of hard currency that foreign banks lent Venezuela, the Venezuelans shipped $1.32 overseas.[16]

The Asian model came to be known as "export-led" growth, rather than import-substituting growth. But neither model was laissez-faire; one worked, the other didn't. One was consigned to a kind of debtor's prison while the other grew wings. Standard economic analysis, conflating two quite distinct characteristics—export-led growth and laissez-faire—assumed that Asian export-led growth must be laissez-faire. After all, it succeeded, didn't it? But Japan and South Korea practiced a model of development that was a far cry from free-market capitalism and brilliantly averted the fate commended by orthodox economists—to fling open their domestic capital and product markets to Western capital and grow by becoming cheap-labor "platform economies" of foreign owners. Rather, they were simply a different type of mercantilist, and far more successful. When their industries reached the point where their consumer products could surge competitively into global markets, their firms were nationally owned and their capital was mostly local.[17] In fact, their refusal to become yoked to global capital markets turned out to be providential in the 1980s, when debt collectors reigned.

Historians and sociologists will long debate how much of the Asian success is cultural rather than economic; how much of the Latin American failure is due to the Catholic legacy of static bureaucracy over nervous entrepreneurship and the different quality of public administration in the two cultures. (There was corruption and authoritarianism in, say, South Korea as well as Mexico in the 1970s, but the one was highly functional for export-led economic growth, while the other was not.[18]) Economists will debate whether the Latin American economic miracle of 1950–70 might have continued had it not been for the OPEC shock. The point is that Latin America's penury in the 1980s offered orthodox opinion an opportunity both to teach an object lesson and to reclaim a continent that had cheekily attempted to devise its own course free from bondage to American and European capital. The lesson was simple: first, to restore confidence you must practice a sound (i.e., austere) macroeconomics (unlike certain hegemonic nations, but never mind); second, you must dispense with mercantilist nonsense, embrace free movement of capital and goods,

and fling your capital and product markets open to foreign private capital.
Privatize. Deregulate. Sell off real assets to pay back debts. Reassure
foreign capital, and you will be rewarded. To a shocking extent, the debtor
nations complied.

The story of how bankers shoveled loans down the throats of Third World
Finance Ministers has already been told in lurid detail by Anthony Samp-
son, Susan Strange, Michael Moffitt, Harold Lever and Christopher
Huhne, among others. Until 1982, when the inability to repay became
obvious, net lending increased every year. Between 1978 and 1982, the
foreign debt of Latin America more than doubled. By 1980, when the cost
of borrowed money began soaring thanks to Paul Volcker's ultra-tight-
money policy, the ratio of external debt to GNP of fifteen highly indebted
countries was already an unsustainable 33 percent; by 1987, it was an
astonishing 50 percent. The fraction of export earnings needed for international debt service leaped from an already excessive 29 percent in 1980 to
an unbearable 50 percent just two years later. And even though real interest
rates subsided, that figure remained at about 40 percent through most of
the 1980s.[19] In 1932, Germany had declared a debt-service moratorium
when its debt-service costs reached 12.9 percent of its exports. By 1982, the
non-OPEC developing countries had a debt-service burden equal to 23.9
percent of exports.[20]

In financial circumstances like these, real growth turns negative, consumption falls, and people suffer, which leads to an overall fall in global
purchasing power. Some statistics convey the unprecedented magnitude of
the shift. Between 1980 and 1983, real income in Latin America dropped
about 10 percent.[21] For some countries, the decade as a whole was an
economic catastrophe. Between 1981 and 1989, Mexico's per capita gross
domestic product dropped 9.2 percent, Peru's 24.7 percent, Bolivia's 26.6
percent, Argentina's 23.5 percent, and Venezuela's 24.9 percent.[22] In the
late 1970s and early 1980s, an average of about $10 billion a year of net
capital was transferred into Latin America; between 1983 and 1989, approximately $150 billion in net capital was transferred out of Latin America,[23]
and less than one-quarter of the interest that the continent owed foreign
bankers was covered by new loans.[24] In 1988, according to the World Bank,
the developing nations as a whole transferred a record $50.1 billion to the
world's richer nations.[25]

The continued penury of Latin America, and the insistence on orthodox
austerity remedies by the IMF, the World Bank, the major creditor banks
(represented by a consortium popularly known as the Paris Club), and the
U.S. government, has not only been harmful to millions of the world's

poorest people; it has also devastated one of the traditionally best markets for U.S. exports. At precisely a moment when the United States' trade balance was deteriorating, it came under further strain because of Latin America's belt-tightening. The nations of the region were placed under great pressure to cut consumption and increase export earnings with which to service debt, and between 1982 and 1984 Latin American exports rose by $11 billion, with 87 percent going to one customer—the United States.[26] In effect, the U.S. manufacturing sector was permanently losing markets so that the U.S. financial sector—the creditor banks—might tread water a little longer.

Because of the weakened hegemonic posture and creditor orientation of the U.S. government and the international lending agencies it dominated, a Keynesian or Marshall Plan type of solution to the debt crisis was out of the question. Instead, the U.S. government, the IMF, the World Bank, and the Paris Club adopted a joint policy of tight discipline and muddle-through. The lending orgy suddenly turned into a debt-collection one, but because the debts were unpayable, the strategy was actually one of lending new money to finance interest payments on old debt, which put the poor nations deeper into hock and reduced their capacity to boost consumption or increase domestic investment. Beginning in 1982, the IMF functioned essentially as a creditors' cartel, lending new money to finance interest repayments on old debts, but not offering any debt relief. The debtors had little choice but to go along. First, they were paying more for oil and paying for it through external debt, which required interest payments that were consuming an ever higher share of their export earnings. Second, they were paying interest at very high rates. Third, they were repaying loans in dollars, at a time when the value of the dollar was unnaturally high and rising. And fourth, their own products were competing in a soft market. Commodity prices fell by one-fourth between 1980 and 1982. (The so-called middle-income nations of Latin America—Brazil, Chile, Argentina, Uruguay—despite their industrialization are heavily dependent on commodity exports of copper, tin, wheat, corn, beef, soybeans, and coffee.)

The laissez-faire counterrevolution did damage in one other respect. Global agriculture, under American prodding, was also deregulating. Nations were urged to abandon price-support regimes and let markets dictate prices, quantities, and market shares. Even more perversely, grain-exporting nations were encouraged to plant more acres and export more crops— the better to earn hard currency with which to service their debt. As a consequence, prices of most farm products fell. As always in agriculture, this produced a self-defeating incentive to keep growing more, not less. Nations like Argentina and Brazil found themselves producing more and earning less in a weak market. Argentina's volume of exports increased by

47 percent between 1981 and 1985, but its export earnings increased just 3 percent.[27]

In the spring of 1985 the Latin Americans proposed a quite sensible remedy. Leaders of eleven Latin American debtor nations, meeting at Cartagena, Colombia, proposed that each nation's total interest payments be limited to a percentage of export earnings. This was widely ignored by the official creditor community. Instead, in October of that year, Treasury Secretary Baker unveiled what became known as the Baker Plan—not a plan at all, but a vague quid pro quo. If the debtor nations would "liberalize" their economies in the Reagan image, the American government would use its good offices to persuade commercial banks, private investors, Western and Japanese multinational corporations, international agencies, and foreign governments to increase the flow of net resources to the region to the tune of about $20 billion. In the meantime, debt workouts and reschedulings would have to be handled "case by case." Emphatically, there could be no blanket debt relief or coordinated write-down.

As the Harvard economist Jeffrey Sachs, an adviser to several debtor nations, astutely observed, "case by case" turned out to mean precisely the opposite. In practice, it meant that every case had to be handled almost exactly like every other case, lest all the other debtors clamor for the same degree of relief given to the worst hardship case. The one exception to this was Bolivia (whose government Sachs advised), where the government simply dug in its heels and refused to pay. Eventually the banks were induced to participate in a "debt buyback" scheme in which the Bolivian government redeemed the outstanding debt at eleven cents on the dollar and wiped the slate clean. Bolivia was a small enough country so that this was not regarded as a precedent; its debt had been considered all but uncollectible in any case.

As the Baker Plan languished, Sachs and countless others, including the Democratic Party's chief expert on global finance, New Jersey senator Bill Bradley, called for genuine debt reduction and relief rather than merely repeated reschedulings and extensions of new market-rate loans. Sachs made the analogy of a bankruptcy: when a company is on the verge of going bankrupt, every creditor tries to collect what is owed him at the expense of every other creditor; only a fool would offer relief unilaterally. The law of bankruptcy, Sachs observed, is founded "on the proposition that efficient debt collection will not normally occur in a decentralized market process, since each individual creditor has the incentive to press for full payment of its own claims, even if it would be in the collective interests of the creditors to reduce the debt burden. The bankruptcy settlement cuts through this fundamental collective action problem by enforcing a concerted settlement on the creditors."[28] This "failure of collective action," he observed, was what prevented the orthodox solution of voluntary, market-oriented negotiation from producing a real improvement in the flow of resources to debtor countries. New creditors are understandably reluctant to provide new loans in the context of a burdensome debt overhang "for fear of having their new loans become part of the overall bad debt,"[29] and existing creditors are unwilling to provide new credits at all, except to finance interest payments on their own back loans.

A bankruptcy settlement, specifically the "Chapter Eleven" version, allows the bankrupt enterprise to reorganize, reduce its debts, and continue operating. Creditors are paid off, in negotiated sequence, at so many cents on the dollar. As Sachs noted, in a bankruptcy "once the existing debts are reduced, the bankrupt firm may *immediately* return to the credit markets for new financing based on a cleaned-up balance sheet."[30] The alternative to a Chapter Eleven settlement is a liquidation. But it is not practical to liquidate entire countries and sell off their fixtures. Sachs's analogy to Chapter Eleven bankruptcies suggested to him that the international lending community should agree to what commercial bankers call a "workout": a reduction of interest rates on accumulated Third World debts; a proportionally equal sharing of the loss among all lenders; and an infusion of new "official" money (from creditor-nation governments and international lending institutions) to increase the flow of new resources to the poor countries.[31]

Dozens of debt-relief plans began to circulate in academic, banking, and government circles. For a time, the journal *The International Economy* even took to keeping a scorecard on them. By the September–October 1989 issue (after which it stopped keeping track), there were twenty-five such plans, most of them calling for some combination of interest-payment forgiveness and new money. Those sponsored by bankers had a rather different flavor: their main objective was gradually to reduce bank exposure, not to promote economic recovery. For a time, bankers were particularly keen on "debt-equity" swaps, in which the local country buys back some of the outstanding debt and in return the bank gets a share in a tangible local enterprise. Far from infusing new resources, of course, this is the equivalent of selling off the fixtures.

Sachs's analysis is instructive on three counts. First, it is an astute discussion of the failure of the conventional approach. Second, he proposes a workable remedy. And third, Sachs is in many respects a fairly orthodox neoclassical economist who takes pains to couple his call for debt relief with an equally strong call for what is delicately known as "conditionality": the new credits should be conditioned upon orthodox "structural reforms." Thus, although bankers excoriated Sachs as a turncoat advising Third World deadbeats how to get off scot-free, there is little ideological dispute between a Jeffrey Sachs and a John Williamson over how an economy ought to be run. Both think it should be operated according to free-market principles, and both think the community of lenders ought to try to make that happen. The only issue is how much pain and suffering should be inflicted in the meantime and how much old debt should be written off. Indeed, when the Solidarity government of Poland hired Sachs to advise them about their many financial problems, Sachs recommended the maximum amount of new foreign credits and the fastest possible transition to a price system and a convertible currency.

When the Bush administration succeeded Ronald Reagan's, and James Baker moved from the Treasury to the State Department, it could be admitted that the debt-relief plan bearing his name was a failure. After a decent interval, Baker's successor, Nicholas Brady, offered another plan, in March 1989, combining token elements of Sachs's remedy of genuine debt relief with the usual bankers' approach. Under the Brady Plan, some reduction of outstanding debt was finally to be forthcoming. The bankers themselves would get to choose from a menu of debt-relief alternatives: either they could reduce the interest or the principal, or they could take debt-equity swaps. The debtor government would then exchange new bonds for old, and repayment of these new, lower-interest "exit bonds" would be partially guaranteed by the IMF and the World Bank. All told, the Treasury estimated, Brady's initiative would cut the outstanding debt owed by thirty-nine developing countries by $70 billion, or about 20 percent of the total sovereign debt outstanding; $20–$25 billion of this new money would come from the IMF and World Bank. Treasury calculated that the package would save debtor nations more than $20 billion in interest payments in 1990–92.[32] Some Japanese quietly noted that this bore a striking similarity to their own Miyazawa Plan, which the United States had rejected a year earlier.

The Brady Plan was widely hailed as a long-needed breakthrough. Mexico, perhaps the gravest case, was designated as the first candidate. The Mexican government, which had been deregulating and privatizing at a rapid clip in order to curry U.S. favor, began negotiations with high hopes. It owed a total of approximately $102 billion and had overseas interest payments of roughly $11 billion. The Mexicans requested debt relief of $15–$20 billion. To restore balanced growth, they really needed perhaps double that—enough to reduce their interest payments to $4 or $5 billion a year, approximately the amount of their trade surplus, at which level they could run balanced external accounts without either inflation or a steady decline in domestic living standards. But the official U.S. debt-reduction goal for Mexico under the Brady Plan was only $10.5 billion of *principal,* or about only $1 billion of interest. The eventual principal reduction was only $7 billion, with a savings in interest payments of about $700 million a year. Mexico then borrowed $5.7 billion from the World Bank, the IMF, and the Japanese Export-Import Bank, at roughly market rates. And the Bush administration's David Mulford managed to infuriate Congress by disguising a $350 million subsidy from the Treasury, which represented the U.S. part of the package. In 1989, Mexico's non-oil exports grew by only 8 percent, its total exports by 15 percent, while its total imports soared by 30 percent.[33] In the end, the banks had taken a very small loss and Mexico had won only a trivial gain, saving at most a few hundred million dollars yearly in interest payments. A similar plan is being negotiated for Venezuela. Sachs, as economic adviser to the new Polish government, urged abrupt convertibility for the Polish zloty and other measures to bring about a quick transition to capitalism, but he has also been pushing for a rather uncapitalist degree of debt relief, far in excess of Brady Plan guidelines. It is, however, politically awkward to justify writing off a Second World debt on terms so much more generous than those permitted the poorest nations of the Third World.

By 1990, it was clear that the Brady Plan, like the Baker Plan before it, had fallen short of solving the problem and that the world's poor countries were in danger of suffering a second "lost decade." Against an accumulated debt of $517.5 billion owed by nineteen "severely debted middle-income countries" (in World Bank jargon), mainly those in Latin America, the Brady package promises to provide something like $30–$35 billion in relief, or less than half its original goal, with about $24 billion coming from the IMF and the World Bank and the rest almost entirely from Japan.[34] At this writing, active Brady Plan negotiations are underway with the governments of only Costa Rica and the Philippines. Banks have continued to reduce their exposure slowly via swaps and write-downs—Citibank had surprised the lending community by deliberately writing down the value of some $3 billion of its Third World debt in 1987. But though this case-by-case, market-oriented muddle-through gradually "solves" the debt crisis from the creditor's balance-sheet point of view, it does little for the debtors. It does nothing to solve Sachs's "collective action" problem and thus does not permit substantial new resources to flow where they are needed.

To the extent that the defined problem has been the exposure of American and European banks, the hard-line policy has succeeded in gradually reducing the banks' vulnerability. In 1985, nine key money-center banks had $60.5 billion, representing 148.6 percent of their capital, tied up in dubious Third World loans; by 1988, this had been reduced to $45.2 billion and 81 percent of capital.[35] Between June 1987 and September 1988, the heyday of the Baker Plan, twenty-nine of the largest U.S. banks succeeded in reducing their exposure by $12.7 billion, or 16 percent;[36] several cut their exposure by more than half, and none increased their net lending. But only in this sense of improving banks' balance sheets has the Baker/Brady Plan "worked." The banks gradually wriggled free of the problem through a combination of debt-equity swaps, write-offs, "buybacks" by the debtor country, and shifting of the debt to multilateral lending institutions. But if the goal was to restore economic growth in the Third World, it failed miserably.

A paper indicative of the orthodox view, written by John Williamson of the Institute for International Economics in January 1990, spoke favorably about the substantial privatization, the new openness to foreign private investment, the deregulation of financial institutions, the reduction of subsidies, the devaluation of currencies, and the embrace of restrictive macroeconomic policies that occurred under the constraint of debt repayment. "There is now a very wide consensus in Washington [sic]," Williamson wrote, "that export-led growth is the only kind of growth Latin America stands any chance of achieving in the next decade."[37] Few would take issue with that, even outside Washington. However, Williamson, like others in the orthodox camp, makes the fundamental mistake of equating export-led growth with laissez-faire economics. The Asian experiences surely prove otherwise. He makes the further mistake of assuming that austerity as a remedy for past debt is a necessary concomitant of a market approach to future growth.

Moreover, as Williamson is constrained to admit, several Latin American nations still suffer from hyperinflation, from capital flight, from a net transfer of resources out of the region, and from declining living standards. Latin America is still getting poorer, still losing control of its own economic destiny, and still dragging down world economic growth. In the 1970s, when the developed world experienced high inflation, Latin American inflation averaged 36 percent per year; in the 1980s, when inflation elsewhere had subsided, annual Latin American inflation was 123 percent. In the "statist" 1970s, Latin American investment as a share of gross domestic product averaged 23.5 percent; in the laissez-faire 1980s, it dropped to 18.7 percent. In the 1970s, annual growth was 3.1 percent; in the 1980s, it was minus 0.8 percent.[38] By 1987, every major Latin American country had an external debt burden equal to more than double its annual value of exports; Mexico's debt burden was nearly four times its exports; Peru's five times; Argentina's nearly seven times.[39] Even from an orthodox perspective, austerity was too much of a good thing, as the World Bank, champion of the "voluntary, market-based" approach, recognized in the 1988–89 edition of its publication on global debt, where it was acknowledged that the current level of debt burden actually "reduces incentives to undertake sustainable long-term adjustment."[40]

. . .

The role of the IMF as agent of austerity, orthodoxy, and private capital is an odd mutation from what was intended by Keynes. Far from being a counterweight to the "bankers' internationalism" of the 1920s, the IMF has been thoroughly captured by private commercial banks and inflation-wary central banks, and its credit agreements are loaded with various forms of "conditionality" imposed on struggling economies. There is an extensive and bitter literature from Third World experts on how IMF stabilizations have crushed struggling economies in order to save them. (There is also a rival self-congratulatory literature on how the IMF dragged statist economies kicking and screaming into the bracing discipline of market pricing and fiscal soundness.)

It now seems painfully obvious that the delegation of such a degree of authority to a supranational institution by the United States was possible only because the institution was in safe, orthodox hands and because the real loss of sovereignty would be inflicted on unimportant countries. The ultraconservative 1980s compounded a long-standing resentment toward the IMF, since the debtor countries were then so desperate and so vulnerable to IMF conditionality.

The IMF first began providing "stabilization" packages to developing nations in the 1950s, and the script has become all too familiar. A nation gets into economic difficulty for one of several reasons: its inflation rate soars, its balance of payments turns seriously negative, its hard-currency reserves evaporate, its domestic budget goes into deficit as it tries a reflationary or compensatory program to make up for the hardship. Sometimes, this pattern of imbalance is the result of foolish policies; other times, it is the result of external factors such as world recession, high interest rates in global money markets, or a deterioration in the terms of trade because of falling commodity prices, all of which are quite beyond the control of the offending nation.

Then an IMF technical mission of experts arrives and prescribes an austerity program. Compliance with the program is the precondition for new financial resources from the IMF and to certify to private lenders that the country is following an acceptable plan for recovery. The IMF package boils down to five recommendations: devalue the currency; operate a tight domestic monetary policy to restrict domestic use of credit; reduce domestic demand—specifically, restrain wages and cut public-sector deficits to dampen inflation, restore private-sector confidence, and free resources for export; cut public spending on social services, housing, education, unemployment compensation rather than balancing the budget by progressive taxation, which might deter entrepreneurship; and "liberalize" by removing state intervention and making economic activity more congenial to foreign capital.

There is a highly ideological agenda concealed in this seemingly technical formula. A left-of-center government that might have been elected on its promise of a development program via, say, public-works spending, land reform, social welfare, domestic industrial development, redistributive taxation, and controls on capital exports—just what Western Europe did in the 1950s—would be judged economically incompetent by the IMF technicians, and denied funds. The IMF formula also has the effect of yoking the nation to global private capital and to one strategy of economic development among many. It suggests that the ceding of sovereignty required for membership in the Bretton Woods institutions is strikingly asymmetrical. Only poor nations (with rare exceptions) find their domestic economic programs dictated by the IMF.

The IMF has been roundly criticized for this from many political quarters—Marxist, nationalist, social democratic—and has also been criticized as resting on dubious economic theory. One of the most sober critiques was made by the 1985 Brandt Commission report, *Global Challenge,* which offered an alternative proposal for global economic recovery. The Brandt report criticized the IMF for putting the burdens of adjustment primarily on the poor countries, for making the adjustment period too short, generating real hardship, and for relying too heavily on devaluation. In theory, a devaluation makes the devaluing country's products cheaper in world markets, allows it to sell more of them, and simultaneously makes imports more expensive. This should be just the right medicine. It should fix the trade imbalance, depress domestic consumption, and restore investor confidence. Unfortunately, however, many poor countries export primary products, for which demand is fairly inelastic. So devaluation is often a false solution to a payments imbalance and often only worsens the terms of trade. The country has to export that much more coffee to earn the same hard currency with which to buy imports. Further, to the extent that the country is trying to industrialize, it is now paying more for imported machine tools. It also now takes more local currency to service preexisting debt. Moreover, when the exporter is a multinational firm rather than a national producer, it often fails to drop its price on world markets in proportion to the devaluation, lest it undercut its own global price—so the gain goes to it rather than to the debtor nation.

As the MIT economist Lance Taylor has observed, in a review of IMF-induced stabilization programs: "Under orthodox stabilization, the main tools . . . are austerity and devaluation. Austere programs often 'work' in the sense of making the trade balance improve. But they succeed by reducing output and capital formation."[41] Moreover, IMF-inspired devaluation typically leads to a decline in real wages and a shift in shares of national income from other wage-earners to the export sector. Unless the government either is highly authoritarian or has highly refined institutions of social bargaining, IMF devaluations lead to demands for compensatory wage increases; often, the government capitulates and the inflationary cycle begins anew.[42] Hyperinflation in Mexico came *after* acceptance of an IMF "stabilization" plan. Politically, to accept an IMF program is to agree to cuts in social spending, low in poor countries to begin with, and this creates massive difficulties for even the most honorable of governments. When the IMF is proposing the same austerity remedy to several poor countries simultaneously, the result is an administered counterpart of the ruinous competitive devaluation that occurred in the 1930s.[43]

The IMF approach reflects only one of several possible theories of how economies work. Most IMF staffers believe in the monetarist explanation of inflation and payments imbalance (this is almost a precondition for working at the place): namely, inflation results because the central bank prints too much money. However, the opposing structural view is that inflation can have any of several causes, ranging from external shocks to conflicting distributional claims on total national income. Sometimes the monetarist cure is inappropriate and does positive harm.[44] Sometimes its distributional effects overwhelm its intended macroeconomic effects. Devaluation is a gift to those who engage in capital flight and to some exporters. It tends to harm ordinary consumers, who face squeezed wages and higher prices for imports. For example, in Argentina, a market-oriented administration working with the IMF announced a policy of gradual depreciation in the late 1970s and lifted capital controls. However, as Taylor recounts, "inflation was structural, and did not slow as the current account deteriorated, fears of exchange depreciation spread, and wealth-holders put their assets abroad. They were rewarded in the end by maxi-devaluation, but not before the government had run up enormous external debts to finance both the current account deficit and the capital flight in the tens of billions of dollars."[45] Mexican economists and many foreign observers blame the collapse of that country's economy after 1982 on IMF-induced deflationary overkill. Indeed, as Taylor drily observes, one unintended phenomenon that prevented the Mexican economy from expiring altogether was that so many Mexicans had moved flight capital into dollars—which made them rich after the peso collapsed; they could then convert back to pesos and go on a spending spree, with Keynesian effect. This was not quite what the IMF team had in mind.

The IMF approach may be dubious theory and often painful practice. As we saw in Chapter 2, a similarly orthodox approach to European reconstruction after World War II would almost surely have slowed growth and increased economic pain. However, if the political goal is to persuade developing countries to pursue laissez-faire policies and link themselves to global capital markets, then the IMF/monetarist theory serves beautifully.

Defenders insist that the pain is proof that the medicine is working. Sometimes, however, pain is applied and economic conditions only worsen, as they have done in the past decade. If a different set of people with a different operating ideology were in charge of the IMF, one could imagine a very different institution, one more congruent with Keynes's ideas in 1944. First, a different sort of IMF, more liberal with credit, could base the adjustments, not on austerity and competitive devaluation, but on growth and mutual expansion of markets. Paul Streeten, a former World Bank official, has proposed, very much in the spirit of Keynes, a two-tier tax to finance new resources for the IMF and the public development banks: nations that ran trade surpluses would have to donate a sum equal to a fraction of their surplus to increase the capitalization of the IMF–World Bank complex. Relative to their GNP, *all* rich nations would pay a small tax that would go to finance the reduction of interest rates on IMF and World Bank credits to poor countries.[46] Surplus nations, after all, tend to export capital in any case. This was the pattern beginning with Great Britain a century ago, the United States a half century ago, and Japan and Germany today. However, Streeten's idea is not to reward chronic surplus nations by allowing them to expand their reach via exports of private capital, but to punish them mildly by tithing some of that surplus for the betterment of the Third World.

Beyond the question of what the strategy of adjustment should be, there is the more fundamental issue of laissez-faire versus intervention. Sachs, for example, opposes austerity but favors laissez-faire. Judging by his writings, Keynes would have been appalled by both. A different IMF committed to cheaper credit and higher growth as the preferred strategy of adjustment would also tolerate mixed economies in borrowing nations and a structural rather than a monetarist view of inflation. For example, an "incomes policy" in which labor and management agree on socially bargained shares of gains from productivity improvement may be a superior way to combine high growth with low inflation. But it is not a laissez-faire solution. Taxing the wealthy may be a superior way of balancing a budget. But orthodox opinion holds that high taxes on the wealthy are bad for the business climate. Even capital controls may sometimes be superior to the inflationary pressures and the outflow of domestic savings that result from premature liberalization (Europe in the 1950s is again a good case in point). But orthodox opinion insists that free capital flows are a sine qua non for efficient markets.

Before about 1980, the World Bank functioned as something of a counterpoint to the IMF. As a development bank, some of whose credits were extended at concessionary rates, the Bank was somewhat more growth-oriented and more sympathetic to public-works spending, to state-led industrialization, and to what some people might see as a dose of mercantilism. The Bank even cared about the plight of desperately poor peoples. But after all, the Bank had been designed as the economic-development rather than monetary-adjustment part of the Bretton Woods schema, and the president of the Bank at the time, Robert McNamara, perhaps atoning for his past as Secretary of Defense during the Vietnam War, was in his own way a social progressive.

But the Bank's operating philosophy has become scarcely different from the IMF's. McNamara's successor, former Bank of America chairman A. W. Clausen, had more of a traditional banker's outlook. Clausen replaced Hollis Chenery, the Bank's chief economist and an advocate of aggressive development lending, with Anne Krueger, a representative of the conservative Chicago school. Krueger believed in traditional comparative advantage, the monetarist view of adjustment, and was extremely skeptical of the ability of state policy to accomplish anything beneficial. It became conventional at the Bank, as well as the Fund, to blame the miseries of the Third World on its nations' overdose of statism. Clausen's successor, former Republican congressman Barber Conable, has been widely criticized for taking this aping of the Republican administration's attitudes even further and considering the Bank a pure instrument of U.S. policy. It was for this reason that—in late 1989, when the Soviet Union began the process of letting its former satellites determine their own course in Eastern Europe—the European Community quickly set up a European Development Bank with the United States included in only a token role; it was imperative to ensure that the World Bank and the Reagan-Bush economic philosophy would not be in charge of the economic recovery of Eastern Europe.


As we look forward to the twenty-first century, we must ask: What currency or currencies will function as the world's money, and subject to what blend of austerity and expansion as the strategy of adjustment and stabilization? What philosophy and what institutions will we have for the economic development of poorer nations—and the transition to market economies in the failed communist regimes? Will global banks like the IMF and the World Bank be engines of laissez-faire or sympathetic to mixed economies? How shall we reconcile systemic needs of world economic growth with the parochial interests of great powers and their multinational firms and banks? As in 1944, the essential choice is whether to leave these questions to the tender mercies of markets and private economic forces or to balance markets with public institutions ultimately accountable to voters.

A related institutional question is how we can address such crucial policy issues as debt, trade, monetary policy, and macroeconomics together. Lamentably, the pressures exerted on poor nations by rich ones in different realms of the economy often operate at cross-purposes. For example, a debtor nation like Brazil finds itself simultaneously pressed to run a trade surplus the better to service its foreign debts—and pressed by the same club of rich nations to throw open its domestic markets to imports when the context is trade negotiations.

From the orthodox perspective, the only way to accomplish all goals simultaneously is for nations like Brazil to become satellites of American, European, and Japanese capital and policy: essentially to turn over their economic development to foreign nations that may not have their best interests at heart; to allow their banks to become branches of U.S., European, or Japanese banks; to import products of the multinational firms and provide them with production facilities and low-wage labor. But it is hardly surprising that the nations of the Third World, which have vivid memories of overt colonialism and gunboat diplomacy, are reluctant to place their fate in foreign hands. Neither would Japan and Europe care to cede their sovereignty to other powers. Nor should the United States.

It seems unlikely that the IMF will change until the political leadership of its constituent nations, or their relative weight, changes. Meanwhile, laissez-faire America is increasingly the odd man out. Europe and Japan, the other members of the emerging concert of great economic powers, believe in mixed forms of capitalism. Ironically, if the Bush administration keeps using its political capital to push for its blend of laissez-faire and austerity, it may get instead a disguised form of cartelization and a world divided into economic spheres of influence. A weak IMF and World Bank or an IMF devoted to austerity creates a vacuum in which impoverished Third World nations make desperate bargains with individual creditor nations that turn out to be far more reminiscent of the 1930s than anything Keynes imagined for the IMF. Surely a growth-oriented IMF is preferable to a new co-prosperity sphere linked to Japanese capital and Japanese companies.

As the era of dollar hegemony, when the IMF and the World Bank were proxies for American power, is nearing an end, we are entering a period when world commerce is denominated in a few "key currencies." The opponents of Bretton Woods proposed something like this in the 1940s as an alternative to Keynes's plan for a central clearing union. A malign version of this system had operated in the 1930s, when there was a dollar area, a reichsmark area, and a sterling area. Now the European Community is becoming a de facto DM area, and the Japanese yen is gradually becoming more widely used in global finance and commerce. However, because of American eagerness to prolong the legacy of dollar hegemony, and there is no policy forcing Germany and Japan to bear hegemonic burdens, there is no rush to a tripartite currency system. According to the IMF, over 60 percent of the world's monetary reserves are still held in dollars; roughly 80 percent of its commercial transactions are in dollars, and virtually all raw-materials shipments are still priced in dollars. Japan, as part of its strategy to hold market share, prices most of its exports to the United States in dollars rather than in yen, so that the Japanese supplier rather than the American customer graciously bears the exchange-rate risk of a strengthening yen and the American customer still thinks of himself as king.

A better alternative would be closer to Keynes's vision in 1944: a supranational institution very much like a world central bank with the power to create reserves that would become a substantial portion of the official reserves of most nations. The IMF has been only a most tepid version of this sort of institution. IMF Special Drawing Rights account for only 3 percent of world reserves today, less than in 1970, and the United States has generally resisted expanding them significantly. Keynes's proposed clearing union was user-friendly, allowing nations freely to draw on a line of credit up to a preset limit. The modern IMF is more like a debtors' prison and should be restored to its original vision.

A true world central bank would require the ceding of a substantial degree of monetary sovereignty, which in turn would mean giving up a good deal of policymaking sovereignty as well. Ironically, of course, the incursion of the global "free market" upon the policymaking capacity of states has precisely this result in any event. As a matter of ideology and nationalism, it is no concession at all for conservatives to let global market forces and private capital gradually assume perquisites that once belonged to sovereign states. It is something else entirely to recognize what is taking place and to make a conscious decision to pool sovereignty the better to counterbalance market forces and private capital.

A good deal of de facto sovereignty has already been ceded to markets. To the extent that sovereignty has been pooled and given to public rather than private market institutions, it has been entrusted to perhaps the most conservative and market-oriented of all public institutions—central banks. Central bankers have an almost fanatical devotion to sound money, a fear of inflation, and an insistence that debts be paid. So although a regime of public and supranational institutions is in operation, the triad of central bankers, IMF, and World Bank has been so thoroughly creditor-oriented that it might as well have been the House of Rothschild or the House of Morgan. (Indeed, there were times in history when the vision of private merchant bankers was rather more expansionary than that of the ostensibly public-minded financial gnomes of our time.)

In one key respect, the club of central bankers in our own era has done rather better than their predecessors of the 1920s. They have at least managed to keep the world's money markets from splintering, and in moments of crisis they have taken necessary steps to keep liquidity flowing. They have operated in relative amity, so that disputes of high politics, of the sort that wracked the capitalist nations during the 1920s, have not interfered with the politics of monetary coordination. But this had everything to do with capitalist high politics being frozen in the Cold War. Now more than ever, the system of ad hoc muddle-through cannot work indefinitely, and to the extent that it works at all, it does so at the general expense of world growth and especially at the expense of the world's poorest people. New institutional arrangements are called for.

A hybrid system based on three key currencies and a stronger world quasi-central bank would provide three benefits we now lack. First, there would be greater stability and less fluctuation in the parities of the three key currencies, since the dollar would be carrying less of the load. Second, there would be more plentiful credit in the entire system—something of immense importance to the former communist nations of Eastern Europe and to the developing world. Finally, the United States would enjoy relief from its obsolete hegemonic responsibilities and would be compelled to undergo the same salutary fiscal discipline as other nations. A plural world financial order is surely on the horizon, whatever the United States does. Rather than clinging to the perquisites of a vanishing order, American policymakers would do well to share in the design of the emerging one.

⁓

# eight

# LAISSEZ-FAIRE AND AMERICA'S
# FUTURE

In this book, I have explored the logical relations between the several strands of America's policy of hegemonic responsibility for the postwar system: its advocacy of a utopian conception of laissez-faire, its military conception of national security, its own economic decline—and the escalating instability of the global economic system. This chain of logic has at last been broken by the end of the Cold War. The military definition of foreign policy and technology policy, as well as the level of military outlay, must change. And the end of the Cold War permits the United States to share the burden of stewardship for the global financial and trading system. In turn, we can acknowledge what our uniquely national economic interests are. For the first time in half a century, we must think through what the dynamics should be for our own peacetime economy to prosper. All of this compels us to accept that the idea of a pure market system is a hopeless and hazardous crusade—that government is necessarily enmeshed in a modern industrial economy.

To be sure, a mixed economy does not mean a statist economy. Markets do many things very efficiently. As classical economics correctly perceives, prices are often accurate signals of what consumers want and of what products cost. Private market institutions—entrepreneurs, manufacturing firms, banks, purveyors of services—are often lighter on their feet than big public bureaucracies. Incentives—the prospect of financial rewards and punishments—influence human behavior, and markets reward innovation and punish failure, whereas state bureaucracies are slower to respond to administrative or political discipline. Centralized Gosplans are dismal failures.

But this is only half the story. To concede the virtues of markets is not to embrace simple laissez-faire. A market system, however inventive, is not self-regulating. It does not add up to a socially defensible allocation of either private income or public investment. It does not efficiently or fairly distribute certain necessary social goods, like education or health or roads or research spending. Left to their own devices, markets do not broker social contracts—which are needed, even in narrowly economic terms, to compensate for the market's own myopia. Markets often punish innocent bystanders and reward unproductive speculators. Market values tend to crowd out social values. Private market institutions do not always grasp new technologies or new opportunities. Certain industries, like agriculture, are vulnerable to cycles of boom and bust, which market pricing only exacerbates. Other industries, like banks and securities markets, are too important to be left to brutal market discipline. Still others, like those that produce toxic substances, must be regulated in the public interest lest they force some of their costs of production onto the public and save money at the expense of public health.

Even institutions that seem to be based on purely private market relationships are usually social constructs. Patents, trademarks, the institution of bankruptcy, the corporation itself, even the concept of legally enforceable private property, are all political inventions. Once laws are passed to restrict the dissemination of "proprietary" information, or to allow commercial failures to escape the full consequences of their failure by declaring bankruptcy, something other than a pure free market is functioning. The real debate is about how to structure the departures from pure laissez-faire, not whether to have them. As we have seen, at the level of the macroeconomy pure market systems are dangerously unstable. And at the level of the international economy, nations have repeatedly demonstrated that they do not trust Adam Smith's famous unseen hand to dictate their fate. In all of these arenas, the challenge is not how to move ever nearer laissez-faire, but how to produce the best blend of a price-auction system of supply and demand and an efficient and just civil society.

As the economy internationalizes, it erodes national sovereignty and the national instruments of a mixed economy. One cannot advocate an interventionist policy domestically without coming to terms with the porous character of the economy globally. Private banks outreach national monetary policy. Private corporations operating worldwide outrun national labor and minimum-wage laws. Free movement of capital and goods undercuts the power of national fiscal policy. An attempt to stimulate a national economy via deficit spending results in substantial "leaks" into the purchase of imports. Just as Keynes feared, a globalized market economy leaves less room for national policy. If one wishes to reclaim the ability of the democratic polity to counterbalance the forces of the private market, there are only two possibilities. Either the nation-state reclaims a measure of sovereignty from private market actors, by limiting the cross-national flow of capital and goods, or it pools sovereignty in supranational public bodies that set common rules. I argue that elements of both approaches are necessary.

To reclaim a mixed economy at home, we must rebuild a global monetary system in which public regulatory bodies are a match for private ones. It is desirable to create a stronger IMF and system of public development banks with a bias toward growth rather than austerity, and a tolerance for institutions of a mixed economy. The skirmish between the United States and the nations of the European Community over the new European Development Bank is highly instructive in this connection. The Bush administration threatened to withdraw its backing if the Bank lent to the Soviet Union, and pressed hard for a policy that emphasized purely private-sector lending, on the model of the U.S.-dominated World Bank. But the Europeans, with a rather different economic philosophy, insisted that the Bank should be able to lend to public infrastructures, and, since in this case they were contributing most of the capital, they prevailed.

As my review of the European Community has suggested, there is a world of difference between simply ceding sovereignty to global private capital and building international institutions of governance that can keep pace with global capital. As markets become global and national economies "interdependent," the practical choice is to pursue pure laissez-faire at the expense of competent governance, risking both instability and inequity; or to let economic outcomes be dictated unilaterally by the relative mercantilists; or to adjust government, both domestically and internationally, to the new realities of global commerce.

In this book, I have suggested several areas of economic policy that cry out for a common set of global rules—trade, finance, national-security export controls, environmental regulation, labor standards, to mention just a few. Almost by definition, these rules cannot be the rules of laissez-faire. There have been a few promising initiatives to build stronger international regimes, in such functional areas as the law of the sea or the common regulation of banks. Thus far, however, the U.S. has stopped well short of leading this effort, because of both its official commitment to laissez-faire as doctrine and its self-perception as a hegemon, with a consequent reluctance to share power. Both of these assumptions have been overtaken by events. The more commerce internationalizes, the greater is the need to harmonize national policies, preferably through international regulatory institutions.

When in 1944 the architects of the postwar world envisioned a geopolitics of peace based on collective security, they invented bold new global institutions that would be governed plurally. And they imagined that each domestic economy would plan for full employment and broadly diffused economic growth. Peace, pluralism, and planning. But instead of peace, we got a forty-five-year armed truce. The Cold War organized the basic East-West alliance system and kept it from degenerating into a hot war. But it also permitted, even exploited, countless regional armed conflicts; the great powers shared an interest, though, in containing them lest they cascade into a general war. Economically, we got a system of dual hegemony: a relatively benign American military and economic protectorate in the West and a Soviet dictatorship in the East, where a deadening combination of totalitarianism, state socialism, and militarism wrecked the capacity of the U.S.S.R. to realize a superpower potential. In the West, the United States underwent a more gentle cycle of decline, but it, too, can no longer be a hegemonic superpower without suffering escalating economic damage.

Instead of explicit global planning aimed at tempering markets, we have had a diversity of national experiences and ideological muddles. In the United States, the Pentagon became the unacknowledged substitute for civilian planning. In other capitalist nations, the planners outnumbered the advocates of simple laissez-faire. Yet even as the United States has weakened, its leaders have continued to try to convert others to the ideal of Adam Smith economics. Our trading partners no longer listen to them, and both the politics and economics of laissez-faire are at a dead end. After a detour of nearly fifty years, we have cycled back to the agenda of 1944: pluralism, peace, and planning.

The coming global economic regime will surely be pluralist, and this can be good both for the United States and for the system. The real issue is whether it will also be stable, equitable, and sustainable. The challenge is the same one Keynes foresaw in 1944: how to gear the system toward both stability and steady, high rates of growth. As I have suggested, we are moving away from a system of dollar domination toward one with three major currencies, and this will benefit America by releasing the dollar from its inflationary burden of financing world commerce and providing the world's monetary reserves and by subjecting the United States to the same fiscal discipline as other nations. That, finally, should end the domestic politics of fiscal gridlock.

Some observers,[1] noting the commercial emergence of Europe and Japan, have gloomily envisioned a future with three tight trading blocs—the Japanese as the regional hegemon of East Asia, the European Community as a continental power expanding eastward, and the United States left with Canada, Mexico, and the debtor nations of South America. But this vision is misleading. Despite the likely emergence of three key currencies, the volume of direct foreign investment and the interpenetration of European, Japanese, U.S., and Third World economies can only intensify. U.S. and European firms will continue to launch joint ventures and invest in each other's economies. Japanese multinationals will continue to operate worldwide. Rather than being divided into spheres of exclusive economic and currency influence, the Third World will enjoy competition among firms from Europe, the United States, and Japan, and the same will be true of the Second World—the former Soviet bloc. There will be more joint ventures between First World and Third World partners, as well as among the industrial nations. Several large nations which are just emerging as economic powers—China and India come to mind—are not firmly in anybody's orbit, and will continue to be the object of commercial rivalry among the economic great powers. Japan may well dominate in parts of East Asia, yet some Asian nations such as Taiwan, South Korea, and the Philippines are intent on preserving both their own economic autonomy and their links with the United States and Europe, precisely to keep from becoming Japanese economic colonies.

The challenge for the trading system is threefold: to stabilize the new global monetary order; to gear it toward high growth, especially for poorer nations; and to fashion a new set of reciprocal rules of trade. A system based on three key currencies is more complex than a system based on one, but it is surely possible to devise such a system, using adjustable, relatively stable exchange rates. To function smoothly, this does require key nations to coordinate their macroeconomic policies and to intervene cooperatively to manage exchange rates. As Europe and Japan increase their global power, they are becoming more outward-looking and willing to share in the responsibility of stabilizing the system. There is still a risk that the Third World will be given short shrift, but if they are wise, the great powers will perceive that a policy of austerity only slows world growth as a whole.

What will the U.S.S.R. and China do in this new trading order? The Soviet Union, if it stays on the course charted by Gorbachev, will continue to absorb capital and technology from the industrialized capitalist nations. Western Europe and Japan are already doing more and more in East-West trade; they have a capital surplus as the United States does not, and they are better positioned as trading states. Although China since the early 1980s has benefited from preferential access to Western capital and technology, thanks to a U.S. policy of playing it off against the Soviet Union, it will be decades before either China or the Soviet Union is strong enough to be an economically great power. It is remarkable how the map of "great powers" changes when one emphasizes geo-economics rather than geo-military politics.

The rules of the trading system, as I have suggested, must necessarily be the rules of a mixed system. Given that nations will continue to seek national economic policies, these rules must be changed to allow for national industrial and technology strategies, and should try to balance these, not banish them. They must allow for such departures from the ideal of laissez-faire trade as development subsidies, content requirements, flexible cartels, and quotas. The key is to put the total calculus of these departures from laissez-faire on a roughly reciprocal basis and to discourage individual nations from running chronic trade surpluses at the expense of the rest of the system. Europe-Japan trade gives a rough model of how such a system might operate.

A globalized market system in which private firms outrun national laws also requires global regulatory standards, so that market forces will not overwhelm those of civil society. Even conservative regulators have begun to acknowledge this. The Bank for International Settlements, the Basel-based "central bankers' central bank," took the lead in sponsoring a treaty that now requires all major banks to have common capital standards. The day is not far off when banks will be subject to common supervisory standards on prudent lending as well. As I have suggested, the trading system lacks a set of common standards on what constitutes antitrust, or "dumping," and the GATT should be strengthened so that predatory practices mean the same thing in different countries; otherwise individual governments are likely to reclaim authority that has been ceded to the private market. The European Community now sets thresholds of "European content" to determine which foreign-owned firms producing in the European market are considered European for purposes of preferential tariff treatment and admission to EC-sponsored research consortia. The United States does something of the same—but only when it has to do with defense, in which case foreign-owned firms often are simply not allowed to participate. The European standard is sensible, while the U.S. approach is self-defeating. The emerging world economy is characterized by joint ventures and cross-border direct investment: if these capital flows are not to be left entirely to the vagaries of market forces or to other nations' industrial policies, and if governments wish to influence the development of key technologies, then we must establish criteria for what are considered "domestic enterprises." In most cases, foreign-owned firms that make products in a host country should receive the same treatment as purely domestic ones, but there should be common, worldwide criteria for this treatment.

It is not hard to imagine a gloomier version of pluralism. Students of the concept of hegemonic stability are divided on whether a global market economy can be stabilized absent a dominant nation supplying capital, credit, security, and asymmetrically open markets, as the United States and Britain before it once did. Geopolitically, a pluralist system might well be less stable than a bipolar armed truce, and some commentators have imagined the end of the Cold War letting loose ancient animosities that were submerged in the artificial unity engendered by an authoritarian regime. The stakes here are far bigger than border skirmishes between Hungary and Romania. The U.S.-Japan relationship might become nasty. A newly united Germany could seem to be a threat to its neighbors rather than a benign engine of economic growth. In other regions, such as the Middle East, flash points might continue to ignite in the absence of any bipolar hegemony.

On the other hand, there is a good historical example of a system that was both plural and relatively stable. The Concert of Nations, negotiated after the end of the Napoleonic wars, inaugurated an era that avoided general war in Europe for ninety-nine years, despite the rise of nationalism and imperial rivalries. In the present situation, pluralism has a better than usual prospect of success. For the first time in more than a century, the great powers are not bent on territorial aggrandizement, as they had been on the eve of both world wars. Nor are there great ideological schisms, except in the Middle East. So the great powers share an interest in containing rather than enflaming conflicts. Fascism and communism are all but extinct as viable political forces. Increasingly, all the great powers save China now believe in some variation of liberal capitalism. The disagreements are over the relative role of state and market.

In contrast to the United States, other nations, with smaller military budgets, have found a way to civilian forms of economic planning. Though Americans briefly flirted with civilian planning in the first Roosevelt administration—the era of the NRA codes and the Reconstruction Finance Corporation—the zenith of American planning occurred during World War II, and we have been moving away from it ever since. But the conversion to a stable peacetime economy requires a dose of planning, and Americans need to get over their antipathy to planning for civilian and commercial purposes. Planning is necessary so that a peacetime economy will not create dislocations in regions that have heavily depended on defense contracts, and two obvious areas of American life—the environment and our decaying civilian infrastructure—will require large public investments in the coming decades.

Domestically, what is the practical alternative to laissez-faire? Critics and theorists have offered ingredients of a post-laissez-faire economic program on an ad hoc basis, in a host of reports and policy platforms. But they have not been fused into a coherent public philosophy or ideology. Meanwhile, the debate about the cause and cure of American economic decline has divided along a clear line: on one side are planners, who believe (as do most of America's trading partners) that government must play a role in an advanced industrial economy; on the other are the true believers in self-regulating markets—macroeconomists, advocates of global capitalism, diplomats schooled in the era of U.S. hegemony. For this latter group, the causes of U.S. decline are clear, and so are the remedies: America needs to reduce its budget deficit and raise its domestic savings rate; as domestic savings rise, so will domestic capital investment; U.S. industries will then become more productive, hence competitive, and there will be less need to import capital; when this is accomplished, markets will determine the "correct" value of the U.S. dollar relative to other currencies, and there will be less reason for governments to meddle in exchange-rate markets. The planners agree that a higher domestic rate of savings is part of the remedy, but they stress other factors that involve the *structure* rather than the macroeconomic balance of the U.S. economy. These include the following:

*A competitive work force.* The overwhelming evidence is that the United States does a good job at schooling its university-educated elite, but a terrible job of schooling the bottom half of the high school graduating class. We also lack a coherent system of ongoing, lifelong training for adult workers. Even standard economics texts acknowledge that training is an "externality"—an investment that will not necessarily be repaid. Firms hesitate to train their workers because there is no assurance that they won't move across the street and work for a competitor. The low level of reciprocity and loyalty between firm and employee in the U.S. industrial culture is compounded at the management level, where executives often rise in their own careers by moving to rival firms.

Other countries compensate for this kind of market failure in various ways. In Japan, a company can invest in the skill levels of its workers without fear of competitive loss, thanks to customary reciprocal loyalties. The worker can seek job protection in skill levels rather than in negotiated artificial job categories and work rules. Even though workers in smaller firms do not enjoy formal guarantees of permanent employment, there are social networks in which big firms take care of supplier firms. Japan's appreciation of the value of this careful networking is precisely what causes the fierce resistance to U.S. demands that it practice an Adam Smith-style economy. West Germany has a system of nearly universal apprenticeship training for students who do not go on to university. The apprenticeship—subsidized by industry, labor, and government—is conducted partly in the classroom and partly in the shop. It produces a high-quality work force and a nationally recognized system of certification. Sweden's "active labor market policy" uses periodic retraining sabbaticals as a way of soaking up excess labor during periods of high unemployment and continuously upgrading the caliber of the work force at the same time. In France companies are required either to spend a specified fraction of their gross earnings on worker training or to pay a tax into a common training fund. There is no single template which fits all countries. But each of these industrial nations has devised an efficient labor-training system consistent with its society and polity.

The United States, in contrast, has some minimal, patchwork job-training programs, but it spends roughly 80 percent of its total labor-market outlays on one big program—unemployment insurance—paying people not to work. Unemployment insurance is an entitlement. You don't need to spend your furlough learning anything; you only have to go through the motions of looking for another job. It is astonishing that a rather conservative society would support this approach in principle. But in standard economics, unemployment insurance is the most "marketlike" of all labor-market public-policy interventions: the unemployed worker is "free to choose" to buy additional training if he or she calculates that this would be useful. Presumably, the individual is behaving rationally. Unemployment insurance also allows firms to shed excess labor during economic downturns without extreme privation to the individual. But reliance on unemployment insurance as society's principal labor-market subsidy reinforces the economy's systematic tendency to underinvest in its human capital. The difference between the labor-market policies of the United States and its competitors helps to explain why the latter have enjoyed higher rates of industrial productivity growth even though they have a lower percentage of university graduates than the United States.

A related structural impediment is the weak linkage between the laboratory and the factory floor. U.S. manufacturing corporations, in the past forty years, have stressed products, not processes. A rich case-study literature has investigated what it is about America's industrial culture that causes this. Among the most prestigious and persuasive of these works was a May 1989 report of an MIT study commission on America's economic future, the first such MIT report since World War II. The makeup of the study panel was significant, since it included distinguished engineers and industrialists as well as economists. The report, *Made in America,*[2] concluded: "There are good reasons to think that the capital-formation problem in the United States may be only part of the story."[3] The study reports case after case of innovations conceived in America which failed to result in American firms' commercializing the mass-market product. The report closely connected this failure to weaknesses in the characteristic American approach to training. In West Germany and Japan, on-the-job training gives workers general as well as special skills. In the United States and Great Britain, in contrast, formal educational institutions teach general skills, whereas on-the-job training is job-specific. This, in turn, reflects the lack of a social contract between industry and labor. Workers are taught only what they need for a given job.

*Capital markets.* Almost uniquely among major industrial nations, U.S. financial markets expect short-term returns, which in turn influences the strategies pursued by corporate managers. There is no reliable source of what has been called "patient capital." The result is that firms make decisions heavily influenced by the prospect of short-run profitability. Critics have recommended not only higher savings rates, which in turn would produce lower capital costs, but a wholly different structure of financial markets and corporate governance.

In competitor nations, entrepreneurs are able to have a longer perspective, in part because of the different operations of banks and equities markets. In Japan, banks are long-term equity investors in Japanese firms. Other large blocks of stock are held by other corporations in the same industrial group. The Japanese stock market has risen prodigiously over the past decade, but it is not driven by frenetic buying and selling. Companies can get away with paying out scant dividends and plowing capital back into operations. When investors do take profits, they realize them from the long-term capital gain in the value of their shares. The Japanese government, through the postal savings system and the Japan development bank, has also been a source of "patient capital."

In West Germany, likewise, the three largest banks are major lenders and major shareholders in big corporations. This has certain drawbacks; it makes banks the de facto planning agency of the national economy, and many German critics have argued that their corporations need to make more use of equities markets and rely less on debt. But as in Japan, the system does have the virtue of allowing companies to focus on the long term. In the United States, unfortunately, firms are accountable mainly to a highly volatile stock market dominated by pension funds and other institutional investors which are exquisitely sensitive to short-term performance. In addition, standard theory in America has taught that managers are supposed to look at their companies simply as a set of fungible assets, almost as a stock portfolio. If returns are low in one sector, this must be the market signaling the company to get out of that line of business and into another. Foreign firms are far more inclined to innovate, to pursue new variations on old products, whereas American firms are more inclined to diversify.

Early in this century, progressives were divided bitterly on the issue of how best to domesticate the giant corporation. Some reformers, like Louis Brandeis, championed antitrust law and said that government regulation could restore the ideal of the nineteenth-century free market by making cartels illegal and reclaiming price competition and consumer sovereignty. Others, like Herbert Croly and later Raymond Moley and Rexford Tugwell, argued that bigness and market power were inevitable characteristics of a modern industrial economy, and that public policy, rather than breaking up behemoth corporations, should turn them to public purposes. But Brandeis and his intellectual heirs won the debate. Antitrust was the more "marketlike" form of intervention than cartelization in the public interest. However, a recent literature[4] argues persuasively that the main effect of antitrust was to encourage corporations to become *horizontal* conglomerates, pursuing lines of business they knew little about. It is interesting that under antitrust law in both West Germany and Japan, well-behaved cartels and bank/corporation interlocks have been tolerated; their corporations have stuck to their knitting, expanding their basic businesses, backed by powerful banks and industrial groups.

In the 1980s, the hostile corporate takeover became a fashionable substitute for more normal forms of corporate accountability. Big institutional investors—pension funds and life insurance companies—loved hostile takeovers, because bidding wars for control of a company tended to boost share prices. The corporate raiders portrayed themselves as virtuous Robin Hoods, acting on behalf of small shareholders and against entrenched management, in order to "maximize shareholder value." They borrowed money and offered to buy shares at a price far above the current market value, which pleased the stockholders. When they succeeded in gaining control, they were likely to sell off divisions, reorganize others, and ruthlessly cut costs. Defenders of the hostile takeover thought of it as both a new form of corporate accountability to shareholders and a new source of pressure on U.S. industry to innovate. Critics, dating back to A. A. Berle and Gardiner Means[5] in the 1930s, have long argued that the notion of shareholder democracy—in which shareholders elect the board of directors and the board hires and fires management—is a fantasy. In practice, corporate boards are self-perpetuating, and small shareholders have only the power to sell their holdings.

Both of these claims are narrowly accurate. Corporate raids do replace managers, and they do temporarily boost stock prices. But as a stimulus to innovation, a corporate raid is like burning the barn to roast the pig. A hostile takeover has the profound disadvantage of creating immense uncertainty and institutional dislocation. If the problem of American industry is the managers' short time horizons, the pressure of hostile takeovers makes them even shorter. The pressure to repay the debt that financed the takeover causes the new owner not just to pare fat but to reduce needed investment.

Pension funds, as a source of financial speculation and an engine of corporate raiding, are also an American anomaly. Pension funds are a quintessential form of long-term capital. Pension contributions are set aside for workers' retirement and may not be withdrawn for several decades. (Life insurance reserves are in the same category.) Logically, these pools of money ought to be the perfect source of "patient capital." Once, institutional investors were just that; they invested in long-term assets such as pools of mortgages. But in the 1980s, pension funds, operated by professional money managers, were the extreme case of *impatient* capital. Quarterly yield was everything, for this is how laissez-faire markets are supposed to operate (and this was how the money managers won their bonuses). We should change the laws that give pension funds and life insurance companies special tax advantage, to require that they behave as patient investors. They could have highly diversified investment portfolios, but to qualify for the favorable tax treatment, each investment would have to be made long-term.

Americans must learn to look at the problems of underinvestment in worker training, dysfunctional capital markets, adversarial labor relations, unaccountable corporate managers, and the chaos of corporate raiding as several facets of a single underlying problem. The individualist American model cherishes what the sociologist Ronald Dore termed "contingent" relationships.[6] Economic man is believed to have no attachments to his fellows, except on a short-term, purely instrumental basis. Every economic transaction is supposed to be a one-night stand, because tomorrow someone might make you a better offer. This operating philosophy is supposed to add up to a socially optimal allocation of resources and a maximum free choice for all players. In this view, *loyalty* is a purely nonrational and sentimental value. The worker and the executive are free to pursue job opportunities in competing firms as they arise. The pension-fund manager is free to tender his shares; the corporate raider is free to borrow money and mount a hostile takeover attempt; the manager is free to relocate his plant. By the lights of Milton Friedman, all this freedom is splendid and a tonic for economic efficiency. However, contingent short-term relationships come at the expense of many other qualities and factors the real economy needs: corporations that can plan for the long term; workers who consider that they have a stake in their company; communities that can count on employers staying put; suppliers who want long-term relations with customers so they can invest in productivity-enhancing capital equipment.

Industrial America needs a new form of social partnership. We need to devise a better form of managerial accountability than *in extremis* selling the entire corporation out from under the manager and dismembering it.[7] It is not as if government is uninvolved. After a hostile takeover, the final referee of the disposal of corporate assets is often a bankruptcy judge or sometimes the taxpayer-funded Pension Benefit Guarantee Corporation, which steps in to bail out raided corporate pension funds. In a different system (not unlike the West German and Austrian ones), hostile takeovers would be unnecessary because managers would be more accountable to their employees. Greater worker participation in management and greater security from the effects of hostile takeovers would give workers more of a stake in the long-term health of the company. That would promote less adversarial labor relations. If these social forms of accountability operated, antitrust would be less important and we could tolerate more joint ventures.

The underinvestment in training is also closely related to our adversarial labor relations. In the United States, workers are generally treated as an expendable factor in production. As a consequence, unions bargain for job security based on job classification, rather than supporting generic training and upgrading that might pay off in higher productivity. In the nonunion sector, there is a notorious lack of job security. A different sort of labor relations requires nothing less than a new social contract between labor and management, in which employment security is not tied to a particular job and training becomes broad-gauge. But first, companies must stop going all out to break unions, and the unions, in turn, must scrap their devotion to defensive and inflexible work rules and job classifications.

Some students of comparative labor policy, such as Harvard law professor Paul Weiler, recommend an American counterpart of the West German "co-determination," using a works council to which all workers in a given enterprise elect representatives, regardless of whether the firm is unionized. According to Weiler, this provides a forum for constructive labor influence; unions in unionized firms can do their job more effectively, and workers in nonunion firms have a greater degree of representation. But such a collaborative style of labor-management relations is hard to imagine in our country without a corresponding change in public policy. As long as firms have no particular long-term commitment to their employees, it is literally irrational for workers to work for productivity improvements, lest their jobs be replaced by machines. Yet, paradoxically, it is machines replacing humans that makes the economy wealthier and more productive as a whole. In other countries, policies—either private paternalism and cultural norms (Japan) or a combination of collective bargaining and public policy (Sweden, Austria, West Germany)—assure that productivity improvements result not in layoffs but in higher living standards and new opportunities for wage workers.

*Public investment and technology.* Among the many things the free market does badly is to allocate investment to public goods. Our infatuation with laissez-faire and starvation of the public sector have gone so far that many critics urge the privatization not just of municipal services like garbage collection but of the building of highways, on the model of eighteenth-century private turnpikes. But this is fantasy. Certain public goods, like roads and railways, are vital to the economy as a whole yet not cost-effective for a private entrepreneur. That is why in every advanced country in the world (including our own) transportation systems, water and sewer systems, bridges, harbors, and so on, have been developed by governments.

In the past two decades, there has been a marked slowdown in public investment in infrastructure—highways, airports, bridges, tunnels, railroads, subways, and other transportation facilities as well as public buildings and gas, electric, water, and sewer facilities. Nonmilitary public capital grew at an average annual rate of 4.1 percent from 1948 to 1969 (greater than the rate of economic growth) but only 1.6 percent between 1969 and 1987. As military public investment took precedence during the Reagan years, the rate slowed still further, to just 0.9 percent per year during the 1980s, or less than half the rate of overall growth.[8] We have been living off our past public investment, as well as not saving enough money to pay for private investment. Recent research by the economist David Aschauer finds a significant correlation between the rate of public investment and the rate of productivity growth. This is only logical, since firms depend on good road, rail, and air transport, on water, sewer, power, and postal facilities, as well as on purely private physical capital. These cannot be left to the private market.

Other nations have deliberately used public infrastructure investment to help develop technologies and production processes for new domestic and export industries. For example, the Japanese state, through MITI and municipal governments, is working with private companies to develop advanced photovoltaic cells that will eventually provide municipal power systems in small cities with an efficient form of solar energy. This will reduce Japan's dependence on imported oil and create yet another export winner for Japanese industry. When the French government modernized the Paris Métro, it took the opportunity to develop technology that would drive a new export industry; a state-led company, SOFRETU, became a world leader in the design and export of underground rapid-transit systems. The legitimacy of planning allowed Japan and France to realize such commercial benefits in these and countless other enterprises.

In the United States, one candidate for this kind of synergy is short-distance passenger rail; but a combination of ideological disapproval and fiscal paralysis makes the project impossible to realize. A consortium of manufacturing, research, and utility companies based in Pittsburgh have come together to create a joint venture called Maglev, Inc. Maglev stands for magnetic levitation, the current technology which can be used to power light rail vehicles at speeds of about 150 miles per hour. The cars run on elevated monorails, floating magnetically just above the rails. The technology was invented at Brookhaven National Laboratory, but the military establishment saw no use for it, and it fell to the West German government and the German firm AEG, a subsidiary of Daimler-Benz, to commercialize it. In Pittsburgh, Maglev, Inc., plans to license the West German technology and to run a demonstration track between downtown and the airport, nineteen miles away, which would carry passengers from the center of the city to the air terminal in nine minutes. This short demonstration track can probably be built with private money. Maglev hopes eventually to spawn a new grid of short intercity rail lines that could carry passengers on busy routes of 250 miles or less, such as New York–Boston, Pittsburgh–Cleveland, Chicago–St. Louis, or Los Angeles–San Diego, more efficiently than air travel.

The sponsors of Maglev point to multiple benefits: improved transportation; the creation of a new manufacturing industry; the reduction of pollution; saved time for travelers. But all agree that at $20 million per mile the only body that can underwrite a Maglev rail grid is the federal government, and the concept of a manufacturing consortium planning to create a new industry on the basis of public outlays violates the prevailing doctrine separating public from private. Ideally, Maglev, Inc., hopes that in exchange for pioneering the venture and contributing the seed capital, its member firms would get the construction and manufacturing business: USX would provide the steel; Bechtel would get the construction contract; AEG-Westinghouse would provide the control systems and the rail cars. This is how consortia work elsewhere, but in the United States economic relations are contingent and instrumental. Public contracts must be put out for bid, and consortia may be in violation of the antitrust laws. Capital spending for mass transit, budgeted at several billion dollars a year in the 1960s and 1970s, has now dwindled to a trickle, a casualty of budget deficits and of ideology—if there were a good reason to finance mass transit, the private sector presumably would find the money.

As I have suggested, technology policy needs to be civilianized: we need an expanded National Institute on Standards and Technology (NIST) or a civilian counterpart of DARPA. We need not put public money into every new technology. And we need to be sure to follow the model of Sematech, where public money flows only when private money flows first. Supposedly, public spending on new technologies might be subject to bureaucracy and gross political intervention, but the studies of DARPA suggest that the scientists there managed to forge valued links with both the scientific and manufacturing communities, were light on their feet, and were remarkably free of political meddling.

*Regulation.* The Reagan administration provided a test of the proposition that a deregulated economy would be more innovative and efficient. The most costly failure of the hypothesis occurred in the banking industry. Savings-and-loan associations, once limited to the narrow business of taking small deposits and making mortgage loans, lobbied Congress to be allowed to take in speculative, large-volume, market-rate deposits and to make loans on everything from ski condos to fast-food franchises. S&Ls used to have limits on the interest they could pay; these were lifted. They used to be nonprofit mutual associations owned by their depositors. Congress permitted them to convert to for-profit, stockholder institutions, usually controlled by a small group of people in real estate. After a decade of deregulation, there was plenty of innovation, most of it directed to get-rich-quick schemes financed by the depositors' money. By the time Congress woke up and reregulated, the nation's savings-and-loan associations had lost a cool quarter of a trillion dollars. The savings-and-loan associations that rode out the storm most serenely were the ones that had stuck to their traditional, unglamorous business.[9]

Airlines were also deregulated. The inspiration for this idea was the claim of standard economics that free competition would provide more consumer choice and lower costs. The economist Alfred Kahn, an architect of deregulation, served as the last chairman of the Civil Aeronautics Board in order to dismantle it. But industries like the airlines, with expensive capital equipment and essentially standard products, can't endure pure price competition. That's why standard fares on competing airlines mysteriously turn out to be identical and why airlines responded to deregulation by introducing Byzantine complexity into their routes and rate structures.

In the first years of airline deregulation, new upstart airlines entered new markets, offering cut-rate fares. But one by one they were gobbled up or driven out by the major carriers. By 1986, the top six airlines had a higher market share than they did in the bad old days of regulation: single airlines, or perhaps two, enjoyed monopolies or duopolies at key airport hubs. Rather than participating in the mutually ruinous competitive free-for-all that Kahn and the deregulators envisioned, airlines tacitly let one another reign supreme in what came to be called "fortress hubs." TWA got to dominate St. Louis. Northwest got Minneapolis. USAIR got Pittsburgh and Charlotte. United got Denver, and so on. On short routes, with a few carriers holding to fixed prices, fares rose to an astronomical eighty cents per seat-mile, or $250 for a round-trip ticket between New York and Boston. In place of a regulated cartel, consumers got a privatized cartel. Airlines monitored one another's fares and engaged periodically in vicious price-cutting—not to benefit consumers but to punish upstart airlines who tried to compete on the basis of promotional fares. According to *The Wall Street Journal,* these punitive fares were sometimes coded "FU."[10] While prices dropped in the first few years of deregulation, by the mid-1980s they were, once adjustments are made for fuel costs, rising far faster than they had in the regulated era.[11]

The twin issues of environmental and energy policy suggest the utter failure of laissez-faire approaches. Pollution is the most widely recognized economic "externality": private decisions that do not take into account the full social cost make it seem rational for the individual business firm to dump toxic wastes, add to ozone depletion, contribute to the greenhouse effect, and so on. All of these problems require both national regulation and global collaboration among governments. Most economists have argued that environmental regulation should be as "marketlike" as possible. They tend to favor tax incentives and economic penalties as inducements to proper behavior, rather than direct regulation. For example, companies can be charged for the right to pollute, and emissions permits may be traded; gasoline taxes can be raised, to induce less gas consumption or more fuel-efficient cars. On the other hand, sometimes direct regulation can get the job done more quickly, as in the law that requires automakers to have a fleet average fuel efficiency of at least 27.5 miles per gallon, or pay a gas-guzzler tax. Utility rates can be structured to make it rational for local power companies to reward their customers for installing more energy-efficient equipment instead of adding to their, the companies', own generating capacity.

The debate over creation of incentives versus direct regulation, of course, misses the point; it is merely a dispute about the best strategy of regulation. Neither of these approaches leaves the problem to the private market—in both cases, government is intervening to change private behavior. Energy presents a closely related case of market failure. Throughout the 1980s, in line with prevailing economic doctrine, the Reagan and Bush administrations insisted that the free market was the best determinant of energy pricing and that the oil cartel would eventually break, since theory tells us that no cartel can last forever. But historically, oil has been cartelized almost since it was first pumped. The reason is that oil, once discovered, costs virtually nothing to extract. If it were produced according to the principles of true supply and demand, that is, if producers pumped all they could and did not conspire to set prices and restrict supply, oil would trade at a few dollars a barrel. This has given producers an immense incentive to cartelize.

In fact, the cartel did briefly break, in 1985–86, leading to volatile prices and political instability among oil-producing nations, and damaging friendly producers in such far and near places as Saudi Arabia, Mexico, West Texas, and Louisiana. The Bush administration, its official doctrine notwithstanding, intervened to help put the cartel back together, working with the Saudis to enforce a target price of $18 a barrel. When the cartel broke again, in mid-1990, the result was the Persian Gulf crisis. In its geopolitics, the United States, even under Republican administrations, has recognized that oil is too important to be left to the invisible hand; but in its economic management, it has, uniquely among the industrialized nations, rejected the idea of a coherent energy policy, insisting that the market is a better determinant of prices and end-uses. As a result, when the third oil crisis struck, in August 1990, the United States had done less to increase energy productivity, or to seek alternative energy sources, than any of its trading partners.

*Health.* Americans pay more and get less for their health dollar than the citizens of any other industrial nation. We spend over 11 percent of gross national product on health—the highest fraction of any nation—but leave out some 37 million Americans; another 15 million are underinsured, and another 10 million are insured by the inferior Medicaid system. Health-care costs have been rising at double the rate of inflation for two decades, and various "cost containments" have proven powerless to brake this escalation.

In its attempt to blend public and private care, the health system in the United States manages to get the worst of both worlds. In 1965 Congress enacted a program of public universal health insurance for the elderly (Medicare). In order to win over powerful health-industry lobbies, Congress had to write a blank check: the taxpayers would pay the costs, but doctors and hospitals remained sovereign in determining what procedures to perform and what charges to levy for them. That system led to a spiral of inflation, and in the early 1980s Congress changed the rules. Doctors and hospitals would be reimbursed according to a schedule of fees, and private insurance companies tried, with mixed success, to subject them to the same discipline. But in an era of ever more technically complex medicine, this strategy failed to contain costs. Instead it led to an interminable, administratively expensive cat-and-mouse game, in which hospitals kept complicating their billing and groups of physicians and laboratories kept inventing new, gold-plated procedures. A decade ago, a hospital bill was a simple page. Today, hospitals charge separate markups on every suture.

In standard economic theory, the buyer disciplines the seller by shopping around for the best product at the lowest price. The seller, meanwhile, maximizes his earnings by shaving his costs. But in the health-care industry, patients do not shop around because they lack the expertise and because they seldom pay the bill directly. By the same token, providers of services maximize their earnings not by shaving costs but by inflating them. The discipline of standard economics does not work in the health-care system. And the American patchwork system of partly private and partly public medicine further complicates the administrative confusion.

A universal health insurance system is not only more equitable but also more efficient. The countries with universal systems, even those that have more generous welfare laws overall, have done better at containing medical costs, and at no cost to life expectancy or public health. Most of them give hospitals overall budgets within which they must live, so there is nothing to be gained in playing the gold-plated reimbursement game. Doctors are paid flat fees based on the number of patients they serve. The total pool of patients in each practice is assumed to be large enough so that time-consuming cases and quick ones average out. Special pools of money are available for unusual cases. Critics of universal health insurance and effective cost containment argue that to impose them in the United States would be tantamount to medical rationing. But such rationing already exists. Medical technology is such that if every available procedure were used on every patient who might conceivably benefit, it would consume 100 percent of the gross national product. Health care will be rationed one way or another—based either on private ability to pay, which strikes most people as brutally unfair, or on some given set of socially determined criteria. A universal system for the United States would be the rational one. But again, this solution is blocked by our ideological commitment to laissez-faire and by our fiscal impasse.

*Savings.* Yes, Americans need a higher savings rate. If we fail to save more and we wish to have even a minimal rate of capital investment, we have to borrow money from abroad; we have to keep interest rates (and hence capital costs) artificially high to keep attracting that capital. Alternatively, we need to sell American industry outright to foreign owners who have the capital to invest.

But there are many routes to higher rates of savings and capital formation. The preferred remedy, and the one advocated most frequently in conservative editorial pages, is to lower taxes on well-to-do investors, so that they will save more. This is the laissez-faire solution. But, of course, there are many other roads to a higher savings rate. If we balanced our trade accounts, that would increase the profits of American firms and hence the domestic savings rate. If we once again raised the income tax for people with incomes in excess of $100,000, that would decrease the public deficit and hence increase the savings rate. If we used Social Security as a pool of social capital rather than as an income stream to offset part of the deficit, that would also raise the savings rate. And if we changed the tax code to punish purely speculative financial investment, that would allow that much more of our scarce savings to go into productive ventures.

What these seemingly disparate ideas have in common, of course, is that they each challenge the idea that the free market is self-regulating and that private market forces maximize outcomes. Each idea calls for some form of government intervention—in education and training, labor relations, the structure of capital markets, public infrastructure, environment financial regulation, health care, trade and technology policy. They all require money, or allocation of resources, which in theory markets ought to, but in fact fail to, make.

Two nagging political questions remain. Who among America's voters will support this conception of a plural world and a peacetime economy? And is the public sector in the United States competent to do what has to be done?

The dissenters who oppose laissez-faire have not quite formed into a coherent opposition, for several reasons. A mixed economy has been out of fashion, and even liberals sometimes find themselves saying that they too favor deregulation, privatization, lower taxes, and liberation of market forces. The politics of campaign finance reinforces this response. Because of the fiscal crisis in the federal budget, many liberals think the main task of government is to reduce the deficit, not to increase public spending. In any event, the people who favor more activist policies in education, training, infrastructure, technology, or trade include groups that are usually ideologically opposed. Business groups that now favor a more assertive U.S. trade policy and a civilian government technology policy—for example, the American Electronics Association, the Semiconductor Industry

Association, the Machine Tool Builders Association, the textile manufacturers, and so on—are in other respects conservative, free-market Republicans; other things being equal, they prefer the usual Republican set of policies: low taxes, minimal regulation, and an industrial climate free from meddling trade unions. On the other hand, supporters of laissez-faire act out of clear ideological certitude and reflect the core interest of the financial and diplomatic establishment.

The balance of political forces is entirely different from what it was forty years ago, after World War II. The antigovernment mood, though less intense than during the Reagan years, has not dissipated. Roughly 80 percent of voters have less real disposable income than they did twenty years ago. Thanks to the tax policies of the Reagan 1980s, the working middle class is also bearing more of the tax load. In this climate, a politics of resistance to higher taxes is attractive to voters who feel the financial pinch. A frustrated citizen cannot vote for a reduction in the cost of mortgage credit or the price of food at the grocery store, but he can vote to oppose an increase in federal taxes.

The Democrats, by and large, are without a coherent political philosophy; they have been battered by the recent wave of conservatism, and are not yet consistently challenging the continuing vogue for laissez-faire. Many American liberals and Democrats have fallen into the self-defeating habit of simply waiting for the next deep recession to create a psychology of throw-the-bums-out, which would presumably give them a turn at governing. But praying for recession is hardly a becoming posture for liberals, and in any event, a deep recession may not come. Indeed, the prospect for the American economy in the 1990s is not a second great crash, but rather a slow bleed. Paradoxically, another great crash is unlikely today precisely because enough remains of the Rooseveltian mixed economy: when the stock market crashed in October 1987, it was not the invisible hand that rescued the real economy, but the Federal Reserve that pumped in credit, social insurance that kept demand high, and federal regulators who contained the damage. When the savings-and-loan associations succumbed to an orgy of speculative excess, federal deposit insurance ensured that this did not become a general credit crunch. Moreover, the new high-tech and service economy is structurally different from the one that came crashing down in 1929. The modern economy is not composed mainly of huge factories that can produce only standardized production runs, that lie idle if demand shifts. In the contemporary economy, capital is more adaptable, and its flexibility also militates against a great crash.

A slow bleed would be simply an intensification of the pattern of the 1980s: gradual erosion of the American place in the global economy; increasing dependence on foreign capital and technology; a slow decline in living standards. The more this syndrome develops, the more government policy will become captive to the idea of the freest possible flow of foreign capital, to denying national economic interests, and to prolonging dollar hegemony in order to finance the debt. The reckoning would be delayed, but the underlying condition of the U.S. economy would steadily worsen. Living standards for the class that includes opinion leaders won't decline, so long as West Germany and Japan continue to lend the United States money. A dramatic crisis may never come, but the damage will persist.

Still, there are now elements of a new and surprisingly potent planning coalition that will tolerate and even welcome an active role for government in the solution to this impasse. This is reminiscent of the New Deal era, when business groups were divided into traditional laissez-faire conservatives and corporatists who welcomed partnerships between business and government. The corporatist tradition was evident in the National Recovery Act, the Reconstruction Finance Corporation, the Wagner Act, and, later, the wartime planning agencies; it lived on, albeit vestigially, in such business groups as the Committee for Economic Development, a rare business supporter of active government-industry partnerships for improved education, training, and public infrastructure investment. It took the decline in U.S. competitiveness in the world economy to activate a broader business disaffection with laissez-faire.

The 1990s offer what may be a brief window of opportunity to re-create a politics of planning. While some U.S.-based industries have been pushed to the brink of extinction, many other firms have sought shelter in junior partnerships with European and Japanese buyers. The more this occurs, the less there will be an industry-wide constituency for a tougher trade policy or for interventionist industrial and technology policies. Some of the same companies that once supported a harder policy to pry open Japan are now Japanese subsidiaries. The industries that favor interventionist policies are ones that still have a distinctively American flavor.

There are signs, however, that a new anti-laissez-faire coalition is growing stronger. It includes not just liberals, trade unionists, and those concerned about redistribution but bankers and industrialists worried about the fate of the American economy. Many students of the welfare state have assumed, mistakenly, that the prime purpose of the mixed economy was redistribution; as the constituency for redistribution weakened, the constituency for a mixed economy necessarily weakened, too. But in reality a substantial public sector in a capitalist economy does far more than advance welfare purposes; it also provides a stabilizing counterweight to the chronic instability of capitalism, and serves as an engine of economic development. In Europe and in Japan, the captains of industry and finance have supported a mixed economy, not out of solicitude for the poor but to promote stability and growth. In the 1930s, many of America's richest and most influential people decided there were worse things than paying taxes. As American competitiveness lags, as the economy slides into recession and dependence on foreign capital grows, the case against laissez-faire grows stronger, and so does its constituency.

If the United States does not act to reclaim industrial leadership in many technologies and industries it once led, the window of opportunity will close. We shall reach a point where we can get back into the business of manufacturing only as an outpost of other, more advanced producers, as has happened in Great Britain. (For example, the British automobile industry has virtually vanished; today, Britain is getting back into the business of making cars, but the nameplates are Nissan and Honda.)

Some have argued that there is nothing wrong with this. My colleague Robert Reich, in an influential article titled "Who Is Us?",[12] makes the case that the global economy has already become such a web of cross-national investment that it is now meaningless to talk of "American" or "Japanese" companies. Indeed, if American managers have become inept, why show them special favor? Reich, generally a critic of laissez-faire, contends that the U.S. government should have relatively interventionist policies, to stimulate advanced technology and improved manufacturing processes, turn out better-trained workers, and then welcome capitalists of whatever nationality who wish to set up shop in the United States. He is mostly right, I think, but his argument begs the question addressed by Mordechai Kreinin of whether these foreign multinational companies really play by the same rules as American companies. The preponderance of evidence suggests that they don't, not yet at least. At some point in the next century, U.S.-owned, European-owned, and Japanese-owned companies may be truly indistinguishable; as global stock markets meld into one big market, stock ownership itself will be multinational. But until that day comes, U.S. policy needs to make sure that American-based enterprises are around to compete.

The who-is-us view strongly implies that it doesn't really matter if U.S.-based firms go out of business as long as foreign-based firms are here providing good jobs for American workers. But unless one is a true believer in laissez-faire, such a benign outcome would require that one of two alternatives obtain, neither of which is likely to do so in the near term, if ever. Either Japanese firms will have to begin behaving just like textbook Western firms and pay no heed to the nationality of suppliers or the national location of production; or the United States will have to embrace an uncharacteristically tough and necessarily bureaucratized "labor mercantilism," in which every major foreign investment is vetted to make sure that it indeed provides high-value jobs for the United States. Otherwise, our industrial fate remains captive to other people's mercantilisms, which still strive very explicitly to keep the high-wage, high-knowledge end of business within their own borders.

As Andrew Grove, the brilliant president of Intel, has observed, Japanese companies have figured out how to design ultra-high-technology products that paradoxically can be assembled largely by uneducated young women, at wages of well under a dollar an hour, in the remote outposts of East Asia. The brains of the operation, however, stay in Japan—the manufacturing expertise, the financial power, the scientific knowledge, the engineering and marketing talent, and of course the flow of profits which then capitalizes the next generation of technical innovation and leadership. It takes the presence of at least some U.S.-based firms if bargaining over technology transfer and location of production is to take place; otherwise, the United States brings nothing to the table. If U.S.-based high-technology firms like Intel are simply driven out of business by the mercantilism of other nations, we will gradually decline to the position of those low-wage East Asian women: assembly will take place in the United States, to the extent that our wages are competitive (i.e., low). But as U.S.-based firms lose their capacity to earn profits in domestic and foreign markets, they lose the capital needed to keep America technologically competitive. And as U.S.-owned firms vanish, the critical cluster of research, science, manufacturing technology, and engineering prowess will gradually migrate to the home offices of foreign firms. Once again, the laissez-faire premise that the nation has been overtaken by the globalization of the economy proves wishful.

American liberals who once scoffed at the idea that "what's good for General Motors is good for the country" ought not to go to the opposite extreme and insist that it simply doesn't matter whether General Motors goes down the drain. The solution is, to be sure, not sentimental attachment to American managers simply because they are nominally our countrymen. As American citizens, our affection for them—as for foreign-owned firms—should be conditional: what are they bringing to the American economy and its work force? That, in turn, requires a functioning social contract anchored in a coherent set of public policies and a competent public sector. In that respect, Reich has it right.

Utopian conservatives make a last-ditch argument against a mixed economy that government, per se, is hopelessly incompetent. More narrowly, they argue that American government in particular is unable to intervene in the market economy without succumbing to diverse political pressures that render the exercise inefficient in practice even if it is possible in theory (or in Japan and Sweden). A new school of political economy, called public-choice theory, has refined this proposition over the past few decades. The core idea is that the polity is a marketplace, just like any other marketplace, and politicians win votes by satisfying vocal constituencies, whether or not their policies make economic sense. The general prescription of public-choice theory is to get as much of economic life as possible out of the political market and back into the private market (by definition optimal).

This school is deeply pessimistic, not just about the prospects of economic planning but about political democracy itself. For if economic decision making in the public sector is hopelessly flawed, then so is every other form of political decision making. We might as well put the government out for bids or appoint a Platonic committee of economists to conduct public business. In most modern economies, the instruments of government have been refined to make constructive social partnerships possible, and they do not in fact lead to government by special-interest groups. Foreign governments, far more explicitly enmeshed in their private economies than ours is, have proven that it is possible to transcend narrow interests to pursue a broad public good—safeguarding the environment, phasing out no longer competitive industry with a minimum of social pain, fashioning health systems that are equitable and efficient. Some aspects of government are indeed inefficient—but so are some aspects of the private market. Most governments have tried to combine the best elements of both—not to vilify democracy for the greater grandeur of pure commerce.

As the political scientist Richard Valelly[13] has observed, the weakness of political and governmental institutions in the United States in recent years and the popular alienation from both government and politics reinforces the claim that social and economic questions, wherever possible, should be turned over to the market. But as Valelly suggests, the unexplored alternative is to reinvigorate the polity. Indeed, any alternative brand of political economy that assumes a role for effective and competent government will be implausible until government is repaired and reclaimed. That reclamation must reach government in both senses of the concept—government as a dispenser of services but more fundamentally government as an instrument of democratic decision making.

The United States invented modern constitutional democratic government. In a world of "developmental states," some argue that our unique system—presidential rather than parliamentary, federal rather than unitary—leads to government by interest group rather than government by national consensus. If our government is indeed less competent than others, then in yet another way we face a competitive crisis. But if we can retool particular industries the better for them to compete, we can retool our democratic government.

The reader should note that this book has not dwelt on the most fundamental indictment of laissez-faire—the fact that it leads to grotesque extremes of wealth and poverty. The oldest chestnut in the conservative mythology is the claim that greater equity unfortunately comes at the expense of efficiency and growth, and that, if we truly wish to help the poor, the best strategy is to stop hobbling the rich, for they are the source of society's wealth and growth. This view, which has timeless appeal for people of financial means, is contradicted by history. At many times and in many places, economies have grown faster by diffusing their wealth more broadly, and in this enterprise government is an essential factor. I have addressed that question in *The Economic Illusion*. [14] This book has not been about distributive justice, but about the systemic dangers of utopian laissez-faire—dangers that resulted in one catastrophe, the Great Depression of the 1930s, and that might produce a very different sort of accelerating decline in the 1990s.

Today American public philosophy is at one of its periodic great divides. We can pursue the laissez-faire solution: balance the federal budget, continue the process of reducing taxes and regulatory constraints on business, and continue to try to sell this philosophy to the rest of the world. We can continue lowering the wages paid to American workers, to compete on the basis of cheap labor because we no longer compete by working smarter. We can continue to pretend that other countries don't intervene in their markets, that there is no effective difference between Japanese, U.S., and European industries. If we follow that route, we will gradually become a poorer and less influential country. Or we can get on with the great challenge of building institutions that reconcile a dynamic private economy with a decent and viable society.

The collapse of world communism has been widely welcomed as a gift for political liberty, for economic enterprise, and for world peace. It is surely all of these. But, just as important, it offers the United States an opportunity to redefine its national purpose in the world and to arrest a dangerous spiral of self-deception and decline. This shift will surely include a welcome end to the arms race, but it must include a new conception of economics as well. The hands that will repair the damage of recent decades must be visible ones.

# NOTES

The sources for the epigraphs to the book are as follows:

Friedrich List, *The Natural System of Political Economy* (originally published in 1837, translated and edited by W. O. Henderson, London: Frank Cass and Company, Ltd., 1983), p. 17.

John Maynard Keynes, "The End of Laissez-Faire," in *Essays in Persuasion* (New York: Norton, 1963), pp. 312, 317–18.

Karl Polanyi, *The Great Transformation: The Political and Economic Origins of Our Time* (Boston: Beacon Press, 1957), p. 73.

## INTRODUCTION

1. See John Gerard Ruggie, "International Regimes, Transactions and Change: Embedded Liberalism in the Postwar Economic Order," in Stephen D. Krasner, ed., *International Regimes* (Ithaca, N.Y.: Cornell University Press, 1983); Charles Kindleberger, *The World in Depression* (Berkeley: University of California Press, 1973), especially Chapter 14; and Robert Gilpin, *The Political Economy of International Relations* (Princeton: Princeton University Press, 1987).

2. Ruggie, p. 209.

## ONE   RELUCTANT STATECRAFT

1. Karl Polanyi, *The Great Transformation* (Boston: Beacon Press, 1944), p. 135.

2. Albert O. Hirschman, *Rival Views of Market Society* (New York: Elisabeth Sifton Books/Viking, 1986), pp. 106–7.

3. See David P. Calleo and Benjamin M. Rowland, *America and the World Political Economy* (Bloomington: Indiana University Press, 1973), p. 11; and Bernard Semmel, *The Rise of Free Trade Imperialism* (Cambridge: Cambridge University Press, 1970).

4. Friedrich List, *The Natural System of Political Economy* (London: Frank Cass, [1837] 1983), pp. 70–71.

5. Ruggie, p. 209.

6. See Richard N. Gardner, *Sterling Dollar Diplomacy* (New York: McGraw-Hill, 1969); for Keynes's view, see Roy Harrod, *The Life of John Maynard Keynes* (New York: Norton, 1951), especially pp. 525–85. Also Robert Triffin, *Europe and the Money Muddle* (New Haven: Yale University Press, 1957), especially pp. 93–142.

7. Quoted in Harrod, pp. 526–27.

8. Gardner, p. xii.

9. Gardner, p. 76.

10. John Maynard Keynes, "National Self-Sufficiency," *Yale Review,* Vol. XXII, No. 4 (June 1933).

11. Harrod, p. 513.

12. Harrod, p. 513.

13. Fred L. Block, *The Origins of International Economic Disorder* (Berkeley: University of California Press, 1977), p. 46.

14. Block, p. 45.

15. Block, p. 45.

16. Harrod, p. 512.

17. Richard J. Barnet, *The Alliance: America-Europe-Japan, Makers of the Post-War World* (New York: Simon & Schuster, 1983), p. 103.

18. Gardner, pp. 349 ff.

19. Winthrop G. Brown, "Why Private Business Should Support the ITO," *State Department Bulletin,* Vol. XXII (1950), as quoted in Gardner, p. 372.

20. Walter Isaacson and Evan Thomas, *The Wise Men: Six Friends and the World They Made* (New York: Simon & Schuster, 1986), pp. 340–41.

21. John Lewis Gaddis, *The United States and the Origin of the Cold War* (New York: Columbia University Press, 1972), p. 180.

22. Gaddis, p. 181.

23. John Lewis Gaddis, *The Long Peace* (Oxford: Oxford University Press, 1987), p. 26.

24. Gaddis, *The Long Peace,* p. 27.

25. Gaddis, *The Long Peace,* p. 27.

26. Isaacson and Thomas, p. 350.

27. Isaacson and Thomas, p. 350.

28. George F. Kennan, *Memoirs: 1925–1950* (Boston: Atlantic–Little, Brown, 1967), pp. 547 ff.

29. Harry S. Truman, *Memoirs: Years of Trial and Hope, 1946–1952,* Vol. II (New York: Signet Books, [1956] 1965), p. 128.

30. John G. Ikenberry, "Rethinking the Origins of American Hegemony" (manuscript), p. 16, quoting Gaddis, *The Long Peace,* p. 58.

31. Ikenberry, p. 17, quoting Kennan, *Memoirs: 1925–1950,* p. 336.

32. Barnet, p. 124.

33. David P. Calleo and Benjamin M. Rowland, *America and the World Political Economy* (Bloomington: Indiana University Press, 1973), pp. 62–63.

TWO    ATLAS ENFEEBLED

1. Paul Kennedy, *The Rise and Fall of the Great Powers* (New York: Random House, 1987), p. 422.

2. Barnet, p. 203.

3. Robert Triffin, *Gold and the Dollar Crisis* (New Haven: Yale University Press, 1960).

4. Block, pp. 109–14.

5. John H. Makin, *The Global Debt Crisis: America's Growing Involvement* (New York: Basic Books, 1984), p. 173.

6. Howard M. Wachtel, *The Money Mandarins* (New York: Pantheon, 1986), p. 74.

7. Joanne Gowa, *Closing the Gold Window* (Ithaca: Cornell University Press, 1983), p. 56, citing Robert Solomon, *The International Monetary System, 1945–1976: An Insider's View* (New York: Harper & Row, 1977), p. 46.

·8. Fred Bergsten, *Dilemmas of the Dollar* (New York: New York University Press for the Council on Foreign Relations, 1975), p. 78, cited by Fred Hirsch et al., *Alternatives to Monetary Disorder* (New York: McGraw-Hill, 1977), p. 40.

9. Gowa, p. 61.

10. William Greider, *Secrets of the Temple* (New York: Simon & Schuster, 1987), p. 340.

11. *The Economist,* December 25, 1971, p. 10, as quoted in Makin, p. 106.

12. Milton Friedman, "The Case for Flexible Exchange Rates," in *Essays on Positive Economics* (Chicago: University of Chicago Press, 1953).

13. Robert O. Keohane, *After Hegemony: Cooperation and Discord in the World Political Economy* (Princeton: Princeton University Press, 1984), p. 179.

14. Ikenberry, p. 3.

15. Harold Lever and Christopher Huhne, *Debt and Danger: The World Financial Crisis* (Boston: Atlantic Monthly Press, 1985), p. 37.

16. Michael Moffitt, *The World's Money* (New York: Simon & Schuster, 1983), pp. 134–35. See also Robert D. Putnam and Nicholas Bayne, *Hanging Together: Cooperation and Conflict in the Seven Power Summits* (Cambridge: Harvard University Press, 1987), pp. 75–92.

17. Moffitt, p. 135.

18. Edward Tufte, *The Political Control of the Economy* (Princeton: Princeton University Press, 1978).

19. Walter Bagehot, *Lombard Street* (1904), quoted in Makin, p. 40.

20. See the author's *The Economic Illusion* (Boston: Houghton Mifflin, 1984).

## THREE  REAGANISM

1. Under Secretary of the Treasury for Monetary Policy Beryl Sprinkel, a strict monetarist, announced on April 16, 1981, that the United States would intervene in exchange-rate markets only to smooth out temporary "disorderly" conditions, not to influence the value of the dollar. *New York Times,* April 17, 1981.

2. I. M. Destler and C. Randall Henning, citing *Dollar Politics: Exchange-Rate Policymaking in the United States* (Washington, D.C.: Institute for International Economics, 1989), in U.S. Department of Commerce, *Survey of Current Business.*

3. Yoichi Funabashi, *Managing the Dollar: From the Plaza to the Louvre* (Washington, D.C.: Institute for International Economics, 1988), pp. 4–21.

4. *National Journal,* February 23, 1985, p. 412.

5. Art Pine, "To Avert a Trade War, United States Sets Major Push to Drive Down

Dollar," *Wall Street Journal*, September 23, 1985. "Although the ministers apparently haven't set any numerical targets for the dollar or the other currencies, they seek to lower the dollar's value significantly or at least prevent its further rise."
6. Funabashi, pp. 4–21.
7. To a lesser extent than the dollar, the German mark functions as a reserve currency. But the Bundesbank does not lend marks to finance interventions by other European central banks for the purpose of maintaining intra-European parities. Coordinated intervention against the dollar made the mark stronger relative to other European currencies and pushed it toward the top of its acceptable range, requiring both the Bundesbank and other central banks to intervene in European markets, usually in dollars (which were losing value). Other European countries needed to buy dollars in order to finance their EMS interventions, and at the same time needed to *sell* dollars to drive down the dollar's value, which put pressure on the Bundesbank. Poehl remained the most reluctant member of the Plaza club. (Author's interview with Karl-Otto Poehl; see also Funabashi, pp. 28–29, and Karl-Otto Poehl, "You Can't Robotize Policy Making," *The International Economy*, October–November 1987.)
8. If, for example, U.S. interest rates rose relative to Japanese rates, capital would pour into U.S. money markets, bid up the value of the dollar, and thereby frustrate the targeting exercise.
9. Funabashi, p. 47. See also *Wall Street Journal*, March 10, 1986.
10. Poehl, "You Can't Robotize Policy Making."
11. Funabashi, p. 149.
12. Funabashi, p. 149.
13. Stephen Marris, *Deficits and the Dollar: The World Economy at Risk* (Washington, D.C.: Institute for International Economics, 1985).
14. For a discussion on instabilities in the market, see Benjamin J. Cohen, *Organizing the World's Money* (New York: Basic Books, 1977), especially Chapter 1; also John Williamson, *The Exchange Rate System* (Washington, D.C.: Institute for International Economics, 1985).
15. Fred Bergsten, *America and the World Economy* (Washington, D.C.: Institute for International Economics, 1988).
16. Author's interview with Bernard Appel.
17. Stuart Holland, *The Market Economy* (New York: St. Martin's Press, 1987), pp. 250–51.
18. Lawrence Summers, "Time for Inaction," *The New Republic*, January 25, 1988, p. 14.
19. See Robert Reich, "An Outward-Looking Economic Nationalism," *The American Prospect*, Spring 1990.

## FOUR   TRADE

1. David Ricardo, *Principles of Political Economy and Taxation* (London, 1817; reprinted, Cambridge: Cambridge University Press, 1951), p. 14.
2. *The Free Trade Debate* (New York: Twentieth Century Fund, 1989), p. 4.
3. See Paul R. Krugman, *Rethinking International Trade* (Cambridge: MIT Press, 1990); Paul R. Krugman, ed., *Strategic Trade Policy and the New International Economics*

(Cambridge: MIT Press, 1986), especially Brander and Spencer chapters; also Avinash Dixit and Gene Grossman, "Targeted Export Promotion Policies with Several Oligopolistic Industries," Discussion Paper 71 (Princeton: Princeton University, Woodrow Wilson School, 1984).

4. See Paul A. Samuelson, "International Factor Price Equalization Once Again," in Jagdish Bhagwati, ed., *International Trade, Selected Readings* (2nd ed.; Cambridge: MIT Press, 1987).

5. Klaus Stegemann, "Policy Rivalry and Industrial States: What Can We Learn from Models of Strategic Trade Policy?," *International Organization,* Winter 1989.

6. Lawrence Katz and Lawrence Summers, "Can Inter-Industry Wage Differentials Justify Strategic Trade Policy?" (Cambridge: National Bureau of Economic Research, September 1988).

7. Krugman, *Rethinking International Trade,* p. 2.

8. Senator William Roth, speech to the Chicago Council on Foreign Relations, April 11, 1989.

9. Paul Krugman, "Is Free Trade Passé?," *Journal of Economic Perspectives,* Fall 1987, p. 143.

10. For a good discussion of the history and the weakness of antidumping, see Steven D. Irwin, "Revitalizing a Private Right of Action in Antidumping Cases," *Law and Policy in International Business,* Vol. XVII (1985), pp. 847–77.

11. U.S. Supreme Court decision in *Matsushita Electric Industrial Co., Ltd., et al.* v. *Zenith Radio Corp. et al.,* October term 1985, 475 U.S. 582 (1986).

12. Ibid., p. 589.

13. Irwin.

14. See Jacob Viner, *The Customs Union Issue* (New York: Carnegie Endowment for International Peace, 1950).

15. Richard Rothstein, "Keeping Jobs in Fashion" (Washington, D.C.: Economic Policy Institute, 1989), p. 25.

16. William B. Cline, *The Future of World Trade in Textiles and Apparel* (Washington, D.C.: Institute for International Economics, 1987), p. 15.

17. John B. Judis, "Bush and Japan Chip Away at U.S. Economic Destiny," *In These Times,* August 15–28, 1990.

18. Albert O. Hirschman, *National Power and the Structure of Foreign Trade* (Berkeley: University of California Press, 1945), p. 78.

### FIVE  NICHIBEI

1. Boston *Globe,* March 17, 1990.

2. Chalmers Johnson, *MITI and the Japanese Miracle* (Stanford: Stanford University Press, 1982), p. 17.

3. Johnson, p. 84.

4. Ronald Dore, *Flexible Rigidity: Industrial Policy and Structural Changes in the Japanese Economy, 1970–1980* (Stanford: Stanford University Press, 1986), pp. 88–89.

5. James C. Abegglen and George Stark, *Kaisha: The Japanese Corporation* (Tokyo: Charles Tuttle, 1985), p. 127.

6. Mordechai Kreinin, *World Economy,* December 1988, pp. 330–31.

7. Kreinin, p. 533.

8. Kreinin, p. 536.

9. See, for example, Ezra Vogel, *Japan as Number 1* (New York: Harper & Row, 1979); Johnson, *MITI and the Japanese Miracle;* Clyde B. Prestowitz, Jr., *Trading Places* (New York: Basic Books, 1988); Dore, *Flexible Rigidity;* and Karel van Wolferen, *The Enigma of Japanese Power* (New York: Alfred A. Knopf, 1989).

10. Dore.

11. "Effect of the Japanese Patent System on American Business" (Senate Hearing 100-874), Joseph Massey testimony before the Subcommittee on Foreign Commerce and Tourism of the Committee of Commerce, Science, and Transportation, U.S. Senate, June 24, 1988.

12. Ibid., p. 23.

13. Ibid., p. 83.

14. "U.S. to Take Radical Path on Japan Trade," *Wall Street Journal,* March 29, 1986.

15. *New York Times,* January 28, 1988.

16. *Wall Street Journal,* January 28, 1988.

17. *New York Times,* January 28, 1988.

18. Boston *Globe,* January 28, 1988.

19. See report on the Structural Impediments Initiative (Washington, D.C.: U.S. Trade Representative, 1989).

20. *United States–Japan Price Survey* (Washington, D.C.: U.S. Trade Representative, 1989).

21. Prestowitz, *Trading Places* (paperback edition), pp. 62–63.

22. Prestowitz (paperback), pp. 61–62.

23. James Fallows, "Containing Japan," *The Atlantic,* May 1989, p. 51.

24. Van Wolferen, p. 5.

25. Van Wolferen, p. 433.

26. Colin Nickerson, "Europe and Its Japan Problem," Boston *Globe,* March 11, 1990.

27. Author's interview.

28. Author's interview.

29. Author's interview.

30. Author's interview.

31. Author's interview.

32. Author's interview.

33. Author's interview with Lars Anell.

SIX    SECURITY

1. "Security Agency Debates New Role: Economic Spying," *New York Times,* June 18, 1990, p. 1.

2. For a discussion of a large defense establishment as detrimental to economic well-being, see Mary Kaldor, *The Baroque Arsenal* (New York: Hill and Wang, 1981); also Seymour Melman, *Profits Without Production* (New York: Alfred A. Knopf, 1983).

3. Cited in Joel S. Yudkin and Michael Black, "Targeting National Needs," *World Policy Journal,* Spring 1990, p. 66.

4. Kennedy, *The Rise and Fall of the Great Powers,* p. 522.

5. *Balancing the National Interest: United States National Security, Export Controls, and Global Economic Competition* (Washington, D.C.: National Academy of Sciences, 1987), p. 107.

6. Ibid., p. 235.

7. Charles Ferguson, "High Technology Product Life Cycles," in *Balancing the National Interest* (Working Papers volume), p. 79.

8. Author's interview.

9. Steven B. Gould, "Foreign Nationals in U.S. Science and Engineering," in *Balancing the National Interest* (Working Papers), p. 14.

10. Ferguson, p. 80.

11. Memo from James Mach, American Machine Tool Builders, March 14, 1990.

12. Cormac Walsh, in *Balancing the National Interest* (Working Papers), p. 143.

13. Author's interview with anonymous working-group member.

14. Anthony J. Blinken, *Ally vs. Ally: America, Europe and the Siberian Pipeline Crisis* (New York: Praeger, 1987), p. 3.

15. Department of Defense Authorization for Appropriations, Fiscal Year 1989, Hearings before the U.S. Senate Committee of Armed Services: Part 7, Defense, Industry and Technology, March–April 1988 (Senate Hearing 100-790), p. 30, citing John Deutsch, "Technology Base Management," Report to the Secretary of Defense, December 23, 1987, p. 43.

16. Yudkin and Black, p. 270.

17. Jay Stowsky, *Beating Our Plowshares into Double-Edged Swords* (Berkeley: Berkeley Roundtable on the International Economy), 1986.

18. "The Navy Initiates a Nuts and Bolts Experiment," Washington *Post,* national edition, December 25, 1989.

19. Jeffrey F. Rayport, "DARPA" Case Study, Harvard Business School, January 18, 1990, citing Department of Defense directive #5105.

20. European Strategic Programme for Research and Development in Information Technology (ESPRIT), 1989 Annual Report (Luxembourg: Commission of the European Communities), Directorate-General XII, pp. 3–4.

21. Rayport, p. 7.

22. Leon Wynter, "Major Revolution in Computers Came from Darpa Work," *Wall Street Journal,* October 24, 1985, p. 6.

23. Author's interview with George Lodge.

24. Department of Defense Authorization for Appropriations, Fiscal Year 1990–91, Hearings before the U.S. Senate Committee of Armed Services: Part 7, Defense, Industry and Technology, March–April 1990 (Senate Hearing 101-251), pp. 14–15.

25. Hearings before the Senate Committee of Armed Services, Fiscal Year 1989, p. 234.

26. Prestowitz (paperback), p. 12.

27. Prestowitz (paperback) p. 13.

28. Deutsch, "Technology Base Management."

29. Rayport, p. 14, citing "Soviet Military Power: Prospects for Change, 1989."

30. "Bigger Role Urged for Defense Department in Economic Policy," *New York Times,* October 19, 1988.

31. Malcolm Currie et al., "Defense Industrial Cooperation with Pacific Rim Na-

tions" (Washington, D.C.: Office of Under Secretary of Defense for Acquisition, 1989), p. x.

32. Currie, p. 16.

33. "A Strategic Industry at Risk," National Advisory Committee on Semiconductors, November 1989, p. 1.

34. Ibid., p. 7.

35. Ibid., p. 5.

36. Ibid., p. iii.

## SEVEN   GLOBAL FINANCE

1. Cohen, *Organizing the World's Money,* pp. 159 ff.

2. Friedman, "The Case for Flexible Exchange Rates."

3. Alexandre Lamfalussy, "A Plea for an International Commitment to Exchange-Rate Stability," Atlantic Institute for International Affairs, 1981.

4. Susan Strange, *Casino Capitalism* (Oxford: Basil Blackwell, 1988), p. 8.

5. Putnam and Bayne, *Hanging Together,* pp. 39–42.

6. See Jacques van Ypersele and Jean van Koeune, *The European Monetary System* (Brussels: Commission of the European Communities, 1984).

7. *ECU Newsletter,* No. 31 (Turin, Italy: Istituto Bancario San Paolo di Torino, January 1990), p. 2.

8. Author's interviews.

9. Quoted in Anatol Kaletsky, *The Costs of Default* (New York: Twentieth Century Fund, 1985), p. 1.

10. Kaletsky, p. 8, citing William Wynne, *State Insolvency and Foreign Bondholders: Case Histories,* Vol. II (New Haven: Yale University Press, 1951).

11. John Maynard Keynes, "How to Mend the Treaty," *The New Republic,* January 21, 1920, p. 220.

12. See Alice H. Amsden, *Asia's New Giant* (Oxford: Oxford University Press, 1989).

13. Gilpin, *The Political Economy of International Relations,* pp. 284–86.

14. Barbara Stallings, *Banker to the Third World: US Portfolio Investment in Latin America, 1900–1986* (Berkeley: University of California Press, 1987).

15. See Jeffry A. Frieden, *Banking on the World* (New York: Harper & Row, 1990), pp. 133–36.

16. Manuel Pastor, "Capital Flight and the Latin American Debt Crisis" (Washington, D.C.: Economic Policy Institute, 1990), p. 8.

17. Amsden.

18. Amsden.

19. Christine Bogdanowitz-Bindert, *Solving the Global Debt Crisis* (New York: Ballinger, 1989).

20. Stephen Schuker, *America's Reparations to Germany, 1919–1933: Implications for the Third World Debt Crisis* (Princeton: Princeton Studies for International Finance, 1988).

21. See "World Imbalances" (United Nations University, World Institute for Development Economics Research Report, Helsinki, 1989); also 1989 World Bank Annual Report.

22. From Economic Commission for Latin America and the Caribbean (ECLA), cited in *The International Economy,* April–May 1990, p. 96.

23. "World Imbalances," p. 83.

24. Kaletsky, p. 10.

25. See World Bank Annual Report; Elaine M. Koerner and George E. Rossmiller, "U.S. Farmers and Latin American Debt," *Resources* (Washington, D.C.: Resources for the Future, Fall 1989).

26. Lever and Huhne, p. 28.

27. "The Impact of the Latin American Debt Crisis on the U.S. Economy," Joint Economic Committee Staff Study, May 1989, Table 1, from ECLA.

28. Jeffrey Sachs, "Efficient Debt Reduction," World Bank Symposium on Dealing with the Debt Crisis, Washington, D.C., January 26, 1989.

29. Sachs, p. 16.

30. Sachs, p. 11.

31. Sachs, pp. 45–46.

32. See various Treasury documents, and also Walter Mossberg, "US Plan May Cut Debt 20% for 39 Nations," *Wall Street Journal,* March 16, 1989.

33. Jorge Castañeda, "The Mexican Free Trade Express," *The International Economy,* June–July 1990, p. 30.

34. Steven Fidler, "One Step Closer to a Lighter Burden," *Financial Times,* January 23, 1990.

35. "World Imbalances," p. 78.

36. Sachs, p. 18.

37. John Williamson, "The Progress of Policy Reform in Latin America" (Washington, D.C.: Institute for International Economics, 1990), p. 21.

38. "World Imbalances," p. 83.

39. Pastor, p. 22.

40. Sachs, p. 1.

41. Lance Taylor, *Varieties of Stabilization Experience* (Oxford: Oxford University Press, 1988), p. 48.

42. See discussion by Ajit Singh, "The Present Crisis of the Tanzanian Economy: Notes on the Economics and Politics of Devaluation," January 1983 (unpublished).

43. Holland, *The Global Economy,* pp. 419–21. Also Michael Manley and Willy Brandt, *Global Challenge* (London: Pan Books, 1985; New York: St. Martin's Press, 1988).

44. Taylor, pp. 11 ff.

45. Taylor, p. 15.

46. Paul Streeten, "Structural Adjustment" (Boston: World Development Inst. Monograph, 1987).

EIGHT   LAISSEZ-FAIRE AND AMERICA'S FUTURE

1. Walter Russell Mead, "On the Road to Ruin: Winning the Cold War, Losing the Peace," *Harper's,* March 1990, pp. 59 ff.

2. Michael Dertouzos et al., *Made in America: Regaining the Productive Edge* (Cambridge: MIT Press, 1989).

3. Dertouzos, p. 37.

4. See Neil Fligstein, *The Transformation of Corporate Control* (Cambridge: Harvard University Press, 1989); see also Robert Bork, *The Anti-Trust Paradox* (New York: Basic Books, 1978).

5. A. A. Berle and Gardiner Means, *The Modern Corporation and Private Property* (New York: Macmillan, 1932).

6. Dore, pp. 88–89.

7. See Louis Lowenstein, *What's Wrong with Wall Street* (Reading, Pa.: Addison-Wesley, 1989); also the author's "A Progressive Labor Agenda after Reagan," *Challenge,* September–October 1988.

8. Alicia Munnell, "Why Has Productivity Growth Declined?," *New England Economic Review,* January–February 1990, pp. 14–15.

9. *Savings Bank Financial Quarterly,* Vol. XXI (Third Quarter, 1989) (IDC Financial Publishing, Inc., January–February 1990).

10. *Wall Street Journal,* June 28, 1990, p. 1.

11. Paul Stephen Dempsey, *Flying Blind: The Failure of Airline Deregulation* (Washington, D.C.: Economic Policy Institute, 1990).

12. Robert Reich, "Who Is Us?," *Harvard Business Review,* January–February 1990.

13. Richard M. Valelly, "Democratic Renewal as a Response to Democratic Decline" (Cambridge: MIT, unpublished monograph, 1990).

14. Robert Kuttner, *The Economic Illusion* (Boston: Houghton Mifflin, 1984).

# INDEX

A NOTE ABOUT THE AUTHOR

Robert Kuttner is economics correspondent of *The New Republic,* a contributing columnist for *Business Week,* and founding co-editor of the new liberal quarterly *The American Prospect.* His weekly editorial column, originating in the Boston *Globe,* is syndicated by the Washington *Post,* and his commentaries are heard on National Public Radio's news program "All Things Considered." Mr. Kuttner has taught at Harvard's Institute of Politics, at Boston University, and at the University of Massachusetts. Previously, he served as chief investigator for the U.S. Senate Committee on Banking, Housing and Urban Affairs and as a national staff writer on the Washington *Post.* He lives in Brookline, Massachusetts, with his wife and their two children.

A NOTE ON THE TYPE

The text of this book was set in a type face called Times Roman, designed by Stanley Morison (1889–1967) for *The Times* (London) and first introduced by that newspaper in 1932.

Among typographers and designers of the twentieth century, Stanley Morison was a strong forming influence—as a typographical advisor to The Monotype Corporation, as a director of two distinguished English publishing houses, and as a writer of sensibility, erudition, and keen practical sense.